GROUNDWORK

GROUNDWORK

*Charles Hamilton Houston
and the Struggle for
Civil Rights*

Genna Rae McNeil

University of Pennsylvania Press

PHILADELPHIA

Published with the support of the Haney Foundation

10 9 8 7 6 5 4

Published by
University of Pennsylvania Press
Philadelphia, Pennsylvania 19104-4011

Permission is acknowledged to reprint excerpts from previously published poems:
"Sympathy," by Paul Laurence Dunbar, copyright 1913, reprinted from *The Complete Poems of Paul Laurence Dunbar* by permission of Dodd, Mead & Co., Inc.
"Dark Testament," by Pauli Murray, © 1970, reprinted from *Dark Testament and Other Poems* (Norwalk, Conn.: Silvermine Publishers) by permission of Pauli Murray.
"Libations," by Jayne Cortez, © 1973, reprinted from *Scarifications* (New York: Bola Press, Inc.) by permission of Jayne Cortez.

Library of Congress Cataloging-in-Publication Data

McNeil, Genna Rae
   Groundwork: Charles Hamilton Houston and the struggle for civil rights.
   Bibliography: p.
   Includes index.
   ISBN 0-8122-1179-0 (pbk., alk. paper)
    1. Houston, Charles Hamilton, 1895-1950. 2. Afro-American lawyers—Biography. 3. Civil rights workers—United States—Biography. I. title.
KF373.H664M3   1983
342.73'0873'0924 [B]
347'.3028730924 [B]
          82-40483
          CIP

To the Memories of
Jesse Jai McNeil, Sr. (1913–1965), my father
Vernon Thomas Rogers (1947–1965), my friend
and Clotill Marconier Houston (1879–1978),
keeper of the Houston tradition

For Charles Hamilton Houston, Jr.
and his children, Caron and Charles III

CONTENTS

ACKNOWLEDGMENTS

The events leading up to the publication of *Groundwork* were set in motion when Vincent P. Franklin, Yale University historian and author of *The Education of Black Philadelphia*, urged John Mc-Guigan of the University of Pennsylvania Press to read the introduction to my manuscript biography of Charles Hamilton Houston. I have no doubt that the appearance of this work in 1983 is the direct result of Vincent Franklin's initial efforts and the enthusiastic advocacy of Derrick A. Bell, Jr., Dean of the University of Oregon Law School, and A. Leon Higginbotham, Jr., Circuit Judge in the United States Court of Appeals for the Third Circuit. When called on by the Press to read the manuscript, each did so with dispatch and was willing to make a case for the value of such a critical biography to historians, lawyers, students, and a wider audience.

In the course of researching and writing this biography, I incurred many debts. Unhappily, I can no longer recall the names of all who assisted me during the twelve years of *Groundwork*'s preparation. I trust, however, that each person who contributed to the completion of this study will understand how sincerely appreciative I am.

I must first acknowledge—and how inadequate the word seems at this time—Charles Hamilton Houston, Jr., who was just six years old when his father died. Charles granted me access to the records of the Houston firm and the Houston family papers, without which this biography could not have been written. Beyond that, he spent hours with me, during at least six years of this project, locating sources, visiting his father's friends, following up leads, answering questions, and helping me to solve mysteries.

This study began as a doctoral dissertation at the University of Chicago under the extraordinarily able and sensitive direction of historian John Hope Franklin. His guidance and that of another committee member, Philip Kurland, a professor at the University of Chicago Law School, were of enormous assistance in the earliest stages of this biography. While researching the Houston & Houston firm records and the private papers of Charles Houston, William Gardner, then the senior partner and now a judge, was the epitome of magnanimity and cooperativeness. He and his junior partner, Annice Wagner, also now a judge, were patient and helpful teachers in response to my daily inquiries about the practice of law. Bernice Gordon, who had been a secretary in the Houston firm for a number of years, was my best informant as I sought out former partners and friends of Charles Houston. During this same period, my sister, Brenna Jean McNeil Jackson, performed innumerable clerical duties connected with researching the case files and compiling data used in tables on Houston's private practice. I thank her for bearing with me and accepting a hurried Chinese lunch in exchange for weeks of work.

Mary Frances Berry, a professor of history and law at Howard University, and Charles H. Long, a professor of religion at Duke University and the University of North Carolina at Chapel Hill, were simultaneously my mentors and my intellectual "sparring partners." To a large extent it is the analytical process for which they were catalysts that was most essential to the making of Groundwork. For this interpretation of Houston's significance, however, I assume full responsibility, while acknowledging the many scholars cited in my bibliography who have written on the history of African Americans and the American legal process.

My decision to seek publication of this biography, despite the vagaries of the publishing world and the impact of American racism on it, was supported over the years by the response of students, professors, and lawyers to lectures and articles on Charles Hamilton Houston. In this regard, I thank especially the 1973–74 Black American Law Students Association of Harvard; the 1977–78 Black Law Students Union of Yale University; Vivian Gordon, Lynn French, and the 1978–79 Black Student Association of the University of Virginia; Ralph Smith of the University of Pennsylvania Law School and his 1980–81 students in the seminar on race and law; the student body of Amherst College and the tireless organizer of that college's 1980 Charles Houston Forum, Mavis Campbell; the National Bar Association; and the annual Charles Hamilton Houston Medallion committees of the Washington Bar Association.

Sixty-one people who knew Charles Houston were sources of valuable information and encouragement, assisting me with my research through interviews, conversations, and correspondence. Although each is identified in the bibliography, I acknowledge with a profound sense of gratitude Henrietta Houston, Clotill Houston, William H.

ACKNOWLEDGMENTS xi

Hastie, Jr., Joseph Waddy, and Samuel Clark, all of whom died before
the appearance of *Groundwork*. I also owe a special debt to three other
people whom I interviewed when this study was in its infancy: Margaret Gladys Moran Houston, Charles Houston's first wife, Dr. Edward
Mazique, Houston's personal physician and friend—who, with Charles
Jr. unearthed the 1949 tape-recorded message—and Benjamin Amos,
a former neighbor and friend of Houston. Despite enormous demands
on their time and attention, Judges William Bryant, Robert Carter,
George Crockett, Margaret Haywood, Constance Baker Motley, Spottswood W. Robinson III, and Juanita Kidd Stout—four of whom at one
time or another worked in the Houston firm—thoughtfully considered
and answered pivotal questions.

Three historians, the eminent Charles Wesley, Ernest Allen of the
University of Massachusetts, and Debra Newman of the National Archives, provided me with primary sources that significantly affected
the interpretation of this study. I am also indebted to the extended
Houston family—particularly Ulysses J. Houston, James Pendergrass,
Ann E. Houston, Thomas Jackson Houston, and Shirley Dickerson—
for doing genealogical research and fieldwork it was beyond my capabilities and resources to undertake and for granting me access to
papers and photographs from their private collections. I cannot give
enough credit to Pearl Walker McNeil, an anthropologist and my
mother, for taking the most primitive of family trees that I had prepared on the Houstons and transforming it into the genealogy that
was the basis for Figure 1 and the continuing research of the Houston
family.

The administrators and staff of each library and institution cited in
the notes helped me unselfishly. Aiding me in special ways were Howard Law School's former Dean, Charles T. Duncan; Dean Wiley A.
Branton, Houston Distinguished Professor of Law Herbert O. Reid, Sr.,
and JoAnne King of Howard Law School; Thomas Battle, Esme Bhan,
Maricia Bracey, Karen Jefferson, Cornelia Stokes, and Michael Win-
ston of the Moorland-Spingarn Research Center of Howard University; Dorothy Porter Wesley and Charlotte Price, formerly of the
Moorland-Spingarn; Ruth Nicholson and Sylvia Render, specialists
in the Manuscripts Division of that library; Debra Newman, James
Walker, Alfred Blair, and Sara Jackson of the National Archives;
Sharon M. Howard and Ernest Kaiser of the Schomburg Center for
Research in Black Culture; Jean Blackwell Hutson, former chief of the
Schomburg Collection, now Assistant Director for Collection Manage-
ment and Development—Black Studies at the New York Public Li-
brary; and Ann Shockley of Fisk University. For permission to quote

from archival and manuscript sources, I thank each library, institution, and individual cited in the notes.

In addition to John Hope Franklin, Derrick A. Bell, Jr., and A. Leon Higginbotham, Jr., five scholars read all or part of this biography at various stages. T. J. Davis of Howard University studied portions of the first revision with careful attention to concerns I had expressed. Jesse Jai McNeil, Jr., analyzed chapters of the study and offered a new perspective on the significance of Houston's work with respect to social change in the United States. J. Clay Smith, Jr., read the entire manuscript and offered comments that gave strength to my revised discussion of constitutional issues and the legal process. I asked Vincent P. Franklin and Mary Frances Berry to read the manuscript in its various forms. Their suggestions and criticisms were helpful in countless ways, and I owe them an incalculable debt far in excess of what is reflected in my notes.

I am grateful for the assistance of John McGuigan, the able acquisitions editor of the University of Pennsylvania Press, Ingalill Hjelm, a meticulous and gently persistent editor, and Peggy Hoover, a skillful and demanding copy editor whose reputation preceded her. They guided me from manuscript to book—sometimes an arduous journey—working closely with me to the end that *Groundwork* tell a clear and compelling story. In addition, I am appreciative of the personal interest that Malcolm Call, Associate Director of the Press, and Debra Kamens, Promotion Manager, took in the timely appearance of this study.

The Central Administration of the New York Public Library aided me in the preparation of this manuscript, and my supervisors were most cooperative throughout the several months of completing the biography. I wish especially to acknowledge, however, my co-workers of the New York Public Library. Debra Carter Wilkerson, Diana Lachatanere, Deborah Willis-Thomas, Cherie Meyer, Berlena Robinson, Richard Salvato, Robert Sink, John Stinson, Anastacio Teodoro, Verna Hodge, Valerie Wingfield, Edith Wynner, and Mary Yearwood demonstrated their concern for me and the successful completion of *Groundwork* on numerous occasions, as I worked with them in Schomburg's Archives and the library's Manuscripts Division.

Friends of long standing and new friends went far beyond the call of duty in assisting me with specific tasks. Janet E. Miles, JoAnn Richardson Joubert, Sharon Howard, and Charles B. Coleman know that the roles they played were indispensable to the completion of the book. I am particularly grateful to Cheryll Y. Greene for serving as my personal editor at crucial points in the process of preparing the final manuscript. For typing and preparing tables for the book at various times, I thank Joyce Evans, Nanette McGuigan, Secily Jones, Bonnie Samuels, and secretaries of the University of North Carolina at Chapel Hill. I also thank for their contributing efforts, all of which enabled me to complete my research and writing, Conrad Harper, Ruth and James Pace, Fran Womack, Charles E. Daye, Nellie Hines, June Patton, Bettye Collier Thomas, Deborah Ragland White, Josephine Ragland, Marshall Grigsby, Jerry A. Moore, Talbert Shaw, Elliott Hall, Edward Kirby, Denardo Coleman, Damon Keith, Lorenzo and Marsha Morris, Linda Edwards, Joseph Joubert, Reuben Brown, Marshall Hawkins, Dennis L. Hite, Khalid Moss, Vivian Browne, Charles Barron, Peggy Agard, Samuel D. Proctor, Calvin O. Butts, and the members of Abyssinian Baptist Church, all of whom prayed for me. My spiritual mentor, Howard Thurman, died before the completion of this study, but his writings and our conversations often were vital to my work, and I pay homage to him for what he so freely gave to me and many others. Close personal friends, whom I have not already named—Wilma and Walter Allen, Barbara and Isaiah Baker, Margaret Ralston Payne, Aseelah Abdul-Mutakabbir Rashid, Tony Martin, Artis Lane, Vince Cannon, Jayne Cortez, Mel Edwards, and Harry Amana—know how deeply indebted to them I am for their constancy in caring.

I have been blessed with an extended family of remarkable human beings. I am grateful to each member for support and interest over the years. I especially acknowledge several members who took the time to respond to my requests no matter how difficult the circumstances in their own lives: Pecic and Elbert McNeil and their daughters, Loretta and Ruth; Alicestine Walker Scott and Stanley; the Charles Walker family; Andrea, Robert, Kim, and Kristy Shepherd; Mentie Bell; Mildred and Thomas Hall; Henry and Ella Mitchell; Mary Thomas Rogers; and my Washington, D.C. "family" of Mrs. Rushie Beasley Andrews, her children and grandchildren, among them, Pauline, Jeannie, Carolyn, Eddie, Donald, Dennis, Denise, Connie, and "Babs." I recall with deep appreciation the late Milton A. Lespere, also of the Washington, D.C., family, who played for all of us music of beauty and grandeur. I also count it a privilege to include member-friends of the Tabernacle Baptist Church of Detroit, Michigan, among my extended family. Of the Tabernacle family, I owe special thanks to the former Minister of Music, Charles D. Coleman; he introduced me to the spiritual "Children Don't Get Weary" and taught me that music too can be a form of prayer.

The boundless and sustaining love of my immediate family—Pearl Lee Walker McNeil, Kenneth Ross, Jesse Jai, Jr., Larke Lynell Turner,

Jai and Kyle McNeil, and Brenna Jean and Carla Jean McNeil Jackson—has been an ever-present help. Kenny, Brenna, Jesse, and Larke I thank especially for listening critically and sympathetically, giving consistently helpful advice, constantly encouraging me and helping me keep this project in perspective. Pearl McNeil, my mother, has been throughout her life an example of strength, disciplined pursuit of knowledge, courage of conviction, kindness, and faith. She has always come to the aid of each of her children and kept us foremost in her daily prayers. I am grateful to God for her and acknowledge her quintessential role in making a way for me to strive for my goals even when there seemed to be no way. My father, the late Dr. Jesse Jai McNeil, Sr., who was a pastor, professor, author, and musician, was the source not only of love but also of inspiration and encouragement for eighteen years. *As Thy Days so Thy Strength* and *Mission in Metropolis* (Eerdmans, 1960 and 1965) were a part of his legacy of spiritual guidance and teachings on the wise and responsible exercise of personal freedom to family, friends, students, parishioners, and a wide circle of Christians concerned about the improvement of the society. I shall never be able to express fully my appreciation for the integrity of his living and the quality of his giving to each of his children and his wife.

Finally, I am aware that God, the creator and authentic source of all blessings, is the *sine qua non* of this work. For God's abiding presence and particular beneficence in my life, I am eternally thankful.

Genna Rae McNeil
New York City
December 1982

The National Association for the Advancement of Colored People made a generous contribution toward the publication of this book in order to make it available to a wider audience.

JOHN McGUIGAN
University of Pennsylvania Press
March 1983

FOREWORD

by *Judge A. Leon Higginbotham, Jr.*

There has always been, and probably always will be, an "explicit . . . conflict between the obligations of law and of conscience—between the commands of law and the claims of justice."[1] I am grateful for Dr. Genna Rae McNeil's superb book, which traces the journey of a heroic lawyer who tried so valiantly to make the American legal process a system that synthesized concepts of moral conscience and justice for blacks within the commands and obligations of law.

Fifteen years after Charles Houston's lamentable and premature death, Martin Luther King, when speaking to the Bar Association of the city of New York, said:

> You should be aware, as indeed I am, that the *road to freedom* is now a highway because lawyers throughout the land, yesterday and today, have helped clear the obstructions, have helped eliminate roadblocks, by their selfless, courageous espousal of difficult and unpopular causes.[2]

The road to freedom that Martin Luther King described as a highway in 1965 was in the early twentieth century not even a discernible path in the jungle of racism tolerated by the American legal process.[3] Among the builders of the early road to freedom, which Martin Luther King significantly extended, no one person played as significant a role as did Charles Hamilton Houston. The primary architects and engineers in building this highway also included William Henry Hastie, Thurgood Marshall, James Nabrit, and at most two or three others. Yet each of these illustrious lawyers would have agreed that Charles Hamilton Houston was the chief engineer and the first major architect on the twentieth-century civil rights legal scene.

Some readers may rebel when I describe our America of fifty or one hundred years ago as a jungle of racism. There is no better way to test this hypothesis, at any time, than by examining the policies of the president of the United States. Grover Cleveland was president when Charles Hamilton Houston was born. During this era, blacks were restricted to the most menial jobs. With only the rarest of exceptions, the professional, managerial, secretarial, and "white collar" jobs were certainly unreachable for even the most talented and competent blacks. From the presidency of Grover Cleveland through that of Herbert Hoover, presidents were either patently hostile or generally unsympathetic to the muted and cautious requests by blacks for some slight improvement of their lot. Even the false rumor that a black had been present at an official White House function was sufficient to drive President Cleveland into a frenzy, and thus he responded: "It so happens that I have never in my official position, either when sleeping or waking, alive or dead, on my head or my heels, dined, lunched, supped, or invited to a wedding reception, any colored man, woman, or child."[4]

In 1904 when a most moderate black leader, Booker T. Washington, had lunch informally with President Theodore Roosevelt, the *Memphis Scimitar* wrote: "The most damnable outrage which has ever been perpetrated by any citizen of the United States was committed yesterday by the President, when he invited a nigger to dine with him at the White House."[5] Senator Benjamin Tillman of South Carolina said: "Now that Roosevelt has eaten with that nigger Washington, we shall have to kill a thousand niggers to get them back to their places."[6] Georgia's governor was sure that "no Southerner can respect any white man who would eat with a Negro."[7]

Not wanting to be outdone by others in racist remarks, Governor James K. Vardaman of Mississippi wrote in his newspaper:

> It is said that men follow the bent of their geniuses, and that prenatal influences are often potent in shaping thoughts and ideas in after life. Probably Old Lady Roosevelt, during the period of gestation, was frightened by a dog, and the fact may account for the qualities of the male pup that are so prominent in Teddy. I would not do either an injustice, but am disposed to apologize to the dog for mentioning it.[8]

Apparently, Woodrow Wilson had no qualms about the plight of blacks. A black newspaper, *The New York Age*, warned that Wilson, "both by inheritance and absorption . . . has most of the prejudices of the narrowest type of southern white people against the Negro." Princeton University, of which Woodrow Wilson was president from 1900 to 1910, was the only major northern school that excluded Negro students. Moreover, as governor of New Jersey from 1911 to 1912, his "progressivism" did not embrace the Negro. Wilson's "New Freedom" had been "all for the white man and little for the Negro." Wilson had not visited "any colored school, church, or gathering of colored people of any nature whatever."[9] During his administration there was a steady "expansion of segregation in the federal department buildings in Washington, a policy which Taft had begun."[10]

The Congress was no better. It "had done nothing to protect civil rights during Republican administrations and did nothing under Wilson."[11] "Neither Harding nor Coolidge had restored Negro patronage to pre-Wilson levels, and in 1928 Hoover bypassed the regular black-and-tan organizations to cultivate white support in the South."[12] Government offices and cafeterias remained segregated; the War Department segregated Negro Gold Star mothers who were traveling to their sons' graves in France; Hoover ignored race problems in his messages to Congress. He made "fewer first class appointments of Negroes to office than any President since Andrew Johnson."[13]

This was the jungle of patent racism confronting Charles Hamilton Houston. Because of his tenacity and genius, he deserves a stature in our nation as significant as that specially reserved for Thomas Jefferson, George Washington, Patrick Henry, or Chief Justice John Marshall. Though Houston did not write the Declaration of Independence, he made life, liberty, and the pursuit of happiness a far more meaningful option for blacks than Thomas Jefferson ever did for his own slaves or for blacks in general. Though Houston was never commander-in-chief of the armed forces, almost singlehandedly he organized and led the legal battalion in the critical early battles seeking equality for black Americans. Though Houston never shouted from the hilltops, "Give me liberty or give me death!", he gave his entire professional life to make the cloak of liberty embrace and protect that race of Americans whom Patrick Henry enslaved. Though he did not have the extraordinary judicial power of Chief Justices John Marshall and Roger Brooke Taney, nevertheless Charles Houston made the Constitution a living and more relevant document to those Americans against whom John Marshall and Roger Brooke Taney so often ruled adversely, dashing the aspirations and hopes of blacks for freedom.

Charles Hamilton Houston was the primary force in designing a strategy to move human-rights concepts from the valley of despair toward "the mountaintop" subsequently envisioned by King. With a systematic approach, Houston slowly and persistently hacked through the forests of racism and oppression; yet few contemporary Americans, including judges, lawyers, professors, deans, or students, know of Houston's momentous contributions. Some weeks ago I had the pleasure of talking to several intelligent and highly motivated black law students at the University of Missouri. I asked them if they had heard of Charles Hamilton Houston and of his involvement with the University of Missouri.[14] Not one student there knew of his role in litigation against their university, and most were unaware of his greater role in constructing the road toward racial freedom.

It is with reluctance that I refer to those marvelous students, because I admired them. I do not mean to impugn them. My point is that they were typical of thousands of students, both black and white, in law school today. Except for the predominantly black schools, I would have received the same response at almost every major law school in the nation. Most colleges and law schools give students no exposure to the black heroes in the law who built the foundation for the later success of blacks in the 1960s, 1970s, and 1980s. Fortunately, with Dr. McNeil's book, that gap of knowledge is being partially filled.

Charles Houston's life was devoted to the cause of freedom. His accomplishments cannot be viewed as aiding only blacks—instead, he helped save all of America. How would America look today in the eyes of the world if United States senators were still urging, as did Senator Ben Tillman, that "we will have to kill a thousand niggers to get them back to their place?"

Charles Houston's legacy for us is the foundation he built almost singlehandedly to deter and eliminate the racial oppression others had enforced through the legal system and through violence. His career is an extraordinary counterbalance to our forefathers' failures in the racial human-rights arena. Because of his leadership in legal education, his vision as a lawyer, his ardor as an advocate, his skill as a strategist, and his compassion for all mankind, we have today the opportunity to make this nation the type of land it must be and what it may never have become but for the efforts of Charles Hamilton Houston and a few other dedicated Americans.

Houston spawned Thurgood Marshall, Robert Carter, and several other great civil-rights lawyers, and he nurtured the William Hasties who, in their respective ways, carried on the battle long after Houston's premature death in 1950 at the age of fifty-four. Hundreds of acts and accomplishments could be cited from his victories in housing, voting, and in the criminal justice system that preserve the rights of all Americans. Most important, however, Charles Houston should be a model as well as a legend. For if he could speak to us in his melodious voice, he might remind us that by the sheerest coincidence we are privileged to have been born in an affluent country and fortunate to have been exposed to a grossly superior educational system. He would stress that all of us, for whom so much has been given, share a special but heavy burden of contributing our skills back to society so as to improve the welfare of others.

Groundwork is more than an excellent biography of a superb lawyer—who happens to be black. Its major contribution is its revelation of the critical battles Houston fought for the ultimate credibility of all America—the tenacious and discouraging fight for equal justice under the law for all Americans. Through Dr. Genna Rae McNeil's descriptions of Houston's extraordinary efforts, most readers will recognize that it required great courage, tenacity, and discipline to move justice forward even a little bit in the trial pits and hostile appellate courts; it required more courage than that displayed by our most revered justices on the United States Supreme Court who wrote in the tranquility of their chambers and were shielded from the harsh diatribes, the financial struggles, and the escalating frustrations that were the daily menu of an articulate, committed black civil-rights lawyer from 1920 to 1950. Dr. McNeil's description of Houston's travail and turmoil presents penetrating insights into the American legal process during the first half of the twentieth century, its rigidity, its callousness, and yet its most important—though sometimes illusory—virtue, the possibility of change for the better through the judicial process.

In another sense, Dr. Genna Rae McNeil has also written a remarkable history of a significant black family, whose contributions would rival and exceed those of almost any family in America, regardless of race. The magnitude of the Houston family's contributions toward the quality of justice in American society probably dwarfs that of any other black family in the country, or, in fact, that of any family in which the members did not control extraordinary material resources or hold major public offices.

In summary, Dr. McNeil has captured the substance and subtleties of these multi-faceted issues and has presented cogently the problem of the duality of black America that Dr. W. E. B. Du Bois once described:

> One ever feels his twoness,—an American, a Negro; two souls, two thoughts, two unreconciled strivings; two warring ideals in one dark body, whose dogged strength alone keeps it from being torn asunder.

> The history of the American Negro is the history of this strife,—this longing to attain self-conscious manhood, to merge his double self into a better and truer self. In this merging he wishes neither of the older selves to be lost. He would not Africanize America, for America has too much to teach the world and Africa. He would not bleach his Negro soul in a flood of white Americanism, for he knows that Negro blood has a

message for the world. He simply wishes to make it possible for a man to be both a Negro and an American, without being cursed and spit upon by his fellows, without having the doors of Opportunity closed roughly in his face.[15]

Houston dealt with this duality from his days at Amherst to that spring day on April 22, 1950, when he died. In Dr. McNeil's references to this duality, there are several other issues intertwined with Houston's efforts and life—the military during World War I, the challenge of black educators and predominantly black universities, the tension for excellence versus the demand for accessibility, the struggles for unity and consensus within a political spectrum running from the middle to the left. Finally, it should be pointed out that this superb work provides a moral for all people of good will, whether black or white. It is the message Houston's life symbolized: the essentiality of labor, the struggle for distant goals, and the inherent financial sacrifices one encounters in seeking to fulfill the dream.

I congratulate Dr. McNeil for tenaciously pursuing and finishing, with such indisputable scholarship, this significant study of an American pioneer. I would also like to commend the University of Pennsylvania Press for publishing, within one year, two extraordinary books[16] involving race and the American legal process that set standards by which future great books in this field should be measured.

NOTES

1. J. Auerbach, *Unequal Justice: Lawyers and Social Change in Modern America* (New York: Oxford University Press, 1977), p. 264. Many of the ideas expressed in this foreword have been discussed in greater detail in A. Leon Higginbotham, Jr., *In the Matter of Color: Race and the American Legal Process* (New York: Oxford University Press, 1978); idem, "Judge William Henry Hastie—One Who Changed the Immutable," *Howard Law Journal* 24 (1981): 259; idem, "Racism and the Early American Legal Process, 1619–1896," *Annals of the American Academy of Political and Social Sciences* 407 (1973): 1; idem, "Foreword," in *Blacks in the Law: Philadelphia and the Nation*, by G. R. Segal (Philadelphia: University of Pennsylvania Press, 1983), p. xiii; idem, review of *Race, Racism and American Law*, by D. Bell, *University of Pennsylvania Law Review* 122 (1974): 1044.
2. M. L. King, Jr., "The Civil Rights Struggle in the United States," *The Record of the Association of the Bar of the City of New York* 20 (1965): 5, 6.
3. Some commentators have stressed that even in the 1960s the road to freedom had not been built and there was a jungle of racism. Professor Auerbach notes in *Unequal Justice*, pp. 264–65, when speaking of the later 1950s and early 1960s that

As the civil rights crusade spread through the South, the relentless prejudice of a Jim Crow bar surfaced. The complicity of the legal profession in preserving unequal justice under law, for whites only, raised questions about professionalism and its social responsibilities. For at least a decade after the *Brown* desegregation decision, Southern lawyers persisted in their defense of "Nordic, White Protestant, Anglo-Saxon Christian values." Few dared to defend advocates of racial equality. Daring was costly: it prompted harassment by courts, legislatures, vigilantes, and fellow professionals (while the American Bar Association shrugged aside the problem as a "political" issue beyond its purview). In Mississippi, the president of the ABA (along with forty other lawyers) refused to represent a civil rights advocate. One white lawyer in the state, one of a mere handful who demonstrated the courage of his professional convictions, was disbarred. A black lawyer engaged in desegregation litigation was harassed by a federal judge whose behavior, according to an appellate court, contributed to the "humiliation, anxiety, and possible intimidation of . . . a reputable member of the bar." The result, not only in Mississippi but throughout the South, was "timid lawyers and neglected clients."

4. G. Sinkler, *The Racial Attitudes of American Presidents, from Abraham Lincoln to Theodore Roosevelt* (New York: Doubleday, 1972), p. 270.

5. Higginbotham, review of *Race, Racism and American Life*, p. 1044.

6. Ibid.

7. Ibid.

8. Ibid.

9. R. Logan, *The Betrayal of the Negro* (New York: Macmillan, 1965), p. 361, quoting A. Walters, *My Life and Work* (1917), p. 257.

10. Ibid.

11. Ibid., p. 363.

12. G. Tindall, *The Emergence of the New South 1913–1945* (Baton Rouge: Louisiana State University Press, 1967), p. 542.

13. Ibid., quoting W. E. B. Du Bois, "Hoover," *The Crisis* 29 (1932): 362.

14. For discussion of *Missouri ex rel. Gaines* v. *Canada*, 305 U.S. 337 (1938), see pp. 143–45, 149–51, 199, 200, 218 of this volume.

15. W. E. B. Du Bois, *The Souls of Black Folk* (New York: New American Library, 1969), p. 17.

16. The other being Segal, *Blacks in the Law.*

PREFACE

The significance of the struggle for the rights that are called inalienable, "life, liberty, and the pursuit of happiness," has always seemed to me quite crucial. This is so by reason of the irony of the contrast between America's original declaration regarding the inalienability of these rights and the protracted struggle of black people in America against their alienation from these rights. In large measure, however, the struggle for these human rights seems crucial because it links us with a process through which, because of which, or in the face of which we all must decide (by action or default) how the entitlement to these inalienable rights is related to morality and truth.

Charles Hamilton Houston was born on September 3, 1895; he died on April 20, 1950. The moral imperative on which he acted was, in his own words, to "reconcil[e] the wants and desires of different human beings, each equally entitled to life, liberty and the pursuit of happiness."[1] As a lawyer for nearly three decades, Charles Houston struggled to protect Americans of African descent and to create for his people "better and broader opportunities . . . without prejudice or bias operating against [them]. . . ."[2] Recognizing "the constructive potential of all the forces he could see working against racism, segregation [and] discrimination," he moved with and defended forces that to his mind were most effectively fighting for African Americans' rights.[3] While following this course, Houston insisted on being an "outside man," free of any permanently confining organizational ties or labels.[4] Nonetheless he was bound to and embraced an ideology. Amilcar Cabral demystifies this assertion: "You have to establish the political aims and based on your own condition the ideological content of the fight. To have ideology doesn't necessarily mean that you have to define whether you are communist, socialist or something like th[at]. To have ideology is to know what you want in your own condition."[5] For black people in the United States, Houston demanded legal guarantees and enforcement of freedom, justice, and equality. For the United States he prescribed a moral legal code of conduct with which the majority population had never been in accord, and he claimed that in the twentieth century the egalitarian language of the Declaration of Independence must embrace all, regardless of race. Even when Charles Houston believed he was speaking modestly about the human estimate, his very words challenged the foundation of the nation.

On the occasion of the formal opening of Howard University's Law School in May 1958, Justice Thurgood Marshall declared that not he but Charles Hamilton Houston was "the First Mr. Civil Rights Lawyer."[6] Houston, however, cared so little about personal recognition that he nearly assured his own future anonymity. To begin the process of rescuing Houston from obscurity, it took not only the reminders of Marshall at Howard in 1958 and on the occasion of the inauguration of the Charles H. Houston Forum at his alma mater, Amherst College, in 1978, but also the recollections of friends, colleagues, and other contemporaries during annual Houston Medallion Award ceremonies of the Washington Bar Association (of which Houston was a founder) and in publications of the 1970s.[7]

It is appropriate that there be a critical biography of Charles Houston. Whenever there appears in history a person whose positive reach extends far beyond the measure of his years, his way of being in the world is worthy of attention. In theory (influencing the black jurisprudential matrix with his philosophy of social engineering) and in practice (laying legal groundwork for African Americans' equal rights under the law), Charles Houston made a marked contribution to the civil rights movement and the struggle against oppression of African Americans, for which he was posthumously awarded the coveted Spingarn Medal of the National Association for the Advancement of Colored People (NAACP).[8] As Harvard's Erwin Griswold explained in presenting the award a few months after Houston's death, "It is doubtful that there [was] a single important case involving civil rights . . . [in] the . . . fifteen years [1935–50] in which Charles Houston [did] not either participate . . . directly or by consultation and advice."[9]

Although biographical, this study does not chronicle Houston's life in exhaustive detail. Rather, it examines the lines along which he decided to live his life, the questions he felt compelled to answer, the choices made and the paths taken. It focuses on triumphs, trials, and errors in the process of growth through inner and outer struggles. In so doing, it focuses also on the manner in which using the law as an instrument of social change became an all-consuming task for Houston. This biography is based on Charles Houston's papers from his home, his firm, his NAACP office, and Howard University, official government records, and the records of organizations with which he was affiliated, state and federal court reports, papers of people who knew him, other selected primary sources, and interviews or conversations with his family, friends, students, colleagues, critics, and admirers. I hope it contributes to an understanding of the black experience in the United States, of the development of constitutional law during the first half of the twentieth century, and of race relations in this nation. At times Charles Houston, although among the oppressed, was in positions that made him like an isthmus between two worlds differentiated not solely by race, but also by class, life chances, life choices, by what they held dear and what they accepted as right, good, and true. Sometimes Charles Houston's experience is recognizable as that of the victim—stymied, variously abused, and oppressed. A collective history of black people in the United States from 1895 to 1950 emerges as Houston is placed in his historical setting with all the currents arising from the social, political, and economic predicament of black people and the temper of the times.

It is hoped that this study will prompt further questions about the movement of African Americans toward freedom, about their struggle for justice, equality, and self-determination, about the degree to which reformist or radical solutions may be applied to the problem of creating a just and egalitarian society, and about the relation of law to morality. Apart from raising such questions, the primary hope is that this biography will assure that Houston's uniqueness does not escape us. In the final analysis, this book is an attempt to acquaint the reader intimately with the indomitable spirit of Charles Hamilton Houston, who struggled against oppression his entire adult life while knowing there was "no tea for the feeble, no crepe for dead"[10] and who discovered, against the background of his early privileges, that "every one to whom much is given, of him will much be required; and of him to whom men commit much they will demand the more" (Luke 12:48).

Do not bind the children within the narrow
circles of your own lives. . . . Make them
understand that it is just a question of
reconciling the wants and desires of
different human beings, each equally
entitled to life, liberty and the pursuit of
happiness.

—Charles Hamilton Houston (1934)

Without . . . sacrifice
without understanding and dreams
emotion and protest
without struggle
there will be no childhood.

—Jayne Cortez (1973)

INTRODUCTION

"We wouldn't have been any place if Charlie hadn't laid the groundwork for it," Thurgood Marshall, Associate Justice of the Supreme Court of the United States, told an audience of blacks and whites assembled to pay tribute to his former teacher and friend, Charles Hamilton Houston.[1] Encountering some puzzled faces following such a sweeping testimonial, Marshall, with his inimitable directness, added:

> You have a large number of people who never heard of Charlie Houston. But you're going to hear about him, because he left us such important items. . . . When Brown against the Board of Education was being argued in the Supreme Court . . . [t]here were some two dozen lawyers on the side of the Negroes fighting for their schools. . . . [O]f those . . . lawyers . . . only two hadn't been touched by Charlie Houston. . . . [T]hat man was the engineer of all of it. . . . I can tell you this . . . if you do it legally, Charlie Houston made it possible. . . . This is what I think . . . Charlie Houston means to us.[2]

Thurgood Marshall, Charles Houston's best-known student, has always been generous with his praise concerning Houston. Some have listened and dismissed Marshall's assessment as the adoration of an admiring student. Others have discounted it as an aspect of the dutiful modesty of a student who surpassed his teacher. Nevertheless, Marshall's words serve to remind African Americans and white Americans, who are insistent about equal and just distribution of civil rights and liberties, that they are recipients of Houston's legacy.

Twenty years after *Brown* v. *Board of Education* and *Bolling* v. *Sharpe*, Justice William O. Douglas joined Marshall in directing attention to Charles Houston as a civil rights lawyer and litigator. "I knew Charles H. Houston, and I sincerely believe he was one of the top ten advocates to appear before this court in my 35 years."[3] In a later autobiography, *The Court Years, 1939–1975*, Douglas vividly recalled that Houston "was a veritable dynamo of energy guided by a mind that had as sharp a cutting edge as any I have known."[4]

When Charles Houston decided to study law so that he could influence American government and protect African American citizens in the exercise of their rights, he joined three traditions. Kenneth Tollett has noted the historical relationship of the legal profession to government and the enunciation of civil liberties.

> Traditionally, lawyers have played a critically important role in the political and economic development of the United States. Twenty-five of the fifty-six signers of the Declaration of Independence were lawyers. Thirty-one of the fifty-five members of the Constitutional Convention were lawyers. The United States House of Representatives and Senate . . . and legislative bodies across the country have had a larger proportion of officials and members from the legal profession than from any other profession.[5]

Houston's choice of career placed him in this one tradition, while his principles and race placed him in two other traditions. Since John S. Rock's admission to practice before the U.S. Supreme Court on February 7, 1865, black lawyers have been attempting to win equal rights for citizens of African descent in the Supreme Court of the United States. Moreover, since Africans' and African Americans' petitions and resolutions to colonial ruling powers, blacks in North America have been protesting denials of liberty and justice in not only courts but also in legislative assemblies. Regarding this third tradition, of which Houston became a part, Derrick A. Bell, legal scholar, has offered critical insights. "The history of black people's reliance on the law in their centuries-long struggle for freedom and equality is a story . . . of slow, painful ascent from slavery . . . and virtually no attention is given to just how little even some of the major events changed or improved [African Americans'] status."[6]

Charles Houston's life and work elucidate the stark reality of the second-class status of African Americans between 1895 and 1950. The difficulty he encountered while advocating human and civil rights for blacks particularly underscores historic oppression and repression. As an attorney, Houston found that the truths labeled "self-evident" and the rights labeled "natural" became arguable issues when he presented claims for African Americans. The basis for this was historical.

The "all men are created equal" of the 1776 Declaration of Independence and the "We the people of the United States" of the 1787 Constitution were not obviously inclusive. The first phrase generally proclaimed a new normative system, while the other described the citizenry, but both were framed by whites with only whites in mind. The generality of the eighteenth-century language provided options to consider or not to consider the humanity of blacks. However, the political and economic affairs of a burgeoning nineteenth-century slave system eroded the options. Because so few challenged either slavery or the racism it bred, in 1857 Justice Roger Taney confidently claimed, for the majority of the Supreme Court, that in early American history a black "had no rights which the white man was bound to respect."[7] As Judge A. Leon Higginbotham, Jr., has demonstrated, there was an "early failure of the nation's founders and their constitutional heirs to share the legacy of freedom with black Americans."[8]

Only after blacks seized liberty and demanded rights during a time of civil strife did lawmaking bodies delineate clearly the citizenship rights of African Americans. The U.S. Supreme Court's *Dred Scott* decision on black citizenship in 1857 was nullified by the collective language of the Thirteenth Amendment abolishing slavery (1865), the Civil Rights Act of 1866, and the Fourteenth (1868) and Fifteenth Amendments (1870). The 1866 statute specified that "all persons born in the United States and not subject to any foreign power" were citizens who, regardless of "race and color," were entitled to "make and enforce contracts, to sue, be parties, and give evidence; to inherit, purchase, lease, sell, hold and convey real and personal property," and to enjoy the "full and equal benefits of all laws and proceedings for the security of persons and property as is enjoyed by white persons."[9] The Fourteenth Amendment to the Constitution not only affirmed the national and state citizenship of African Americans, but also prohibited any state's action to "make or enforce any law which shall abridge the privileges or immunities of citizens . . . , deprive any person of life, liberty, or property, without due process of law . . . [or] deny to any person within its jurisdiction the equal protection of the laws." Finally, the Fifteenth Amendment to the Constitution provided that interference with voting on account of race or color was illegal. By 1870, African Americans were citizens with equal rights on paper. The laws of the land conceded their personhood and citizenship.

In less than four decades, the "gains made by blacks—political, legal and social—were erased . . . [and] the Supreme Court and the lower courts confirmed in their decisions . . . that the citizenship [blacks] had been granted, which they believed they had earned through the blood of thousands of black men who had died fighting on the Union side during the [Civil] War, was citizenship in name only."[10] Unless they were acting on behalf of a state, white Americans could discriminate against blacks, and forced separation of people on the basis of race and color became perfectly legal. The Civil Rights Cases of 1883 and the *Plessy* v. *Ferguson* case of 1896, respectively, permitted state and private discrimination and segregation.[11] White racist force, wealth, and power effectively disfranchised blacks in the southern states, where over 75 percent of the African American population lived, and the federal government failed to invoke its considerable legal powers to prevent violation of black people or their rights.[12] Likening the United States to the Republic of South Africa, the late William H. Hastie, Jr., the first black appointed to a federal judgeship, summarized the status of African Americans, and the conditions under which they lived in the early twentieth century: "The effective institutionalization of racism was the common experience of most Negroes. . . . [A]partheid seemed as irradicable and almost as pervasive a feature of the American legal order as it appears to be in South Africa."[13]

Because of institutionalized racism in America, two of the consequences of Houston's choice to complete law school and become a practicing attorney were his double exclusion and double minority status. As a black man, he was excluded from full participation in American society, and as a black lawyer he was excluded from full participation in the predominantly white American bar and the legal process. As a black man, he was part of a group that constituted only 10 percent of the American population, and as a black lawyer he was part of a group that constituted less than 1 percent of the American legal profession. This situation placed in the path of any black lawyer obstacles impeding successful advocacy of the rights of African Americans.

Between World War I and the end of the postwar decade, white Anglo-Saxon lawyers who dominated the profession were engaged in a campaign against any racial minority and aliens under the guise of patriotism, professionalism, and higher educational standards. The American Bar Association, having already barred blacks from membership, was sufficiently racist and xenophobic to encourage lawyers interested in a countermovement. In 1925 black lawyers founded the National Bar Association, and in 1936 the ethnic, religious, and racial underclass of lawyers formed the National Lawyers Guild. Jerold Auerbach has discussed the remarkably enduring influence of such bias among the elite of the legal profession. In the United States,

> justice has been distributed according to race, ethnicity and wealth rather than need. . . . The professional elite bears a special responsibility for this maldistribution. Their efforts, in conjunction with the limitations of an adversary process, . . . crippled the capacity of the legal profession to provide equal justice under law or fulfill . . . paramount public responsibilities.[14]

Owing to the unequal justice that characterized the American legal process and the responsibility white lawyers bore for this, the African American civil rights movement in the 1930s depended largely on the 1,175 black lawyers of the United States.

The first phase of the modern, organized civil rights movement of African Americans began in the midst of, and among proponents of, equal rights and desegregation advocacy. The elective branches of the government were ill-disposed toward taking responsibility for full enforcement of the rights of Americans of African descent. This necessitated fighting many battles in the U.S. Supreme Court, where all questions about the constitutionality of laws were ultimately resolved. Because the aggrieved parties basing their claims on the Constitution were blacks, judicial review became less a perfunctory examination and more a challenge. As Mary Frances Berry explained, "The need to respect constitutional government ha[d] been . . . twisted and perverted" for the "promotion of white nationalism" and the "American government and people ha[d] persistently defended the repression of blacks in the name of law and order" for centuries.[15] Moreover, since the U.S. Supreme Court historically had tolerated, condoned, and been an accomplice of such racial injustice, the arguments of blacks were affected adversely not only by the case litigation method but also by the policies and the composition of the Supreme Court. The policies of the Court to follow principles laid down in previous decisions and to avoid rendering a decision on constitutional grounds whenever possible presented constant problems. Often the justices themselves were a problem. The legal battles of African Americans gave new meaning to the wisdom of Oliver Wendell Holmes: "The felt necessities of the time, the prevalent moral and political theories, intuitions of public policy, avowed or unconscious, even the prejudices which judges share with their fellow men, have had a good deal more to do than syllogism in determining the rules by which men should be governed."[16]

During the 1930s and 1940s participation in a civil rights movement, which used every available legal means to establish and guarantee enforcement of nondiscriminatory laws, was one of the few alternative approaches to doing something about the quality of life for African Americans in the United States. Other choices included advocacy of black separatism, accommodation to the system, collaboration with the predominantly white working-class movement to which matters of racial injustice were secondary to class issues, or affiliation with groups promoting justice for all through the overthrow of the government. In a time for action, this was the essential predicament of African Americans.

This brief overview of the legal status of African Americans before 1950 and the relationship of the legal profession to it provides a general historical backdrop for understanding the significance of Charles Houston's role in the early phases of the modern civil rights movement. To this must be added, however, a few final comments on African American culture during Houston's period, 1895–1950, for the context of his life and work is social as well as political. Relationships with the dominant white society did not fix the perimeters of African American life. A whole series of social relations persisted through time: The black community embraced duties for its members at every stage of life; social stratification within the structure yielded classes and social antagonisms; belief systems created and supported institutions and leaders while also providing concepts for patient endurance, daily perseverance, and hopeful struggling. The black community's network, its forms of self-expression, and its members' feelings and behavior went far beyond reactions to exploitation and oppression. And although, as philosopher-theologian Howard Thurman describes, "white and black worlds were separated by a wall of quiet hostility and overt suspicion," in the black community there was room for personal identity, fellowship, and shared responsibility.[17] Houston cannot be understood in isolation from any of this.

Born in 1895, Charles Houston's childhood spanned years of the black community's confrontation with virulent white supremacy and accommodationism as a white-approved solution. Paul Laurence Dunbar—who for a time lived in Houston's hometown, the District of Columbia—spoke for many members of the community when he explained in his poem "Sympathy,"

> I know why the caged bird sings . . .
> When his wing is bruised and his bosom sore,—
> When he beats his bars and he would be free;
> It is not a carol of joy or glee,
> But a prayer that he sends from his heart's deep core. . . .[18]

The years during which Charles Houston attended high school and college, served in the army, and studied for his law degrees brought important changes, even if racism was continuous. A new racial cohesiveness, consciousness, and self-assurance were reflected not only in protest and resistance, but also in a reaching up and out (and back) to Africa and race pride. A black officer of the National Association for the Advancement of Colored People (NAACP), W. E. B. Du Bois convened a Pan-African Congress in Paris during 1919 to stress the unified determination of blacks to be free. Marcus Garvey, effectively teaching the dignity and beauty of being black and initiating business ventures with Africans, attracted the loyalty of over 1.5 million African Americans before the U.S. government used its power to jail him and eventually deport him. Garvey's importance eluded neither the masses nor Harvard's black law students. During Houston's tenure at Harvard

Law School, he arranged a luncheon for fellow black students at which Marcus Garvey was the guest of honor. Speaking on another occasion, Houston explained: "Prior to Marcus Garvey . . . Madame Walker had made a million dollars making ble[a]ches and straightening hair. But Marcus Garvey . . . claim[ed] his black skin as his proud birthright and distinction. . . . Garvey, by turning the Negro's attention to the beauty of the color of his skin, has had a profound influence on Negro thought."[19] Everyone did not embrace Africa and blackness so that they evoked permanent pride and a sense of past glory, but some Americans of African descent felt a newness in the discovery of this old tie. There was a knowing of "rivers ancient as the world and older than the flow of human blood in human veins" because of a history linked to the Gambia, the Niger, the Senegal, the Congo, and the Nile.[20] Other blacks could take pride in their African heritage and adopt radical analyses in response to conditions in the United States. This was the case with the New Negro Harlem Radicals, headed by Chandler Owen and A. Philip Randolph of *The Messenger*, who were ideologically opposed not only to nationalists, but also to the West-Indian-dominated Marxists of the African Blood Brotherhood.

Throughout the 1920s and the 1930s the "new Negro" movement of the political arena radiated into Harlem and beyond to create a black renaissance. The artists of the era were sometimes crusaders, but not always. This liberating milieu was a time for expressing one's spirit and consciousness with a variety of talents for a variety of reasons. The musicals of Noble Sissle and Eubie Blake, arrangements of spirituals by Harry Burleigh and Nathaniel Dett, the blues of W. C. Handy and Bessie Smith, and the singing and acting of Paul Robeson revealed dimensions of African American creativity to black and white audiences. Books by James Weldon Johnson, Jean Toomer, Jessie Fauset, and Zora Neale Hurston, with the poetry of such writers as Claude McKay, Countee Cullen, Anne Spencer, and Langston Hughes, described black life in its diversity and provided insight into the black ethos. The paintings of Laura Wheeler Waring and Aaron Douglas, the photographs of P. H. Polk and James Van Der Zee, the sculpture of Meta Warrick Fuller, and the dancing of Josephine Baker made a powerful statement about the wholeness and distinctiveness of black people. They "were able to find the means to sustain a far greater degree of self-pride and group cohesion than the system they lived under ever intended for them to be able to do. . . . Black Americans forged and nurtured . . . a rich expressive culture."[21]

Despite the impact of the Great Depression, the late 1930s and 1940s gave way to both an explosion and a flowering. The NAACP, with local branches throughout the nation and under black leadership, declared war on segregation, while black artists—poets, painters, sculptors, musicians, actors—insisted that the black presence be recognized in all fields of creative endeavor. America could not seem to make room for all the talent, but Roland Hayes, Marian Anderson, Ella Fitzgerald, Billie Holiday, Nat King Cole, Billy Eckstine, Sarah Vaughn, and Lena Horne sang black life and shared black feelings in prestigious and ordinary settings. Dizzy Gillespie, Louis Armstrong, Count Basie, Duke Ellington, Thelonious Monk, and Charlie Parker ("Bird") played the highs and lows, the sorrow, the breaking of bonds, the breadth of African American life, on the road or at the Savoy, Apollo, and Howard theaters, while the implications of Richard Wright's *Native Son* and *Black Boy* reverberated inside and outside black neighborhoods. Because of Hollywood movies and publicity, the names of some blacks became household words. Despite stereotyped roles, Hattie McDaniels of *Gone with the Wind* fame, Bill "Bojangles" Robinson, "Stepin' Fetchit," and Dorothy Dandridge exhibited great skill, and blacks watched them enthusiastically.[22] Observing the community that idolized its "Brown Bomber," Joe Louis, and mobilized in the thousands to march on Washington for jobs and a national fair employment policy, such black poets as Sterling Brown, Pauli Murray, Melvin Tolson, Robert Hayden, Gwendolyn Brooks, and Margaret Walker used their talent and skill to underscore the sameness and the changes of the passing years. Painters and sculptors—among them Charles White, Romare Bearden, Charles Alston, Augusta Savage, Richmond Barthe, Selma Burke, and Elizabeth Catlett—viewed African American life sensitively and mirrored or translated its depths and horizons.

Throughout this discussion, reference has been made to a racist status quo undergirded by law and protected by the white American majority. The language of groups—white and black—facilitates summary but diverts attention from the individuals in these separate but intersecting worlds. Racial hatred may become an act of self-affirmation, particularly when all around ruling powers and instruments of government work in behalf of such a feeling about an entire race of people. But no doubt damage is done to the human spirit. Willing black people to be nonhuman has always been a futile exercise, and vital energies have been irretrievably lost in negative encounters. In contrast, love of self and of fellow blacks as well as purposeful commitment to responsible activity are acts of self-affirmation that can create energy and dissipate fears regarding untried endeavors. So often W. E. B. Du Bois's description of African American identity has been assumed to be valid for virtually all blacks prior to the "Black Revolution." He believed there was a personal duality: "One ever feels . . . two-ness . . . ; two souls, two thoughts, two unreconciled strivings; two warring ideals in one dark body. . . ."[23] Yet those whose history and present were linked with struggle also laughed, loved, and grew on a number of levels in the years between 1895 and 1950. Many African Americans believed that the duality was not so much theirs as the nation's:

> This is America, dual-brained creature
> One hand thrusting us out to the stars,
> One hand shoving us down in the gutter.[24]

Because the black community defined itself in many ways, it could foster an analysis of race relations that identified America's schizophrenia as the problem.

Committed black struggle grew out of health, not pathology, even in the period between 1895 and 1950, during which black inferiority was a pervasive doctrine. And despite all the sameness that racism bred, changes did occur. Some came in relation to sweeping political, social, and economic forces that transformed the United States from an emerging industrial, newly expansionist nation to an arrogant, imperialistic power with designs on overseas territories identified as vital to national interests and security.[25] Other changes came as a result of African Americans' resistance to and assaults against racist oppression.

Charles Hamilton Houston's life is a chapter in a story never completely told. Americans of African descent have embraced, resisted, called into question, and advocated much in the process of moving toward freedom. In comparison with the "by any means necessary" aggressive civil/human rights struggle of the 1960s and early 1970s, these decades of slow beginnings may seem lacking in boldness. Nonetheless, without such steady attacks—

> chipping at the stones earnestly, tirelessly
> moving with the changes of the hours
> the days
> the seasons and years[26]—

who knows how long twentieth-century America would have remained smugly oblivious to black shouts and content in spite of national atrocities?

PART ONE

Prologue to Struggle: The Formative Years 1829–1924

I was determined that if I lived I was going to have something to say about how this country should be run.

—Charles Hamilton Houston
Recollections of World War I—"Saving the World for Democracy," 14 September 1940

CHAPTER I

The Inheritance

The story of Charles Hamilton Houston—"Charlie" to those who knew him well—begins long before his birth. Who he was and how he met life and handled its changing fortunes were, in part, givens. Charles Houston was more than the sum of his experiences. No one could know him without being struck by the Houston tradition he proudly carried on and the Hamilton legacy announced and celebrated by his presence. These were deeply rooted and basic.

The Houstons emerge from anonymity when Thomas Jefferson Hunn, born on 10 August 1829 to slave parents in Kentucky, resolved to run away and change his name. Bound to a cruel and violent master in Missouri at an early age, he never viewed his slave status as something he could accept for life. It seemed to him that animals could be bought and sold and beat into submission by an owner, but human beings were different and were—or ought to be—free. Finding himself in this predicament, Hunn resisted his bondage and oppression in a way that was to set an example for his progeny.[1]

"Absolutely unafraid," the young Hunn quietly attempted to free himself by a variety of means at every opportunity. He had run away, gotten caught, been jailed, and been returned to the plantation so often that in the circles of the white authorities he was known as a repeater. Frequent attempted escapes netted him more cruel treatment, but each attempt served to narrow the viable strategies and strengthen his resolve. One night, after an unusually vicious beating by his master, Hunn attempted another escape that proved to be the final one. Seeing that the beating had left Hunn's right leg badly injured, his master left him to suffer the pain. Determined to bring an end to far greater pain, Hunn found a loose stick, which he used as a cane, and during the night he left Missouri. He had not gone far before "[h]e broke his right ankle . . . [but] he could not risk medical aid for fear he would [be] . . . arrested as a fugitive slave." "With a limp which he would have the rest of his life," Hunn walked toward Illinois and took a new surname, Houston. No one in the family remembered the reason for that choice of name, but the purpose had been explained: "to throw the slave hunters off his track."[2]

A man of "deep and provoking faith" in the providence of a just, beneficent God, Thomas Jefferson Houston "became a conductor on the underground railroad between Missouri and Illinois, repeatedly crossing the Mississippi River to bring slaves into free territory."[3] He was, above all, disturbed by the moral and spiritual questions raised by slavery as inhumane oppression, and as would become characteristic of future Houstons, he felt compelled to act in accordance with fundamental convictions. This he did with courage and resoluteness. In later generations, when among some Houstons religious fervor waned, this moral sense endured.

On one run as a conductor, Thomas Jefferson Houston returned to his former master's land and carried his mother and brothers Charles, Henry, and Chester to Cairo, Illinois, where Thomas made his home whenever he was not on a run. After aiding the family in escape, Thomas Jefferson—known to his family and friends as T.J.—was joined by his brother Charles in the underground railroad work. Although it was T.J. who was called to preach in 1849 and ordained as a Baptist minister, Charles carried the Bible on their frequent trips, while T.J. carried a gun. The gun was a form of protection, but not frequently used in the underground railroad work. In connection with their dangerous work, T.J. Houston started a family tradition of using clever and persuasive arguments to accomplish a task when the odds were against success. On one occasion, after the onset of the Civil War, he ran into Union troops as he was taking an unusually large number of fugitive slaves to a river crossing and safety in Illinois. According to family oral tradition, at that moment Thomas Jefferson Houston relied on God, a quick wit, and a remarkable resemblance to Ulysses S. Grant. He calmly informed the officer in charge that he was a friend of Grant awaiting an escort to cross the river with his contraband. He secured not only safe passage but also a meeting with Ulysses Grant later. Thereafter, out of his zeal to support a war that might bring slavery to an end, T.J. attached himself to Grant's troops, which were based in Cairo. In 1862 he served as a teamster in the Battle of Corinth and became General Grant's unofficial personal bodyguard, remaining with him—for the most part—through the fall of Richmond in April 1865.[4]

As were other black men traveling with the Union troops—especially those unofficially attached—Houston was sometimes permitted to "pass the lines."[5] In most cases this happened on national holidays or when there was family business to which a man needed to attend. In Houston's case, however, his temporary leaves were prompted by his faithfulness to his "call to preach" and his decision to minister to blacks miles away. It was on such an occasion that T.J. Houston first saw Katherine Theresa Kirkpatrick, who later became Mrs. Thomas Jefferson Houston. Katherine Theresa was a lovely almond-brown young lady, the eighteenth offspring of Minerva and Reuben Kirkpatrick. She was born on 10 August 1849 in Burkesville, Kentucky, at the plantation of Milton King. When yet a girl of seven, Kate's slave parents, grieving and bitter, were forced to say good-bye to her, as King sent Kate to serve his son, who was moving to Paducah, Kentucky. Good fortune came to Katherine later when the entire King family moved to Paducah, reuniting Katherine with her mother and siblings. The move was not without its sadness, however, for it was Milton King's decision to leave the husband and father, Reuben, behind. Because her marriage was ended by a forcible separation, Katherine's mother could remarry without the stigma of sin. After some time, Katherine's mother married Reuben Harris and bore two children for him.[6] Pondering that mode of human relationships and King's obliviousness to the human feelings of his slaves, Katherine wrote much later, "[T]hey were very very cruel to us in a good many things. . . . Strange that they should have been so cruel to my mother when my mother nursed [the] mistress."[7]

The death of her mother and the cruelty of her owners compelled Katherine to run away. In 1862, with the help of "Uncle Pete" Andrews (a brother-in-law's father), who worked as a porter on a boat, the girl of slight build managed to hide aboard the *General Anderson*, which ran on the Ohio River from Paducah to Cairo, Illinois. In Illinois, Katherine hired herself out, but found each succeeding employer more inhumane. So when the husband of one of the King daughters approached Kate about living with them in St. Louis, Missouri, she told him she would. Victoria King Sweetney and her husband seemed more considerate; Katherine welcomed relief from constant abuse. Yet in the months to come she found she simply could not feel satisfied or safe with the Sweetneys.[8] At first this was merely an uneasiness; later she felt that she must move on. One evening, as if her mother were in the room, Katherine heard her mother warn, "Marse Milton is coming after you and is going to take you as far south as he can to sell you." Katherine forthwith announced to her mistress that she was leaving the Sweetney household. She collected her few belongings and "went away out on Olive Street." She later recalled, "I got a place just by going from door to door where I worked and kept myself hidden. I was on the street one day and got a glimpse of Mr. King who was my master. I guess he was looking for me. . . . [But] I kept out of sight."⁹

One night, when Katherine and her girlfriends attended a church service celebrating the Emancipation Proclamation, Thomas Jefferson Houston first saw his wife-to-be. He noticed her dress, her hat, her coat—every detail. Katherine was so striking. She, on the other hand, "did not know him [and] [n]ever thought of him. It never occurred to [her] that anybody was paying any attention to [her] whatever." Yet, as fate would have it, in three years the two were brought together again. Katherine returned to Cairo, Illinois, and who but Thomas Jefferson Houston was the new pastor of the church she had chosen to attend. When she was taken to meet the pastor, he said, "I have seen you before." She replied, "No, I think not." He then asked her if she recalled the meeting in St. Louis three years earlier, and he described precisely her attire. A three-month revival was held at the church, and during that time Katherine "professed religion." After her profession of faith, the Rev. T.J. Houston, twenty years her senior, proposed to Katherine. She recalled,

> [H]e asked me when could I be ready and I told him in about a year. That did not seem to suit him. I asked would six months be soon enough. He said, "I could be married and forgot in that time,["] so we were engaged. I told him to set the time. We were engaged on Wednesday night and married the following Sunday afternoon [29 April 1866].¹⁰

Over a year after the end of the Civil War, these two escaped slaves began a new life together as legally free people. No longer needing to run and hide, Katherine and Thomas moved into a one-room cabin in rural Illinois and readied the land for crops. Thomas worked his Illinois farm all week and then on Saturdays traveled on horseback and by canoe to Cape Girardeau, Missouri, where he preached on Sundays. Every Sunday evening he then crossed the Mississippi River again and traveled all night until he reached home on Monday. After 1868, Thomas came to be in greater demand, and so he traveled to churches in Cape Girardeau and also in Metropolis, Illinois, on alternate Sundays.¹¹

Between 1868 and 1887, T.J. and Katherine moved often. They lived in Metropolis, Mound City, and Cairo, Illinois, before traveling to Paducah, Kentucky, and Evansville, Indiana, in search of better opportunities. During this time Thomas learned a new trade and worked weekdays as a renovator of featherbeds and pillows. He loved his church work, but by 1887 Katherine had given birth seven times, and he had five children to feed, clothe, and educate: Evangeline Leque

(1868), William LePre (1870), Clotill Marconier (1879), Ulysses Lincoln (1881), and Theophilus Jerome (1885).[12]

Before Theophilus reached school age, the family moved away from Evansville, Indiana. Katherine was constantly talking with her husband about making possible more advantages and, above all, more education for their children. In July 1890, after consultation with her husband and with his consent, blessing, and the tools of her hairdressing trade, which he had purchased for her, Katherine Houston went to Washington, D.C. She "left husband and children [none of whom were infants] and everything behind until [she] could . . . look over the city to see what she could do in [her] line of business." Many "banged their doors in [her] face" before Katherine Houston found one friendly patron.[13] She confidently persevered, armed with "her bible and her faith in the Lord."[14] After she began practicing her trade in Washington, her reputation for fine work in the "weaving of hair, braides, curls, switches and puffs" led her to become the hairdresser for the wife of President Grover Cleveland.[15] In December 1890 the success of her business and the financial assistance of her son William enabled her to bring her four younger children to Washington, D.C. They shared rented dwellings and waited for Thomas Houston to settle business affairs in Evansville. He joined them early in 1891 and soon after was called to the pastorate of the First Baptist Church of Bladensburg, Maryland. By March of the same year, the Houstons were able to rent their first home in Washington, D.C., at 1607 Nineteenth Street, Northwest, near Q Street.[16] Thus it was that Katherine and Thomas Jefferson Houston paved the way for a second generation's less arduous sojourn in the nation's capital and became an enduring source of strength and inspiration for their descendants.

For William Houston, the eldest son of T.J. and Katherine, the decision to move to the District of Columbia was a less difficult one. It was the sole municipality providing opportunities he believed essential to his future well-being, although it held the dubious distinction of being glaringly at variance with the *professed* ideals of the nation. By virtue of an act of June 1878, the federal government shared the expenses of the District of Columbia in exchange for total control over purse strings and policy. Ultimate authority for the governing of Washington, D.C., was vested by the Constitution in the Congress of the United States. Pursuant to the 1878 Organic Act and an 1874 act of Congress, the District was presided over by three presidentially appointed commissioners with no accountability to the local populace. (Earlier, local autonomy had been part of a Reconstruction experiment, and as a consequence the District, having then an aggressive black electorate, had municipal programs and even ordinances that attempted to improve the quality of life for all residents and prohibit discrimination.) By 1890, the 75,572 black and 154,605 white residents were virtually powerless, and racial discrimination was not unusual.[17]

Powerlessness was practically the only thing whites and blacks of the District held in common. Whereas once blacks (admittedly depending on color, class, and position) and whites might be seen in some of the same restaurants, theaters, and hotels, by the 1890s proprietors in Washington, D.C., began to separate blacks and whites. This Washington, D.C., could no longer boast of having black elite in the *Social Register*, a black president of Georgetown University, a black opera company performing at Ford's Theater or nationally prominent politicians gathering at the prestigious Wormley Hotel (owned by a black entrepreneur) to discuss the nation's future.[18] Although "lines weren't drawn in [all] the hotels . . . [or] the National Theater" to exclude blacks absolutely, antidiscrimination statutes of 1869 and 1870 were often conveniently ignored by whites.[19]

Blacks in the District, generally speaking, were less well-to-do than whites. For numerous reasons—not the least of which were racial discrimination, color prejudice, and a high rate of illiteracy among blacks—conditions began to worsen in the decade before the turn of the century. Blacks did not have equal access to employment opportunities and, as compared with their numbers in the populace, they remained grossly underrepresented in professions, skilled and semi-skilled trades and manufacturing occupations. Yet, black people from the states migrated to what they perceived to be a more advantageous location.

Black migration to the District from the states such as those in which the Houstons had resided—Kentucky, Illinois, and Indiana—was to some extent justified by the economic and educational conditions for blacks in those states by the last decade of the nineteenth century. Cities in these and other states provided fewer occupational and educational opportunities for blacks than the District. This was true for at least four reasons. First, the larger District black community had a consequent greater need for services. Second, there was an extraordinarily large class of whites who, either because of wealth or position, employed blacks in domestic and personal service. Third, the employment of blacks in a sizable number of lower-level positions by both the federal government and District government was a source of security. Generally, only custodial, clerk, typist, or messenger jobs were open, but any kind of government employment meant occupational longevity and security. Finally, since 1867 Washington, D.C.,

had become the site of Howard University, a major university open to
all qualified people regardless of race, but particularly established with
funds from the federal government to aid in the higher education of
freed and free blacks.[20]

William Houston left his job in Paducah, Kentucky, in 1890 to move
to the District of Columbia because such a move suited his needs:
Washington, D.C.—with its government jobs and Howard University's
evening Law Department—might even be the town where he could
seek his fortune. Just as the Houstons before him, William possessed a
certain boldness, ambition, and sense of adventure. How could he remain safely in Paducah as a school principal while his parents set out
for a better life? Ever since a distinguished Indiana attorney, Charles I.
Wedding, and his wife had warmly encouraged a young William Houston to pursue a law career, he had dreamed of becoming a successful
lawyer. After two years as a teacher and principal of a Paducah high
school for blacks, and after witnessing his parents' fearlessness, William knew it was time to pursue his own dream. He had met an attractive young teacher, Mary Ethel Hamilton, and he was anxious to
marry her and move ahead with his life. William took and passed a civil
service examination, and by October 1890 he was a War Department
Record and Pension Office clerk during the day and an enthusiastic
candidate for a Bachelor of Laws (LL.B.) degree during the evening.[21]

William was pleased with himself and his progress at the end of his
first of two years at Howard, for he was doing a creditable job in the
Pension Office and seemed to have an aptitude for law. He had very
little money, but he was getting worried about how long he could expect a young lady with Mary Hamilton's intelligence and beauty to
wait. Perhaps he also was lonesome; it might even have been spring
fever. William wrote Mary that he believed their separation and engagement had been long enough; he asked her to join him in the District and become his wife. Mary Ethel Hamilton and William LePre
Houston were married on July 16, 1891.[22] This Hamilton-Houston
union shaped and refined the inheritance of the next generation.

As far back as anyone could remember, life had not been easy for
the Hamiltons. Mary Hamilton's grandmother had been a slave and in
those days had been "lashed unmercifully . . . for mutilating her master's hand when he attempted to impose his will on her."[23] Jesse Hamilton, a free black, met Mary's grandmother, fell in love with her, bought
her freedom and married her. In the 1840s a son was born and named
Amaziah. Jesse, who was determined that his family never become the
chattel of any man, considered it unwise to continue to farm in the
South with his son, particularly after the Fugitive Slave Act of 1850

and the infamous *Dred Scott* decision of 1857, which together proclaimed a clear national policy of the denial of human rights to blacks.
He sold his farm in Rock Hill, York County, South Carolina. Prior to the
Civil War, Mr. and Mrs. Jesse Hamilton and their teenage son Amaziah
traveled by wagon to Green County, Ohio, in the vicinity of Wilberforce. At one stop in Kentucky, Amaziah met the lovely but quite young
Joanna Berry. It was one of those magical meetings that lasted long
enough for the two to know that, despite their youth, they were des-
tined to be together. Promising to return and pledging love one to the
other, Amaziah went on to Ohio with his parents and Joanna waited.
After the Civil War, Amaziah returned to Kentucky to ask properly for
Joanna's hand in marriage. After marrying, the two settled in Kentucky. There, Mary Ethel, the first of ten children, was born in 1867.
During their daughter's infancy, Amaziah decided—and Joanna agreed
—that Ohio was a better place to raise a family. The three Hamiltons
first moved to a small farm three miles from Wilberforce. Amaziah labored, saved a considerable sum of money, and eventually purchased a
farm on Tarbox Road, near Cedarville, Ohio. Everyone welcomed the
move to a larger house, and the twelve worked together to make a success of the farm.[24]

Mary helped in the home with chores and the care of the nine
younger children. She completed her secondary school work and matriculated at Wilberforce in Ohio. However, she did not have the opportunity to complete her course in the Normal Department of Wilberforce because, as the eldest offspring, it was her responsibility to find
work and assist her parents financially. She took her first job in a country school near her home, where she taught some of her siblings. After
one year, she accepted a teaching position in Mayfield, Kentucky, but
she remained there only one year before transferring to a Paducah,
Kentucky, school in 1888. She cheerfully and proudly sent part of her
earnings to her family during the three years she taught there. It was
not that she had so much extra that made her so unselfish, but rather
the memory of her parents' sacrifices and the love they all shared.[25]

While teaching in Paducah, Mary met the ambitious and charming
William Houston. A ripening friendship led to their engagement in
1890, and during the summer of 1891, her love for William made her
willing to give up her plans for a wedding in Ohio and settle for a simple ceremony in the District. Her income following their marriage
went to keep the William Houstons out of dire financial straits until
William finished Howard's Law Department in May 1892. She was no
longer in a position to send money to her aging parents.[26] Fortunately,
as her siblings grew they took on more responsibility for the welfare of

the entire family. They had been taught from the earliest years not only to trust God to do his good work but also to perform their own Christian duties and help themselves as much as possible. This set Mary's mind at ease after a while, although in her first years of marriage she could not help but worry from time to time and feel sad that she had no more to give. Mary Hamilton, as her parents and her parents' parents, was strong but very sensitive. Indefatigable in her work and in her giving, she was an unceremoniously devout Christian. Quietly and simply she loved God, family, and husband. Gently, amiably, devotedly, and steadfastly she supported William's—as she would later support her son's—aspirations and dreams. And although she did not lack intellectual curiosity, she concerned herself more with that which affected the human heart.[27]

The Hamilton-Houston union was not the merging of two totally opposite traditions or two identical ones. It was rather a coming together of sensitivity, unselfishness, determination, and an accepting faith with a keen religious-moral sense, initiative, fearlessness (mixed with noticeable stubbornness), and courage of conviction to reenforce a shared devotion to family and duty, perseverance, intelligence, and a finely honed sense of justice and right. To these traditions Charles Hamilton Houston was an heir. (See Appendix 1.)

CHAPTER II

Charles Hamilton Houston

Charles Hamilton Houston was born on 3 September 1895 in the intimacy of the Houston home at 1444 Pierce Place, Northwest (later renamed Swann Street) in Washington, D.C. His name, the result of careful pondering, paid tribute to Charles I. Wedding, the attorney who had inspired William, and the long line of free Hamiltons, Mary's side of the family. Mary, William, Katherine, Thomas, and Clotill, William's younger sister, greeted the first male of this Houston generation joyfully and prayerfully. All knew that, because of the times and his race, much would be required of Charles.[1]

In 1895—as in other years since Reconstruction—the months came and went with increasing pain to the spirits of black Americans. Slavery had been replaced with tenancy, peonage, occupational ceilings for the race, and unemployment. Where once there had been promises and expressions of lofty ideals, the rhetoric of white supremacy rang, lynch mobs became self-appointed juries, disfranchisement spread, the color line assumed greater national importance, and Booker T. Washington, white-ordained spokesman for the race, emerged preaching accommodation as the solution to the "Negro problem." Yet making a way out of no way was part of what it had always meant to be a black person in America. As they always had, the Houstons faced this harsh reality and set about planning to give Charles Hamilton Houston every initial advantage they could muster.

Completing his law studies and being admitted to the bar of the District of Columbia in 1892 had not established William L. Houston securely in the professional or middle class. His accomplishment, however, had facilitated his escape from a lower-class, hand-to-mouth existence. In two years after his son's birth, although he was forced to continue work as a clerk in the Record and Pension Office instead of solely practicing law, William had saved enough money to move out of his parents' home and into his own home at 1705 Tenth Street, an equally respectable part of town for educated blacks.[2]

Practically every activity in the Houston's Tenth Street home revolved around the child "Charlie." Even as a small child he had a winning way. Mary was devoted to her son and more often than not humored him. William was more firm, but not harsh. He was busy so much of the time that he delighted in his home life and especially the hours spent with his boy. Grandfather Houston was one of Charles's most attentive and fun-loving playmates for the first three and a half years of the boy's life; the eldest Houston always found time to spend with his first grandson despite his church work in Bladensburg, Maryland. Understandably, a gloom set in for little Charles and the whole Houston family when on 19 February 1899 the patriarch died. The *Colored American* newspaper reported the attendance of one thousand people at the funeral of Thomas Jefferson Houston, in whose death "the church and community suffered an irreparable loss."[3] Whatever the loss to the community, it was not as deep and shattering as to the family. Yet Katherine Theresa Kirkpatrick Houston, although left to live without the husband she loved, continued to call forth the immense strength and faith deep within her and to shun grieving before it became its own sickness. She soon found for herself never-ending tasks to perform and, during daily visits with her sons, exhorted them likewise to hard work and faith. After Thomas's death, Katherine became more and more involved in her children's and grandchildren's lives. Between Evangeline and William, Katherine had three granddaughters, Frances, Eunita, and Christine Young, and one grandson, Charles—who seemed more like Thomas as the months went by—to keep her alert and busy.[4]

The boy Charles was full of life. He reveled in the company of his first cousins, whom he called "[his] only little sisters." With Christine, Frances, Eunita, and a small circle of friends, Charles enjoyed the wonder, the gaiety, and the innocuous mischief-making of childhood. Although he was not a tough little boy, Charles could hold his own in outdoor sports. When playing outside with his cousins was not exciting, a naturally curious Charles loved visiting the zoo, attending concerts and theater matinees, and reading titles of books and any sign he could see when out walking with his father. As he grew older, he read so much he was called a bookworm. He got along well with relatives and friends of any age; Mary saw to it that he respected and appreciated differences. But even as a child he was a private person. There were many days when he preferred to spend hours alone practicing the piano. Often Charles seemed a "serious-minded child; . . . that was . . . characteristic."[5]

Charles received his primary and secondary education in the segregated school system of Washington, D.C. During Charles's public school years, the administration of the District's schools was under the direction of an appointed board of trustees and after 1906 a board of education. The board was initially charged with the responsibility of providing "suitable and convenient houses or rooms for holding schools for colored children," employing and examining teachers, paying necessary expenses, building or renting school facilities out of school funds, and endeavoring "to promote thorough, equitable and practicable education of colored children." In 1901, when Charles began school, a dual system had been established, and the board's responsibility to black children was being carried out within divisions numbered 10 through 13 under the auspices of Assistant Superintendents W. Scott Montgomery and Roscoe C. Bruce. With Congress controlling the budget and having little concern for the needs of a voteless people, the regular cutting of the budgetary requests of the District commissioners led to the annually predictable result of gross inequities between the two divisions (i.e., 1 through 9 for whites, 10 through 13 for blacks) in the disbursement of appropriations, the placement of equipment, and the ratio of personnel to students.[6]

Even given this state of affairs, Charles was fortunate enough to attend Garrison Elementary, a grade school in which he was allowed to work at his own pace. The bright and alert youngster, by attending summer school, completed the eight grades of primary school at the age of twelve. In February, 1908 Charles was prepared to enter the remarkable M Street High School.[7]

During Charles's high school years, his father's professional status and economic situation changed for the better. By 1909, William Houston had saved enough money to resign from his government position. During that year and 1910, he practiced law in Chicago, Illinois, under the tutelage of a successful black lawyer, Edward Morris. When he returned to Washington, as had more than two dozen other blacks trained in law, William began to devote his time to a law practice in the District; he was listed in subsequent current editions of the city directory as "Houston, William L., Lawyer. . . ."[8]

The first years of practice at 1314 V Street, Northwest, were, according to William, the "short grass years," when he could take on a case, handle it well, and still make only a three-dollar profit. Moreover, as a consequence of his taking the advice of Charles Wedding—who when giving William his first law book admonished, "Only . . . civil lawyers have lasting reputations"—William turned away potential clients if their concerns appeared to be criminal matters. Nevertheless, William's practice grew as his reputation for being an astute advocate and law professor (he also taught law in the evenings at Howard University's Law Department) spread throughout Washington's black community.[9]

During these same years the income of the William Houston family was supplemented by Mary Houston's earnings. Charles's mother learned the hairdressing trade from her mother-in-law, Katherine. Mary maintained a highly selective clientele; her patrons included the wives of senators, diplomats, and cabinet officers. In the course of her work, she came in contact with a high standard of living and refinement, which she not only admired, but also desired for her son. In William and Mary's home nothing less than the standard of her patrons was acceptable. She had determined that Charles should be brought up as the best. Both William and Mary worked with almost boundless energy so that they could give Charles in his early life what their own parents had been unable to give them. Perhaps because they strove to shield him from difficulty and disappointment, and perhaps because each of Charles's parents sacrificed for the well-being of their families and remembered well "doing without," they sought to move whenever possible to better neighborhoods until they and their boy were situated comfortably in the narrow and secure environment of Washington's black middle class.[10]

From the example of a father who worked ceaselessly to place his family beyond the reach of severe economic proscriptions and assume a notable position in the professional class, Charles learned much about the industry and persistence of strong black men. From his mother's example, Charles learned much about the dignity of being identified as a Negro. Although Mary Hamilton Houston—in physical appearance—was hardly distinguishable from a white person, she always insisted on being known as a "Negro" by her white patrons. She never hesitated to inform these patrons that she expected to be called "Mrs. Houston," not "Mary," to be admitted through their front doors, and to work without having to listen to disparaging remarks about the Negro race. From his father's and mother's frequent and fond references to a mainspring, a parental source of strength, Charles learned that there was cause for great pride in his own heritage: In spite of racial hostility, brutality, and daily personal indignities thrust on them because of their race, the Houstons and the Hamiltons had struggled and endured. Yet while Charles was affected by the vivid stories of his grandparents and parents, these stories had none of the immediacy of his own experiences. They did not cause him to be pensive beyond his years, nor did they weigh so heavily on the conscience of the boy that he, at twelve years old, determined he would aspire to fight for his race. The development of a militant racial consciousness would come some years later, when Charles could understand what Grandmother Houston's stories about slavery and white obliviousness to the humanity of blacks meant for the shaping of his own life.[11]

There was never any question that the offspring of the Houston-Hamilton line would go to college and aspire to greater heights than his forebears had been able to reach. For that reason Charles had been sent to summer school. Afterward Armstrong, the technical high school, had never been considered. Charles was enrolled at M Street High School so he could prepare for college.

M Street was *the* classical high school for black children throughout the District and adjacent Virginia and Maryland cities. The high school's students and their parents understood its purpose to be "to prepare boys and girls for college."[12] M Street "was the first black high school in the United States and it was an academic school from the beginning—fiercely resisting recurrent pressures upon it to become vocational, commercial or 'general.'"[13] During the years of Charles's attendance, M Street continued to be "traditionally classical in its curriculum" including such subjects as English, Latin, French, Spanish, Greek, German, history, mathematics, the sciences, the arts, music and physical education.[14] "The curriculum [for each student] was based on college entrance requirements and those for Miner's Teachers College: two years of a foreign language, one of which was modern, were required."[15] M Street drew its students from the entire black community of the District, although primarily they came from the more fortunate black economic groups. "A large segment of the students had one or more [parents working as] government employees for support . . . these employees were messengers and clerks, with few exceptions."[16] Some other parents were professional or semiprofessional. In M Street, however, there were students from all economic classes because "brains were recognized, not money."[17] Neither was color a major factor. Contrary to popular belief, light-skinned students did not constitute the majority.

The faculty of M Street was composed of exceptionally well trained teachers; practically "every leading college" was represented.[18] "Segregation and discrimination gave [M Street] . . . a captive market of . . . teachers" in that Negro graduates were excluded from most university and college faculties. It was not unusual in a parent-teacher association meeting to discover that the teacher of one's child either held a doctorate or had studied abroad.[19] The school's pupils were dependent on the skill, sensitivity, breadth, and sagacity of their teachers to lessen the negative effects of limited facilities and inadequate financial support for M Street High School. To a large extent, an exceptional faculty was responsible for expanding students' cultural horizons.

In the early twentieth century, black Washington, D.C., was a separate—and for most white District residents—"secret" city. This second city had its own appeal. Distinguished scholars of the race engaged in debate and dialogue concerning a variety of topics under the auspices of the American Negro Academy.[20] A college preparatory high school and Howard University afforded quality education for youth, while other members of the community pursued their varied cultural and intellectual interests as participants in historical associations, artistic societies, literary clubs, and choral societies. Mu-So-Lit, a predominantly Republican and exclusively male social organization, invited lecturers to present discourses on musical, social, political, and literary matters. African Methodist Episcopal, Methodist, and Baptist churches, and Greek letter fraternities and sororities, were important cohesive elements in the social network of the black community. The press, particularly the *Washington Bee* in this era, both kept the community informed on broad national issues and provided residents with "intelligence" on the affairs of the distinguished families, the community leaders, and the rising professional class. After the first decade of the twentieth century, when racial barriers in concert halls, theaters, and other places of public accommodation denied students opportunities to attend many events or see or hear significant figures in world affairs or the arts, many teachers at M Street—recognizing the nature and kind of handicaps created by segregation in the District—encouraged students to visit municipal and federal buildings, museums, and art galleries and arranged for programs with distinguished speakers, artists, and successful alumni or alumnae. Teachers and administrators were particularly interested in students' having an opportunity to interact with M Street graduates who had achieved prominence.[21]

Charles was not a brilliant student in high school, but he did well in many subjects. Bertha McNeill, who taught French to Charles in his second year, recalled that having earned a G (good) from her, "Charles must have been very good."[22] "My philosophy was that a student was there primarily to learn, and that it was my obligation to teach according to the highest standards. . . . The subject matter was either 'absorbed,' 'learned,' 'understood' or it was not."[23] Charles learned his lessons and was on time, prepared, cooperative, pleasant, and succinct. He usually had a ready smile for friends and teachers, but sometimes in classes he seemed quite "nonchalant."[24] Because of his summer school work, Charles was younger than most high school students, and he had days when he was more interested in pranks and attention than in poetry and algebra. "Charles' persistently annoying conduct both in the classroom and especially in the Study Hall makes it necessary for me to write you," Jessica Fauset advised Charles's mother so that she might speak with him about his "nonsense and trifling."[25] At times Charles's teachers were almost certain that he had already expended most of his energy getting to school, since it was all he could do some days to "sit in a slouched position with his elbow on the desk and his head in his hand." Yet even Miss McNeill, who was known to be "hard," knew it must have been somewhat uncomfortable for boys such as Charles, who seemed to have the longest legs and the shortest seats.[26]

The restlessness associated with adolescence was evident in the grades Charles made during his four years at M Street High School. His English performances, for example, fluctuated from excellent to good to fair to good, while he excelled in such subjects as algebra and Greek. By his senior year, however, Charles settled down. He took the maximum five-course load, earning no grade lower than G, and participated as a first lieutenant in Company B of the extracurricular military cadet organization. On 11 June 1911, at the age of fifteen, Charles was graduated from M Street High School.[27]

Most black high school graduates, in contemplating their higher education, were faced with the serious problem of inadequate funds. For this reason, teachers and principals at M Street made special efforts to maintain ties with their colleges and universities, which included Amherst, Bates, Brown, Dartmouth, Oberlin, Williams, the University of Pennsylvania, and the University of Pittsburgh. Occasionally, as a consequence, scholarships became available to bright, motivated M Street students who wished to continue their education and had demonstrated need or great ability. Charles was the recipient of one such scholarship to the University of Pittsburgh, but his parents had encouraged him to apply for admission to a more prestigious institution. Individual blacks who could meet the admission standards and whose parents could afford it had been tolerated at such institutions as Harvard, Dartmouth, and Amherst, if they were inconspicuous. Those who could fulfill the academic requirements and endure the racism could graduate. Mary and William wanted Charles in one of these colleges; it was in keeping with their desire to give Charles the best.

According to the family decision, Charles applied for admission to Amherst, was accepted, and turned down the scholarship to Pittsburgh. Garnering their resources, Mary and William in the fall of 1911 sent their son off to be educated at Amherst. From September 1911 to June 1915, Charles was an Amherst man with no financial worries.[28] For the experience of working, during one summer Charles worked in his father's office as "Journal Officer," and during another summer he was a playground assistant, but "the question of a dollar, the value of a dollar . . . [Charles] never had to think about."[29]

Charles could hardly contain his excitement as he boarded the train for Amherst on 13 September 1911. When he arrived, the campus, studded with multicolored trees so characteristic of New England autumns, held a special beauty.

Charles had been at Amherst only a brief time when he sought a special conference with his mother. It was customary for all students to have a nice room at the college, but it seems that Charles had decided that he really needed more than that if he were to be a good student. Charles "got in touch with his mother and told her he would like to have an extra room" for working on his lessons. Charles's mother, not mentioning it to his father, made the arrangements. On one occasion, Charles's father had an opportunity to visit him, and Charles proudly showed the elder Houston his living quarters. His father said, as he looked in the direction of an adjoining room, "Whose room is this?" "This is my study," replied Charles, completely unruffled in the face of his noticeably shocked father.[30]

With or without a special study, Charles would have made his parents proud of him. He had good study habits, considerable ability, and more time than his white counterparts to devote to his courses. There were no other black students in the class of 1915. He had "very few friends in town and rarely paid a social visit."[31] Often he could be found in his room writing letters to his mother or father. Although letters could not replace the regular conversations Charles had been accustomed to having with his parents, letters kept him involved in family matters. During his sophomore year, Charles read with some alarm of his father's time-consuming efforts as a Grand Master for the Odd Fellows of America and volunteered some advice:

[I]f I were you I would make my plans on myself, for myself and by myself—to paraphrase Lincoln. By that I mean, I would do my own planning, and have my plans ring around me or rest the responsibility upon me, then try to carry them out myself. I have found . . . to the best of my knowledge where you have relied on someone else you have never gained a complete victory. . . . Inexperience hampers the judgment of my statements, but eagerness and sincerity for your welfare lead me instinctively to [these] few conclusions.[32]

Charles had been quite independent as an only child, but he was counseling a self-reliance bordering on complete self-sufficiency. A year as the only student of African descent at Amherst had taught Charles lessons not assigned by any professor.

Charles was a likeable young man, intelligent and pleasant. Among the students, despite his race, he had a number of acquaintances and a few friends. In those days, Charles—"about 153 lbs. stripped"—prided himself on keeping in shape and following a fairly strict regimen.[33] A similarly physique-conscious friend sometimes joined Charles when "on good mornings [he would] get up at 5:40 to play tennis until 7:00."[34] However, genuine comradeship and friendship were difficult to sustain because "the fraternity life in college was strong and the boys moved into the fraternity houses at the opening of the second year. [Charles] had to live in the dormitory." As he described himself, he was either "too shy or too proud . . . to visit . . . classmates very much in their fraternity houses. [His] contacts with . . . classmates [were] limited chiefly to classroom and other common college exercises or functions." In contrast, Charles's classmates unhesitatingly joined Charles in his dormitory study whenever they needed assistance.[35]

Although his race set him apart in some ways, Charles was known to his teachers because of his good work, not merely his race. In some instances there was quite a good rapport between Charles and his professors. From time to time his parents received gratifying reports.[36] Charles knew that his parents had not sent him to Amherst to be a mediocre student. All three, having a great deal of race and family pride, wanted Charles Hamilton Houston of the class of 1915 to be— and be remembered as—an exceptional Amherst man because of demonstrated ability. The alienation born of racism continued to be a catalyst for Charles's academic and personal self-reliance. On his own at Amherst College, he refused to harbor any debilitating feelings of inferiority. "Let us . . . , since we believe that we are as divine as possible in this generation, resolve . . . to depend upon ourselves exclusively as much as possible, in all walks of life," he declared to his father.[37] Occasionally there were professors who simply could not believe that a black student could be worthy of a better-than-average grade, but the Houston standard was always excellence. As Charles made his way through a very white Amherst with toughness, he explained to his father, "Anything that is worth having is worth sacrificing for. . . . Genius is not half so much inspiration as it is the culmination of endless, painful and infinitely careful application."[38]

His classmates recognized Charles's studiousness and success. In the 1915 *Olio*, the Amherst yearbook, the staff wrote: "'Charlie' is one of the hard workers of the class and expects his reward along about February unless 'Emmie' grants special dispensation and holds a special election to Phi Bet sometime previous to the scheduled affair. He has led a very quiet life during his stay with us and certainly deserves anything that his scholarship may bring him."[39] Charles maintained an A average in German, Spanish, Latin and music and a B average in English, mathematics, chemistry, Greek, and French. The anomaly of Houston's academic career while at Amherst was a C in public speaking. On this he did not comment in letters to his parents, probably determining that he would handle this atypical evaluation in another way.[40]

In Charles's senior year, because of an excellent grade point average by the 1914–15 academic year and good moral character, he was elected to Phi Beta Kappa and chosen one of the revered "Bond Fifteen" scholars. He communicated a clear message to his speech professor when from among the Bond Fifteen he was selected, by means of an oratorical competition, to be one of the June commencement speakers for the class of 1915. After deliberation, Charles determined that the subject of his commencement address would be the life of Paul Laurence Dunbar. Charles later told his family that it was not without difficulty that he was able to give the address of his choice. "The faculty, not being well acquainted with [Dunbar] wanted [Charles] to change to another topic. They said, 'Mr. Houston, we don't know—' He said, 'I know it, but you will know him when I've finished.'. . . [H]e succeeded in keeping [Paul Laurence Dunbar] as a topic."[41]

At the end of June 1915, William Houston closed his office for two days. He and Mary took an early morning train to Amherst, Massachusetts, to attend their only son's commencement exercises. Before meeting his parents' train, Charles walked through the campus one more time. He detoured from the natural surroundings only long enough to climb the alluring tower of Johnson Chapel, and, as he had been told was traditional, he climbed to the top to carve his initials and the year of his graduating class inside. As he joined his "CHH '15" with the carved inscriptions of nineteenth- and twentieth-century Amherst graduates before him, Charles did so with a great sense of accomplishment and finality. He descended the rickety wooden stairs of the tower to see his parents, who had made such sacrifices for his four years of full-time study. The ninety-fourth commencement program noted final honors in English to Charles Hamilton Houston, who graduated magna cum laude—"a rank fixed at 88 percent"—with the degree Bachelor of Arts.[42] Charles's father made a special note in his diary under Wednesday, 30 June 1915: "Chas graduated from Amherst at 9:45 A.M. He spoke 'Looking Ahead.'"[43] Throughout his adult life, Charles made contributions to his alma mater and from time to time kept in touch with friends from his class.[44]

During the summer of 1915, Charles took a well-earned vacation from academia. With his mother he visited the Hamilton relatives in Cedarville, Ohio. Grandpa Hamilton had died in 1901, and since that time Grandma, Joanna Hamilton, had run the farm and "worked in the fields the same as a man . . . until she was crippled by a runaway horse."[45] Charles so rarely saw his mother's family that this summer visit was very special to him. (It was to be his last visit with his maternal grandmother; she died in 1916.)

Although it disappointed his father, during the summer of 1915 Charles came to no definite conclusions about his career. His Aunt Clotill was a magnificent teacher who had an impact on many lives; sometimes her nephew Charles seriously considered the teaching profession. He had taken French, Spanish, and German because he thought he might want to be a diplomat. Since childhood he had been hearing about his father's dream, a law firm, "Houston & Houston." But Charles preferred creating music—performing at the piano—to the adversarial role and almost any other job he could imagine. Often he was more certain of his contentment with playing the piano than he was of anything else. Did he dare choose a concert career? In any case, both he and his mother just enjoyed the music in the Houston home again. William Houston grumbled, but he was not going to disown his son if he did not make an irrevocable decision during his first summer since college graduation. William also did not worry about his nineteen-year-old son because, in Charles's behalf, William had already made inquiries about a suitable position. Teaching at Howard University and serving a number of professional clients in his private law practice, William was in a position to assist his son in finding an interesting temporary job with a reasonable salary until he was ready to make a firm commitment to a future course of action.[46]

CHAPTER III

"Army Justice"

Having a father with influence could at times make the path to success a bit easier, and Charles benefited from having such a father. Ambitious for his son, William Houston never considered leaving to chance or to Charles the matter of a good job after graduation. Having heard about the prospective leave of a Howard University English professor, G. David Houston (no relation), William Houston met with G. David, several other professors, an influential trustee, and the university's president, Stephen Newman, during Charles's last semester at Amherst. By 1 June the board of trustees had confirmed the appointment of Charles H. Houston "as substitute for G. D. Houston at Howard Univ."[1] Charles was given the title Supply Instructor in English for the 1915–16 academic year; his salary was to be set by President Newman.[2]

Since its founding in 1867, Howard University had become one of the most prestigious black institutions for higher education in the United States. It was no small accomplishment to be a member of Howard's faculty; some worked for years to merit such a position. Charles recognized that he had to prove himself worthy of the faith in his potential which the president and board had expressed by accepting the recommendation of G. David Houston. He settled down and accepted what seemed to be a multitude of new responsibilities, none of which was related to practicing the piano or a career as a pianist. Charles, however, only nineteen years of age, had no doubt that his father had the best interests of his son at heart. Anxious to be somewhat independent, Charles met the challenge of teaching at Howard determined to prove that his lack of experience was not a major handicap. Any insecurity he might have felt was probably minimized by his confidence in his undergraduate education and his assignment to

Howard's Commercial Department. In addition to offering liberal arts courses and graduate work in medicine, law, and religion, Howard— like a number of universities during the late nineteenth and early twentieth centuries—developed programs for students who were interested in training for business and commerce and who were not yet ready for work toward the bachelor's degree. The Commercial Department had as its primary purpose the preparation of students for business and "practical life," providing instruction in shorthand, typing, mathematics, history, and English. It also was a stepping-stone for students who aspired to higher academic pursuits, because the department had secondary rank but offered courses for which students could receive credit if they wished to enroll in either the College of Arts and Sciences or the Teachers College.[3] Charles had the opportunity to prepare students for regular college work, and he willingly handled the tasks of meeting the students' needs. Resolute, intelligent, and creative, Charles not only taught the required English courses but also developed a specialized course in "Negro Literature."[4]

When the United States entered World War I in 1917, Charles, still teaching and twenty-one years old, was eligible for the draft. He knew enough history to know that for a black man service in the army usually meant an endless succession of labor details, front-line duty, or personal service to high-ranking white officers. This war "was . . . not [his] fight." As he understood the dynamics of the relevant international relationships among England, France, Germany, and the United States, the war was about saving American credit, maintaining a European-American alliance, and "fighting . . . for a bigger share in the exploitation of the weaker people of the earth." For such a war, Charles was not prepared to be drafted and "herded into the Army." Besides, how could he be moved by Woodrow Wilson's appeal that American men ought to risk their lives to save the world for democracy if the President could not even make nondiscriminatory, democratic plans for blacks at home? Charles decided he would be an officer if he had to serve.[5]

Charles was not alone in his feelings about the war or his resolve to be more than one of the herd of drafted privates. In the effort to have officers, Charles and other young black college graduates were encouraged by Joel E. Spingarn. He was advocating a separate officers' training camp for blacks because he believed blacks were capable of commanding troops and was not convinced that the government would permit blacks and whites to train together. All this he did in an unofficial capacity, not as the board chairman of the National Association for the Advancement of Colored People (NAACP). Even so, many believed it incongruous for the prominent white leader of the NAACP, a biracial organization founded in 1909 to address the issues of racial discrimination and equality under the law, to promote a Jim Crow officer training camp. Yet for the young black men such as Charles, Spingarn's position was welcome. Charles and several of the young men similarly situated formed the Central Committee of Negro College Men to press the War Department for a training camp. Accordingly they lobbied among elected officials and sponsored black mass meetings to gain public support and enlist volunteers for a reserve officer training camp.[6]

> The Howard girls sold tags ["I am for the Colored Officers Training Camp, are you?"]; the Howard Dramatic Club through the courtesy of the managers of the Howard Theatre . . . gave a benefit performance to raise money to defray the expenses of the delegates to the other [black] colleges to obtain volunteers.[7]

Draft-age instructors and students at Howard formed a training battalion. They drilled—"no guns or uniforms, but [they] drilled just the same." Classwork on the campus was practically at a standstill. "The struggle for the training camp crowded everything out of . . . the minds" of the students and draft-age instructors.[8]

Public opinion was divided over the issue of black officers, and black opinion was more sharply divided over a separate training camp. Pointing to the potential of blacks who had served in the regular army during the Spanish-American War, Baltimore, Boston, Cleveland, and New York black newspaper editors rebuked advocates of voluntary segregation. Believing it "sometimes better to endure disadvantages than to yield to a principle that might lead to greater disadvantages," some black professionals were skeptical about supporting such separation based on race.[9] Nevertheless, Charles and other draft-age Howard men refused to back down. Although opposed to segregation, they knew that the War Department was going to put them in Jim Crow units anyway, and if they had to be segregated then they were going to fight to have Negro officers for Negro units.[10] The young men of the Central Committee were not to be shamed by talk about principle from older men who would not be called to serve, or by people alarmed about a new Jim Crow precedent: "They say we are sacrificing principle for policy. Let them talk. This camp is no more 'Jim Crow' than our newspapers, our churches, our schools. . . . Our great task is to meet the challenge hurled at our race. Can we furnish officers to lead our troops into battle; or will they have to go again . . . under white officers?"[11]

On 12 May 1917 the War Department notified Howard's President Newman that a camp would be established and on 19 May a Des Moines, Iowa, location was announced. Charles and other members of the Central Committee celebrated, but not for long. They soon learned that the War Department had set a minimum age of 21 and a preferred age of 25 to 40 for candidates; this excluded most of the Central Committee's volunteers, whose ages ranged from 18 to 25. The committee sent out an impassioned appeal. YMCAs and churches throughout the United States became temporary recruiting centers. To ensure that candidates met the physical requirements of the army, the committee even set up in Washington, D.C., a candidates' examining office staffed by black doctors. When the call came, there were more than enough volunteers. The qualified applicants were so plentiful that only one man under the age of twenty-three was included among the first candidates selected for Des Moines from the District of Columbia.[12]

Rejected, Charles faced the option of enlisting or being drafted into the regular army. Neither appealed to him. Charles—who if he had inherited any trait from his father had inherited stubbornness—refused to accept his exclusion from the first group of trainees. He somehow perceived a man's service in his nation's armed forces to be a prerequisite for having "something to say about how th[e] country should be run."[13] And having every intention of promoting black rights, he would not be denied admission to officer candidacy. It was that simple. Disappointed and anxious about his son's future, William took mental inventory of assets and allies available. William knew he could call on a senator, a colonel, and one or two party men. In a few days Charles and William had a plan. Partly by persistence, partly by using friends and their contacts in high places, the two Houstons arranged a meeting for Charles with the adjutant general on Governor's Island. But it was actually an accident that led to Charles's enrollment in the first group of black officer candidates. He recalled:

> The adjutant told me there were no vacancies but I could wait. . . . I had waited nearly all day when a New York boy who had been accepted . . . wanted to postpone his enrollment . . . so he could get married. When he was told he had to report or forfeit his place, he handed in his acceptance and I got it.[14]

Charles bypassed ceremonies and parties for the departing candidates. He "was not taking a second chance on being rejected as too young. . . . [He] started for Fort Des Moines as soon as [he] got [his] acceptance papers . . . merely changing trains in Washington to tell [his] family goodbye. [He] arrived . . . a full day ahead of the Washington contingent and the majority of the candidates." Upon his arrival,

Charles met Francis Dent, an Amherst College senior, who had been transferred from Fort Meyer, where as the only black candidate he was treated in a discriminatory manner. Together they filled out Charles's papers and waited for the training camp to begin officially.[15]

Training at the Des Moines camp began on 18 June 1917. The War Department selected Colonel Charles C. Ballou, Infantry, to take command of the camp for an enlistment period of three months. With high morale, determined to receive their commissions, 1,250 men got up not later than 5:30 A.M., performed assigned duties for ten hours, and studied until lights out at 10:30 P.M. Not unexpectedly they showed greater enthusiasm for the few Saturdays when they could socialize with the young ladies of Des Moines' black community. Nevertheless, they trained for their commissions with resolute spirits.[16]

Pursuant to orders from the adjutant general in July, Colonel Ballou reported on the candidates' progress. While he praised the "conduct" and the "zeal" of the camp squads—40 percent of whom were college graduates, including lawyers, physicians, dentists, architects, engineers, and clergymen—he was careful to emphasize that instructors' reports did not justify great expectations. Unquestionably some men capable of developing into officers of infantry, artillery, and engineers were in the camp, he indicated, but "the average character of the personnel of this training camp [was] not so high as to lead to the belief that so small a camp [could] provide material for all the company, Troop and Battery officers of a Division."[17] Actually, Ballou doubted whether many candidates would develop into officers of more than mediocre efficiency. He believed they lacked the "mental potential and higher qualities of character essential to command and leadership." In view of this he recommended that the army "undertake the raising of a complete division of enlisted personnel, but to count on white officers of artillery and engineers, and also white sergeants—until experience and training have developed colored men to replace them."[18]

Relying on the concluding recommendations of Ballou and the concurring recommendation of the commanding general of the Central Department, the adjutant general of the army secured an order from Secretary of War Newton D. Baker for concentration on the training of "officers of colored infantry."[19] Meanwhile, unaware of their superiors' reports on them or decisions regarding them, Charles and other candidates who had applied for engineering and artillery officer training waited restlessly for specialized training to begin. Their visits to the commander's office for the purpose of inquiring about this became so regular that they were eventually told about the secretary of war's order and given the choice of either following the order or resigning.

"[W]e knew instruction in the other arms of the service was being withheld from us solely because we were Negroes," Charles recalled, but after considering the prospect of service without any commission, it seemed "better to go to war as infantry officers than to be drafted . . . into labor battalions."[20]

After four months (instead of the originally scheduled three) of infantry officer training, in October 1917 some 204 second lieutenants, 329 first lieutenants, and 106 captains were commissioned in infantry. Charles Hamilton Houston became a first lieutenant. The black community of Washington, D.C., held a gala welcome reception for its nearly one hundred commissioned black officers of the Seventeenth Provisional Training Regiment. Although not especially excited about parties, Charles attended this one because it was held at Paul Laurence Dunbar High School (formerly "M Street") and was an opportunity to see old friends. Having met that social obligation, he spent the remainder of his furlough turning down invitations so he could spend time with Uncle Theophilus, Dr. Ulysses (another uncle), Aunt Clotill, Grandmother Katherine, and his father and mother. Charles also saw quite a bit of "Buster" because she was at his mother's side constantly. She did not seem much like a "Buster" anymore; she had really become quite grown up and attractive since she had come to live with William and Mary Houston. Her real name was Margaret Gladys Moran, so Charles gave this young lady from Virginia (for whom his parents had been providing because her parents had not been able to do so) a new nickname, "Mag." Charles saw little need to seek the company of other young ladies. Mag looked remarkably like his own mother, whom he believed to be exquisitely beautiful. Even in manner, Mag seemed to have a similarly arresting warmth and charm. Besides, although his father did not want his son to become engaged before he determined some profession to pursue, his mother seemed pleased about his interest in this young lady.[21]

Assigned to Company G of the 368th Infantry, Charles reported for duty at Camp Meade, Maryland, in November 1917. No sooner had he arrived than he was rudely shaken from his resolve to be content with his infantry commission. Someone in the army hierarchy had decided to create his own self-fulfilling prophecy by assigning some of the Des Moines Camp infantry-trained black officers to artillery units at Camp Dix. When the inevitable occurred—poor and failing performances in the command of men in the 349th and 350th Field Artillery—the army pointed to Camp Dix as proof of the unfitness of black officers for non-infantry commands. The army's unfair assignment of these infantry officers and its disparaging reports regarding the ability of officers and officer-candidates who were black to train in special services offended and provoked Charles so much that he decided he would not do less than become an artillery officer. He asked his father to write letters protesting the arbitrary assignments and the racial discrimination.[22] Charles, in contrast, "raised hell about it in so far as one can raise hell inside the army."[23]

"Raising hell" was not well received at Camp Meade. Before Charles heard any news about a transfer, he was reprimanded, harassed, abused and exposed to a special brand of "army justice" for blacks.[24] While an infantry officer, he and the other black officers were housed separately, far away from white officers of the regiment. But it was not complete segregation. In the Negro regimental area, the army also housed the conscientious objectors who—so far as the army was concerned—were at best "cowards" and at worst "scum."[25] After his long months of training, Charles resented this insult to himself and his fellow black officers. Yet the army had a strange effect on feelings of racial solidarity too, Charles discovered. Charles's immediate superior, a black officer who had worked his way through the ranks of an army to which he was absolutely loyal, assigned the most distasteful and difficult tasks to Charles for the duration of his infantry career because Charles had dared to criticize the army publicly.[26] It seemed that the only benefit of service in the American Expeditionary Forces to date had been the army allowance covering all the expenses of his mother's injury when she "fell and dislocated her knee" in November.[27] Charles continued to push for a transfer to field artillery, the specialty in which he was originally interested.

The last straw in this burdensome, embittering infantry experience was Charles's appointment to the position of judge-advocate for the army in the cases of two black soldiers. Although the duties of an army judge-advocate were to investigate and prosecute, Charles learned that when blacks were involved investigation was of no importance whatsoever. The cases arose out of a Thanksgiving furlough incident during which blacks were engaged in alleged disorderly conduct. Charles conducted a thorough investigation and could not find sufficient evidence to convict the two accused soldiers; the men were acquitted. When Charles reported to the white adjutant, the adjutant simply and abruptly told the young lieutenant he was "no good" because he had not secured a conviction in spite of the evidence.[28] A companion case was more offensive. A black sergeant on trial for disorderly conduct and insubordination, although investigation revealed he was one of the best noncommissioned officers in the company and was arrested while carrying out the orders of his superior officer, was found guilty and sentenced to imprisonment with a year of hard labor, loss of rank, and forfeiture of two-thirds of his pay. Charles could only silently despise the manner in which the army with apparent ease (and a blatant lack of fairness) destroyed the reputation and showed no concern for the life of a man who sought only to serve his country. Thereafter Charles routinely went by the stockade and—contrary to regulations—said a few words to the condemned sergeant. Charles later wrote, "I made up my mind that I would never get caught again without knowing something about my rights; that if luck was with me, and I got through this war, I would study law and use my time fighting for men who could not strike back."[29]

Although racial discrimination permeated Charles's Camp Meade experience, when persistence won him a transfer to field artillery officer-training and it happened to be with the 351st stationed at Camp Meade, he was too serious about proving something to the army to be saddened by the location connected with the opportunity. On 1 June 1918 he relinquished his rank in the infantry and began training to become a field artillery officer. By the end of two months of rigorous, intense training at Meade and later Camp Taylor (Kentucky), Charles was commissioned a second lieutenant. Following a brief furlough, thirty-five black artillery officers in the 351st began the voyage to France.[30] From that moment they "became the unwanted step children of the Army [who] [n]obody wanted . . . to help win the war."[31] Racism was with them on the ship and in Europe; the white Americans saw to that. The fusion of the 368th and 351st in the 92nd Division even began ignominiously: The white artillery officers chose to wear a swastika (a symbol of good luck) as their emblem instead of the buffalo which the majority—black soldiers—had selected for the 92nd because it paid tribute to the courage and fighting spirit of blacks in earlier Indian wars.[32]

This was only an omen of things to come. As a second lieutenant overseas, Charles Houston encountered racism, more virulent than he had ever known before, practiced by Red Cross workers, white enlisted men, and his fellow white officers. Because of his race, his color, the texture of his hair, and myths about his sexual prowess and inferior intelligence, Charles, like all the other black men in the American Expeditionary Forces, personally suffered daily arbitrary indignities and exposure to mortal danger. Talent, ability, and character were of little significance; race set men apart from one another. As they marched in a circle from camp to camp in France, Charles and other black artillery officers—such as Joseph L. Johnson (who would earn a Ph.D. and M.D. at the University of Chicago and become dean of Howard University's medical school), Rayford W. Logan (who would become a professor of history at Howard and an author of national reputation), James Austin Norris (who having graduated from Yale Law School in 1917 would become a prominent Philadelphia attorney with special expertise in taxes and editor-in-chief of that city's edition of the *Pittsburgh Courier*), and Hilary Robinson (who would become a well-known architect in Washington, D.C.)—quickly learned that racism often meant nearly insurmountable difficulties. Army traditions and regulations regarding the treatment of officers were violated at virtually every turn. Jim Crow policies were the rule in army camps, Red Cross–controlled hotels, and even some small inns where owners had been carefully warned about blacks by American whites. American artillery instructors humiliated, abused, and unfairly evaluated the black officers in advanced artillery classes. White American officers and enlisted men spread their racist ideas among Europeans and German prisoners of war; it was explained that black officers were of an inferior grade to whom no respect was owed. To French women, it was explained that black men wearing the uniforms of the American Expeditionary Forces had a peculiarly lecherous nature.[33]

Unwilling to let the racism of the army keep their spirits down, the black officers entertained themselves in camp. Shortly after Christmas at Camp Meucon they organized daily seminars, "each man talking for an hour and a half on the subject he [was] most interested in." Charles was particularly impressed with the talk of Albert Cassell, a graduate student on leave from Cornell's School of Architecture, and was looking forward to the next seminar on the Reconstruction period of U.S. history.[34] On New Year's Day 1919 the black officers organized a "[Harry] Burleigh Glee Club," and by 3 January had done so well in rehearsals that they presented themselves in concert "before the 7th F[ield] A[rtillery] B[attalion]." Charles did all the accompanying but had mandolins substituted for his scheduled solo, "Ragging the Scale," because he "did not feel sure of [him]self."[35] Since most black units seemed to produce minstrel shows for entertainment, the black officers of the 7th F.A.B. were quite proud of the alternative they had put together. Perhaps this highlighting of black culture was too far afield from white perceptions, or the black officers were too demonstrably proud. After the program, each officer had more problems securing permission to go to town.[36] As mess officer for his detachment, Charles, who spoke fluent French, was permitted to go to town for a while. When they were moved to another camp, however, still having seen no action, the black officers found themselves with an order "relieving colored . . . from duty." They were left with "nothing to do but eat and sleep."[37] The black officers were not always treated as pariahs in France. On one occasion they were amused and flattered when the "French girls anxious to learn [black American] dance . . . came after the [officers] in taxis and begged them to dance," Charles carefully noted in his diary.[38] But the amusement would not last. American racism would not let the white soldiers sit still for white women—even if French—seeking out black officers and in some instances preferring them to white men.

Second Lieutenant Houston recalled vividly one final horror in the nightmarish experience of organized American race prejudice. One particular Saturday Charles and a friend, Mortimer Marshall, were returning from the late showing of a French film when they happened on two white captains and a black lieutenant. On the side stood two French women who, Charles and Mortimer later discovered, had deserted the white captains for the company of the black lieutenant. The black officer who by this time was involved in a heated exchange with one of the captains summoned Charles, Mortimer, and one other black officer, Henry Collins. As incredible as it seemed, the next thing Charles knew white enlisted men were surrounding the four black lieutenants in the empty plaza of Vannes, France, screaming "niggers" and swearing it was "time to put a few in their places, otherwise the United States would not be a safe place to live" and then calling for the lynching to begin right away.[39] There seemed no way out when Charles turned and saw a beautiful sight—a French Guard squad marching toward the plaza. But the squad was about as much help as a mirage to a thirsty man in a desert; the men—rifles and all—marched with great precision straight past the lynch mob, deeming it improper to interfere in the American army's internal affairs. Charles felt absolutely alone and without hope, but one other quick-thinking lieutenant, Henry Collins, was able to win a few more precious minutes by accusing the white officers of cowardice when faced with a man-to-man fight with the black officers. The mob got louder and more restless, while the white officer retorted that he wouldn't think of lowering himself to fight with "niggers." "Attention!" the loudest Charles had ever heard it, seemed to come from nowhere, just as did the single figure who shouted the command. The captain of the American military police ordered the enlisted men back to their quartermaster trucks parked two blocks away, lectured the officers about degrading the uniform of the American Expeditionary Forces, and ordered them to return to their respective hotels. No formal action was ever taken.[40]

The less spectacular indignities and regular absurdities born of racial prejudice continued to occur until the black officers—having marched around France, but never really having engaged in battle or command as part of the war effort—were ordered home. Charles reported to his mother that he had read about Robert Russa Mot[o]n speaking in France before the troops began to pull out. "He is preaching his old doctrine of conciliation and humiliation. Let him preach. . . . I don't expect to become a Bolshevik, but I am going to do my best to secure what belongs to me. And whosoever Major Mot[o]n may represent he certainly doesn't represent me."[41] Charles left France on 8 February 1919 and disembarked in Philadelphia on 22 February.

Although he was obligated to continue on with the unit to Camp Dix, New Jersey, Charles was given a forty-eight-hour pass shortly thereafter. On the train southbound to Washington, D.C., Charles and his travel companion, another black officer, were unceremoniously welcomed back to the United States. Starved for nonarmy food, they went immediately to the dining car. Charles had no sooner sat down with his friend across from a middle-aged white man when the man demanded that the waiter find him another table. Sitting there in uniforms with overseas chevrons on the sleeves, Charles politely explained to the man that they were officers who had just landed from overseas and then asked if he were going to insist on having his plate moved. He couldn't help it, he explained. He was from the South. He moved; Charles and his fellow officer ate their meals. Charles never forgot his visceral reaction to the whole army experience: "I felt damned glad I had not lost my life fighting for this country."[42] In April 1919, Charles Houston left the army with his honorable discharge, an impatient and bitter young man.[43]

CHAPTER IV

Studying Law at Home and Abroad

The tension between Charles Houston and the white American in the dining car was unfortunately not unusual for postwar America in 1919. A general fear of foreigners, Catholics, Jews, poor or striking workers, radicals, and blacks led to intolerance and government repression. Dissenting radicals and alleged radicals, in particular, were being hunted down by the government, creating a nationwide "Red scare." Blacks, regardless of their politics, were being lynched, burned, and variously abused. Black soldiers were returning to secure democracy for themselves and other black Americans. In stark contrast, most whites maintained prewar racial attitudes and wished not only to guard their liberty but also to "see that there should be no wholesale distribution." While blacks wanted the nation to focus on the war years not only so that America's shortcomings and hypocrisy could be faced squarely but also so that genuine change might be effected in the United States of America, most whites were more interested in the old ways and greater prosperity. Although labor leaders and "progressives" talked about planned reconstruction from spring 1919 on, regulation and reform were abandoned after a brief period. The majority of Americans turned their attention to and placed their hopes in the "free" capitalist market economy, which following a brief slump was slowly moving toward a boom. What caught the attention of black Americans and what were their hopes? The postwar black American reality was discharged soldiers needing jobs, canceled government contracts creating a new group of dismissed employees who also needed jobs, and entire families needing almost everything for mere survival, and there were painfully few exceptions.[1]

Returning to civilian life, Charles examined law schools and with his parents decided he had nothing to lose by applying to Harvard for the fall of 1919. Blacks had occasionally been admitted. To support himself, Charles looked for a teaching job. His "old position at Howard was no longer available to [him, so he] . . . secured a position teaching English in the Dunbar High School, Washington, D.C." Unfortunately, having a hernia and chronic rhinitis, as Charles later explained to the Veterans Bureau, "the state of [his] health made it impossible for [him] to retain [his] position. The long hours, five classes reciting daily, disciplinary problems incident to high school work, crayon dust from blackboard exercises wore [his] strength away. [He] had to give up [the job]."[2] While waiting, Charles was not without second thoughts about law. He remembered the stand he had taken about studying law, and his father constantly reminded him of the dream of "Houston & Houston, Attorneys-at-law." But Charles did not feel driven to a career decision based on emotion. Neither did ambition or family loyalty inspire him to single-mindedness about a career in law. Before Charles heard from Harvard, he shared his feelings with Mag. He had veterans benefits for his education, so it was not a real money problem. He simply still was considering some alternatives, such as diplomatic service and teaching. He realized that music was out of the question for a number of reasons, and it had ceased to be even a satisfying dream. The war had definitely affected his view of himself and career options with which he could live. The United States of America was for him a battleground. This was confirmed by his first summer home.[3]

As James Weldon Johnson, secretary of the NAACP, observed, it was a "Red summer," which did not end until the nation witnessed approximately twenty-five race riots.[4] Since 1914 and especially after U.S. entry into the war there had been a steady migration of rural blacks to northern cities. A labor depression in the South, boll weevil damage to the cotton crop, and a labor shortage in the North created by a sharp decline in foreign immigration in addition to racial injustice in the South had prompted blacks to seek a better life in the urban North, which had been proclaimed a land of promise. Although new black city-dwellers frequently earned more money than ever before, this did not make Chicago, New York, Philadelphia, or Washington, D.C., the promised land. The southern black migrants moved into overcrowded, rundown apartments and tenements recently abandoned by the poorest foreign immigrants. The same white immigrants, learning to be Americans, soon began automatically to look down on blacks who had lived in the United States for centuries and helped to build it into the modern, powerful nation it had become. With native-born whites, white foreign immigrants resented the flood of blacks who at the end of the war were threatening white employment and wages. Greater resentment led to racial tensions as black ghettos grew and spilled over into white neighborhoods; rents increased in the segregated residential areas almost as rapidly as competition for fewer jobs. While the war for democracy abroad had fostered a militancy among returning black soldiers and fed the hopes of those who remained at home, that hope of democracy and freedom at home which caught the imagination of black Americans was murdered summarily in 1919. The summer of 1919 "ushered in the greatest period of interracial strife the nation had ever witnessed."[5]

Beginning in June 1919, race riots—some large, some small—flared up in various urban centers of every section of the nation. Homes were burned and blacks were flogged, shot, tortured, and lynched as mobs took over cities for days. Many blacks who defended themselves against lawless whites were injured or lost their lives in the process. In July, race riots occurred in Longview, Texas; Chicago, Illinois; and Washington, D.C. In the District, groundless newspaper stories of black men assaulting white women precipitated three days of violence during which white mobs primarily of sailors, soldiers, and marines "ran amuck through the streets . . . killing and injuring" black Americans.[6] On the third day of the racial violence, blacks retaliated against whites who attempted to storm and burn black residential areas. As a direct consequence of black resistance, a number of whites were among the wounded and killed. Owing to continued white terrorization, casualties and fatalities rose considerably before normal relations were restored in the nation's capital. National black (and predominantly black) organizations including the Universal Negro Improvement Association (with over one million members and the charismatic Marcus Garvey at its head), the National Equal Rights League, and the National Association for the Advancement of Colored People protested this persistent racial violence and the failure of the government to protect black citizens.

In the aftermath of such violence, Charles, more the realist than ever before in his life, expected that blacks of the District would fare no better. But he could not help but be disturbed when his father returned to their V Street, Northwest, home one day seething with rage about T.S. Jones. Twenty-five years of age with only a fifth-grade education, Jones had only in May 1919 come to Washington, D.C., from Norfolk, Virginia. On the night of 21 July he went to the vicinity of the Gem Theater to look for the children of a friend and return them to their parents, who were justifiably worried about their children being out in riot-torn Washington. Failing to find the thirteen-year-old girl and her brother, Jones was returning to the house of the parents when a mob began to chase him. He took refuge in his friend's home, but desiring to get to his own home he left after a short rest. Outside he was confronted with stones and shots from an angry mob. Contrary to his assumption, the mob had not dispersed while he was inside, but increased. Jones was terrified as "Kill the nigger, kill the nigger" rang through the air. Someone in the mob hit him with an iron pipe. Fearing for his life, he drew and fired a revolver he had been carrying for protection ever since he had been attacked one night early in July. The mob scattered, and Jones ran to another friend's house for refuge that night. Following the incident he was arrested, charged, and indicted for the first-degree murder of a nineteen-year-old white man. The absurdity and injustice of this led Charles's father to break his rule of practicing only civil law. William Houston (with two other attorneys) took Jones's case but was unable to save him from a conviction.[7]

The army experience, the riot, and the unjust indictment and conviction of T.S. Jones intervened in the comfortable life of the young Charles Houston and changed it with startling completeness. In a deeply personal sense, Charles understood racism as an irrational, ubiquitous, external force that violated human beings, disrupted plans, bred bitterness, and destroyed dreams. Yet at his very center he also knew that he could not be defined by that kind of assault on his spirit. Charles had been jolted, but his future had not been wrenched from his control. With a new sense of authority he took his stand. The racism that permitted the race riots and the victimization of a T.S. Jones had to be eliminated. The laws that buttressed stifling, oppressive practices and policies had to be fought immediately, directly, and persistently if the opportunities of America were to become options for black Americans. This he would do after law school.

The evening of 18 September 1919, Charles left home to begin his first year of Harvard Law School. Charles had selected Harvard because of its excellence, and his parents agreed that was where he ought to be. Although Harvard admitted a few academically qualified blacks, this did not mean Harvard was without racism. Harvard, as did Yale, Columbia, Princeton, and other private institutions with reputations for excellence and elitism, "discriminated against applicants on the basis of their nativity and religion. . . . As for blacks and other racial minorities, a handful were tolerated as long as they remained inconspicuous; too many blacks, it was feared, might change the 'complexion' of the campus."[8] It would be important for Charles to be in a position to study without holding an outside job, the Houstons decided. All three used their resources to make this possible. Charles had some savings and his veterans' benefits. William had discretionary funds because of his successful practice, and Mary had ample earnings to assist her son from time to time because of her established reputation as a hairdresser and occasional needlework she did for fees.[9]

The sacrifices of his parents did not go unrewarded. Undaunted by the rigor and the pace at which Harvard legal education was conducted, Charles "soon proved himself to be an outstanding student despite the keen competition of a remarkable post-war student body." By the end of his first year, Charles had earned one A in contracts and another in property at a time when "[the] grading system [at Harvard Law School had] long been such that an 'A' [was] a mark attained by only a small percentage of the students." Thereafter he kept in his files a memento of his freshman year, an A examination in liabilities signed by a professor whom he admired greatly, Joseph H. Beale.[10]

More comfortable in the Harvard setting during his second year, Charles moved into an apartment with a black classmate, Jesse Heslip. Often when the two left their 1556 Cambridge Avenue apartment they ran into a tall, lanky, but handsome and outgoing young first-year student on his way to the law school. Raymond Pace Alexander (who one day would become president of the National Bar Association) always had something to say or some idea to share. Once he had gotten into a fairly strict study discipline on weekdays, he began to search for less demanding activities on the weekends. Having discovered that more black students—particularly female—lived and attended school in or near Boston, he became noted for his attendance at that city's Cosmopolitan Club weekend parties. The graduate and professional students were not overly fond of liquor during the school term; it didn't mix well with their work and enrollment at predominantly white institutions. For that reason most parties were tea parties, and for his attendance record, Alexander earned the nickname "T.P." Some Saturday nights, "Charlie," T.P., and Jesse, who became quite close, left their Cambridge rooms and books for less metaphysical pleasures. Although Charles was not a "great socializer," as Alexander recalled, "Charlie" was certainly no wallflower. He did less than his share of dancing and more than his share of conversing with the young ladies, and he took turns with T.P. at the Cosmopolitan Club's piano. Enjoying social life in Boston, Charles even "crossed the burning sands" and for the first time as a student had fraternity brothers, Alpha Phi Alpha.[11]

Charles Houston never spent much time on extracurricular activities. Although they had had their ups and downs, Charles and Gladys Moran (who still preferred to be called Mag when they were together) had been relatively serious about each other since his Amherst days. It was a relationship he understood and with which he was rather comfortable. Not being a ladies' man, he never appeared too anxious to seek out new challenges, and actually, as an older student, he wanted to concentrate primarily on his law studies. Charles felt that he was at some disadvantage to begin with because he had worked two years and spent two years in the service since his graduation from Amherst. To this was added the obvious obligation imposed on him because of his race. He had learned in the army that an individual black was so often seen as the representative of the race's abilities and potential.[12]

It did not take long for Charles and other black students at Harvard to discover that there was a dividing line between whites and blacks and to observe that lines were drawn even with respect to such quasi-academic activities as law clubs. One did not come to Harvard and forget one's racial heritage. Because of Harvard's practices, and because of the pride in his race Charles had and knew other black students shared, during his second year Charles took responsibility for a special meeting of black students. He was "agent-organizer" for the "luncheon to be given for the Honorable Marcus Garvey at the Harvard Union."[13] The black students assessed themselves two dollars to defray the expenses, which they paid to Charles, and "Charles H. Houston covenant[ed] to give each and every one of [the] subscribers due notice of said luncheon, to render a true and full account of all expenditures incurred, and to refund all monies not expended."[14] Twenty-two black men of Cambridge entertained Marcus Garvey. The total expense was $43.20, and Charles covered a deficit from a taxi for Garvey and his guests to and from Boston.[15] Charles would never forget the experience, and in later years he spoke proudly of Garvey's contribution to black people.[16]

Infrequent socializing, hard work, seriousness, and discipline in relation to his law studies despite obstacles or other obligations earned Charles five As and one B, "something which few students are able to do," Dean Roscoe Pound was eager to point out in a letter of recommendation for Charles.[17] This honor average in his second-year work won Charles election to the editorial board of the *Harvard Law Review*. He became the first of his race to be so honored. Alexander remembered how proud the black students were when this happened, for Charles had not only done his own studying, he had also willingly assisted other students and particularly younger black students who looked to him "as a guide post."[18] In talking with white students, black students found that their friend Charles Houston was considered by students and faculty alike "one of the brightest men on campus."[19] "All of his teachers speak highly of him," Harvard dean and renowned scholar Roscoe Pound reported.[20]

Charles's third year of law school, 1921–22, was incredibly busy. Editing volume thirty-five of the *Harvard Law Review*, one of the most prestigious journals of scholarship on the law, was both an honor and a heavy obligation. It required an extraordinary number of hours a week beyond regular studies. Researching legal questions, analyzing cases, evaluating articles written by law professors throughout the country, editing those accepted for publication, reviewing books, and writing lengthy "notes" on issues of law put Charles under constant pressure. Being the first and only black on the *Law Review* made it even more difficult. After a few months, Charles wrote his parents and was very candid: "The editors on the *Review* didn't want me on this fall; now all is one grand harmony. But I still go on my way alone. They know I am just as independent and a little more so, than they. My stock is pretty high around these parts. God help me against a false move."[21]

Although Charles certainly had more than enough to do, he was persuaded that a law club for students excluded from the established clubs was an important part of the legal education. Black and Jewish students had none of the opportunities for outside legal activities such as investigating cases and researching legal authorities for cases being handled by practicing attorneys. White students were able to do these things because of a number of law clubs open to them and because they had constant support from attorneys in the Boston-Cambridge area. His *Law Review* status notwithstanding, Charles had never been approached about a law club. In fact, there had never been invitations extended to nonwhites or non-Protestants. Raymond Alexander, although he had a job and not as much time for activities beyond assigned studies, was sensitive to the significance of this exclusion. He and Charles spoke with other students and, according to Alexander, owing to Charles's efforts both on and off campus, eleven Harvard blacks succeeded in establishing a Dunbar Law Club (named for a Jewish lawyer in Boston who came in and acted as adviser to fourteen students of African and Jewish heritage).[22]

For more nights than he cared to remember, Charles was buried under conflict of laws, constitutional law, corporations, and equity and surety books because he had one other project on his mind. He wanted to do graduate work. His father was practicing and teaching at Howard. Charles believed he might fulfill some of his professional goals by doing the same. Charles explained to the Veterans Bureau in his application for an extension of his vocational training period:

My reasons for desiring graduate work are both personal and civic . . . a deep desire for further study in the history of the law and comparative jurisprudence . . . [and the belief that] there must be Negro lawyers in every community . . . the great majority [of which] must come from Negro schools . . . [where] the training will be in the hands of Negro teachers. It is to the best interests of the United States . . . to provide the best teachers possible.[23]

In this ambition Charles was encouraged by his dean and mentor, Roscoe Pound. With Pound praising Charles's "excellent work" and stressing that "I should undoubtedly offer him a scholarship if he wishes to stay for another year," Charles Houston qualified for and won the Langdell scholarship.[24] The financial award enabled Charles to study for his doctorate at Harvard in preparation for both practical and scholarly pursuits in law. Ranking in the top 5 percent of his class, Charles graduated with his LL.B. (Bachelor of Laws) cum laude (with honors).[25]

In September 1922 Charles became a candidate for the degree of Doctor of Juridical Science. He again distinguished himself, making a 79 graduate average (75 was equivalent to an A). He took five courses, and professors consistently evaluated his work as excellent or superior. This was no small accomplishment, since these courses included Roman Law and Jurisprudence taught by Roscoe Pound, who had recently published *An Introduction to the Philosophy of Law*, and Administrative Law and Public Utilities under the instruction of Felix Frankfurter. With Frankfurter as an adviser, Charles prepared a doctoral thesis titled "Functional Study of the Requirements of Notice and Hearing in Governmental Action in the United States." Although he was a doctoral candidate from 1922 to 1923, Charles maintained contact with black students in the classes below him because he believed some unity was very necessary. He kept abreast of the underclassmen's progress through Raymond Alexander. When called upon, he met with them to protest racial discrimination in the freshman dormitory. Later he assured the younger students of his support and interest in their welfare by joining the newly created Nile Club (named after the river in Africa) for Harvard students of African descent.[26]

Charles was determined to obtain as broad an education as possible. As he approached the end of his fourth year, he became fascinated with the idea of using his languages and continuing his graduate law studies. When the faculty of Harvard awarded Charles the coveted Sheldon Travelling Fellowship ($1,800 for study at any university in Europe), he selected Spain and the University of Madrid's civil law program. William and Mary Houston, Louis Wright (a physician and William's friend), and Mag saw Charles off at the pier. He sailed from New York for Barcelona, Spain, on 6 September 1923. There he caught a train on to Madrid, where he remained for nine months. During that time he was enrolled in law courses for one academic term (approximately eight months), the entire course of which required at least six years of prelaw and law studies. Nevertheless, Charles was serious about his studies, not only because he had an interest in Spanish civil law but also because he hoped that at some time in the future he would have an opportunity to practice law in one of the Spanish-speaking countries of the western hemisphere.[27]

Charles never rushed to classes at 51 Calle de San Bernardo. He and the Spanish men and women in the advocacy curriculum spent a lot of time talking outside the "plain, stone building dingy with the dirt and weathering of many years."[28] At first, as he told Pound in a letter, it was annoying to Charles, but later he began to understand the Spanish lifestyle better and adjusted to the loss of class time. Students stood around and talked among themselves because courses were scheduled for one and a half hours but only taught for one hour. The extra half hour was used for the arrival of the professor. Among Charles's professors were some of the more prominent legal scholars of international reputation; it was out of deserved deference that a half hour was allowed for their arrival. During this time, in conversation with students outside he learned a great deal about the differences between American and Spanish curricula. All students had compulsory courses in the department of philosophy and letters. Advocates were to be broadly educated people; a liberal arts background was essential. There was a different rationale supporting the education of lawyers in Spain. Charles took advantage of those aspects which were distinct and felt very fortunate that he was good in languages. All courses— Roman law, civil law, and philosophy of law—were offered in either Spanish or French. Just as at any other university, the lectures varied in quality and appeal; they certainly were not all stimulating, but there were moments when the classes even seemed to move forward with "zeal."[29]

Coursework was not the most significant or memorable part of Charles's experience abroad. Charles was enamored of Spanish culture—its richness, its longevity, its appreciation of variety and beauty. His experiences in Spain "colored [his] entire life on the race question."[30] His friends in Madrid did not seem at all bothered by his color. And there was time, after the academic term, to travel. This Charles really loved. He went from Italy to France to Tunisia and Algeria, sending postcards he had promised to mother, father, grandmother, aunts, and uncles. Reaching the shores of northern Africa held tremendous significance for Charles Houston. He spent hours sitting in on court sessions in Tunisia and Algeria, but he spent more time walking through cities of an ancestral homeland. Tunisia was not West Africa, but being on the African continent gave Charles an inexplicable sense of belonging to something vast and permanent, a sense of continuity. "Thank God," Charles wrote his grandmother Katherine Houston, "one of the Houston clan stands back on native soil. I count it a happy privilege."[31]

In June 1924, Charles Houston left the easy pace of Europe and northern Africa to return to an America experiencing the roaring twenties in full motion. While most white Americans, culturally, seemed caught up in a home-grown superficiality, blacks were variously exuberant. Although their daily tribulations came with the same regularity as the sunrise, folk tales, spirituals, and the blues lightened and softened rural black life as the race pride of the Garvey Universal Negro Improvement Association still stimulated urban masses despite a federal government and integrationist "Garvey Must Go" campaign. In New York City a variety of bohemian and/or well-to-do whites even sought out blacks of Harlem. Harlem and some aspects of black culture were in style—Mamie and Bessie Smith's blues, Paul Robeson's singing and acting, Bill "Bojangles" Robinson's dancing, the jazz of New Orleans, Chicago, and Harlem nightspots, and the work of Harlem Renaissance writers. There was an audience for more than Sinclair Lewis's *Main Street* and F. Scott Fitzgerald's *The Beautiful and the Damned*, as the poetry and prose of Countee Cullen, Langston Hughes, Zora Neale Hurston, Claude McKay, and Jean Toomer attracted white money and readers of both races. In this mood, the America to which Charles Houston returned was both the same and different.[32]

When Charles returned to Washington he found Calvin Coolidge presiding over a nation that was in the midst of Republican conservatism, isolation, and intoxicating prosperity (blacks excluded). Radical labor activity and criticism of the nation were eschewed, and business, technology, and speculation were supported in this era. The frenzied xenophobia of "Red scare" days had been replaced with an antiforeign immigration policy, anti-Semitism, and the Ku Klux Klan, which was less hysterical but decidedly more violent. Prosperity seemed to be the economic trend, and the majority of Americans were enjoying the good times that were the result of technological advances and easy-payment plans. Many white Americans believed permanent prosperity was just around the corner—at least that was the promise. But prosperity was uneven. Blacks remained in genuine poverty, real wages for working-class people—farmers and laborers—did not rise sharply in proportion to profits, and for all of them, purchasing power frequently faded in the face of inflexible prices. It was to the black community of Washington, D.C., that Charles would be turning for the building of his practice. As in other black communities, most of its residents were not in any position to live carefree, buy-now-pay-later lives. Few were focusing on suits or injustices that meant paying fees to attorneys. Whatever was left over after rent, food, heat, doctor bills, insurance, and church dues was sought after by so many and the advertised good life was so alluring. With a restless spirit, Charles read newspapers, listened to Coolidge's policy statements, and observed big business for some insight into this paradoxical postwar era. Although he was glad to be home with his family and friends, he was troubled by the state of the nation and the conditions under which black people lived. But he did have his plans.

Charles was admitted to practice in the District of Columbia on 9 June 1924. William had a new sign made for the office on F Street; the firm "Houston & Houston" was born. In the summer of 1924, Grandmother Katherine, William, Mary, Clotill Houston, and friends, when they visited, spent hours during the evenings listening to "Charlie's" endless stories about Spain. Charles devoted his time to the family, the firm, and Mag (more beautiful than ever). Less than two weeks after Katherine Houston's seventy-fifth birthday was celebrated there came another festive occasion for the family. On 23 August, Charles, Margaret Gladys Moran, and William and Mary Houston drove to the home of Bishop Jonathan Hurst in Baltimore, Maryland, where Charles and Mag, the daughter of the late Charles and Margretta Moran of Warrenton, Virginia, were wed in a private ceremony.[33]

There were no more preliminaries. Married, ready to settle down in Washington, no more degrees to be earned or university studies to be done, Charles Houston joined his father in the Houston law offices. The elder Houston had a well-deserved reputation for being a skilled, wise attorney. His son's Harvard background and good character were well known. Charles's responsibilities were multiplied, and the challenge was considerable. He wanted the United States to be a home for blacks, not just a land for those either brave enough to stay or with no other place to go. It was time to begin working out for himself the full meaning of his earlier resolves.

PART TWO

Developing Cadres: The Howard Years, 1924–1935

Due to the Negro's social and political
condition . . . the Negro lawyer must be
prepared to anticipate, guide and interpret
his group advancement.

—Charles Hamilton Houston,
"Personal Observations on . . . Howard University
School of Law," 28 May 1929

CHAPTER V

Houston & Houston

Five minutes from the District of Columbia Municipal Court House, on F Street, Northwest, number 615, at the top of a long flight of stairs in the Helpers Building, William L. and Charles H. Houston shared law offices. William believed that blacks ought to invest their money wisely, and as far as he was concerned, owning downtown property was the better part of wisdom. For some time he had had his eye on a building down the street from his first downtown 639 F Street office. By 1921, William persuaded the Supreme Order of the Helpers, a black "fraternal beneficial association" which he, his brother Ulysses (a medical doctor), and seven other men had incorporated in 1915, to purchase the impressive three-story building.[1] William set up his law office on the second floor, while the Helpers rented the third-floor apartments. When the father and son formed their partnership in 1924, William was comfortably settled at this prime location with a well-established reputation as a legal counsellor for "middle-class Negroes" and some whites. Not forgetting who helped him get his start, William still handled the legal affairs of his first clients— maids, chauffeurs, lower-echelon government workers, and laborers. William's practice was a general one, including matters of negligence, domestic relations, trusts, estates, and real property. When Charles entered this general practice it expanded, but it did not change greatly.[2]

Charles benefited from his father's reputation and experience. There was a steady flow of clients, and William was always willing and able to advise his son on the practical matters of legal work. Charles learned in a short time how to assess the merits of claims and how to negotiate to avoid any unnecessary litigation. Both Houstons believed in the value of detailed and accurate work. They sought to make all their cases as tight as possible so there would be no error or omission on their part that would lead to costly court sessions or adverse decisions.[3]

William was an expert office manager. (He taught the office management course at Howard Law School because of his expertise.) He kept impeccable records, and on any day of his years of practice he could tell where the firm stood in its accounts. Since the Houstons did not begin with a surplus of money, their fees were not large, and prompt payment was not always a realistic expectation. The elder Houston believed that he personally had to keep close watch over all expenditures. The office was run on an austere budget, Judge Margaret Haywood (then a secretary) recalled. That budget allowed for meager salaries for secretaries and a barely adequate allotment for office supplies. William "Chief" Houston was strictly business and so seriously opposed to wastefulness that he kept postage stamps in his locked desk drawer to be distributed only after he was certain that the correspondence was properly weighed work for Houston & Houston. Most important, William did not believe in free legal advice. "The services rendered were worthy of the fee," he frequently reminded clients and colleagues.[4]

Charles Houston's procedure was quite different, Juanita Kidd Stout, one of his secretaries (who would later become a judge in Philadelphia), recalled. The son seldom inquired about the ability of the client to pay, and "if you had a *good* case, Charles never asked you if you had the money."[5] Regarding the collection of fees, the two Houstons never saw eye to eye. Nonetheless, Charles was sensitive to his father's desire to maintain a secure and successful law firm. While Charles Houston defined success in terms other than being financially well-to-do, he recognized that his father's concern was both for himself and for his family's future. The "short grass years," which were still a painful memory, drove William Houston to work, save, invest, and regularly urge his son to be cognizant of his responsibility to his wife and the children to come.[6] Too frequently for William's taste, he transferred carefully noted sums from the "William L." accounts to the "Charles H." expenses. This displeased and worried William. But the two understood each other quite well.[7]

Charles did his fair share of work even if the fees did not come in on time. He liked practicing law. Advising people of their rights, negotiating settlements when claims warranted it, and doing battle in court when the cause was just seemed to be the most fulfilling work he could do. It was not always exciting, but it did not have to be in order to be worthwhile. Being excellent at his work had its own rewards. Besides, in these first years Charles was establishing himself. Beginning in the summer of 1924, Charles took a number of routine cases his father did not have time to handle. Trust and estate matters, which had to do with the preparation of wills, contested wills, estate administration, or trustee appointments, took up almost a quarter of Charles's time. William usually turned over a number of indebtedness disputes and debt-collection cases to his son. Soon there were clients who came directly to Charles also. Some were more comfortable with a lawyer of their own race because they were not always certain there was a case but they wanted to discuss how they believed they had been wronged in connection with an accident, slander, false or malicious prosecution—that is, tort claims—and find out if they should sue. Others were having troubles with landlords. Actually, landlord/tenant cases, real property transactions, trusts, estates, debts, and torts made up the bulk of Charles's legal practice, although he handled a few divorces, separations, partnerships, and breaches of contract. When criminal practice was no longer taboo after 1919, Charles had a few opportunities to be a defense attorney. As he grew more interested in civil rights causes, the character of his practice would change, but as a young lawyer Charles had an ordinary case load (see Appendix 2).[8]

With the two Houstons, so good at their work but also so different in style and temperament, the 615 F Street law office had greater appeal. There was a marked increase in the number of clients. Many younger people and District residents in lower economic brackets sought out William's son. During the first decade of his practice, over eighty-five new clients came to talk to Charles about some legal matter. Among these were men and women from age nineteen to forty-nine. Most of them were black, although not all. Many were married with children, but some were separated, widowed, or single. Neither their occupations nor their incomes seemed to determine whether they would litigate if they believed they had grievances against a person or company they wanted redressed. One client Charles represented was a twenty-four-year-old trucker who brought home $19.50 a week for his family (a wife and two children), while another black woman, thirty-eight years old, explained in her first interview that she was recently separated, working in a laundry, and earning only $18.00 to $20.00 a week with which she provided for six children. Class seemed not to have been a determining factor for Charles in accepting clients. He negotiated legal matters and litigated cases for a seamstress, a baggage hostler, and a cook on the Atlantic Coastline Railroad, as well as clergymen, lawyers, teachers, and doctors.[9]

Charles's method of building up a practice and selecting clients did not always mean he would bring in enough cash to take care of monthly expenses. However, his policy regarding fees and cases did not work a major hardship on the firm if annual income were considered. William could afford to advance his son funds for office expenditures in February or May because the fees paid in other months amply covered any advance. On the one hand, the firm did not suffer; on the other hand, the younger Houston and his wife could not have lived comfortably on Charles's net cash income. (See Appendix 3 [10]). Luckily, after the summer of 1924 he would almost always be able to supplement his income from his private practice.

As a welcome and challenging diversion from his local practice, in his third year of practice Charles worked on his first U.S. Supreme Court case. At the request of a former classmate, Samuel Horovitz, he assisted in the preparation of a brief to be presented to the Supreme Court, *Bountiful Brick Company et al.* v. *Elizabeth Giles et al.* during 1927. Pleading for the Industrial Commission of Utah and widowed Elizabeth Giles in the case involving the death by accident of her husband, Nephi Giles, Houston and Horovitz argued the legality and justice of the lower court's finding of negligence on the part of the brick company in the death of Mr. Giles. Giles, an employee of Bountiful Brick Company, taking the shortest path to work, as many employees had a practice of doing with the company's knowledge, entered the Bamberger Railroad Company's right-of-way on 17 June 1925. He was struck by a train and killed. The Industrial Commission awarded Mrs. Giles compensation because her husband's death came about "out of or in the course of employment." On appeal of a lower court's decision the brick and insurance companies sought to have the previous decision overturned by arguing Giles's negligence, illegal intrusion on the company's property, and an insufficient causal connection between the injury and employment. Despite these contentions, the Court handed down an opinion that the brick and insurance companies should have been held responsible. Houston and Horovitz won their case. [11]

The U.S. Supreme Court victory was exhilarating, but writing briefs for the Court was not something Charles Houston planned to do with any regularity early in his practice. It would be very different in years to come, but for the time being he had committed himself to other tasks in the District of Columbia. Only during the summer of 1924 did he devote all his energies to his practice. By fall 1924, Charles Houston could be found during the day at 615 F Street, Northwest, and during the evening at 420 Fifth Street, Northwest, the Howard University School of Law.

CHAPTER VI

The Transformation of Howard University Law School

When Charles Houston was still young enough to think himself wise beyond his years, he confidently told Sterling Brown, a Dunbar High School student (who would later become one of the nation's foremost poets), "He who can does and he who can not teaches."[1] That was long before Houston came to know and esteem such professors of law as Joseph H. Beale, Roscoe Pound, and Felix Frankfurter. While attending Harvard Law School, Charles Hamilton Houston was challenged to a new appreciation of teaching, particularly, law teaching. For some reason (perhaps because of William's emphasis on practice) it just had not occurred to Charles before (during the years his father regularly spent evenings at Howard Law School) that the formal teaching of law was so important. But he knew better by 1922. He understood that if it were not for teachers and scholars, the law might never be more than precedent—judgments confirming the correctness of earlier judgments.[2]

So it was that in the midst of his Harvard years Charles had pondered his commitment to the use of the law in the struggle for rights and in its relation to the education of lawyers. So it was that he decided it was important not only to practice but also to teach law, and therefore went on to do graduate work at Harvard and the University of Madrid. It was important to him to be more than competent; he had to have a thorough grounding in law so he could teach and practice with authority. When he believed he had virtually met this self-imposed standard, he requested that Roscoe Pound and Felix Frankfurter send letters of recommendation to Howard's Dean Fenton W. Booth in support of his application for a faculty position. Pound did so "without qualification" in December 1923. He and the Harvard faculty had deemed it appropriate to show "their appreciation of [Houston's] work as a student and their confidence in him by giving him about every honor that it is possible for a law student to take while in the institution." Pound had carried on lively exchanges with Charles while he attended the University of Madrid. He personally considered Charles Houston "a remarkable man" also because he "combined a high order of scholarship with solid good sense and capacity for seeing things as they are."[3] Felix Frankfurter, who recalled that Charles Houston was one of the best doctoral students he had taught at Harvard Law School, had written Charles in January 1924 that "it will be a pleasure for me to write to the Dean of Howard Law School. . . ."[4] With such recommendations, Charles looked forward to his application being favorably received.

The enthusiasm was mutual when Charles Houston, A.B., LL.B., S.J.D., accepted the dean of Howard University Law School's offer in 1924. Dean Fenton W. Booth, also a judge on the District's Municipal Court, was under some pressure to hire more full-time faculty members and upgrade Howard's Law School. Despite Howard's admirable record as a part-time evening school, it was under attack. By the 1920s it mattered only slightly to the accrediting agencies, the American Bar Association (ABA) and the Association of American Law Schools (AALS) that Howard—since the establishment of the law department in 1869—had graduated over 700 men and women, black and white, and trained more than three-fourths of the nearly 950 black American practicing attorneys in the nation. As a consequence of the Carnegie Foundation study of legal education prepared by Alfred Z. Reed, "Training for the Public Profession of the Law," all part-time afternoon/evening law school programs were suspect. He had found that they generally operated with lower educational standards, inadequate libraries, and insufficient full-time faculty and staff.[5]

The ABA and AALS—for which such findings provided ammunition in the elitist offensive called a drive for "higher standards" and "professionalism"—soon prevailed within the profession, and their approval became a must for every "good" law school. And they disapproved of part-time education with few exceptions. This hit home in 1920, when one of Howard's law students was required to repeat studies at Fordham because his previous work had been done at an unaccredited evening law school. Howard Law School's dean, Benjamin Leighton, and President J. Stanley Durkee needed no further warning. It was obvious that the repetition was predicated on the assumption that courses at an unaccredited part-time school could not be equivalent to those of ABA/AALS approved institutions. They immediately evaluated the Howard program and concluded that substantial upgrading of the physical plant, admission standards, library holdings, and the curriculum, which was substantially similar to other part-time law schools, was needed and that the faculty could be improved. For those reasons, at a June 1920 meeting the university trustees had voted that "steps be taken to so advance the School of Law that it may become eligible for membership in the American Association of Law Schools."[6] Thus while the timing of Charles Houston's application was determined by entirely separate factors, his addition to the Howard law faculty in 1924 proved to be auspicious.

Although Charles knew that as a new member of the faculty he would have little choice in courses, he had hoped that he could teach one of the courses for which he had applied, "The Interstate Commerce Act." Both he and Frankfurter believed Charles was "admirably equipped . . . to give this course."[7] Apparently the dean had other plans. Charles devoted his first year to the teaching of "Agency," "Surety and Mortgages," "Jurisprudence," and "Administrative Law." His students included first- and second-year LL.B. candidates and graduates seeking the masters in law (LL.M.).[8]

In Charles Houston's first years, Howard was at best "a very good, but in no way exciting part-time law school," although a sizable element of the District's black bourgeoisie was fond of calling it "Dummie's Retreat."[9] Yet Charles Houston respected the institution both for what it had done and for what it had already been for his people. From Howard's Law Department had graduated William H. Hart (LL.B. 1887, LL.M. 1894), who while a professor at Howard successfully litigated *Hart* v. *State (of Maryland)*, a Jim Crow rail transportation case in which the court upheld Hart's contention that forced separation of the races was unconstitutional as it affected interstate travel. Howard also could count a governor of West Virginia, a U.S. Registrar of the Treasury, several municipal judges, and the first woman admitted to practice in the District of Columbia among its graduates. Howard had given Charles's father, a high school principal, an opportunity to study law and become one of the District's best and most successful black lawyers.[10] Charles Houston also respected Howard for what he believed it could become—the school that would produce lawyers who would be excellent in their profession and fearless in their struggle against racial discrimination. His affection and respect for the institution helped this Harvard graduate as he mingled

with his new colleagues. The modest young man "was very highly regarded . . . by the members of the faculty . . . and recognized . . . as a
very brilliant scholar."[11]

Charles Houston was extremely serious about his teaching at Howard. He worked the students as if he believed they had no choice about
becoming first-rate lawyers. His distant cousin by marriage, William
Henry Hastie, Jr., who followed in Charles's footsteps, remembered
that Charles knew that "in the world nobody's going to make allow-
ances. . . . The world takes no excuses even for understandable shortcomings." Naturally, because of this, there were some students who
had difficulty with Dr. Houston and others "who disliked him because
of his toughness and unwillingness to accept the mediocre."[12] Yet certainly everyone knew, as A. Mercer Daniel, Howard Law graduate
(1909) who later became a professor and law librarian, recalled, "It
was no easy task to study law when the student had to work eight
hours during the day, as most of them did, and go to school from 5 P.M.
to 9 P.M. three or more days a week."[13] But Charles Houston asked no
more of his students than he expected of himself, and for that reason,
while "students were sometimes driven to swearing" at Houston "they
also swore by him."[14]

Charles Houston "was a law teacher all of his days. . . . Surrounded
by an aura of extreme competence, his very presence in legal dialogue
commanded respect. His wise advice, accompanied by explanation of
analysis and synthesis . . . , was a revelation in itself."[15] He was "in the
law school night and day."[16] He devoted many hours, beyond his practice, to preparation for his courses, both when large numbers of LL.B.
students were concerned and when a few graduate students were dependent on him for advanced study. He made detailed and extensive
notes for jurisprudence lectures, and his examinations were indicative
of the kind of critical thinking he expected of his students.[17] In the jurisprudence course, for example, less than two months into the term,
Houston presented his students with an examination of four questions
about material he had covered. Two were "Compare the doctrine held
and set forth by the nineteenth century historical school with those
held by the nineteenth century analytical school" and "Sketch the philosophy of Kant."[18] By December of the same year, he called on his students to analyze and discuss their lecture and reading materials in
answers to such essay questions as "Which nineteenth century school
of jurisprudence emphatically denied the power of conscious effort to
change or modify the course of law, and why?" "Contrast the principles common to the various schools of sociological jurisprudence of
the twentieth century with the principles common to the various

schools of jurisprudence of the nineteenth century," and "Write a short discussion of the sociological aspect of capital punishment as applied under our present form of the administration of justice in criminal cases."[19]

As Charles Houston developed his courses over the years, he increasingly insisted that the students think about the broad spectrum of societies, laws, and classes of people. In the course on administrative law he stressed the elements of expediency, social interest, and spheres of influence to illustrate the growing importance of administrative law to black people.[20] Focusing on a related concern in a jurisprudence final for 1926, he asked, "Can you trace in the course any evidence of an extension of the protection of the law to wider and less-favored classes of men from the days of the Greeks to the present?"[21] (He would in later years implement changes at Howard to assure that its program of legal education was consistent with an understanding of the interrelationships of race, class, and law in the society. This meant offering standard courses but also providing a different emphasis and through standard courses and new courses focusing on the application of the law to the plight of black people.[22])

Charles Houston was concerned about both the training of excellent lawyers and their continuing education. This concern manifested itself in activities outside the firm and Howard Law School. When he was admitted to practice in the District of Columbia, there was no local bar association in which Houston or any other black attorney was welcome. The D.C. Bar Association, a private voluntary professional organization, excluded nonwhites. In 1925, Charles Houston, with fellow District lawyers who were black, such as George E. C. Hayes, Louis R. Mehlinger, and J. Franklin Wilson, organized and incorporated the Washington Bar Association. The "objects" of the association as stated in the charter included "improvement or enhancement of professional skills as well as professional and citizenship responsibilities of the members; . . . advancement of the science of jurisprudence and administration of justice; continued improvement of the standards of legal education; [and] encouragement of legal research."[23] Consistent with these aims, Houston, for the Washington Bar Association, communicated with the D.C. Bar Association and such distinguished attorneys as Felix Frankfurter in an effort to have the D.C. bar library facilities open to black lawyers upon application.[24]

After three years of local practice and teaching, Charles Houston wanted more involvement in the effort to train blacks for law and encourage their participation in the struggle for liberty and the improvement of the quality of black life in the United States. The official approval of a legal survey which the School of Law at Howard proposed to conduct provided such an opportunity. Given the assent of the executive committee of the board of trustees of Howard, in 1927, Charles enthusiastically assumed the directorship of a "Survey of the Status and Activities of Negro Lawyers in the United States."[25] It was to be an extensive study, but its main thrust would be examination of the training and activities of black lawyers in relationship to other black Americans and their communities.[26] To gather data for the survey, Charles began a personal tour of seventeen cities, including Birmingham, Alabama; Atlanta, Augusta, and Savannah, Georgia; Louisville, Kentucky; New Orleans, Louisiana; Jackson, Mississippi; Charlotte, North Carolina; and Nashville, Tennessee, in November 1927. Upon his return to Washington, D.C., he visited the Association for the Study of Negro Life and History, whose director, Carter G. Woodson, graciously placed at Houston's disposal the facilities of the association. At the conclusion of Houston's survey of the "Status and Activities of Negro Lawyers" under the Laura Spelman Rockefeller Memorial grant, Houston, as director, submitted three studies. His work of nearly a calendar year yielded data on "Negro Law Schools," the "Negro Lawyer," and "The Negro and His Contact with the Administration of Law."[27] For his own institution, Howard, Charles completed a special "Survey of Howard University Law Students."[28]

Charles Houston was in his element as a lawyer, professor, and scholar when he became ill. His wife had not been pleased with his physical condition for some time. Charles had been coming in at the end of his long days totally drained. This was particularly alarming because earlier during his spring trip as director of the survey he seemed to have contracted either influenza or a mild form of pneumonia. At that time he complained of congestion, but he later claimed to be stronger. Now with constant coughing and almost total exhaustion, Gladys wanted to put him to bed. Charles kept going out and working on his survey as if its completion were more important than his health. She did not like what was happening. The way he dismissed her serious comments with some nonspecific reply and used her nickname Mag, to tease and change the subject made Gladys suspicious about the gravity of the situation. Finally, one day, although he had planned a full evening of work, he felt so badly he seemed to have only enough energy to go to bed upon Gladys's insistence and let her call the doctor and his parents.[29]

In early June 1928 it appeared that Charles Houston had a "tubercular condition in [his] left lung resulting from influenza and exposure during service in France," so he spent eight days at the Edgecombe

Sanitarium in New York under the care of Dr. Louis T. Wright.[30] A second physician, James Miller, was consulted, and together Wright and Miller determined that Charles should go home for a month of bed rest and return for a second examination afterward. But by the end of June, Charles was in Mount Alto Hospital for further diagnosis. The Mount Alto doctors failed to find "sufficient symptoms to justify a diagnosis of tuberculosis." Charles, who found it next to impossible to accept his need for months of bed rest, hoped to get back to Howard by October.[31] He had been too quick to believe what he wanted instead of how he felt; a final diagnosis in August confirmed Wright's original opinion. A "minimal lesion in [the] left lung and a case of active tuberculosis" left Charles Houston no alternative but to take off at least part of the 1928–29 academic year.[32] (Charles actually had no energy. Dr. Wright was adamant about rest. And under the laws of the District, a tubercular patient could not enter a school in any capacity.) Charles Houston assured the Rockefeller Memorial and his family, colleagues, and friends that the prognosis was favorable, but he did rest during an official leave of absence without pay from the Law School. Even in January 1929, although he wanted to be up, his health did not permit either attendance at any social affairs or extensive work.[33]

Charles Houston, as did other Howard Law School faculty and the new university president, Mordecai W. Johnson (Howard's first black president, educated at the University of Chicago, Harvard, and Rochester Theological Seminary), continued to follow with interest the ABA and AALS discussions of recommendations regarding higher standards. Both Johnson and Houston were anxious about the impact of the "professionalization" thrust on Howard, which was taking slow steps toward achieving accreditation. Thus the reaction was one of pride and concern when Howard Law School's dean, Fenton Booth, was elevated to the position of Chief Justice of the United States Court of Claims, for it created a vacancy in the Law School's administration at a crucial period in its history. Howard was obligated to act on the recommendations for upgrading if it were to be a useful and significant institution in the future. Degrees viewed as suspect by the ABA and AALS could hardly help the university or the aspiring lawyers enrolled there. The trustees' Law School Committee persuaded Booth to stay on as acting dean, both to allow for a smooth transition in the administration and to help implement changes for mixed curricula—three-year day and four-year evening programs—which might be approved by the AALS.[34]

Although still recovering from his bout with tuberculosis, Charles Houston was anxious to involve himself once more in the work of the

Law School. He had been talking with Mordecai Johnson about the
ABA developments and the Carnegie Report done by Alfred Reed.
(Charles had had ample time to study and evaluate it during the past
year.) Charles's emphasis on the improvement of the Law School was
constant. He also knew that Johnson's unofficial adviser, Justice Louis
Dembitz Brandeis, was pressing for higher standards, stiffer admission requirements, and conversion to a three-year day school. Johnson's advocacy of accreditation for Howard Law School against some
opposition seemed an encouraging sign to Charles. In May 1929,
Charles completed his "Personal Observations on the Summary of
Studies in Legal Education as Applied to the Howard University
School of Law" for the perusal of the law faculty and the president. In
his twenty-page statement he discussed the status of legal education
at Howard, the faculty, the library, the alumni/ae, the objectives and
aims of the school, prelegal education, student admissions, law school
curricula, methods of legal instruction, auxiliary research aims, and
plans for Howard's coming academic year. His provocative ideas, his
commitment to the institution, and his seriousness were recognized
by the university. On 4 June 1929 the board appointed Charles H.
Houston Resident Vice-Dean in charge of the three-year day school
and the law library.[35]

As resident vice-dean he attempted to create a program that would
demonstrate Howard Law School's societal significance and establish
its excellence in education. His far-reaching goals were based on assumptions articulated in his "Personal Observations": "first, that every
group must justify and interpret itself in terms of the general welfare;
and . . . second, that the only justification for the Howard University
School of Law, in a city having seven white law schools, is that it is
doing a distinct, necessary work for the social good." Charles Houston
accepted the sociological view that lawyers serve as "reinforcement
units in the social structure." Given that view, he had sought to underscore that his survey had revealed an appalling paucity of Negro lawyers "to meet the group needs." Legal representation of black people
and advocacy of their rights were, to Houston's mind, essential to the
race's eventual eradication of legal racist discrimination, and Howard
Law School's "indispensable social function" was to train lawyers for
these tasks. Some 25 percent of black law students in the nation during 1927–28 were attending Howard, and if this were to continue
there was even more reason for Howard to meet the challenges of the
society and the times.[36]

A specific conception of the role of the black lawyer provided the
basis for Charles Houston's proposals regarding the future of Howard

University Law School. He maintained that in addition to taking care of legal matters revolving around the individual client's personal problems with individuals or society,

> [the] Negro lawyer must be trained as a social engineer and group interpreter. Due to the Negro's social and political condition . . . the Negro lawyer must be prepared to anticipate, guide and interpret his group advancement. . . . [Moreover, he must act as] business adviser . . . for the protection of the scattered resources possessed or controlled by the group. . . . He must provide more ways and means for holding within the group the income now flowing through it.[37]

Thus, Charles Houston proposed that the "immediate objective" of the school should be "to make itself a more efficient training school" in order to fulfill the race's need for "capable and socially alert Negro lawyers." As a training school, Howard Law School should seek to "equip its students with the direct professional skills most useful to them" and, stressed Houston, to "give them as deep and as broad a societal background as possible." In its courses, Houston believed Howard Law School should include basic economics, "drilling in the application of law to the simpler business relations," instruction in administrative law that would emphasize inherent and societal limitations with respect to the legal process, and practical training beyond moot court. Forced out into private practice directly from school, because racism usually eliminated most clerkship opportunities, black law students needed training with particular attention to the "legal aspects of Negro economic, social and political life."[38]

The continuing growth of the day school enrollment and the decline of the evening school enrollment during the drive for accreditation of Howard Law School prompted Houston, President Mordecai Johnson, and others to urge that the law school concentrate on being a first-rate full-time day school. Both Johnson and Houston were painfully aware of what this meant in relation to the Howard Law School tradition. Howard's evening school had created the opportunity to study law for most of the formally trained black lawyers in the United States. Charles Houston's father, William, was able to continue working as a clerk in the Record and Pension Office of the War Department during the day because classes were conducted at Howard during the evening. Yet possibly William Houston understood as well as his son that day school (and accreditation) constituted the wave of the future. Neither oral tradition nor extant records reveals a controversy between William and Charles regarding the necessity to move forward with a day school program, even at some sacrifice. Certainly Charles Houston was not alone in seeing that much of Howard Law School's importance was connected with its potential. Charles Houston had a vision, and Mordecai Johnson was persuaded by Houston's observations and those of Justice Louis Brandeis. Brandeis and Johnson had frank discussions on the subject of black Americans' rights and the law. Brandeis's emphasis on the importance of well-trained black advocates to argue constitutional principles before the Supreme Court of the United States and his compelling arguments regarding quality legal instruction pointed to fundamental change in the Law School, the president of Howard University concluded.[39]

Armed with supportive evidence provided by a Supreme Court justice and a young black Howard faculty member educated at Harvard Law School, Johnson presented his case for a full-time day school and an improved faculty. The university could not have it both ways. The more stringent admission requirements, which were adopted following the trustees' 1928 mandate to seek membership in the AALS, had precipitated a decline in enrollment. In 1928–29 twenty students registered in the day program, and nine registered in the first-year evening class; at the beginning of the 1929–30 academic year, again twenty registered for the first year of the three-year day curriculum, while only one registered for the evening school. The expense of running the two programs concurrently was prohibitive and could not be justified by enrollment. On 4 February 1930 the trustees voted to abolish the law school's evening course as of 6 June 1930. After protest by students in the program, however, the board of trustees of Howard University, meeting on 5 June 1930, amended their action to permit men registered in the evening course to continue until graduation or transfer into the day school. At this same meeting the recommendation of President Johnson that Charles Houston be appointed vice-dean of the Law School for the coming academic year was accepted.[40]

From the day after the meeting, President Johnson, Houston, and all other day school proponents were under attack. The *Washington Tribune* editorialized:

> The decision of the trustees of Howard University to eliminate the night law classes is one that seems to be against the needs of the people. Ever since the law department was established in Howard University there has [sic] been night classes. It is only recently that the day classes were established. Many of the country's best lawyers among our people secured their training by being able to work in the day and attend evening classes. Our economic condition is such that few of our young men have the means to attend college in the day time.[41]

The *Tribune* continued to focus on the Howard Law School in a feature article captioned "Alumni Protest Abolition of Night Classes." It reported that the Alumni Association members were emphatic in their "collected disapproval of the proposed discontinuance of the evening classes of the University School of Law." The article cited one of the chief reasons for discontinuance, namely, "that each year the enrollment in the first year class of the evening school becomes small and . . . at present there are only six second year men in the evening school, and only one first year student." However, most of the article was devoted to the arguments of students opposing the proposed change. Adamant alumni made new arguments that "among the two groups, those who pursue their law study in the day and those who take advantage of the evening possibility, the latter are in most cases more conscientious . . . because the men . . . realize better the advantage to be gained" and that "with the abolition of the evening classes, the Law School faculty will suffer the loss of such sterling professors as Dean Fenton W. Booth, George E. C. Hayes, Judge J. A. Cobb, [and] W. L. Houston." Regarding the latter contention, the alumni/ae had not interviewed the professors named, but speculated about their resignations because of a conflict between day classes and other work.[42] The ensuing months at the Law School did not vindicate the Alumni Association's position. As prominent Washington attorney Belford V. Lawson, Jr., recalled, black graduates of other law schools supported accreditation of Howard and a day program despite the hue and cry about "Harvardizing the Law School."[43] After the resignations of a number of white professors for reasons undisclosed to the press, rumors about discrimination and Houston's unfairness led to speculation that came to be printed. In the face of innuendo, Mordecai Johnson consented to an interview. Although he explained that the regrettable loss of the white professors was attributable to "pressure of outside business" which made it impossible for them to "devote more time to teaching," the *Washington World* reported that Johnson had "tried to conceal the real reason for the resignation of the white members," the acceptance of which had caused widespread dissatisfaction. The article concluded with an allegation regarding Mordecai Johnson's denial of free speech.[44]

Since Mordecai Johnson had been named the first black president of Howard University in 1926, race had been an issue at Howard. It was becoming more sharply an issue at the Law School, as Booth assumed less importance and power and a young black vice-dean with considerable power seemed to be ushering in a new order. (No member of the press published comments of Chief Justice Booth, with whom Charles Houston had good relations that continued after Booth assumed his full-time Court of Claims duties.[45]) Race was not the only

issue, however, and certainly not the key. Many responsible people—
both black and white—believed the abolition of the evening school to
be an effort to "Harvardize" the law school to its own detriment. By
stiffening admission requirements, changing the hours, and attempting to model the curriculum and classroom expectations after Harvard,
opponents of the evening school abolition believed the new Howard
Law School administration was eliminating the greatest opportunity to
"render the service for which it was organized and is now maintained
by public appropriation."[46] All seemed to be attributable to actions approved by the first black president, Mordecai Johnson, who according
to the evening school advocates was a man "led up a blind alley" by a
"fortunate" but "insensitive" Harvard graduate.[47] A few dissenting
voices came from the press. The *Palmetto Leader*'s editor presented
both pro and con arguments and reminded his readers that doctors,
dentists, and clergymen attended day school as part of the necessary
sacrifice for training. He concluded with praise of Charles Houston as
"eminently qualified" to make the proper prescriptions for Howard
Law School's improvement.[48]

Houston could not help but be affected by the dissatisfaction and
unrest. Yet he was persuaded that to discontinue the evening curriculum for a time was appropriate. Given the issues of accreditation and
funds, Houston believed, in the final analysis, that it was of service to
the university to call for the best possible education during the day.
The evening class had died from lack of enrollment, and "from an
academic standpoint it [was his] judgment that, other things being
equal, three years of day work [were] better than four years of evening
work."[49] Although he continued to be attacked as an insensitive elitist,
Houston went about his daily administrative chores and continued his
close supervision of the accreditation drive.[50]

In regard to accreditation, Houston focused primarily on the forthcoming inspection of the law school by the American Bar Association's
Will Shafroth, adviser of the section on legal education and admission
to the bar. This was the first time the ABA had made such an inspection of a predominantly black law school. Moreover, only seventy-one
law schools in the United States were ABA-approved. Nevertheless,
Howard Law School anticipated the inspection with some confidence,
for its drive to become accredited by the AALS had simultaneously become an effort to meet the standards of the ABA. The American Bar
Association required that entering students have at least two years of
college, that there be a minimum of 7,500 approved volumes in the law
library, that three full-time instructors be employed, that there be ade-

quate housing for the school, and that any day program be conducted for three years and any evening program be conducted for four.[51]

To become a member of the Association of American Law Schools, institutions similarly were required to have students with two years of college and adequate facilities and housing for the school, but in addition, by September 1932 requirements included a minimum of 10,000 volumes in the library, with a portion of these volumes being a complete national reporter system, supreme court reporters, federal statutes and digests, reporters for the state in which the school was located, published records of decision of courts of last resort in half the states, and at least six legal periodicals. Moreover, AALS was requiring that a minimum of $10,000 be spent within five years for additions to the library. A minimum of four full-time instructors and, over and above that, one full-time instructor for each one hundred students had to be retained in order to be approved by the AALS. Membership would finally be granted only after for two consecutive years the school had complied with the standards set out in the articles of the AALS.[52]

In 1928 Howard had instituted its full-time three-year law school program, and by the month of inspection, October 1930, Howard boasted four full-time professors, one full-time librarian, a library of 10,000 volumes, part-time instructors, and an adequate separate facility on Fifth Street, Northwest. In a summary of the 1930–31 report of President Johnson to the U.S. secretary of the interior, it was noted that the "work of the school of law was examined by the council of legal education and admittance to the bar of the American Bar Association [and] was found to maintain standards acceptable to that body, and was accredited by them."[53] Full accreditation and approval was accomplished at the end of 1931. The adoption of stiffer entrance requirements by Howard permitted the ABA's Council on Legal Education and New York State to approve all the work of Howard students effective 14 April 1931. The AALS granted membership in December of the same year, with retroactive approval of the work of those students currently attending the school.[54]

CHAPTER VII

"Dean" Houston's School for Social Engineers

Howard's accreditation was a genuine triumph for Charles Houston and all who shared his vision for Howard Law School. But there was still much to be done if the Law School, as Houston envisioned, were to offer "superior professional training and extraordinary motivation . . . to prepare the professional cadres needed to lead successful litigation against racism as practiced by government and sanctioned by law." Making this vision a reality was "Dean" Houston's great challenge. He sincerely believed, as his cousin recalled some years later, "first rate people with first rate training" would actually accomplish "such a transformation in American law and in the society it regulated."[1]

Approval of the program at Howard was in part predicated on the strength of its faculty and curriculum by the time of the inspection. Nevertheless, both still required attention if accreditation were to be maintained. Houston took it on himself to contact his former law professors and arrange meetings with administrators at Michigan, Yale, and Columbia "to inquire about fellowships for teachers" at Howard. This would lead to post-LL.B. fellowships for several Howard faculty members and alumni.[2] Remembering the creativity of his M Street teachers, who fought disabilities resulting from racism by bringing excellence and breadth to their students, Houston became a proponent of special lectures. He had no intention of permitting Howard students to be stymied and to suffer "ceilings on their ambitions or imagination[s]."[3] Opportunities ordinarily denied he would create. To this end he sought to expose Howard students to the best in the field. He set up the special lecture fund and, as his best-known student, Thurgood Marshall, remembers, Charles Houston "secured the services of . . . great lecturers such as Roscoe Pound, Clarence Darrow, Arthur Garfield Hayes [*sic*] and others."[4]

Clarence Darrow, the eminent trial attorney of the Scopes "monkey trial" fame and outspoken advocate of civil liberties and civil rights, confirmed his 1931 lecture series for Howard even before full accreditation. In his own inimitable style, Darrow addressed the Howard faculty and students and the larger Washington legal community. Darrow spoke on "Preparation for Trial," "The Court and Jury," "Examining the Witness," and "Evidence," emphasizing the inequities in the criminal justice system, the disabling effects of poverty and blackness in the United States, and the imperative need for lawyers to understand not merely the intricacies of law but also the complexities of life—its psychological and sociological aspects as well as political-economic realities. One lecture was particularly sensational as Darrow presented his views on jury selection. He asserted that knowledge of psychology and biology was a most important asset for the ambitious litigator (particularly the defense attorney) and then proceeded to give examples of good and bad risks for jurors. Lawyers should try to begin a case with jurors they believed prejudiced in their favor, he proclaimed with no hesitation. Houston, who presided, probably flinched noticeably as Darrow seriously suggested that students spend more time developing their wits, because at least nine-tenths of what one was up against in the courtroom was anything but law. Yet the students appreciated Houston's zeal in their behalf and never forgot that he gave them opportunities to question and intellectually spar with lawyers who had proven themselves top-flight litigators and scholars.[5]

Concerned about the "essentially formless" curriculum, Charles Houston undertook a thorough "study of the entire curriculum" in order "to give [it] a more functional aspect."[6] Specifically he sought to "coordinat[e] the subjects and eliminat[e] the waste." For these purposes he requested that the faculty supply him with, first, text and case materials used in each course for the first semester; second, the cases assigned and covered in connection with each chapter and section; third, any special review work or mimeographed materials; fourth, an informal, brief memorandum of the instructor's opinion on how much work can profitably be covered in the semester and how best to cover it; fifth and finally, any suggestions for the current term.[7]

This survey during February 1931, and the conclusions drawn from it, led Houston to believe that adequate training demanded longer terms. He lengthened the term and became the object of criticism once again. The press kept its readers informed about Howard Law School's difficulties:

> Increase of the academic year at the school from October 1 to June 15, instead of to commencement day, as customary, has just been disclosed in a bulletin prepared by Vice Dean Charles Houston.
> This lengthening of the school year to 32 weeks for day students and 36 weeks for evening classes has caused concern among the student body, which has filed three petitions already for less work assignments. . . .
> Other petitions have been filed with the vice dean because of a heavy schedule of eighteen hours a week in day classes, recently inaugurated.[8]

Dissension spread beyond the Law School's walls; by 31 March 1931 there were rumblings of discontent which affected the president of Howard University. Some alumni of the university opposed the naming of a black man to head Howard, a university of two thousand students and three hundred faculty members. Others, who were impatient with Johnson's tolerance of Houston's changes at the Law School, advocated the resignation of Mordecai Johnson and the appointment of a white successor. One of the major grievances cited was Johnson's policy of appointments with respect to faculty and deans. According to the *Washington Times*, "many of the alumni . . . felt . . . that Dr. Johnson seeks to elevate to the higher positions at the university any scholar who had been able to receive a doctor of philosophy degree . . . [and] previous experience of members of the faculty is disregarded."[9] Dissidents seized on Houston's charge of incompetence in law librarianship against James C. Waters as a prime example of the administration's disregard for experience and service to the university. Waters, the law librarian and professor of law, was indeed known by faculty and staff because of habitual lateness and a lack of formal training in law librarianship, according to Houston. Since the beginning of the accreditation drive, the specialized holdings of the law library had increased, as had the need of students for assistance from a trained librarian. Nonetheless, few alumni were willing to admit that objectivity and sincere professional interest in the institution had any connection with Houston's call to review Waters's performance of his duties. James Waters spoke for a number of people at the law school when he claimed that personal dislike, elitism, and a predisposition to maintain both "honor men" from Harvard or Columbia, and others who had Phi Beta Kappa keys but no experience, were the reasons for Houston's demand for a review of Waters.

Outspoken in their criticism of Vice-Dean Houston following his extension of the law school term and his charges against James Waters, the students aired their grievances to the press. One of the students advised a reporter that "the Vice Dean was more of a machine than a man."[10] Houston stood his ground on both issues. Thirty-two weeks for day school students (and thirty-six weeks for the remaining evening school students) became the requisite academic year, and James C. Waters, Jr., was given a leave of absence for the year 1931–32, during which time he was to be engaged in law library administration studies.[11]

Anti-Houston and anti-Johnson elements sought the removal of Johnson and some tightening of the reins on the vice-dean. But the trustees were apparently not inclined to do either. No meeting resulted in the removal of Houston or Johnson. Despite the unrest, Mordecai Johnson asked Houston to consider accepting the position of Dean of the Law School.[12] This was the first time Houston refused the promotion. "Actually, he never held and several times refused to accept the official rank and title of 'Dean.'"[13] Although he was already doing the work, Houston wanted to make a point. He could not take the title of dean until all Law School faculty and staff salaries were raised to a level of compensation equal to the minimum a "poor school" would pay, and he thought that additional money should go to hiring the best-qualified professors for Howard's Law School.[14] The significance of the compensation argument is illustrated by the pay scale established for 1931–32 as it appeared in one of Charles Houston's memoranda to the faculty and staff:[15]

Faculty

Charles H. Houston, Assistant Professor and Vice Dean	$4,500.00
William E. Taylor, Assistant Professor	3,500.00
Milton A. Kallis, Instructor	3,000.00
Leon A. Ransom, Instructor	2,500.00
James A. Cobb, Professor	1,600.00
William L. Houston, Professor	1,500.00
George E. C. Hayes, Assistant Professor	1,500.00
Nathan Cayton, Lecturer and Judge of the Moot Court	1,500.00
Theodore Cogswell, Lecturer	700.00
William H. Hastie, Lecturer	1,500.00

Administrative Staff

James C. Waters, Jr., Librarian (on leave of absence 1931–32, to pursue studies in Law Library Administration)	2,500.00
A. Mercer Daniel, Acting Librarian	500.00
Two student assistant librarians at $350.00 each	700.00
Ollie M. Cooper, Secretary to the Dean	1,200.00
William Lee, Janitor	1,080.00

To students, faculty, and staff, Charles Houston was "Dean Houston." He worked constantly to keep Howard out of jeopardy and maintain full accreditation. Houston's good record at Harvard and his rapport with the professors there led to an understanding with Harvard that they accept and financially provide for the graduate law studies of a Howard instructor. For accreditation purposes, Houston maintained the requisite high entrance requirements for Howard Law School, specifying the number of years of college necessary for admission according to a sliding scale which was based on the quality or rating of the institution the prospective student was attending. Additional volumes were carefully selected for the law library according to the stipulations of the AALS. Plans were made to lease an annex, give faculty merit raises, create a scholarship and loan fund for students, and continue overhauling the curriculum.[16]

Charles Houston performed his duties with greater confidence because he was fortunate enough to have as his secretary Ollie M. Cooper, whom he affectionately and respectfully called "Dean Cooper[,] . . . the real boss of the Law School."[17] As secretary to the various deans of the Law School since 1918 and a lawyer (Howard '21), her knowledge of the Law School was vast and her ability and understanding superior. Years later she admitted being hesitant to work for Houston after Booth resigned and left the Law School. Houston had a reputation for being "a man who insisted on perfection."[18] People had told Ollie Cooper that Houston was not a "nice person to work for," but after she became his secretary she discovered "there wasn't a nicer person." He was punctual and expected others to be on time. He was neat and he liked things in order, Ollie Cooper recalled. He often worked late, and since her duties included keeping records of the school, collecting money, making payments, and typing all examinations, correspondence and "those long forms for accreditation," she worked late too. But on such days it was not unusual for Houston to get her sandwiches and coffee; "he was very thoughtful."[19] The long hours and the intense work had their reward. By 1932, Houston could report that Howard Law School was "the only approved law school in the country serving Negro students in particular. Except for Howard . . . there is no approved law school where Negro law students can matriculate south of a line running from Philadelphia on the east, west through Pittsburgh, Columbus, Cincinnati, Kansas City to Los Angeles. . . . Thus Howard University School of Law [was serving] more than four-fifths of the entire Negro population."[20]

Mordecai Johnson, Charles Houston, and Ollie Cooper consequently faced their share of problems between 1932 and 1934. Enrollment declined, as a result of the elimination of the part-time evening school, the raising of standards of scholarship for admission and continuance, the exclusion of 50 percent of the colleges and universities from which students had been accepted, and the economic depression. Student enrollment dropped from 61 to 37, and the number of graduates decreased by eleven, from 18 to 7.

The Law School was commanded to reduce its budget in 1933 by $3,750.[21] With considerable difficulty, Houston and his committee—Nathan Cayton, James Cobb, William Taylor, and Alfred Buscheck—worked out a budget cut of $3,600 but advised the board that "it [was] with great sacrifice . . . that they had so reduced [their] budget, and that such reduction [might] be attended with grave consequence, for which [they could] not assume the responsibility."[22] The budget reduction weakened the practical aspect of the law students' program because it necessitated the elimination of a portion of moot court time. Houston, who had in 1929 stressed the importance of equipping students with direct professional skills, was compelled to ask the judge of the moot court, Nathan Cayton, a judge in the Municipal Court of the District, to limit his offering of moot court to one semester and accept compensation of $500 until his regular salary and semester hours of teaching could be restored.[23] The budget reduction, furthermore, meant that the full-time faculty for 1933–34 would be cut to four teachers, the salaries for whom had never been ideal or even the norm. Now it seemed that dedication was almost the only thing that would hold faculty members at the Howard University School of Law.[24]

Houston was fortunate that continued full membership in the AALS was not dependent on a higher standard of interpretation of "adequate facilities."[25] Trustees, faculty, and staff had recognized and agreed by 1933 that the institution had outgrown the physical plant at 420 Fifth Street, Northwest. The trustees, in the same year, voted to move the school to the campus as soon as the money became available, but it hardly seemed that it would be immediately forthcoming. Budgetary concerns in the summer of 1934 were interfering with other vital areas of the Law School's operation. Houston's requests for a full-time teacher and a full-time librarian in 1934–35 were turned down because of lack of funds.[26]

One of the few bright moments in the summer of 1934 came when Houston found that his spring 1934 tour of fourteen colleges, including South Carolina State at Orangeburg, Shaw University in Raleigh, North Carolina, Virginia State at Petersburg, Virginia, and Virginia Union in Richmond had been fruitful. Admissions records indicated that there was an increase in the number of applicants and applications accepted. By July, nine had been accepted, eight were pending, and only four rejected.[27] At the beginning of the academic year 1934–35, the elder Houston wrote, "The freshman here in the law school showed an enrollment . . . of more than double the number that matriculated in 1933; which is directly traceable to [Charlie's] trip."[28]

After juggling administrative budget details and coping with administrative problems, it was almost always a pleasure for Houston to meet with his students for classes. During his vice-deanship, Houston offered "Criminal Law Laboratory," "History of Law," "Legal Bibliography and Argumentation," and "Evidence" to first-year students. He instructed second-year students in "Common Law Pleading" and third-year students in "Conflict of Laws" and "Municipal Corporations" during the times when the latter was not duplicated in other courses.[29] Extant class rosters reveal that Houston taught a number of young men who were to become prominent in the field of civil rights: Thurgood Marshall, Oliver W. Hill, Leslie S. Perry, Coyness L. Ennix, Edward P. Lovett, and James G. Tyson.[30]

Charles Houston is remembered best by those students who encountered him during the formative period of the modern accredited Howard Law School. Few of them were without mixed emotions while going through Howard as its first accredited classes, because Dean Houston was ferocious in his insistence that no one be a mediocre Howard Law graduate. As these students recalled, he "ran Howard the same way Harvard was run" and was quite at ease while telling first-year students, "Look to your left and look to your right . . . next year one of you won't be here."[31] He never seemed to be at a loss for sobering tenets or alarming witticisms as he "worked the students without mercy." His favorite expression was "No tea for the feeble, no crepe for the dead."[32] He also reminded them with shocking regularity that "doctors could bury their mistakes, but lawyers couldn't."[33] Thurgood Marshall, Houston's student and later his colleague, remembered that "Houston's drive earned for him the affectionate nickname 'Iron Shoes.'"[34] Houston simply "rejected out of hand all complaints that work was too difficult or assignments too long."[35] And he had no tolerance of carelessness, laziness, or lack of attention to detail. Oliver Hill, distinguished Richmond, Virginia, attorney, loves to tell the story of Houston (whose office was on the second floor) sending to the homes of his students (who all generally studied and attended classes on the first floor of the Law School) special delivery registered letters with return receipts in order to be certain that they were advised of his desire to meet with them in his office.[36] (Although to his students it seemed at best an idiosyncrasy, it was certainly an unmistakable lesson on documentation.)

Nor did Dean Houston's intolerance of mediocrity and laziness change after the first three-year day school class' graduation. In an unambiguous notice to a subsequent first-year class, Houston warned that "the class must from this date cease any attempt to slide by on work. . . . A faculty meeting will be called on the class after Thanksgiving. . . . If it is necessary to cure the temper of the class by making examples of some of its members, this action will be taken."[37] As more than an afterthought, Houston also served notice on the second- and third-year students who had developed a custom of following with interest the litigation activities of their professors on behalf of the NAACP, so that times and courses for less diligent studying might be selected. "[T]he attitude. . . that the students need not be as accurate and punctilious about their assignments as in former years . . . is a very great mistake. . . . If as a last resort it is necessary to take disciplinary action, the action will be swift and severe."[38] To the end that Howard Law School become and remain a first-rate law school, graduating lawyers of the highest quality, "Charles Houston, the law teacher, was an unremitting task master."[39]

Dean Houston was painfully conscious of the need for black lawyers to be "not only good but superior, and just as superior in all respects as time, energy, money and ability permit."[40] This viewpoint transformed itself into demands that could become hardships on some of the students who while serious about the law and law school had to work at night. One such student was William Bryant, who was to become a partner in the Houston firm and the first black Chief Judge of the U.S. District Court for Washington, D.C. "How many of you work?" was the question that preceded Houston's survey of the freshmen class when Bryant began law school in 1933. Eventually reaching Bryant, as the others before him he was called on to answer questions about work. "How long do you work?" inquired Houston. "Twelve A.M. to eight A.M.," Bryant replied. "You can't work and go to law school. Don't get any notion that you can," Houston told Bryant. Bryant, who had already worked a full year doing manual labor in order to save money to attend Howard's Law School, wanted clarification because he did not intend to waste his time or hard-earned money in a no-win situation. "Are you telling me I can't work and go to law school or are you telling me I can't work and get the law?" he asked, and then quickly announced, "I'm not asking for any favors." Houston went on to the next students. After class, fellow students warned that one just did not "cross the Dean." Everyone was so adamant about it that Bryant began to wonder if his law school career would come to a quick, unglorious end. In reflection, Bryant remarked that what Houston did not know was that the job Bryant held was at a Howard University dormitory switchboard where, after about forty minutes to an hour, there ceased to be any telephone calls. "I wasn't a whiz kid that defied Charles Houston. I studied, read, and had no interruptions." At first Bryant was "a little paranoid." What William Bryant and his classmates did not know initially but would learn was that Charles Houston was not unfair or "vindictive." He was just a "perfectionist" who believed the law was "a jealous mistress." There was "no place in his mind for the law accommodating any weakness." Certainly there was no such thing as grading on a curve, because Houston "t[aught] the law as it had been taught to him." Nevertheless, William Bryant got "some of [his] best grades from Charles Houston" in such courses as "legal bibliography," "history of law," and "common law pleading."[41] Houston remained a demanding teacher, but Bryant "got the law, graduating first in his class."[42]

Most of Houston's students came to know him when outside the classroom, as both "sociable and humane." "His purse was never very full, if only because he so often emptied it to tide a student over an emergency."[43] Nor could Mag count all the times Charles called to let her know the students would be coming over so she should prepare something.[44] Marshall recalled, "He was a sweet man once you saw what he was up to. He was absolutely fair and the door to his office was always open."[45]

Charles Houston was much more than a good teacher and dean. He was a man possessed by his vision and confident of the nature of his special mission. With as much fervor as his grandfather had preached the Christian's duty of loving God and neighbors as self, Charles Houston preached the lawyer's basic duty of social engineering. Required courses included trips to the Federal Bureau of Investigation and penitentiaries. No student left Howard during Houston's tenure without considerable understanding of the workings of the government with respect to race and justice.[46] And why? "There was a social engineering job which they could not avoid."[47] Not for a moment did Houston equivocate. "A lawyer's either a social engineer or he's a parasite on society," he told all students.[48] "What is a social engineer?" was a question that was answered before any could ask. A social engineer was a highly skilled, perceptive, sensitive lawyer who understood the Constitution of the United States and knew how to explore its uses in the solving of "problems of . . . local communities" and in "bettering conditions of the underprivileged citizens." As he explained to his students, discrimination, injustice, and the denial of full citizenship rights and opportunities on the basis of race and a background of slavery could be challenged within the context of the Constitution if it were creatively, innovatively interpreted and used.[49] The "written constitution and inertia against . . . amendment give the lawyer wide room for experimentation . . . and enable [black people] to force reforms where they could have no chance through politics."[50] (That is how he summed it up some years later.) In his writings he was even more specific about the task of social engineering. It entailed duties to "guide . . . antagonistic and group forces into channels where they will not clash" and ensure that "the course of change is . . . orderly with a minimum of human loss and suffering."[51] A social engineer by definition was to be "the mouthpiece of the weak and a sentinel guarding against wrong."[52] The black social engineer further was called on not only to "use . . . the law as an instrument available to [the] minority unable to adopt direct action to achieve its place in the community and nation," but also consistently and competently to interpret the race's rights, grievances, and aspirations.[53] Preeminently, Charles Houston's presence was synonymous with this conviction about the moral obligation of black lawyers, and emanating from Houston was an intensity that inspired serious commitment to freedom and justice from his students and associates. And he knew well, as he taught those around him, that the struggle for fundamental change should not be deferred. This accounted for his restlessness after eight years at Howard. His mother understood it, as did his wife. As for Charles's father, he saw it in his son, but the nation was in the throes of an unprecedented economic depression, and one just did not give up fees, on any regular basis, even to save the race.[54]

CHAPTER VIII

The Limitations
of American Law

What was happening was worse than a nightmare because it was unadulterated reality. William actually knew he was lucky to have money to do anything. As Franklin D. Roosevelt reported in his inaugural address of March 1933, "Values ha[d] shrunken to fantastic levels; . . . the means of exchange [were] frozen; . . . farmers [found] no market for their produce: the savings of many years in thousands of families [were] gone. More important, a host of unemployed citizens face[d] the grim problem of existence, and an equally great number toil[ed] with little return."[1] All but a few black Americans were among those who were facing the "grim problem of existence" because of both economic and racial oppression. Survival had superseded every other concern.

Both William and Charles Houston were disturbed about the Depression. On the one hand, clients were having difficulty paying bills for services, which made it hard for William to take care of home and office expenses, pay the staff salaries, save money, and from time to time subsidize Charles, who was to William's way of thinking too generous with his time and money. On the other hand, the NAACP had begun calling on Charles regularly to assist the executive secretary, Walter White, and to serve on the National Legal Committee. Blacks knew that the NAACP had not been formed by the masses of black people. The NAACP had come into being largely as a result of a combined black intellectual middle class and white liberal and radical abhorrence of racism, to which was added the noblesse oblige of some of the whites on the founding committee. Initially its leadership was predominantly white. Although several prominent blacks had been pivotal to early meetings, including Ida B. Wells, Francis Grimke, and Bishop

Alexander Walters, only W. E. B. Du Bois was part of the first group of officers and leaders as he assumed the position of Director of Publicity and Research in addition to editor of the NAACP's official publication, *Crisis*. Between 1916 and 1920, however, James Weldon Johnson, a well-known black writer, increased the NAACP's membership tenfold through branch organizations, and under his leadership as field secretary, some blacks in nearly every region of the United States were encouraged to be part of a coordinated biracial battle against racial discrimination. Although the NAACP did not attract the numbers that Garvey's Universal Negro Improvement Association (UNIA) did at its peak, the NAACP did emerge from the 1920s with a sizeable black constituency because its leadership had not, as had the UNIA, suffered attacks on every side. More important, its program to secure rights for blacks could already boast consistent support of antilynching legislation and some successes in resort to court for redress of grievances related to disfranchisement and residential segregation. By the time Walter White had succeeded Johnson on the staff, it was clear that the NAACP had increasing credibility, but it still needed talent in its ranks, greater resources, and effective access to the political system.[2] During 1932 and 1933 the NAACP was involved in protesting racial injustice and Jim Crow public accommodations and denial of employment to and racial discrimination in the treatment of black workmen at government projects—Hoover Dam, the Mississippi Valley, and the Tennesse Valley in particular.[3] As Charles traveled across the United States assessing the conditions under which the masses of black people were living and—when they could find jobs—working, he seemed consumed by the primary importance of eliminating racially discriminatory policies and laws. Charles Houston insisted that "the privilege of piloting the race in its persistent march toward full citizenship [was] its own compensation for any hardships the lawyer may have to undergo."[4] William Houston wondered why, if "saving the race" was its own compensation, Charles had to borrow so much money![5]

Charles Houston joined black scholars and leaders in the summer of 1933 for the Second Amenia Conference. Just as the first Amenia Conference was called in 1916 at Joel Spingarn's estate so that leaders concerned about the plight of blacks could engage in free and frank discussion regarding a program of reform and action, so were the conferees of this second Amenia conference assembling to make "a critical appraisal of the Negro's existing situation in the changing American and world scene and . . . consider underlying principles for future action."[6] Among others, William Pickens, James Weldon Johnson, W. E. B. Du Bois, and young Howard radicals or activists including Sterling Brown, Ralph Bunche, Abram Harris, and Charles Houston met and, according to Du Bois, failed "to find a common language in which they [could] approach each other."[7] After three days the conference "resolved that it could not resolve" and went down in history, Houston reported, as the "anemic conference of Amenia."[8] The statement prepared for the press noted tactfully that "[N]o attempt was made to lay down a concrete program for . . . action by any organization or group."[9]

Disappointment with the Amenia Conference gave way to more aggressive struggle when in Tuscaloosa County, Alabama, a white lynch mob murdered two blacks who were in sheriff's custody and left a third for dead as they vented their rage inflamed by the June murder of a white girl. Incensed by the disregard for the lives of black people, Charles Houston and a Washington radical, George B. Murphy, Jr., of the *Afro-American*, had called at the White House. With the backing of Roger Baldwin, President of the American Civil Liberties Union, Houston and Murphy sought "an engagement for President Roosevelt to receive a delegation of representatives from various organizations which desired to protest the lynching evil and submit . . . proposals [for] . . . the protection of Americans."[10] They were told to return next morning. When they complied with that request by returning to the White House the following day and advising the receptionist of their presence, the initial response almost made them wonder if they were invisible. Although the demands on their time, as a lawyer in private practice and a newspaper man, were great, Houston and Murphy waited for more than an hour. Then they approached a secretary and were asked before they could say a word, "What do you boys want?"[11]

Attempts of black Americans and civil libertarians to persuade the federal government it had an obligation to protect black people from lynching had never fared well. The ineffectual responses and non-responses of the government to Ida B. Wells-Barnett's crusade against lynching and her *A Red Record* at the end of the nineteenth century, and to the NAACP's more recent twentieth-century protests and publications exposing the crime of lynching, served to remind Houston and others that harboring any great expectations was ahistorical and unrealistic.[12] Nevertheless, pressure had to be applied. Houston persisted until with Murphy and Baldwin, among others, he met with an assistant attorney general. Subsequently the special delegation met with the U.S. attorney general, Homer Cummings, who challenged Houston to defend his positions in a memorandum brief to the federal government. Members of the delegation gave Houston free rein in research and writing, so he enlisted the aid of two Howardites, a former student, Edward Lovett, and a professor, Leon "Andy" Ransom. To-

gether they worked assiduously to prepare a brief on Tuscaloosa showing the legal authority for federal prosecution of the Tuscaloosa sheriff
in charge.[13] After the state of Alabama failed to take action against
those guilty of the lynching, the authors constructed an argument in
which they used legal documentation to "make the South condemn itself."[14] During the course of the controversy some civil libertarians began focusing on the right of people to present their opinions and to
have full and free disclosure. But Houston, co-author of the brief,
spoke strongly to this point: "The one thing I want to emphasize is that
the brief is not a matter of free speech and free press with me, but a
fundamental matter of human life and orderly government. We have
had too damn many words without action already." Most important, it
was clear to Houston that "the law and constituted authority [were]
supreme only as they cover[ed] the most humble and forgotten citizen." Among white citizens, even in the federal government, a "traditional policy of temporizing with injustice and disrespect of the law"
was exhibited and Houston believed it largely "responsible for the
moral collapse . . . [observable] in so many quarters." Unhesitatingly,
Houston expressed these views in a letter to one of President Roosevelt's staff assistants.[15]

In October 1933 the authors of the forty-seven-page memorandum
brief argued the sheriff's guilt under section 52, chapter 3, title 18 of
the U.S. Code (willful subjection of a citizen to deprivation of rights,
privileges, and immunities protected by the Constitution and laws of
the United States). They further declared that if the federal government did not suppress internal violence and violation of federal statutes, "the Negro race in America will be driven to the conclusion that
the guarantees of the federal constitution and laws are labeled 'For
Whites Only.'"[16] (Believing it crucial to gain widespread support, the
NAACP printed and circulated widely the brief Houston had submitted to the attorney general. Nevertheless, it would be February 1934
before Houston and Ransom could confer with Assistant Attorney
General William Stanley, who would inform the attorneys that he did
not believe they were entitled to know the department's decision. Even
later in the spring, Houston would learn that the Justice Department
had decided not to prosecute.[17])

The completion of the Tuscaloosa brief in October 1933 came none
too soon. As a member of the NAACP National Legal Committee,
Charles Houston had already assisted with several important NAACP
cases, including those of Willie Peterson and Sam Jones, accused of
murder. Yet Walter White was refusing to take no for an answer in the
matter of the NAACP's new *cause célèbre, Commonwealth of Virginia*
vs. *George Crawford.* Earlier in the year, Houston had become familiar

with the case because he had assisted with a petition of habeas corpus and a legal maneuver to block extradition.[18] During that period, Houston had prepared a statement suitable for mass meetings in Crawford's behalf that explained the originally perceived legal and social significance of the case:

> The position of the N.A.A.C.P. is that a state cannot appeal to and nullify the Constitution at the same time; if it invokes the Constitution or any part thereof, it must do so subject to the limitations of the remaining parts. This question has never been passed upon by the United States Supreme Court on the particular combination of facts present in the Crawford case, and is a constitutional case of first impression in the Federal courts.[19]

The federal courts had not been persuaded by any NAACP arguments on appeal, and George Crawford had been returned to Virginia for a double murder trial.[20] Crawford would have to face the judicial system of Virginia. The executive secretary and the National Legal Committee were of the opinion that an attorney from "the North" should not be sent into Loudoun County. After all, it was a case in which two white women, Agnes B. Isley, a woman of considerable status in Virginia society, and Mina Buckner, her companion, had been murdered. The national office called on Houston partly because of his residence in neighboring Washington, D.C., his familiarity with some aspects of the case, and his professional ability. But when White first sought Houston's participation he had thoughtfully replied: "This case is far too big to be sloppily prepared. I would not be equal to the task because it would mean that I would have to give up all work here at the University. It would be impossible to do both jobs at the same time."[21] For Walter White's consideration Houston added that Howard Law School men believed "if Crawford could be defended by all Negro counsel it would be a turning point in the legal history of the Negro in this country." But he again emphasized it would be impossible for him to consider heading the case unless he had a leave of absence.[22]

Despite Houston's personal reservations, less than a week thereafter the NAACP had thanked and dismissed Crawford's Massachusetts attorneys, J. Weston Allen and Butler Wilson. Walter White released a press statement that "Charles H. Houston . . . [would] be in charge of the defense."[23] As of 20 October 1933, Houston found himself chief counsel for the Crawford case—an accomplished fact, it seemed. It was too late to think about securing a leave for the academic year 1933–34. Houston assumed the new position believing he knew as much if not more than any other attorney about the case and looking forward to the opportunity of having Negro co-counsel because he had made that a condition for holding the chief counsel's post.[24] These factors, for a time, overshadowed the potential danger.

On 6 November 1933 the Circuit Court in Loudoun County heard arguments in the first phase of the Virginia case. Charles Houston raised the issue of unconstitutional jury exclusion in a motion to quash the indictment against Crawford. In oral argument based on the motion, Houston stressed that Negroes were not included in the lists from which the judge of the court was charged to select grand jurors and that as a result of this exclusion no Negroes served on the grand jury returning the indictment. He also pointed out and presented witnesses to confirm that there were numerous blacks qualified for service. Finally, he forcefully contended that Virginia was permitting a caste system to interfere with its constitutional duties.[25] Nevertheless, the motion was overruled and the exceptions of defense counsel noted in the record. It was reported later,

> The court found the exclusion of Negroes, that there were qualified Negroes, that there was a caste system; but refused to find that Negroes had been excluded solely on account of race on the ground that to exclude, one had to bear in mind and consider, to pass judgment upon; and that since Judge Alexander did not consider Negroes in selecting the grand jury, did not have Negroes in mind, he did not work a constitutional discrimination, although uniformly he had selected white men only.
> Houston said . . . [the] ruling on the Crawford indictment is a dangerous technical legal stand, which, if established firmly in law without successful challenge, may give the state the right in the future to ignore Negroes altogether in jury service.[26]

The defense counsel had been prepared for an adverse ruling. After arraignment, on 7 November, the defense offered immediately another plea to the effect that George Crawford need not answer the indictment since Negroes were unlawfully excluded from the jury and this was highly prejudicial to the accused. Again Houston was overruled; counsel for Crawford entered a plea of "Not Guilty."[27] After adjournment, reporters crowded around Charles Houston. They wanted to know if he was going to move the trial to another county. To the question "Will you seek a change of venue?" Houston gave an unequivocal response. "Loudoun County and Virginia justice were as much on trial as Crawford," he insisted, and he and his co-counsel were going to argue the case in Loudoun County "if [they] had to cram it down the County's throat; . . . the crime [was] committed there and since Crawford had been charged with it, there . . . he should be tried."[28]

Failing to save Crawford from trial in Virginia on constitutional grounds or a legal technicality, Houston turned all his energies to creating a strong defense and assuring Crawford a fair and impartial trial—as far as it was within his power. Charles did not have enough experience in criminal law to be absolutely certain of the best procedure. He had never been in charge of a double murder case. Upon his recommendation, the defense had been investigating the case of the prosecution against Crawford in order to develop a defense that took into account all details. Defense counsel scrutinized the prosecution witnesses' stories, examining them about the course of events as related by their client. More than a few discrepancies appeared. Houston sent James "Pete" Tyson and Andy Ransom to verify the Boston alibi, which had seemed incontrovertible when presented at the Boston hearings. Because of circumstances apparently beyond their control, Tyson and Ransom were unable to see two key Boston witnesses. Since time was limited, the two lawyers gathered what they could and returned to assist Eddie Lovett and Houston with the argument for the December trial.[29]

In the midst of finalizing arguments and refining items for cross examination of prosecution witnesses, Houston was confronted with yet another problem. Bertie de Neal, Crawford's erstwhile sweetheart, had turned state's witness. Houston had an opportunity to talk with her, but so had the sheriff. The next thing Houston knew there was no alibi. Crawford's friend placed him in the vicinity of Middleburg at the time of the murder. A confused Houston went to George Crawford's cell and confronted Crawford with the new development regarding Bertie de Neal and the alibi. Crawford confessed to his presence in Middleburg and the burglary.[30]

The facts were suddenly very unclear. Crawford's story had changed. It now seemed that at least part of the confession was true. Houston, who had worked so hard and argued so zealously before the trial, believing in Crawford's total innocence, was not certain how he should proceed. After discussion with co-counsel, the decision was made not to offer the Boston alibi since certain damaging contentions of the prosecution were objective facts:

> 1. On Christmas eve, 1931, the Isley cottage in Middleburg was entered and a gold watch stolen. In January, 1932, shortly before the murders, Crawford turned up in Lynchburg at Coleman's home and pawned *this same watch* to Coleman for the price of a bus ticket to Richmond. . . .
> 2. About 4:00 A.M. on the night of the murders two Negroes abandoned a Ford car on the Virginia side of the Potomac River just outside of Washington, D.C. This was Mrs. Isley's car. It was searched, a note indisputably written by George Crawford was found on the floor. . . .
> 3. Crawford's clothes were discovered in Washington, D.C., where he had abandoned them when he fled from Washington.[31]

On 12 December 1933 the *Commonwealth of Virginia* vs. *George Crawford* was called to trial in the Leesburg, Virginia, courthouse. Ransom, Lovett, and Tyson accompanied Houston to the trial and joined him at the defense table. The atmosphere in the entire community was hostile and tense. Counsel commuted daily between Leesburg and Washington (over an hour's drive) because blacks in the locality were afraid to provide living accommodations to these men who were the first blacks to argue in the Leesburg court. Whites in the vicinity did not like the whole situation, and rumors about "running the 'Nigger' lawyers out of the county" had wide currency. It took enormous physical courage simply to go to Leesburg for the trial.[32]

Although they did not expect success, the defense counsel argued a motion to quash the all white petit jury on the basis of unconstitutional exclusion of blacks. Judge James McLemore heard the arguments, overruled them, and the jury was impaneled. Several questions had to have gone through Houston's mind. Would the power of the law be used to ensure Crawford anything remotely resembling a fair trial? Would the judge impartially instruct the jury that it could return either a verdict of "Not Guilty" or a verdict of "Guilty" with a recommendation of a life sentence in lieu of the death penalty if it so desired? Would any verdict other than the death penalty be acceptable to the southern whites who were bent on a black man's paying for this ultimate "violation of southern womanhood?" From 13 December through 16 December 1933 Houston and his co-counsel were in a trial pervaded by a sense of danger and challenge. The evidence of the prosecution was heard first. The prosecution presented nineteen witnesses who swore that Crawford was in Virginia between 24 December 1931 and 13 January 1932, although no one actually saw Crawford commit any murder. With the weight of the circumstantial evidence and the all-white jury, the issue was convincing the jury that there was reasonable doubt sufficient to save Crawford's life. The defense counsel cross-examined witnesses, pointing out weaknesses, where possible, in the testimonies. Only two witnesses surprised defense counsel when they testified, and they were successfully impeached. The testimony of one black man, Robert Hutchins, a principal witness against Crawford, was thoroughly discredited. Leon Ransom's able cross examination of the state's pathologist and Charles Houston's exceptional conduct in the courtroom controversy over the admission of the Boston "confession" obtained under duress were noted by reporters covering the case.[33]

Yet neither Houston's nor Ransom's handling of the prosecution's witnesses could fill the void left when the defense rested without calling Crawford or any other defense witness. In lieu of placing Crawford on the stand and risking his perjuring himself or collapsing under the pressure of the prosecution's cross examination, Charles Houston and Ransom decided counsel should defend Crawford in their closing arguments. Houston presented a lengthy but not particularly strong argument. More than once he mentioned the possibility of guilt for the lesser charge—larceny—then quickly added that of course he was not admitting the guilt of his client. (He seemed in some sense unnerved by the private confession of Crawford to the burglary.) Nevertheless, he concluded his argument with fervor: He was fighting to save the *life* of his client; George Crawford was not a killer type. George Crawford was a poor, hungry, jobless black man, but certainly not a killer.[34]

After less than three hours, the verdict was returned. George Crawford was found guilty of the murder of Agnes B. Isley. The jury recommended life imprisonment, although it could have recommended death. Houston immediately moved for a new trial; the motion was overruled and Houston's exception was noted by the court. The sentence was imposed and George Crawford was remanded to the custody of county officials. In confinement Crawford would await his second trial. State police guarded Houston, his co-counsel, and their wives as they left Leesburg.[35] (Although the press followed the case closely, it did not report any threats to the members of the jury, which underscored even more dramatically the circumstantial nature of the evidence and the probable weakness of the prosecution's case.)

For different reasons, neither George Crawford, Charles Houston, nor the state of Virginia was anxious to go through another such trial. Nevertheless, the final decision was Crawford's to make. His wishes were to enter a plea of "Guilty" rather than risk a trial for the murder of Mina Buckner with a less sympathetic or more racist jury. Although the *Norfolk Journal and Guide* carried an interview with Crawford on 10 February, in which he allegedly claimed he had been framed, Crawford repudiated the interview. On 12 February 1934 Crawford was unceremoniously sentenced to life in the Richmond State Penitentiary.[36]

Although Walter White proclaimed the case an "outstanding example of successful legal defense," Houston could hardly feel exuberant.[37] He just believed, as did his wife, co-counsel, and many others, that counsel had saved Crawford from a death sentence. Houston presented Crawford with all the facts of his situation regarding his rights, should he wish to appeal, and the possible consequences. Crawford was ill-disposed to "take a chance on the electric chair" if the sentence were reversed on appeal and remanded to trial.[38] He resigned himself to the consequences of his decisions. Justice had not been served, but Houston had followed his client's wishes. Houston let go of the Crawford matter and turned to the case of a fellow attorney, Bernard Ades.

The problems and pressures of the Crawford case had drained Houston physically and emotionally, but they had no corrosive effect on his desire to use his skills on behalf of those whose civil rights and liberties were not being properly defended. Prior to the Crawford jury trial in 1933, Houston had indicated to Bernard Ades of the radical International Labor Defense (ILD), that it would be both an honor and a pleasure to serve in the capacity of chief counsel in disbarment proceedings against him.[39] Houston was putting himself in a difficult position. The ILD was considered too radical for a temperate liberal. Houston, however, saw a need for this temporary association because the disbarment—as he understood the charges—was not justified. No state court had even complained about Ades's conduct. When Howard University's president, Mordecai Johnson, inquired about the law professor's affiliation with Ades and the ILD, Houston explained that Ades, a practicing attorney and a member of the ILD, had "rendered significant service . . . in exposing certain discriminations which Negroes used to suffer in Maryland courts."[40] On one case, Ades had consulted with Houston about saving a black from execution and gone to the U.S. District Court for a writ of habeas corpus. Ades's zeal had been rewarded with suspension under arbitrary circumstances by the federal judge and a disbarment hearing for unethical conduct.[41] "It is," Houston insisted, a "matter of principle vitally affecting the rights of any lawyer who espouses an unpopular cause that he be freed from the threats of arbitrary pressure of the Court. . . ." This was important to black Americans.[42]

When the hearing was called in February, Houston was to defend Bernard Ades against the general charges of "professional misconduct, malpractice, fraud, deceit and conduct prejudicial to the administration of justice." The opposing attorneys had prepared well and seemed to have built a case for professional misconduct on one or two counts. Ades and Houston conferred before Houston answered the charges. Houston indicated to Ades that the loss of one count might mean some problems. As Houston recalled, Ades, very nervous about the continuation of capriciousness and possible disbarment, agreed that Houston might suggest a reprimand for a count that counsel and Ades could not forcefully counter. Regarding the 1931 case of Euel Lee, Ades had approached Lee (whom Ades had unsuccessfully defended against a murder charge and who had been sentenced to death) about being named Lee's beneficiary. This was done on the day before Lee's execution and without Lee's request. Having been named beneficiary in Lee's will, Ades sought in legal proceedings to secure the body for a memorial meeting in New York City. On that one count the judge asked Houston's personal opinion, and he admitted that a reprimand might be in order. In contrast, on all other counts including such matters as soliciting clients and making accusations about the discriminatory conduct of the state of Maryland in "railroading" blacks to jail, Houston refused to make concessions.[43] For every count, Houston insisted that there was but one point. Ades provided unselfishly able defense for poor black clients who otherwise might have been deprived of effective legal representation. In addition, Houston reminded the judge that Ades "established two fundamental liberalizing principles in Maryland jurisprudence," namely, the right to change of venue as a substantial right and the right to jury service for black state citizens.[44] Finally, in a piercing indictment of the Maryland judicial system Houston declared:

> [The] real basis of attack on Ades [was] Ades' insistence on exposing officials with a dual standard of public morality—one for whites and one for blacks. Real enemies are men . . . who cannot conceive that Negroes are entitled to full citizenship. They cannot stand publicity and maintain their respectability therefore they want to remove Ades from the bar so they can rest in their hypocrisy.[45]

Having directed Soper's attention to official racism, Houston hoped that the judge would examine the evidence and arguments and find no bases for sustaining any counts against Ades.

The Ades's case was not the first time in February that Houston found himself locking horns with state officials because of dual standards. In an important address of 1934 to the Virginia Commission on Interracial Cooperation, he had taken issue with the governor of Virginia declaring that NRA (President Roosevelt's New Deal National Recovery Administration) actually meant "Negro Robbed Again."[46] The white South seemed to be forcing "the Negro to accept smaller wages while at the same time he is forced to pay the same prices for food, etc.," and more than that "attempting to make the Negro a landless, . . . unemployed class."[47]

In the same month, Charles Houston testified before a subcommittee of the Senate Judiciary Committee in hearings on national antilynching legislation, the Costigan-Wagner Bill (S1978). Houston was called on to "discuss the international and domestic implication of lynchings in the United States, and to point out . . . why federal legislation must be enacted and then firmly enforced."[48] First he emphasized the international implications. "The failure of the country to suppress . . . lynching" crippled U.S. prestige, exposed hypocrisy as the nation interfered with internal affairs of Central America and the West Indies, and further made it possible for foreign nations to "gamble on the possibility of Negro defection" as a result of racist treatment in their homeland.[49] In case no one took seriously the possibility of Negro defection as a response to government unwillingness to protect black people, Houston assured the senators that disillusionment and distress was the mood of black people, and not merely among radicals or southerners. He vividly illustrated this point:

> Only last Sunday . . . Congressman DePriest gave a musical in the Auditorium of the New House Office Building. A large gathering of Negroes of the City were there; all the Negro officials almost. Mr. William Tyler Page, former Clerk of the House, was the principal speaker. After the proper oratorical approach he swept to his climax that the Negro had never deserted the country in time of need and the United States can always count on his unwavering loyalty. Not even a decent ripple of applause trickled through the room.[50]

As Houston saw it, in an international crisis America might yet "reap the lynching harvest."[51] Second, he asked the Senate Committee to consider the domestic implications of lynching and the urgent need for enforcement. Using the Tuscaloosa incident as an illustration, he pointed out the way in which lynching had become such an accepted manner of dealing with black people accused of crimes that local officers could neglect their constitutional or statutory duties with local support.[52] Third and finally, he insisted that lynchings were not the last resort in punishment of sex crimes, but rather for the protection of both southern profits and southern exploitation of blacks.[53] "If the Department of Justice does not do anymore with the new legislation than it has done with the legislation already on the books," Houston stressed, "the law will be a dead letter."[54]

Charles Houston longed for time to handle the affairs of Howard Law School and Houston & Houston. With all his testifying before Congress and his NAACP and civil liberties activities, he was away from his Howard and firm duties more than he liked. The students were not performing up to par when they noted his absences and outside litigation. There were any number of wills, estates, and suits to attend to for his regular clients. He welcomed the end of his extra responsibilities for a time and was anxious to receive Judge Morris Soper's decision in the Ades case so that it could be closed. Ades was performing an important service to Maryland blacks in his vigorous defense efforts. Yet when the opinion was handed down it was not exactly what he had hoped. Morris Soper clarified the right of the accused to have counsel of his or her own selection even if counsel is supplied by an independent organization, and the right of counsel to volunteer his services in exceptional cases particularly when assistance is needed or important issues are involved. Yet, Soper stressed that the attorney's actions, not motives, were to be judged. Therefore he held that two counts had been sustained: first, soliciting the body of a former client who was to be executed so that the body might be used in a public meeting regarding racial prejudice and injustice, without full disclosure of intended use; second, publicly accusing Maryland County officials of railroading one of Ades's clients to the electric chair.[55] For the two offenses the judge reprimanded Ades.[56] Despite the reprimand, Houston believed that this opinion from U.S. Circuit Judge Soper might be of interest to the *Harvard Law Review*. He wrote the editorial board:

> Judge Soper's opinion raises some very fundamental questions: how far radical organizations may go in tendering their services to indigent, friendless prisoners; the right of an indigent prisoner to counsel of his own selection; the province of the court to inquire into the tenets and political beliefs of an attorney or organization volunteering to defend a person accused of crime.[57]

Houston had hardly dropped that letter in the mailbox before he received a letter from Lawrence Emery of the ILD. Houston was stunned by the contents of the statement. In addition to criticizing the official reprimand, the statement contained a strong condemnation of Soper and Houston:

> The hypocritical decision of the capitalist Judge Soper is designed to furnish an excuse for those other agents of capitalism, the N.A.A.C.P., to persuade the Negro people to put their faith in the courts. It is only by maintaining such faith in the courts and in the ruling class officials who administer the laws and "justice" that the masses of people can be kept back from the militant struggle which alone can result in real liberation for oppressed peoples and classes. . . .
> Dr. Houston, as an N.A.A.C.P. leader, was quite willing that Ades be reprimanded because the reprimand was a notice in so many words that efforts to destroy the faith of the masses in the courts must cease.[58]

Houston wrote William L. "Pat" Patterson, national secretary of the ILD, protesting misstatements. So did Houston's friends, such as John P. Davis of the Joint Committee on National Recovery, and Isadore Polier of the International Juridical Association (IJA). All were distressed by the charges against Houston made by the ILD. Patterson's replies to Davis and Polier indicated exactly where the ILD stood on the matter. Yes, Houston had "defended Ades upon the invitation," but certainly that is no cause for a special show of "gratitude to a man who voluntarily enlists in a struggle for . . . [black American] rights."[59] A letter that focuses on Houston, Patterson told Polier, has the problem of "turning the attention . . . from the major issue. I am fully in sympathy with the charges made against Houston. The statement issued by us was based upon a report made by Ades himself. . . . A careful reading of the record shows no basis for a censure but demonstrates that the constitutional guarantees to Negroes and to white workers are openly flouted."[60] Meanwhile Houston and Ades corresponded regarding Ades's scheduled hearing before the Grievance Committee of Maryland's Bar Association and Ades's representations to the ILD constituency. Houston asserted, as he wrote Ades on 1 May, "I do not feel free to represent you. . . . If you are not satisfied . . . it would be unfair for me to represent you on substantially similar charges before the . . . Committee."[61] Ades attended the 4 May 1934 Grievance Committee hearing alone, while Houston, deciding the matter was closed, went to Philadelphia to address an International Young Women's Christian Association (YWCA) Convention.[62]

Houston was sensitive to the radicals' criticism of his methods. He understood their viewpoint, although he was forced to bear the burden of public criticism. Therefore, in an address to the YWCA's thirteenth annual convention Charles Houston used the theme "An Approach to Race Relations" as a vehicle for expressing his views on a number of diverse and controversial issues. He called attention to economic discrimination—wage differentials, cotton acreage allotment abuses, exploitation of tenant farmers—and the failure of the government, employers, and owners to combat the devastating effects of the Depression in a nonracially discriminatory manner.[63] Although he believed "communism . . . too new and Negroes . . . too conservative to rush into any radical, revolutionary program," Houston praised the militant activities of Communists who were fearlessly promoting "mass resistance and mass struggle" against oppression. He asserted that they were compelling other Negro leaders to firmer stands and bolder action.[64] Yet in the same address he clarified the significance of Marcus Garvey, the Jamaican leader based in the United States who, a little more than a decade ago, had commanded the loyalty of over a million black people. Too many whites and blacks had failed to understand this man's importance because of the attacks on him by respected Negro leaders, the U.S. government's handling of him, and the movement's "visionary Afri[c]an empire." Marcus Garvey's movement was "a black man's dream; . . . it made a permanent contribution in teaching [the] simple dignity of being black." Marcus Mosiah Garvey claimed "his black skin as his proud birthright and distinction." It was immaterial that some considered Garvey a charlatan or fool, because "Marcus Garvey by turning the Negro's attention to the beauty of the color of his own skin has had a profound influence on Negro thought."[65] Finally, regarding better race relations, Houston asserted the necessity of freeing the young from the "blight of race prejudice, . . . senseless phobias and . . . contemptuous arrogance." "I ask you to take the question out of the realm of abstractions and to restate it in terms of human relationships. . . . [U]nderstand that it is just a question of reconciling the wants and desires of different human beings, each equally entitled to life, liberty and the pursuit of happiness."[66] On this last point he was emphatic. "We are not attempting to push you to the point of destruction. But we do emphasize that leadership in time of stress inevitably involves . . . risk. And the only way you [the YWCA] can remain a potential social force . . . is to accept responsibilities and [the] risk that incorruptible, courageous leadership brings. We are not asking you to take up the cross out of any sentimental interest in the Negro. . . . We do expect you to throw all your energies twenty-four hours a day in a fight for elemental justice without regard to race, class or creed."[67]

This was more than a speech. It was a conversation Houston was holding with his heart. Defending black rights, fighting against racial discrimination, working for better race relations—what were these tasks he set out to accomplish except expressions of a deeply rooted and personal ultimate concern about freedom and the quality of human life? This speech also represented political growth. But he was not able to reflect on the Philadelphia experience for very long. Ades and the ILD had more to say on Charles Houston's alleged subordination of the rights and struggles of blacks to the reprimand controversy. It was only later in June 1934 that Ades was able to engage in tempered dialogue with Houston.[68] As Ades reflected on it, "Houston . . . put up a good defense . . . in Court. . . . The deviations . . . from . . . agreed tactics were . . . his personal opinion. . . . The complaints [of] the International Defense were . . . not . . . against his professional integrity, but against his personal viewpoint."[69] Houston was pleased. He would represent Bernard Ades "either alone or with Joseph R. Brodsky as associate" regarding the Baltimore Bar Association charge of "stirring up race prejudice" (a form of professional misconduct) because "the principle of fighting segregation is paramount to any personal consideration."[70]

In his own struggling for elemental justice Houston found that his views were in conflict not only sometimes with radicals but also with other black NAACP leaders. Certainly they were not consistent with W. E. B. Du Bois—although on such matters as the race's equality and black pride, dignity, and worth they had no argument. Houston was opposed in principle to proposals of a separatist nature because of the subordinate status of the black minority in the United States and the impossibility of effecting justice in the context of legal segregation. Believing that the NAACP ought to be "for its greatest effectiveness . . . of the Negroes, by the Negroes and . . . for all the Negroes" and have a program of "[i]ntelligent leadership plus intelligent mass action" never meant, for Houston, the exclusion of whites.[71] Rather, it meant that whites must understand that if blacks were to be "advanced" they should have the leadership roles in guiding that advancement.[72] Actually Houston saw himself closer to some of the positions espoused by A. Philip Randolph and William "Pat" Patterson. Randolph believed that "salvation must and can only come from within," but he did not desire legislation to exclude anyone on the basis of "race, creed, nationality or color" from a union of sleeping-car porters.[73] Patterson, since Sacco and Vanzetti's political persecution, conviction, and execution, had been persuaded that there were many commonalities in the oppression of working-class blacks and whites by the class controlling the means of production. He further believed that some education and action toward working-class unity and replacement of capitalist exploitation with a more equitable socioeconomic system would be necessary if blacks were to be genuinely liberated in the United States of America.[74] Houston believed that both elements of black self-determination and periodic alliances with whites similarly oppressed were dictated by the realities of the plight in which black Americans found themselves during this period.

W. E. B. Du Bois, in contrast, had recently been writing editorials in *Crisis*, the official publication of the NAACP, that proposed "voluntary segregation" as part of the solution to the problems of black Americans. Houston had read with interest Du Bois's editorials, through which he asserted that the black American "must . . . voluntarily and insistently . . . organize . . . economic and social power, no matter how much segregation it involves," since it was not the case that in the near future black Americans would be in a position to choose between segregation and "no segregation." Nevertheless, Houston did not believe that the exigencies of the 1930s justified diversion of energies from action for a free, just, egalitarian, and desegregated society in the United States.[75]

In 1934 the NAACP hierarchy wished to have this matter addressed during or before its annual conference by a Negro leader of prominence. Walter White called on Charles Houston. Houston was hesitant to agree to deliver a "general speech." His preference was a "strictly professional" speech on the legal activities of the NAACP. Yet he did believe he had an obligation to speak to the NAACP members attending the conference. Houston wrote Roy Wilkins in May to indicate that being "more effective," not the Du Bois–NAACP controversy was the issue. He actually wanted to ignore formally what he called the Du Bois "attack." By so doing he "was not running from Du Bois," he told White.[76] Something positive needed to be stressed. When he spoke at the end of June he was very clear: "If the Negro is to make any further progress against the obstacles set up by private prejudice and public administration . . . he must unite with the 'poor white.' . . . [Although] the minds of both the poor whites and the Negroes have been poisoned against each other, . . . the attempt must be made." He further asserted that although the order of society was being affected by government programs during the economic crisis, black people should not be deceived. The place reserved for blacks is still "the bottom."[77]

Despite his May and June pronouncements regarding the Communists and the need for class unity, Houston was still far from the point of friendly dialogue with ILD members and black radicals. Some who had desired continued appeals in order to uphold George Crawford's constitutional rights, vindicate him in the face of the murder charges, and make his cause one with the masses refused to let the Crawford matter rest. Two who had done investigative work on the case, Helen Boardman and Martha Gruening, and pushed the issue believing justice had not been served, wrote Walter White and conferred with Houston, who made trial data available to them. In addition, Houston attended two conferences in New York with Boardman and Gruening, despite their scathing critique of the NAACP and Houston in the last June issue of *The Nation*. Boardman and Gruening—who were associated with the ILD—had concluded their article with a challenge to the NAACP and Houston:

> We realize that this was a difficult case and that any course Crawford's counsel might take had its dangers, but Mr. Houston's failure to appeal shows that he dared not put Virginia justice to any real test.
> The choice in such cases is not between surrender of the client's constitutional rights, and mass pressure and agitation regardless of the client's interests. . . . The precedent established in the Crawford case is, to the best of our belief, a new one in the history of the N.A.A.C.P. Its fine record of militant defense in the past is illustrated by the Arkansas riot cases. . . . Is this policy to be exchanged for one of abject surrender? Has the N.A.A.C.P. decided on retreat?[78]

Obviously the attack could not be ignored. Houston and Ransom carefully drafted a reply that appeared in the next July issue of *The Nation*. They stressed that four errors of the court with respect to jury exclusion and evidence constituted a basis for appeal, but that Crawford did not want to risk his life and counsel took orders from the client. While admitting that in not appealing the NAACP was party to a compromise, they did not concede it was a "retreat." The decision involved "not only questions of law, but also . . . [the] goodwill of the dominant majority."[79] They argued that the problem before the NAACP was not simply to force the jury issue—that issue had been forced in *Ex parte Virginia* (an 1880 case in which the action of a county judge to exclude blacks from a jury was declared violative of the Fourteenth Amendment)—but to force it in such a manner as to provoke the minimum resistance. There were indications that jury exclusion was breaking down in Virginia and other states of the south, they noted, giving examples and statistics of the breakdown without public resentment. They believed that it was important to weigh the sentiments and attitudes of the dominant majority. Moreover, they believed that the NAACP existed largely because of the tenet "The Negro can attain full citizenship and equal rights . . . with the cooperation and goodwill of the dominant majority." As practicing lawyers they emphasized that "[t]he law itself is a powerful weapon, but it has certain definite limitations when it comes to changing the *mores* of a community."[80]

In conclusion, they expressed some of their concerns and upheld the position of the NAACP in its legal program. They returned to the underlying theme of the dominant majority as they emphasized their consideration of the local community, noting that "sometimes in major social movements it may be necessary to sacrifice the peace of a community in the greater interests of the whole, but the decision would be made after great deliberation."[81] They went on to distinguish the Crawford case from the Scottsboro or Elaine, Arkansas riot, cases. Finally, they insisted that the Negro citizens of Virginia knew that the NAACP had neither retreated nor "dropped the jury issue," but was "in the fight to stay until every Virginia Negro enjoys all the rights, powers and privileges of every other citizen of the Commonwealth."[82]

Despite the questions left unanswered by Houston's response, he believed that the *Nation* rebuttal would end the long controversy. In the final analysis, Houston had acted in accordance with his client's wishes. Under a headline in the *Negro Liberator*, however, "Houston Indicts NAACP Leadership in Statement," black Communists of the League of Struggle for Negro Rights claimed that Houston had admitted betraying Crawford and bartering his rights away. The *Nation* article was such "evidence . . . of the traitorous role of the NAACP leader," they declared, that no other evidence "need be given."[83] The International Labor Defense published criticism and attempted to interview George Crawford, while the League of Struggle, through the *Negro Liberator*, continued to decry "the Crawford case [as] the worse betrayal that the N.A.A.C.P. leaders have ever perpetrated against the Negro masses." Charles Houston, an editorial declared, "was guided in the Crawford case not by the interest of George Crawford and the constitutional rights of the Negro people, but by the 'good will' of the boss court of Virginia. Houston did nothing which he thought would antagonize the lynch bosses of Virginia."[84] Moreover, while Houston attempted to move beyond the Crawford affair and continue with the business of fighting segregation in its various manifestations as best he could, the League castigated him for "trying to crawl back."[85]

There seemed to be no way to halt the criticism of his radical brothers. (As late as 29 December 1934 the League was still writing about Houston. It awarded a "bandanna" to Houston for being one of the "Uncle Toms" of the year in his conduct of the Crawford and Ades case.[86]) He had in the Crawford case and the Ades hearing tried to be professional and objective, to see both sides and then do the ethical and conscionable thing. He was reminded of George B. Murphy's admonitions about politics and the struggle. Murphy had insisted in 1933 that it was Houston's role not to decide on guilt but to defend vigorously his client and forward the struggle for human rights. George Crawford's cause was the cause of numberless poor blacks, Murphy maintained. The masses had seen and responded to the call to fight for the constitutional right of jury inclusion and, should they become accused of crimes, judgment by a jury on which blacks served.[87]

The Associated Negro Press, through Percival L. Prattis, voiced its opinion that it was out of naiveté that anyone would try a balancing act between the NAACP and radicals and that such an act was doomed to failure. Prattis wrote to tell Charles he hoped he would soon give up and leave "the Reds" alone,[88] but that was not Charles Houston's style. He did not give up on or dismiss issues until he could satisfy his own mind and conscience. He knew Benjamin Davis, Jr., a fellow Amherst and Harvard Law School alumnus who had joined the Communist party. Ben had defended for the ILD the young black labor organizer Angelo Herndon in 1932 and become part of a team of radical lawyers working on behalf of the oppressed masses. Both Ben Davis and Pat Patterson were black lawyers concerned about justice for black people in the United States. Houston felt he could cooperate with such men even though he chose not to be a Communist. The friendship of the Houston and Davis families, and the respect the three lawyers had for one another made a difference to Charles Houston.[89] To turn his back on the ILD and black Communists or the NAACP and the Associated Negro Press would solve nothing. This was an issue with which he must grapple, and he would.[90]

CHAPTER IX

Matters of Conscience

Charles Houston's experience with the League of Struggle for Negro Rights and the International Labor Defense was not altogether unique. Neither were the League and ILD responses to Houston's handling of the Ades and Crawford cases singular. The League of Struggle for Negro Rights had been formed in 1930 to develop a broad-based radical race movement in the United States. Among other things, its goals were to eliminate "white supremacy ideology 'with its attendant instruments of terror against Negroes,' . . . [demand] 'complete economic, political and social equality,' . . . [and insist on] 'equal protection of Negroes in all walks of life,' with a guarantee of freedom of speech, press, assembly and petition."[1] The ILD had been formed in 1925 to develop "a mass political and legal defense in . . . cases of . . . the class struggle," and to combat "legal and extralegal attacks against Negro people by K.K.K. elements, acting either as outright lynch mobs or as lynchers clothed with the garb of legal authority." Under Executive Secretary William L. (Pat) Patterson, the latter purpose assumed increasing importance. The Communist party "took the initiative in the establishment of the I.L.D." and the League of Struggle for Negro Rights. However, the ILD was "a united front organization of workers and middle class elements, of Negroes and whites of various political groupings."[2]

Given such aims, both the League and the ILD were in competition with the Urban League and the NAACP for black support and black talent. Before Charles Houston rose to prominence in the NAACP's National Legal Committee, William L. Patterson sought Houston for the ILD collective of black lawyers. Earlier, American Communists sought to bring William Pickens and W. E. B. Du Bois into the Party.[3] In the early 1930s all three rejected formal affiliation with the ILD, the

League of Struggle for Negro Rights, and the Communist party. Although membership in the ILD or the League would have not been membership in the Party, membership in either, for these three men, would have appeared to be acceptance of the Party's position on the "Negro question." Both the ILD and the League embraced the program of the Party set forth during the Sixth World Congress of the Communist International: "full emancipation" through "national self-determination in the southern states, where the Negroes form a majority of the population."[4]

For Houston, as for other blacks, rejection of formal affiliation with the three organizations was a decision predicated partly on the proposition that self-determination in the context of an independent black nation within the United States was not the answer for black Americans. It also was an affirmative response to two preeminent ideological questions. First, could one "wring a higher standard of living out of the Industrial Revolution for all people within the framework of constitutional government and capitalism?"[5] Second, could one achieve and guarantee freedom and justice for all regardless of race or class within the framework of such a system?

Allying himself with the reformist tradition in the 1930s, Houston, as were Pickens, Du Bois, and Walter White of the NAACP and Lester Granger of the Urban League, was attacked by the League of Struggle and the ILD. It was a time when, having abandoned the "boring from within tactic," the Party and related radical organizations had concluded that discrediting reformist black leaders and organizations was as necessary to the promotion of revolutionary programs as developing a radical popular front.

In 1933 Communists were less than gracious in describing Pickens, Du Bois, White, and Granger and in discussing their work for black people. "[Booker T.] Washington's scraping before the ante-rooms of the mighty is faithfully aped today by leaders of the [NAACP], the Whites, the DuBoises, the Pickenses. . . . The efforts of the present day 'leaders of the race' to chain the Negro people to the chariot of American imperialism, to perpetuate and build further the . . . antagonism towards white workers of the country, must be smashed."[6] Lester Granger of the Urban League at one point was declared the "Judas" of the race.[7]

Between 1933 and 1935, the League of Struggle and the ILD demonstrated an indecisiveness about how to proceed with the task of full emancipation for blacks. The discrediting of leaders of reformist groups ofttimes militated against the development of the united front for freedom and equality which was recommended as a tactic by the Comintern executive committee in 1933. Yet until the formation of the National Negro Congress in 1936, the ILD and the League approached the hierarchies of the NAACP and the Urban League with both occasional cooperative overtures and frequent criticism. In retrospect, William Patterson, who was affiliated with the ILD, the League, and the Party, allowed, "I think that perhaps on some occasions in our zeal to create a united front we were too sharply critical of some of the forces with which we worked."[8]

This overzealousness in discrediting non-Communist or socialist activists in the struggle and the apparent tactical confusion or ambiguity, as Charles Houston viewed it, were related to the primary dilemma of Communist and Communist-related organizations. The organizations were "subject to remote control," while their effectiveness was directly related to the adoption of a program that would speak to unique conditions in the United States.[9] This troubled Houston.

Houston, however, refused to be anti-Communist or anti-ILD. He could not endorse the view of Walter White, who was not interested in the kind of "popular front" the Communist party seemed to have in mind. Communists, White warned socialist Norman Thomas, "whenever it appeared to them to be advantageous . . . would indulge in sabotage attacks, lying and other tactics of that sort."[10] Neither could Houston support the position of Percival Prattis, although there was much with which Houston did agree. In one letter Prattis wrote, "I am not against the Reds. I'm for them. They're acid in the cleansing process. I'm not. . . . We all seek an ideal of racial justice, our group (let us say) in one way, and the Communists' group in another." "[B]ut," he insisted, "the methods of the two groups are not emulsive [sic]. We should . . . not fight each other, nor get mixed up."[11]

As far as Houston could see, objective reality dictated another course of action. The reality was that Communist party and ILD members were more often than not in the forefront demanding freedom, justice, and equality for all. This was sufficient justification for continued efforts toward cooperation. For that reason, Houston and his students joined Scottsboro marches. For that reason, in 1932 and 1933, Houston assisted William Patterson and the ILD by sending financial contributions "for the Scottsboro case . . . [and] any case the ILD [was] defending," supplying lists of authorities for use in defense of the "Scottsboro Boys" and discussing with Patterson and his other comrades points of law and politics.[12] After one such work-visit of Patterson and other ILD members, Patterson wrote: "I more than appreciate every courtesy you extended both Comrade Haywood and myself while in Washington, as well to the other comrade who found your advice and assistance of an extremely welcome character."[13] Although a member of the NAACP National Legal Committee, Houston deemed the cause of justice for the Scottsboro Boys too important to wait and find out what official stance was agreed on by the NAACP hierarchy.

Early in his association with the NAACP, Houston discovered that sometimes principles would create serious rifts between himself and others in the organization. Such was the case when William Pickens published in the *American News* of 24 May 1933 a castigation of the ILD for its use of Ruby Bates, one of the complainants in the Scottsboro case, in parades and mass gatherings. In Houston's opinion, Pickens's "Reflections" showed a lack of perception.[14]

Olen Montgomery, Haywood Patterson, Clarence Norris, Ozzie Powell, Charlie Weems, Eugene Williams, Willie Roberson, and Andrew and Leroy Wright (all between the ages of thirteen and twenty) were the "Scottsboro Boys." They had been indicted on the testimony of Victoria Price and Ruby Bates that they had been raped repeatedly by the black youths on 25 March 1931. The nine did not even recognize the two women. Yet on 9 April 1931 they were tried at Scottsboro and, on the basis of the testimony of the two women of questionable moral character, all but Leroy Wright, thirteen years of age, were judged guilty with a penalty of death by the electric chair on 10 July. The frame-up of the Scottsboro Boys was first exposed in April 1931, and on the day of sentencing the ILD sent counsel to demand a stay of execution. There followed incessant quarreling between the radical ILD and the cautious NAACP, with political slurs and maneuvers—particularly involving the Communists—interfering with the efficient handling of the Scottsboro case until the ILD secured written retainers from the youths and their families.[15] The legal battle was injected with new life when Ruby Bates confessed perjury. She became, in April 1933, a witness for the defense. Shortly thereafter she began appearing at ILD-sponsored mass meetings. Yet what was most impressive to Houston was the response of the masses to the call of the radicals for support of these innocent young men. Protests and demonstrations from Berlin, Germany, to Chattanooga, Tennessee, in response to the Communist and ILD call to "Unite and Fight" forced the case to a new level.[16] Scottsboro "caught the imagination of Negroes as nothing else within a decade."[17] And as the black and white masses clamored for justice it became clear to Charles Houston that cases could be judged and disposed of by juries outside the courtroom. When in 1933 William Pickens of the NAACP criticized Ruby Bates's public appearances and Communist involvement in the cases, Houston publicly denounced Pickens's position in the *Amsterdam News*.

Pickens seems to think that justice for the Scottsboro boys can be obtained in Alabama without outside pressure, and that the association of the [ILD] with the case hurts the boys' chances. I disagree. What sort of justice did the boys obtain in Alabama before the [ILD] entered the case? And so far as Ruby Bates' public appearances and speeches are concerned, Dean Pickens forgets that she is now testifying before that jury which will ultimately dispose of the Scottsboro cases: that is, before the public opinion of the world.[18]

Houston maintained that it was immaterial whether Ruby Bates was being promoted by the Communist party, the ILD, a national committee of liberals, or all three. The more important point was that Ruby Bates, as "a living example of the results of the oppressive system of the South by which the working classes white and Negro are set at each other's throats in order to perpetuate the system of discrimination and exploitation," exposed that system publicly.[19] She exposed an oppressive system by marching at the head of the Washington, D.C., Scottsboro parade, by volunteering as a witness for the defense, and by proclaiming the innocence of the youths to both the Speaker of the House and to the White House. Houston reminded the editor that this was not sensationalism: "It is not beyond the realm of possibility," he argued, "that if these Scottsboro cases proceed and the boys are actually threatened with execution, an American president [might] yet have to intercede . . . in Alabama lest America be condemned before . . . the world." Houston further stressed that none of Ruby Bates's activities interfered with her value as a trial witness and that in fact her real value as a witness "lies in her testimony before the people of the world outside of Alabama."[20]

In subsequent months, Houston was encouraged by the addition of the experienced criminal attorney, Samuel Liebowitz, to the forces, Judge James E. Horton's order for a new trial for Haywood Patterson, and by marches, rallies, and petitions on behalf of the Scottsboro Boys. Houston urged Walter White in November 1933,

> [r]egardless of any division of opinion between the NAACP and the ILD [relative to funds, attorneys, or tactics], . . . use all of the Association's press contacts to guarantee that the third [Scottsboro] trial will be covered. . . . [G]et . . . the Branches to move, send telegrams, protests, etc. . . . It needs all the steam which the Branches can raise to insure publicity which will protect Liebowitz and the rest . . . in Alabama.[21]

The year 1934 having been a difficult year for Houston and for the Scottsboro Boys, Houston found it problematic to keep on top of all that had to do with the Scottsboro trials, convictions, and dissension among the forces fighting for the youths' freedom. As months elapsed, he was unable to obtain direct information on Scottsboro from Pat Patterson or Ben Davis, Jr., not only because of Houston's own troubles arising out of the Crawford and Ades cases but also because of another schism in the ranks of those defending the Scottsboro Boys. When two ILD attorneys were arrested on the charge of attempting to bribe the remaining prosecution witness, Victoria Price, and Liebowitz publicly broke with the ILD and Communist-sponsored attorneys, Walter White was confused as to whether he should keep the NAACP clear of the controversy or support the Liebowitz/anti-Communist, anti-ILD group. He turned to Houston, who advised him to "keep out" but indicate that after the controversy was settled, the NAACP "stands ready to help."[22] Houston's position was predicated on what seemed a common-sense approach to the NAACP's best interests.

> As the case now stands I have some doubts whether the boys are any better off with Liebowitz in and the Communists out, than with both of them in. . . .
> Finally, if the communists are put out and the boys finally lost, you have played right into the hands of the I.L.D. It would say as long as the working classes had the case mass pressure kept the bosses from the boys' throat; but that the NAACP as the bosses' minion formed a conspiracy to destroy the boys and betray the class struggle, etc., etc. No use of that.[23]

While Houston preferred that the NAACP as a black rights organization maintain its credibility through nonalliance until the Scottsboro youths selected counsel or the Supreme Court ruled on the appeal before it, he personally was very worried about the impact of the infighting on the cases and the masses. He did not commit himself to any group, but he spent a good deal of time talking with groups and deliberating about an effective role he might play to assist in the legal battle to free the youths. It would be criminal for them to be lost as a result of fighting among friends of their cause.[24]

Houston's constant civil liberties, civil rights, and antidiscrimination activities kept him on the go. Some of his Howard Law School students resented these other involvements that claimed so much of the vice-dean's time. They began to complain about his "absenteeism." In the midst of Houston's planning period for direct action against the upcoming federal crime conference because of its failure to deal with lynching, disgruntled Law School students threatened a strike because of the alleged racial prejudice of a white professor, Alfred Buscheck, and the "absenteeism" of their "dean." William Bryant remembered that Buscheck was a professor who taught very much as Charles Houston did. He knew his material. He presented it. He had no curve

and no lower expectations just because the majority of the students
were black. You either passed because you demonstrated that you
knew the law, or you failed. All the students knew that Dean Houston
had other involvements, but he was not negligent. Houston was beginning to sense that he had done all he could do at Howard as the chief
administrator. It was time to move on to the next challenge. Although
he felt obligated to finish the academic year at Howard, this student
protest and his response to it convinced him that he was right about
needing to leave Howard Law School. A menacing student uprising
notwithstanding, Houston considered picketing the federal crime conference more crucial than rendering an immediate decision on Buscheck. It was unbelievable to many students, but Houston's priority
was strategizing and staging a street demonstration to direct attention
to lynching.[25]

The strike was averted as a consequence of the assistance of alumni
Edward Lovett and Thurgood Marshall, practicing attorneys with a
special interest in civil rights and liberties. But it was an uneasy calm.
Marshall wrote to Houston: "If you need me to give anybody *hell* just
let me know."[26] Houston, who had prudently nurtured Howard Law
School to a level of excellence, felt pulled to the broader struggle of
black Americans. How could the grievances of the students be more
pressing than the Justice Department's omission of extralegal attacks
on and murders of black Americans from its conference agenda? This
omission had national implications. It underscored that the last place
in Washington where a black could look for protection was the Justice
Department. Yet this was the era of "Tuscaloosa," "Scottsboro," and the
Costigan-Wagner antilynching bill. Houston masterminded the picketing by blacks with nooses and placards. City-wide press coverage directed attention to the issue of antilynching legislation, as Houston
had planned. The seriousness of the concern of black Americans was
underscored by the picketing and arrest of Roy Wilkins (from the
NAACP's national office), Emmett "Sam" Dorsey (prominent Howard
University professor), George B. Murphy, Jr. (Washington, D.C., radical and member of the family that published the *Afro-American*), and
Edward Lovett (recent Howard Law School graduate and civil rights
lawyer). As a result, lynching came before the public and the federal
crime conference despite the agenda. Houston was certain that "not a
word would have been said about lynching during the Conference and
certainly not even an indirect mention would have been made in the
resolutions" if direct action had not been employed.[27]

Throughout the Howard Law students' protest they had insisted
that Charles Houston's first duty was to the Howard University Law

School. It could be argued that as vice-dean it should have been. Yet the Howard Law School no longer claimed Houston's first loyalty. Although he had not made a public announcement, his relationship to the NAACP had changed, and accordingly he had incurred obligations necessitating attention to a number of disparate problems. On 26 October 1934 he had presented to the Joint Committee of the NAACP and the American Fund for Public Service a memorandum regarding the expenditure of an appropriation to the NAACP for a national legal campaign against racial discrimination in the areas of education and transportation. His memorandum had met with the approval of the Joint Committee, the members of which were Roger Baldwin, Morris Ernst, Lewis Gannett, James Weldon Johnson, James Marshall, Arthur Spingarn and Walter White, and Houston had accepted the offer to direct the NAACP's legal campaign.[28]

In 1930 the NAACP had been voted a special grant from the American Fund for Public Service. This fund, established in 1922 by Charles Garland, who had resolved to use his inheritance (in excess of $1 million) for philanthropic purposes, had as its policy the dispersal of money to individuals and groups for the benefit of mankind. Specifically, Garland stipulated that gifts and loans from the Fund should be used to benefit "poor as much as rich . . . [and] black as much as white" and that recipients "shall be trusted not to use [any gift or loan] to the advantage of . . . one class or nation as opposed to another."[29] Such a policy inspired criticism of Charles Garland and the Garland Fund. Critics, in correspondence and through the print media, impugned the motives of Garland and the Garland Fund for its alleged communism and support of alleged communist activities. The Board of Directors—which included among others, Roger Baldwin, Morris Ernst, Lewis Gannett, James Weldon Johnson, Clarina Michelson and Norman Thomas—countered the allegations with facts about the composition of the board, the Fund's policy and recipients of appropriations. The chief work of the board, however, was review of applications from individuals and groups seeking support for a variety of projects. Subcommittees concentrated on areas of particular concern, civil liberties and the plight of black Americans. Morris Ernst, Lewis Gannett and James Weldon Johnson, the Committee on Negro Work, functioned with interest akin to zeal in researching the Fund's support of blacks, studying their legal status and socioeconomic conditions, reviewing the organizations that made appeals to the Fund and considering projects or approaches that might be pursued by organizations to alleviate racial oppression. The three men surprised the remainder of the board when the Committee proposed that a minimum of $294,000 be spent on a program to obtain for blacks equal rights through the courts with emphasis on such tactics as taxpayers suits and direction of the campaign by the NAACP, a previously-funded bi-racial organization dedicated to the advancement of black Americans. The board sent the Committee on Negro Work back to deliberate, after reading its October 1929 memorandum, and further stipulated that it try to meet with the Committee on Civil Liberties whose members held the view that the problems of blacks should be tackled from the economic end with work through labor organizations. The two committees came to no compromise so the Committee on Negro Work presented a revised proposal by means of a second memorandum in the winter of 1930. The board eventually approved the release of $100,000 to the NAACP for taxpayer suits to challenge the dual school systems in the South, for legal protection of blacks' civil liberties, for litigation seeking an end to segregation and jury exclusion, for attacking American imperialism in the western hemisphere, particularly Haiti and Nicaragua, and for propaganda in support of the legal campaign. A joint oversight committee with members from the Garland Fund and the NAACP was to secure an attorney to head the nation-wide campaign.[30]

On October 4, 1930, the oversight committee, known as the Joint Committee, selected Nathan Margold of Harvard, a very capable white scholar with expertise in constitutional law, to study the state of the law in regard to blacks' civil rights and direct the NAACP's legal campaign. Margold prepared a "Preliminary Report for the Joint Committee Supervising the Expenditure of the 1930 Appropriation by the American Fund for Public Service to the NAACP" in installments that incorporated the findings of extensive and thorough research on civil rights, with particular attention to equal protection case law, in areas of jury exclusion, jim crow transportation, residential segregation, disfranchisement and unequal apportionment of school funds. (A first draft also included some unenthusiastic reactions of white sociologists and philanthropists to the proposed legal campaign.) Margold quoted from the Committee on Negro Work's memorandum of 1930. He, then, pointed out that it was flawed in its selection of states for taxpayer suits to attack the dual school systems, stressed that the Committee had underestimated the number needed if such suits were to make a meaningful difference, discussed the inevitable proliferation of suits if the Committee's approach were used and proposed instead a direct constitutional attack on segregation when coupled irremediably with discrimination.[31] Arguing for an immediate, direct challenge based on the 1886 Supreme Court equal protection decision in *Yick Wo* v. *Hopkins*, Margold wrote:

It would be a great mistake to fritter away our limited funds on sporadic attempts to force the making of equal divisions of school funds in the few instances where such attempts might be expected to succeed . . .

On the other hand, if we boldly challenge the constitutional validity of segregation if and when accompanied irremediably by discrimination, we can strike directly at the most prolific source of discrimination.

We can transform into authoritative adjudication the principle of law, now only theoretically inferable from *Yick Wo* v. *Hopkins*, that segregation coupled with discrimination resulting from administrative action permitted but not required by state statutes, is just as much a denial of equal protection of the laws as is segregation coupled with discrimination required by express statutory enactment . . .[32]

Strategy and tactics became increasingly important when the originally-approved $100,000 appropriation was substantially reduced after the Depression affected the Fund adversely.[33]

In 1933, having completed his report, Nathan Margold notified the Joint Committee that he would not be available to direct the legal campaign he had proposed because he had accepted an appointment as Solicitor of the Department of Interior. Margold's departure led to the consideration of Charles Houston to direct the legal campaign for the NAACP. Houston was not the first choice. The Joint Committee had offered the position to Columbia University's Karl Llewellyn, also white, whose expertise in constitutional law was well known and highly regarded. It was his spring 1934 refusal on the basis of insufficient courtroom experience that made Houston a frontrunner.[34] As early as July 1933, Walter White had reported on the NAACP's choice for Margold's successor, Charles H. Houston, in a letter to Roger Baldwin, a member of the Garland Fund board of directors as well as the Joint Committee and the chief executive of the American Civil Liberties Union:

> . . . Felix Frankfurter says he [Charles Houston] is one of the most brilliant and able students at Harvard within his memory. . . . His very deep interest would enable us not only to secure a man who would have all the intellectual and legal background necessary but one who will have a definite personal interest which would cause him to do the job better. . . .[35]

On 22 October 1934 Margold also strongly endorsed Houston.

> In connection with the choice of an attorney to take charge of the campaign to establish various fundamental constitutional rights of Negroes, I wish again to bring to your attention my hearty endorsement of Mr. Charles H. Houston for the position. Houston was one year my senior at the Harvard Law School. During his third and my second year at the School we were co-editors of the *Harvard Law Review*. During that period, and on many occasions since then, I have had ample opportunity to reach an informed opinion concerning Houston's ability as a lawyer and

character as a man. His qualities in both respects are superlative. He is, moreover, possessed of unusual tact and personal charm, by reason of which I believe him well equipped to overcome, in large measure, the unreasoning prejudices which he, and indeed anyone else in his position, would encounter in the course of the campaign.[36]

The memorandum that Charles Houston presented to the Joint Committee in October, 1934 set forth two approaches to the legal offensive within the framework of a reduced appropriation of $10,000. Believing it difficult to execute with such limited funds, an effective program of litigation attacking discrimination in more than one area, Houston, first, expressed this view in his memorandum. Thereafter, he presented one budget proposal to spend the entire amount on a campaign against discrimination in education while an alternative proposal specified a division of the appropriation for campaigns against discrimination in both education and transportation, the areas targeted by the Joint Committee.[37] Houston's memorandum revealed a strategy, tactics and a philosophy at variance with Margold's. Desiring to see black institutions and students receive more funds and secure enlarged educational opportunities even within the context of an objectionable and racially discriminatory system, Houston suggested that the attack against racial discrimination begin with the issue of unequal apportionment of school funds in the South, preparation of a model bill and brief seeking state grants-in-aid for black students legally barred from admission to state universities attended by whites and suits on behalf of teachers who were victims of discriminatory salary differentials. The educational proscriptions deserved primary attention, he argued, because of their effect on an entire generation of black people. Secondarily, he noted how court challenges to racial discrimination in rail and water transportation might be handled during the campaign. While Houston urged that the entire appropriation be used for the fight against discrimination in education, he emphasized that whichever issue or issues were chosen, the NAACP-American Fund campaign ought to be an expression of the NAACP's commitment to protracted struggle *for and with* black people. The "aims," under Houston's auspices, would be "(1) to arouse and strengthen the will of the local communities to demand and fight for their rights; [and] (2) to work out model procedures through actual tests in court which can be used by local communities in similar cases brought by them on their own initiative and resources."[38]

Houston's emphasis on black people in their local communities was critical and seminal. Given this singular opportunity coupled with very limited resources, legal soundness would be an insufficient measure of an effective program. Effectiveness in this campaign against racial discrimination also meant waging battles that reflected the concerns of black people and encouraged some commitment of time and individual or community resources. After the depletion of the Garland Fund appropriation, a "concentration of effort" and additional funds to "sustain persistent struggle" and develop model procedures for use in various localities would be crucial to success nationwide. Houston understood, as well as Margold, that in the American legal system "isolated suits [would] mean little . . ." What was of importance to Houston, however, was a planned legal program that laid a "foundation" with respect to research, cases and community involvement in struggle against racial discrimination and for equal rights. Given pervasive racial discrimination and the economic depression in the United States, the NAACP should begin fighting segregation under the prevailing separate but equal requirement (which had been enunciated in the 1896 *Plessy* v. *Ferguson* decision of the U.S. Supreme Court) and in that regard even taxpayers suits could be useful, Houston stressed. The NAACP obviously did not endorse segregation, but, Houston further explained, the campaign ought to make segregation with inequality a target of litigation, make segregation with equality too expensive to maintain and use legal papers in every situation to make plain the desirability of the elimination of segregated—dual—systems. Proceeding on such a basis to attack inequalities resulting from racial discrimination was consistent with the sentiments—and even the recent activity—of some blacks and Houston was concerned about not only a legal but also a "moral effect." Ultimately, he believed that "the inspirational value of a struggle is always greater when it springs from the soil than when it is a foreign growth."[39]

Following the presentation of his conception of the legal campaign, Houston indicated that his commitment to Howard University would necessitate his being a part-time counsel to the NAACP until 30 June 1935, after which time he would begin a leave of absence from Howard "in order to devote his entire time to the work [of the special legal campaign]."[40] The selection of Charles Houston to direct the NAACP's legal campaign against racial discrimination was simultaneously endorsement of his proposal to place major emphasis on educational inequalities and fight racial discrimination by means of "a carefully planned [program] to secure decisions, rulings and public opinion on the broad principle instead of being devoted to merely miscellaneous cases."[41] Equally important, the selection of Houston represented the adoption of his strategy and philosophy regarding the struggle of his people against racial discrimination and for equal rights. The NAACP would commit itself to the elimination of segregation through a protracted struggle, which Houston and others understood would be carried on beyond the period of funding by Garland. That struggle would incorporate local communities' initiation of litigation, community political education and participation with the guidance and assistance of the NAACP and the gradual evisceration of the separate but equal doctrine by means of test cases successively litigated. The direct constitutional challenge would follow such groundwork and Charles Houston, as the head of Howard's Law School and a proponent of "social engineering," looked forward to directing the campaign.[42]

It was Houston's acceptance of this new responsibility with the NAACP that caused such conflict in his dealings with Howard students. He had promoted seriousness about education for racial uplift, protection and struggle. Because he had not resigned, Houston owed the institution and the students more time and attention. Yet he was now formally allied with another tradition of organized protest and struggle against racial discrimination and injustice on a national level. The holiday season came none too early. Between Christmas and New Year's Day he put in many hours preparing for courses, thinking about how to handle the transition from Howard to the NAACP and making plans for the legal campaign.[43]

In the new year the first issue Houston met head-on was Scottsboro. He had not been satisfied with his efforts on the youths' behalf, but he had not had sufficient information on which to act. The U.S. Supreme Court decision to review the convictions of Haywood Patterson and Clarence Norris prompted Houston to write an appeal for Scottsboro defense funds. He disclosed his sentiments to the International Juridical Association (IJA).

> As long as there was any question as to who represented the boys in the United States Supreme Court I remained silent. . . . But now that the United States Supreme Court has decided to hear the cases again, the point is clear. The records and petitions in the . . . Court were filed by . . . lawyers retained by the International Labor Defense. . . .
>
> [O]ur relations have not always been cordial. But my personal interests are immaterial in comparison with the defense of the Scottsboro boys.[44]

Carol King and Isadore Polier of the IJA "both felt [the] appeal was a bit half-hearted." They drafted another version, which Houston agreed was "better in principle than the draft [he] submitted.[45] Houston explained to Walter White of the NAACP, "I prefer for it to be personal with me taking the whole responsibility. I don't expect thanks from the I.L.D. but I do expect to satisfy my conscience."[46]

Having indicated his interest and goals regarding the Scottsboro cases, Houston decided to attend to other pressing issues. He had two Senate hearings in the same month. First, Charles Houston was to represent the NAACP during hearings on a bill "To Alleviate the Hazards of Old Age, Unemployment, Illness and Dependency, To Establish a Social Insurance Board in the Department of Labor, To Raise Revenue for Other Purposes" (S1130). As he studied the provisions of the bill for the aged, the unemployed, and blue-collar workers, he found them to be woefully inadequate. Qualifications for casual, agricultural, and domestic workers rendered the bill at best harmful to black workers and the black aged. As he viewed S1130, the NAACP could not support it because "the more [the NAACP] studied . . . , the more holes appeared until from a Negro's point of view it looks like a sieve with holes just big enough for the majority of Negroes to fall through."[47] Second, there were points he had failed to emphasize the previous year when he appeared before the Judiciary Committee. He began to prepare new remarks on lynching as not only a national emergency but also a threat to the economic security of labor and an example of the federal government's dereliction of duty with cases such as that of Claude Neal of Alabama who was transported across the Alabama state line and lynched in Florida.[48] In the midst of preparation for a February Senate Hearing, Houston was contacted by Walter Pollack, an attorney with the ILD. While some ILD members did not trust Houston at all, others wanted to make use of his expertise. On 4 February, following the expressed wishes of Scottsboro attorneys Samuel Liebowitz, George Chamlee, Walter Pollack, and Osmond Fraenkel, Charles Houston appeared in the Supreme Court to present a motion for the withdrawal of the appearance of Pollack and Fraenkel and the substitution of Liebowitz and Chamlee as counsel in the Norris case. The motion was granted, and Houston advised the men of such. He refused compensation; it was a matter of principle.[49] He noted in a letter to a staunch supporter of the Scottsboro Boys, "My satisfaction comes from the fact that I was able to do a little something to help the boys."[50]

Many things were coming together for Houston in the year 1935. A better understanding of Scottsboro in relationship to lynching and discrimination led him to participate in a curious public meeting with Bernard Ades. The Liberal Club of Howard University had called on the two men to debate Scottsboro, but there seemed to be no significant difference of opinion in that matter, so they debated only when the broader ideological position of the Communist party on the separate Negro nation was brought up. In addressing the gathering about Scottsboro, Houston first stressed that he and the NAACP were inter-

ested in the welfare of the boys and justice. Organizational rivalry had
to yield to these more significant issues. Thereafter Houston praised
the ILD for demonstrating that Scottsboro was not "an isolated instance of a miscarriage of justice," but an aspect of "the oppression of
the American Negro." He credited the ILD with revealing this oppression as a "worldwide issue through . . . demonstrations and mass protests in Europe, South America and all over the world" and exposing
"the American hypocrisy which can play missionary to the heathens
while at the same time it winks at the exploitation of its Negro citizens." Scottsboro, Houston contended, "emphasized the essential unity
of interest" between the poor and the oppressed "white and black
workers," while it made the "rank and file Negro" take an "active part
in his own fight . . . realize his own power and [catch] a new sense of
his own importance."[51] Houston's final Scottsboro remarks were the
product of reflection and careful analysis.

> By its uncompromising resistance to Southern prejudice the I.L.D. has
> set a new standard for agitation for equality. It has . . . demonstrated to
> the Negro bourgeoisie just how shak[y] its claim to race leadership really
> is. Through its activity in the Scottsboro case the I.L.D. has made it im-
> possible for the Negro bourgeoisie in the future to be as complacent and
> supine before racial injustices as it was prior to Scottsboro. It has intro-
> duced the Negro to the possibilities and tactics of mass pressure. It has
> changed the emphasis of the Negro question from a race issue to a class
> issue.[52]

Only days later, Houston, Ades, and all others who had been calling
for the freedom of the Scottsboro Boys received with enthusiasm the
decision of the U.S. Supreme Court. The court held that blacks were in
fact excluded from the grand and petit juries that had indicted and
tried Clarence Norris and Haywood Patterson. It reversed the conviction of Norris and remanded Patterson's case to the state court. This
small victory had come about through persistence, hard work, and perseverance of the masses. Through Scottsboro attorneys, and with the
guidance of the ILD, the Communist party, and the liberal American
Scottsboro Committee, farmers, workers, housewives, and others used
telegrams, rallies, parades, and the like to demand that the nine black
youths, falsely accused of raping two white women, not be sacrificed
in the name of an oppressive system and that the racism, which rendered the women's stories credible to Alabamians, be exposed and
fought. The power of the masses, inside and outside the continental
United States, brought to bear on the issue created an atmosphere for
a profession of truth by Ruby Bates, for closer scrutiny by appellate
courts, and for a judicial concession in at least two cases. This was as

gratifying to Houston as it was to counsel, the ILD, and the countless people struggling together on behalf of the Scottsboro Boys.[53]

Some years later, talking with a friend, Houston reflected on the ways in which Scottsboro marked "an historic departure." In an era "when the Negroes in the South had lost their franchise and the masses of Negroes in the South had ceased to be vocal, articulate, and powerful in the sense of their being masters of their own destinies," Scottsboro cases handled by the ILD raised their consciousness and inspired action. "There was the identification with the struggle, the recognition of the struggle [and] commitment to the struggle." With conviction, he stated, "[N]obody who ever sent a telegram of protest to any of the Scottsboro judges . . . ever inside himself accepted the fact that he was willingly from then on going to tolerate the system and the oppression to which he hitherto had been unresistingly subject." More fundamental, whereas prior to Scottsboro the masses of blacks in the South tended to "stay away" from blacks in trouble "with the idea of not letting trouble spread and also with the idea of avoiding consequences to themselves," they united to fight on behalf of the Scottsboro Boys because they "were made to feel that even without the ordinary weapons of democracy . . . [they] still had the force . . . with which they themselves could bring to bear pressures and affect the result of the trial and arbitrations." Significantly, "the people who up to that time had been considered to be almost unorganizable," taught not only that "the southern government was an instrument which was designed to . . . keep them . . . subject to domination, but also that the courts were instrumentalities of the status quo," became an "articulate protesting mass bent upon their own freedom." Finally, despite the outcome of the judicial process, Scottsboro was positive because it identified "the masses of the world with the struggle of the masses of the Negroes in the United States."[54]

After 9 April 1935 there was little time to reflect, for on that day official word came down from the Howard University board of trustees regarding Houston's application for a leave of absence. His leave of absence for the purpose of accepting full-time employment with the NAACP as of 1 July 1935 was approved, and Johnson was requesting the Law School annual report before that date.[55] Moreover, the case of Jess Hollins, supported by the NAACP, was on its way to the U.S. Supreme Court, and the recent *Norris* and *Patterson* opinions relative to unconstitutional jury exclusion had to be incorporated into the *Hollins* argument. This case was of considerable urgency because Jess Hollins, a black Oklahoman convicted of rape, was alive because of a stay of execution granted pending the high court's decision. Houston enlisted Edward Lovett's service, and he did something he rarely did in civil rights cases for which there was no compensation: He turned to his father, William, for help. The three petitioned to proceed *in forma pauperis* (in other words, with no costs to be charged to Hollins because of his poverty) and filed for a writ of certiorari requesting a hearing in the Supreme Court. This was the first case in which the NAACP had employed exclusively black counsel before the U.S. Supreme Court. As the current vice-dean of Howard Law School, Charles Houston did not share the anxiety of some members of the NAACP. His co-counsel were very able, and he had already outlined the procedure for attack on unconstitutional exclusion of blacks from juries. Using this procedure he had developed with Leon Ransom during the Crawford case, Houston and co-counsel demonstrated in the brief for Hollins that no black had ever served on a jury in Okmulgee County, where Hollins was indicted and tried, since 1907. Yet blacks constituted 17 percent of the county's population, and many of them met the qualifications for jury service. Houston stressed this in oral argument, insisting that there was an official policy of segregation. On 13 May 1935 the decision of the Court reversed the lower court's ruling and remanded the case for further proceedings nonviolative of Hollins's rights. This case for which Houston was chief counsel established the important precedent that illegal jury exclusion was a sufficient basis to warrant the overturning of a conviction.[56] Charles Houston later remarked in a legal report to the NAACP that the Hollins case "illustrat[ed] how close we were to a miscarriage of justice; and illustrat[ed] further how lack of funds and lack of personnel probably cause many cases of miscarriage of justice, just as flagrant, to pass unnoticed and unredressed.[57]

Returning to his Howard Law School administrative duties, Houston was finding it difficult to leave the Law School, where he had labored for its complete transformation from an unaccredited evening school to a fully accredited and nationally known and respected law school. Aside from resolving administrative problems and assisting Ollie Cooper, his secretary, with preparations for his successor, he wanted to spend as much time as possible with his faculty and student body. There was not a great deal of time left in which to make certain that students had access to information gleaned from the survey of black lawyers he had begun for Howard earlier in his professional career.[58]

Houston sought to talk with Howard faculty and students in the same vein as in his recent *Journal of Negro Education* article titled "The Need for Negro Lawyers."[59] In this article, based on his continuing research with respect to the status and activities of black lawyers, Houston reported that there were only 1,230 black lawyers in 1930. Further statistics tragically revealed that there were only 487 black lawyers below the Mason-Dixon line, and in Oklahoma and Mississippi there was only one black lawyer for every 236,308 and 168,286 blacks, respectively. Thus, if a black law school were interested in making a contribution to black people and the social system, Houston argued it should train its students and send them into the South, where the pressure was greatest and the racial antagonisms most acute and therefore the service of the black lawyer as a social engineer most needed. The primary social justification for a black lawyer in the United States, Houston maintained,

> [is] the social service he can render the race as an interpreter and proponent of its rights and aspirations. . . . Experience has proved that the average white lawyer, especially in the south, cannot be relied upon to wage an uncompromising fight for equal rights for Negroes. He has too many conflicting interests, and usually himself profits as an individual by that very exploitation of the Negro, which, as a lawyer he would be called upon to attack and destroy.[60]

Following final discussions and conversations with students and colleagues, there were only a few weeks left to complete administrative tasks for the academic year. Houston returned to the preparation of his 1934–35 annual report and a review of the records of the students planning to graduate. Although less inspiring than teaching and engaging in exchanges on law and political economy with students, these too had to be done.

Despite Houston's administrative work and instruction at Howard, litigation of racial discrimination cases, national political activities, and day-to-day affairs of his private practice, he had by no means been unmindful of his civic obligations. As his father had served on the Board of Education from 1921 to 1924, Charles Houston had been appointed by the six Supreme Court judges of the District on 30 June 1933 and served two years of a three-year term on the District of Columbia's Board of Education.[61] He had taken this appointment seriously and had become an active and outspoken member. As chairman of the committee on student activities, he worked conscientiously and regularly studying proposals for scholarships, essay contests, recreational and cultural activities, high school fraternities and sororities, and cadet organizations in order to make recommendations in the best interests of the students.[62]

On many occasions, with an evident sense of responsibility to his own people, Houston spoke to matters of actual or potential inequities.

He emphasized the importance of the drama program for divisions 10 through 13 (black student divisions within the dual system), whose students "[did] not have adequate access to theaters," and he strongly suggested that the board and the local press promote the need for equipment to establish and maintain such programs within those divisions.[63] He called for the superintendent to investigate the circumstances under which black children were chased off the grounds of a neighborhood white public school, Alexander Shepherd, and the reasons for their exclusion from the playground of Shepherd after school hours and during summer vacations. In addition, when a report regarding a new stadium for the area of the Young-Brown-Phelps school group was made, Houston immediately inquired as to the availability of the play area for not only the white students but also the black students.[64]

Houston did not hesitate to condemn the District of Columbia Repair Shop for making heating repairs on the black Shaw Junior High School during school hours and thereby causing the closing of the school and loss of valuable class time. It was extremely difficult to believe that such action was inadvertent, in the light of the recent reports of discrimination in the D.C. Repair Shop itself. On 21 March 1934, Houston had found it necessary to speak frankly about a petition brought before the Board of Education for support that called for the employment of black building mechanics in repairing the school buildings of divisions 10 through 13, and he called on the board to resolve that "the Board of Education is opposed in principle to any discrimination against Negro labor in work on public school property or public school projects."[65]

For the entire two years of his service on the District's Board of Education, Houston worked vigorously to impress on the other board members and the Public Utilities Commission the dangers not only of heavy vehicular traffic but also of bus routes in the immediate vicinity of elementary schools. Following the deaths of two black pupils—one from the Mott School in 1933 and another from the Young School in 1934—the board took more seriously the need to approach the Public Utilities Commission and the Washington Railway and Electric Company in order to make an appeal for the rerouting of buses and/or the prohibiting of traffic during particular school hours.[66] Moreover, despite the waning and sometimes lack of interest of board members in the formal grievances of black teachers and racial discrimination in the educational system, Houston tried to protect the rights and interests of black constituents.[67]

Although the entire board expressed opposition to commissioners taking control of the schools, as the black member of the board Houston went on record with his special objections to the "Prettyman" Bill, which in one of its sections proposed that the District commissioners—none of whom were black or seemed, to Houston and other blacks, sympathetic to the concerns of the black populace—have ultimate authority over the actions of any employee, official, agency, commission, committee, or board financed in whole or in part from District revenue, with the sole exception of judges, employees of the courts, and the Public Utilities Commission. Whenever the commissioners deemed any action to be in the public interest, according to the Prettyman Bill, they would be authorized to instruct recipients of District of Columbia revenue to pursue such actions.[68] Houston pointed out that the "Negro citizens . . . [did] not believe they [would] receive the same consideration from the Commissioners which they . . . receive under the administration of the Board of Education." Black District citizens had proportional representation on the board, but to date there had not been "a single Negro citizen in any position of major responsibility under the direct control of the Commissioners of the District."[69] In conclusion he clarified his position on segregation (as in the dual school system) and control of the segregated schools by advising supporters of the Prettyman Bill that he was "opposed to segregation, because a minority group never has full equality of opportunity under a segregated system." Finally, he warned that any attempt to transfer ultimate control of Negro schools in the District of Columbia to an indifferent, unsympathetic Board of Commissioners will meet with a storm of opposition from Negro citizens throughout the country."[70]

On fewer occasions, but no less adamantly, Houston spoke out on sensitive political issues that to his mind were significantly related to civil liberties. He proposed in the spring of 1935 that provisions be made for an antiwar organization, "United Strike Committee," to be heard by public school students as well as the proponents of military preparedness and Army Day enthusiasts.[71] He vehemently protested the restriction of freedom of speech in the public schools—supporting the use of a public high school building by the liberal "Washington Open Forum" and denying the validity of arguments of board members who claimed the forum was "too revolutionary" or held "filthy discussions" on such topics as "sex and communism."[72] Houston opposed a rider to the District's appropriation bill which would have prohibited the payment of salary to "any person teaching or advocating Communism." In discussion with the other members at the 12 June 1935 meeting, he addressed himself to the rider, expressing the opinion that "[i]f the proviso carried the language 'advocate communism,' . . . the meaning would be a 'different thing.' But if the proviso refers to the subject as 'a matter of familiarity with one of the forms of government, then it is unsound. . . .' It is much better for children to be taught and to learn the principles . . . than to get hysterical notions which may be from biased reports." Houston further observed that he was convinced that the restriction of classroom teaching about communism as a subject constituted "restriction of intellectual freedom." Moreover, if this restricted teachers' activities outside the schoolroom, then it constituted "unwarranted restriction of freedom of speech and action." He was unsuccessful in persuading the board, but he nonetheless had taken a firm, principled stand.[73]

Prematurely, the blacks and civil libertarians of the District lost this special spokesman, for Charles Houston resigned to assume his NAACP duties one year before the end of his term. The vacancy created by Houston's resignation was filled by Benjamin Gaskins, another black lawyer who was highly respected by the District's black community. As the appointee of the District Supreme Court, Gaskins completed Houston's unexpired term. Houston subsequently turned over most of his private practice to the firm and began his leave of absence from Howard.[74]

Just before moving to New York, Charles visited Gladys, his wife. It was an awkward meeting. They had been living apart for some time. One perilous and frightening pregnancy that yielded no offspring had taken the joy out of childbearing for Gladys. Charles loved Gladys and wanted her to be happy and healthy, but he also wanted a child. Gladys refused to attempt to carry another child, fearful that a second pregnancy might be permanently disabling or fatal. Charles and Gladys had both heard the same doctor's warning about complications, but Charles probably believed that Gladys's response of such enormous fear was unwarranted. Many years later, as Gladys Houston remembered, she was not bitter, but she certainly had felt hurt and it had caused her great sadness that a child would mean so much to Charles. Neither husband's love nor wife's love was nurtured as they grew less affectionate and Charles became increasingly more involved in any number of issues pertaining to the protection of black people, the work of the Howard Law School, and his private practice. Charles was teaching four hours in the evenings and then spending twelve to fourteen hours either in the firm or in Howard's library. His students and secretaries saw more of him than his wife for so long that eventually Charles and Gladys knew that sharing the same living quarters was virtually all that they did together. They decided on a separation to give them a new perspective and time to think about their situation. Nevertheless, when it was time to move to New York City, Gladys could see no point in her going. Charles wanted to try again, but for Gladys it was too late. She would not point an accusing finger as she thought about it later. There was just too great a distance for touching but too much emotion between them for an easy permanent parting.[75] Charles, challenged by the new work—and glad that it would be so all-consuming—made arrangements to live at the 135th Street YMCA in Harlem. He had agreed to take on this Herculean task at the national headquarters of the NAACP and there was no turning back.

At two in the morning on 11 July 1935 Houston registered at the YMCA, where Walter White had reserved a room for the new Special Counsel. Exhausted, Charles delayed settling in to sleep only long enough to give the switchboard operator a telegram to send to his family on S Street: "Trip in rain . . . report to work in morning. . . ."[76]

PART THREE

Struggling on Diverse Fronts:
The National Years,
1935–1950

I am much more of an outside man than an
inside man. . . . Certainly . . . I will grow
much faster and be of much more service if
I keep free to hit and fight wherever the
circumstances call for action.

—Charles Houston to William Houston,
   14 April 1938

CHAPTER X

"This Fight . . . Is Not an Isolated Struggle"

As he stood by an open window watching a shrieking fire engine speed through the city, Charles Houston could hardly contain his excitement. It was skillfully but not entirely masked from his secretary, Lucille Black, who waited for him to continue his dictation. To her, Charles Houston was "a very genteel person" but she also recognized "he had no special airs."[1] Charles Houston felt not only excited but also exhilarated, stimulated, and eager about being in New York City at this time in his life. He was in New York because the NAACP national office was located at 69 Fifth Avenue and the NAACP had hired him to do what he had been wanting to do for some time. He was counsel in charge of the campaign against legalized racial discrimination. He had more thinking and planning to do. He finished the letter and decided to go out for lunch in the neighborhood; it was something he had not been able to do while working out of his downtown offices in Washington because of segregation.[2]

In July 1935, Charles Houston joined the staff of the NAACP national office in New York both to "advise on the regular work of the NAACP" and to direct the NAACP–Garland Fund battle for black American rights.[3] The creation of the salaried position of Special Counsel greatly facilitated the legal defense work of the association. From 1911 to 1912 the NAACP had carried on its legal defense work by engaging counsel as the need arose. The legal bureau was established in 1912, and thereafter various lawyers of distinction assumed responsibility for the NAACP's legal defense program. The association also created a National Legal Committee, which grew to be a standing committee of well-known and highly skilled attorneys constituting a legal resource as well as an advisory body for the NAACP. Serving on the National

Legal Committee at various times were prominent trial lawyers and such legal scholars as Clarence Darrow (the widely acclaimed litigator), Felix Frankfurter (Houston's former professor, who would later, as a Supreme Court Justice, hear Houston argue against racial discrimination), and William H. Hastie, Jr. (who was a Harvard Law graduate and would become the first black man to be appointed to the federal bench).[4]

With a Special Counsel based at the national headquarters in New York, inquiries could be directed to one office and legal efforts could be better coordinated at the NAACP. Attorneys in branches as well as those on the National Legal Committee could determine more easily their own responsibilities regarding cases and discuss them with the Special Counsel. During the course of every year, the NAACP received numerous letters from blacks in prison and those facing criminal charges; often concerned relatives wrote on behalf of those unable to communicate directly with the NAACP. The period of Charles Houston's Special Counselship was no exception. With the cooperation of other executive officers and lawyers, Houston sought to identify those injustices about which the NAACP might do something and then recommend or initiate action which might provide relief. In any given day before returning to his YMCA room in Harlem, Houston found himself responsible for decisions about one black man's parole, another's exoneration, and some other's life or death. Whether handling criminal cases, testifying in Congress on bills concerning black Americans, or attending NAACP mass meetings, Houston worked selflessly.[5] Roy Wilkins recalled, "Charlie was on a grant which was exclusive of whether the NAACP took in 25¢ or took in $60,000, [yet] he spread himself over the whole periphery—not just legal work and education."[6] (See Appendix 4.)

Despite these activities, which alone could fill the hours of an ordinary work week, Houston had been appointed and salaried for another purpose. As Special Counsel his purpose was to carry out a planned legal campaign against discrimination in education and transportation. The "more acute" issue of discrimination in education received the greater portion of his time and attention. Although he had observed the evils resulting from discrimination in transportation and did not wish to minimize them, Houston had also seen the pressure of an economic depression lead to the sacrifice of black education in order to preserve white education. Houston insisted that black people could not let this continue. "Since education is a preparation for the competition of life," he noted, a poor education handicaps black youth who with "all elements of American people are in economic competition."[7]

From 1935 to 1940, Charles Houston established himself as the "architect and dominant force of [this] legal program" of the NAACP.[8] He devised the legal strategy, charted the course, began a program of political education for the masses, and handled the civil rights cases. He called on former students to accept the challenge of civil rights law and brought into the campaign eager, alert, and astute lawyers. He advised and directed black lawyers throughout the nation about their local campaigns against discrimination in education, transportation, jury exclusion, and denial of the vote. With his philosophy of social engineering, Houston was confident of his cause, his strategy, and of his ability and that of his cohorts to engage in meaningful and successful struggle against segregation and inequality. For a myriad of court battles outside the field of education, he also was a cohesive factor for black people seeking equal protection, equal access, and equal opportunity. Houston's commitment to the NAACP campaign against racial discrimination was inextricably bound to a deeply personal disquietude about society and the relationships of human beings to one another. His commitment to this legal struggle was a commitment to the larger struggle for freedom and was fundamentally rooted in respect for human life. In the final analysis, slavery, exploitation, and oppression were morally wrong. But law, Houston believed, should be an "aspect of civilization which had as its chief purpose . . . reconcil[ing] conflicting human interests and control[ing] the antagonistic individual and group forces operating in the community, state and nation."[9] Given an immoral America, the NAACP campaign required that lawyer–social engineers use the Constitution, statutes, and "whatever science demonstrates or imagination invents" both to foster and to order social change for a more humane society. This "Houstonian jurisprudence" pervaded all Houston did in the NAACP campaign.[10]

Charles Houston introduced his 1935 special appeal for support of the NAACP's legal work against discrimination in education with the words of Frederick Douglass, a central figure in the nineteenth-century struggle for the liberation of black people, who had died in the year of Houston's birth:

> To make a contented slave you must make a thoughtless one, . . . darken his moral and mental vision, and . . . annihilate his power of reason. He must be able to detect no inconsistencies in slavery, . . . It must not depend upon mere force; the slave must know no higher law than his master's will.[11]

It seemed to Houston that a new form of slavery still existed in the South and that greater oppression would await blacks throughout the nation if they did not ceaselessly protest discrimination and fight for "identical quality and quantity of educational opportunity [for] all citizens regardless of race, color or creed." Democracy and ignorance cannot "endure side by side," Houston insisted.[12] If ignorance prevails among masses, among any race, they become "the tools of a small exploiting class."[13]

Houston was persuaded that failure to eradicate inequality in the education of black youth would condemn the entire race to an inferior position within American society in perpetuity. The white man claims black American slowness, backwardness, and lesser intelligence to justify "poorer teachers, wretched schools, shorter terms and an inferior type of education" for blacks, Houston declared, but the reason for such treatment has nothing to do with alleged black inferiority.[14]

> Discrimination in education is symbolic of all the more drastic discriminations which Negroes suffer in American life. And these apparent senseless discriminations in education against Negroes have a very definite objective on the part of the ruling whites to curb the young [blacks] and prepare them to accept an inferior position in American life without protest or struggle. In the United States the Negro is economically exploited, politically ignored and socially ostr[a]cized. His education reflects his condition; the discriminations practiced against him are no accident.[15]

This assessment of American conditions and the black American reality informed Houston as he sought to determine limited objectives and the ultimate goal of the NAACP campaign against unequal, discriminatory, segregated public education. Clearly, he asserted, "equality of education is not enough. There can be no true equality under a segregated system. No segregation operates fairly on a minority group unless it is a d[o]minant minority. . . . The American Negro is not a dominant minority; therefore he must fight for complete elimination of segregation as his ultimate goal."[16]

Having set this goal, the Special Counsel, understanding that the "[l]aw [is] . . . effective . . . always within its limitations," selected as his second task devising "positionary tactics" or "the steps [one] takes to move from one position to another"—and clearly articulating the rationale for these tactics.[17] Houston had accepted the position on the condition that the program of litigation be conducted as a protracted legal struggle based on the planned, deliberate prosecution of test cases to secure favorable legal precedents, and thereby lay a foundation for subsequent frontal attacks against racial discrimination and segregation. He developed a plan of attack in accordance with this view.

After a great deal of thought and study, Houston committed himself to this action, for he was very aware of the degree to which it differed from ideas of other civil rights/civil liberties lawyers.[18] His white predecessor, Nathan Margold, had suggested in his "Preliminary Report to the Joint Committee" that an immediate and direct attack on segregation be made, since it was unconstitutional when it involved inequality.[19]

Nevertheless, Houston believed the step-by-step process would have greater long-range effects, first because it would take into account the lack of tradition for equality within the American system. Addressing the National Bar Association, Houston indicated that it was not realistic to expect that an immediate, direct attack on segregation would be sympathetically heard by judges.

> We must never forget that the public officers, elective or appointive, are servants of the class which places them in office and maintains them there. It is too much to expect the court to go against the established and crystallized social customs, when to do so would mean professional and political suicide. . . . We cannot depend upon the judges to fight . . . our battles.[20]

Second, Houston preferred the protracted struggle because he did not view the campaign as an exercise in "legal hand[i]work."[21] An effective program must involve the masses of blacks with their role being the initiation of action against inequalities and discrimination in education subsequent to the exposure of the evils. Yet in the course of his work Houston found many black people fearful of militant action within their own communities, and others, who were not directly facing debilitating discrimination, seemed apathetic about struggle. "This means that we have to . . . slow down until we have developed a sustaining mass interest behind the programs. . . . The social and public factors must be developed at least along with and, if possible, before the actual litigation commences," Houston reported to the Joint Committee.[22]

Third, Houston sought to proceed slowly building precedents to support equality because to his mind it was also important to neutralize the poor white masses and persuade them of the logic and justice of the NAACP position. There would be no true educational equality until racial discrimination in mixed schools also was attacked and eliminated, for it was racial prejudice bolstered by inequalities which in part caused poor whites to be blinded to mutual interests with blacks. It was Houston's position that the achievement of democracy, equality, and justice in education, as in other areas, required the recognition that poor whites and most blacks were in the same economic condition and that unified action could advance their common interests. Such tactical and ideological considerations affected the handling of the NAACP campaign. Pursuant to these views, Houston determined that any program put forward, any case presented, any "proposition . . . for public action, should be interpreted not simply as a Negro proposition, but as a proposition affecting the majority of the people: all the poor people of this country, white and black alike."[23]

The concurrent recognition, by Houston, of the NAACP's limited funds and personnel, the separate (i.e., segregated) schools in a large section of the nation and racial discrimination in educational systems throughout the entire United States, led Houston to make specific choices regarding the objectives and tactics of the NAACP's attack on discrimination in education and transportation. In his opinion there were three possible objectives. First, the direct, immediate result such as a court ordering admission of a student or equalization of salaries in a school system could be the object of litigation. Second, the NAACP could go to court realizing the high probability of losing but making use of the case to achieve beneficial by-products such as calling attention to the evil, using the court as a forum, building public sentiment around the case, and creating a sufficiently strong threat for some temporary ameliorative action to be taken, for example, suing for admission of a student to a university and losing but having legislation for out-of-state scholarships put on the state's books.[24] Third, the NAACP could go to court in order to use the court as a laboratory to extract information. For example, explained Houston:

> We have very little money, very few trained investigators. But all we need is about $10.00, then we can file a case in court. Five dollars more, and we can bring the whole state education department into court with all its records, put each official on the stand under oath and wring him dry of information.[25]

The "positionary tactics" devised by Houston—within the context of a basic strategy of judicial precedent-building for the erosion of the "separate but equal" principle and establishment of the unconstitutionality of segregation—constituted the program of the NAACP for the legal struggle against educational discrimination for the period of Houston's Special Counselship and subsequent years. He selected

> three glaring and typical discriminations as focal points for legal action . . . ; [(1)] differentials in teachers' pay between white and Negro teachers having the same qualifications, holding the same certificate, and doing the same work; [(2)] inequalities in transportation facilities which lie at the basis of all problems of consolidation of rural schools; [(3)] inequalities in graduate and professional education usually offered white students in universities supported by state funds, while Negro education is cut off with the undergraduate work in college.[26]

Houston selected the differential in teachers' salaries because the salary scale was generally regulated by law and it presented a definite, concrete issue. On the teachers' salary cases Houston framed three litigation alternatives: First, a suit by the teacher who is still in service, with a mandamus to equalize his or her pay, or a suit by the teacher, after he or she has left service, for the differential in back pay; second, a parent's and a student's suit to equalize salaries on the ground that equal education with regard to teaching cannot be obtained on the inferior pay scale for black teachers; and third, a taxpayers' suit which will allege that the state can obtain adequate public teaching service on the black teachers' salary scale and therefore it is a waste of taxpayers money to pay white teachers more than blacks.[27] With respect to the third alternative, Houston further explained that the NAACP intended not to bring the pay scale down but to "shock" the white teachers into some kind of serious consideration of raising the salaries of black teachers.[28] Houston was severely criticized for proposing the third alternative by a Howard University student, Lyonel Florant, who identified himself as a member of "the international movement for working class emancipation." Houston, in reply to Florant, explained that this suit was to be filed concurrently with the suit by a black teacher to bring black teachers' salaries up. The real objective of the third alternative was to "convince the white teachers that they cannot remain upon their high pedestal of high salaries without bringing the salaries of Negro teachers up."[29]

For two reasons Houston wanted to focus some attention on discrimination in transportation. First, as he understood it the success of the consolidation of rural schools is dependent on getting children to and from school within a reasonable amount of time. Second, "there is a psychological aspect to white children being transported to school in busses while Negro children plod along the road. An inferiority complex is installed in the Negro children without one word being said about the difference between the races. It does not have to be said to either white children or Negro children who have ridden to a consolidated brick school for eight years, clean and dry, in busses furnished by the county while the Negro children have trudged along the road . . . to a little ramshackled, wooden, one-room school house."[30] With cases such as *Dameron* v. *Bayliss* holding that black children having to walk farther than white children in order to attend school did not constitute a sufficient reason for abolishing segregated schools, the difficulty of successful litigation relative to transportation was apparent. However, Houston indicated that a lawsuit to compel transportation for black children at public expense was most likely to produce beneficial results.[31]

The court attack on graduate and professional schools of state universities was selected because of the general failure of states to furnish to blacks either professional education or graduate education and because of the urgent need for blacks to have access to professional and graduate training for personal development and for leadership positions. "[T]here [was] not a single state-supported institution of higher learning in any one of 17 out of 19 states, requiring separation by law," Houston noted, "where a Ne[g]ro [might] pursue professional or graduate training at public expense," in 1935. Three "southern" or "border" states—West Virginia, Missouri, and Maryland—by this same time were making a pretext of equalizing the graduate and professional studies for blacks by providing so-called out-of-state scholarships that covered tuition but not travel or maintenance outside the state. To Houston's mind this meant whites were taxing blacks "to educate the future white leaders who are supposed to rule over" blacks. Houston insisted, "We must break this up or perish."[32]

In 1935, under the aegis of Houston, the NAACP launched its legal campaign against the established policy of the southern and border states to provide fully at state expense professional or graduate training for white college graduates only.[33] The first case was filed against the University of Maryland on behalf of Donald Gaines Murray, a black Marylander, grandson of a prominent African Methodist Episcopal bishop, Abraham Gaines, and graduate of Amherst College (1934), seeking acceptance of his application to the law school of the University of Maryland and examination of his credentials.[34]

Not only did Donald Murray have a good college record and the desire to fight for his right as a state citizen to attend the University of Maryland Law School, but also his situation met the NAACP's requirements for a test case. The situation represented a "sharply defined issue" which could be "supported by demonstrable evidence." It presented "key discriminations" while it both provided an opportunity for enforcement through "auxiliary legal proceedings" and "furnished a focus or springboard for extending the attacks on a larger front."[35] The case first came to the attention of Thurgood Marshall, who was practicing in his hometown of Baltimore. He recommended the case to Charles Houston, who accepted the case for the NAACP. Houston believed it "a chance to develop under oath by examination of witnesses and . . . documents, the discriminations from which Maryland Negroes suffer."[36]

The groundwork having been flawlessly laid by Marshall, the NAACP, aided by another attorney, William I. Gosnell, filed a petition without reference to race and color which asked that the court compel the university authorities to receive Murray's application, consider in regular order Murray's application, and admit him if he met the general standards. *Murray* v. *The University of Maryland* was heard on 18 June 1935 in a relatively empty courtroom. After all testimony had been taken and the arguments heard, the presiding judge directed the university to admit Murray—in accordance with his constitutional right—pending appeal. The appeal was argued on 5 November 1935 after Murray had been attending the university for over a month. Holding that the out-of-state institution scholarship provisions made by Maryland for Negroes did not afford Murray equal protection as guaranteed by the Fourteenth Amendment of the Constitution, the Maryland Court of Appeals affirmed the writ of mandamus on 15 January 1936. Murray's case set a significant legal precedent; further state actions regarding the graduate or professional education of blacks might be judged by the Maryland court's decision. Donald Murray's attendance at the university law school without racial incident would become a key social precedent in a later law school case, *Sweatt* v. *Painter*.[37]

After the court of appeals affirmed the decision for Murray, Charles Houston was as much concerned about his people's understanding the victory as he was about the future cases of the NAACP's campaign against discrimination in education. He decided to air his views through the official magazine of the NAACP, *Crisis*. In an article entitled "Don't Shout Too Soon," he warned that the fight was just beginning:

> Law suits mean little unless supported by public opinion. Nobody needs to explain to a Negro the difference between the law in books and the law in action. In theory the cases are simple; the state cannot tax the entire population for the exclusive benefit of a single class. The really baffling problem is how to create the proper kind of public opinion. The truth is there are millions of white people who have no real knowledge of the Negro's problems and who never give the Negro a serious thought. They take him for granted and spend their time and energy on their own affairs.[38]

Houston's suggestion regarding a remedy for this problem was that black people, their friends, and civil libertarians seek opportunities to state their case to the white public since the old channels of publicity were inadequate and the radio was not customarily open for discussions or speeches promoting the concept of racial equality. Houston also encouraged blacks to "cooperate in public forums,' . . . agitate for more truth about the Negro [in educational institutions and] . . . [a]long with this educational process . . . be prepared to fight, if necessary, every step of the way." Finally, Houston reminded the readers, "This fight for equality of educational opportunity [was] not an isolated struggle. All our struggles must tie in together and support one another. . . . [W]e . . . [must] remain on the alert and push the struggle farther with all our might."[39]

Such articles were not atypical, for in conjunction with the litigation program, Houston regularly attempted to inform the black community and involve local blacks in each struggle. Early in the campaign, Houston made a film exposing racial discrimination in the rural schools of South Carolina and favored making more such films. An ardent believer in the power of the media, Houston maintained,

> Motion pictures humanize and dramatize the discrimination which Negroes suffer much more effectively than any corresponding amount of speech could do, and films would be serviceable in working for equal rights both in showing the evil results of discrimination and, constructively, the advancement of living and social standards when discrimination is removed.[40]

The small working force of the NAACP's national office and the staff's heavy schedules thwarted plans for any series of films on racial discrimination. In keeping with his desire to disseminate information, however, Houston proposed to Roy Wilkins of *Crisis* that a photograph contest be sponsored. It was Houston's idea to ask the Garland Fund or the Rackham Fund to subsidize monthly prizes (first prize, five dollars; second prize, one dollar) for "snapshots illustrating discrimination in education . . . Negro and white schools and other activities showing discrimination in education. . . ." These pictures would then appear in *Crisis*.[41]

Knowing that it was not enough to plan cases and programs from the national headquarters, Houston also went out on the road. With a three-dollar per diem and assurances of four cents per mile reimbursement, Houston traveled—sometimes alone, other times with a colleague such as Eddie Lovett—nearly 25,000 miles for the campaign against discrimination in education and transportation his first year as Special Counsel. He spoke to civic bodies, teacher associations, interracial councils, church congregations, and student groups in North Carolina, South Carolina, Tennessee, Kentucky, Maryland, and Virginia about the general legal campaign and its relation to their particular situations.[42] Now and then, when speeches went well and meetings did not become long or problematic, Houston would stop to visit his former student Oliver "Peanut" Hill in Richmond or drive through Baltimore to see Thurgood "Turkey" Marshall. He also made time to stop in Washington, D.C., to check on the firm and see his parents. Whenever there, he called and went by the residence of Gladys, his estranged wife. Neither seemed to regret the decision to live apart, but each tried to remain cordial.[43]

In several capacities, "field investigator, lawyer, speaker . . ." and in-house journalist, Charles Houston publicized "the ultimate objective" to abolish "all forms of segregation in public education."[44] As he defined the national office's role, it was not "to force a school fight upon any community," but rather "to expose the rotten conditions of segregation," "to point out the evil consequences of discrimination and injustice to both Negroes and whites," "to map out ways and means by which these evils [might] be corrected," and to aid the local community should it decide to take action.[45]

Houston stressed that where segregation was firmly entrenched by law the NAACP would not only resist it but also plan to use "every legitimate means at its disposal to accomplish actual equality of educational opportunity for Negroes," and this included specific aims:

   (a) equality of school terms;
   (b) equality of pay for Negro teachers having the same qualifications and doing the same work as white teachers;
   (c) equality of transportation for Negro school children at public expense;
   (d) equality of buildings and equipment;
   (e) equality of *per capita* expenditure for education of Negroes;
   (f) equality in graduate and professional training.[46]

In a statement that might be contrasted sharply with a position he had taken a little over a year regarding the Crawford case, Charles Houston expressed his feelings about race relations and civil rights.

> The N.A.A.C.P. and all Negroes desire to live at peace with their white fellow citizens. They crave amicable race relations, but they want them founded on dignity and self-respect. *Real amicable race relations cannot be purchased by the surrender of fundamental constitutional rights.*
>
> The N.A.A.C.P. appreciates the magnitude of the task ahead of it, but it has its duty to its constituency and to the America of the future. It conceives that in equalizing educational opportunities for Negroes it raises the whole standard of American citizenship, and stimulates white Americans as well as black.[47]

In a later article, Houston indicated steps black citizens could take to secure better schools. He emphasized that "the first item on any program for improvement of public schools for Negroes must be convincing the mass of Negroes themselves that they are part of the public which *owns* and *controls* the schools." Although there were some public schools administered and attended exclusively by blacks and other public schools administered and attended exclusively by whites, "both schools belong to one and the same system, and the system belongs to the public," he reminded his readers. Next, he outlined in simple terms an eight-step procedure for attacking discrimination in county school systems which instructed black citizens to (1) "get the facts" by examining state and county board of education records, including budgets for a ten-year period; (2) prepare their own equitable, reasonable budget in proper form not only according to present needs but also in light of discrimination revealed by examination of records and present it to the division superintendent early enough to be included in his budget; (3) get the cooperation of a maximum number of groups and then request a hearing before the division superintendent and county school board; (4) if the board excludes the budget items suggested for equalization of provisions or fails to provide for equality in any other way, have five heads of families with children in school appeal the decision of the board; (5) if the division superintendent grants the items but the board of supervisors refuses to include it in the county levy or make an appropriation, have fifty eligible voters and taxpayers petition the circuit court for a special election; (6) if all this fails, make an appeal to higher courts for remedies; (7) meanwhile, pay poll taxes, register, vote, organize nonpartisan political clubs for support of a program for equal provisions for black schools, and get allies among community groups; (8) "Do not lose heart if victory does not come at once. Persevere to the end."[48]

As the director of a campaign supported by a special appropriation, Charles Houston was acutely aware of the need to sell the program to his people. Philanthropy could not be counted on for the protracted struggle. Yet despite the miles covered, speeches made, articles written, the few financial contributions of blacks to the support of the legal work disheartened Houston. As Walter White remarked to an Urban League friend, "When Charlie first came to [the NAACP] he felt that the enormous significance of the fight against educational inequality would be so readily apparent at least to the fairly well educated Negroes that there would be an overwhelming response."[49]

Houston never voluntarily gave up on any worthwhile project. He prepared "A Program Against Discrimination in Public Education," outlining a plan of action for the national organizations of the black Greek letter societies—Alphas, Omegas, Kappas, Sigmas, AKAs, Deltas, Phi Beta Sigmas, and Zeta Phi Betas—and arranged for such prominent friends and staff members as Marshall, Hastie, Wilkins, and Juanita Jackson to speak at national conventions. The main thrust was an appeal to make equality of education a priority, and the means suggested included commissions, studies, public meetings, fund-raising for test-case participants, and full support behind drives for the admission of qualified Negroes to state universities. By January 1936, Houston's idea netted over $1,200 and full access to the memberships of fraternities and sororities. The money was pledged none too soon, for the Garland Fund had only appropriated $10,000 for 1935–36, and it was unlikely that a large appropriation would be available during 1936–37.[50]

The *Murray* decision had been only a stepping-stone in the process of gaining admission of blacks to state universities. A suitable case to take to the U.S. Supreme Court had to be found. With black lawyers from Tennessee, Missouri, Maryland, and Washington, D.C.—Z. Alexander Looby, Carl Cowan, Joseph Settles, Sidney Redmond, Thurgood Marshall, Leon Ransom, and Eddie Lovett—Charles Houston explored the merits and chances for successful litigation of cases against the University of Tennessee and the University of Missouri. The former case of William B. Redmond, III, who sought admission to Tennessee's School of Pharmacy, would be lost on a technicality ultimately, but with the University of Missouri case the story would be entirely different.[51]

Subsequent to a favorable decision in Murray's Maryland case, Houston had authorized Sidney R. Redmond, an attorney from St. Louis and fellow member of the National Bar Association, to investigate exclusion of blacks from the University of Missouri. Redmond's report had indicated that the educational situation was sufficiently inequitable to justify NAACP commitment to a test case. Lloyd L. Gaines, who met the requirements for admission to the university's law school and the requirements established by the NAACP for a test litigant (having superior qualifications so that no possible objection, except that of race, could be raised) filed suit against S. W. Canada, the registrar of the university, and the curators of the University of Missouri following the curators' rejection of Gaines's application. That case was set for argument in July 1936. In addition to Redmond and Houston, Henry Espy of St. Louis worked on the Gaines brief.[52]

Between the regular legal defense work and other cases in the Joint Committee's campaign against discrimination, Houston found it impossible to get away to work exclusively on the Gaines case until July. He worked in St. Louis from the sixth to the tenth of the month, the day scheduled for the trial. Up at 4:15 A.M., weary but prepared, Houston, Redmond, Gaines, Espy, and Robert Witherspoon of the Mound City Bar Association set out for the courthouse in Columbia at 6:00 A.M. and arrived a little after 9:00 A.M. Redmond, making a strictly factual statement, opened for Gaines. Talking more to the press table than to the court, William Hogsett opened for the defense. With a dramatic and driving style, he called it "laudable" that "Mr. Gaines" wanted to prepare himself to practice law and that he had every right to a legal education, but that he was seeking remedy against the wrong institution. For one hundred years the University of Missouri had been white, and in 1921 the state had given Lincoln University the same powers as the University of Missouri so that facilities could be expanded for blacks. Gaines, maintained Hogsett, had no action or claim against the University of Missouri; he should have applied to Lincoln or for a law school training scholarship.[53]

Houston argued the constitutional merits of the suit, including the Missouri obligation to provide equal protection of the laws for all its citizens. He called witnesses for examination to attest to the superior resources available at the University of Missouri Law School for one seeking to practice in that state. Dean William Edward Masterson of the law school, S. W. Canada, university registrar and the assistant secretary of the university, suffered "the most complete lapse of memory [Houston] had ever witnessed." None was able to tell the court details governing law school admissions or the law school budget, and when the dean was asked about special instruction in Missouri law for people wishing to practice in the state, "Masterson wiggled like an earthworm . . . and made just about the sorriest and most pitiable spectacle."[54] In contrast, counsel for Gaines produced facts regarding the forty-five black lawyers in the state, thirty of whom were in St. Louis and only three of whom had been admitted since 1931. Houston, Redmond, and Espy countered the state university's lawyer on all points concerning the university's law school, the state bar examination, and Lincoln. At the conclusion of the trial in the Circuit Court of Boone County, however, the judge indicated that he was interested in two questions: (1) "whether the act of 1921 establishing Lincoln U[niversity] expressed the state policy to exclude Negroes from [the] U[niversity] of M[issouri] taken in connection with the state constitution, laws and uniform educational policy" and (2) "whether pending development of Lincoln U[niversity] the state scholarships offered equal protection under the 14th Amendment." He requested trial briefs from both sides on these questions.[55]

Houston already had written in his memorandum to the New York office, "It is beyond expectation that the court will decide in our favor, so we had just as well get ready for the appeal," and was not surprised when the judge dismissed the petition for a writ of mandamus to compel the state university to admit Gaines to the school of law. With Redmond and Espy, Houston continued work on an appeal to the Supreme Court of Missouri and supervised the NAACP's other legal matters.[56] Houston needed help. On 17 September he wrote Thurgood Marshall:

> I went to New York to do the special job of the educational campaign. By the time I had been there a week I was doing all the legal work of the Association.

The Association needs another full-time lawyer in the national office. I am not only lawyer but evangelist and stump speaker. I think this work necessary in order to back up our legal efforts with the required public support and social force. But it takes me out of the office for long stretches at a time, and slows down the legal work in New York. . . . I will be glad to recommend to Walter and Roy that just as soon as possible they give you an opportunity to come to the national office at $200 per month for six months if that interests you.

I don't know of anybody I would rather have in the office than you or anybody who can do a better job of research and preparation of cases. . . . Two lawyers would always put one in the office, except in rare instances when both might be away for a few days in actual trial.

You have been more than faithful in giving your time to the Association and I know this has meant a sacrifice of private practice, so you can be assured I will do everything in my power to try to make some provisions for you.[57]

Walter White, the NAACP's board, and the Joint Committee were persuaded by Houston's argument that he could not handle the NAACP's education cases, other phases of the legal campaign against discrimination and legal defense matters. Thurgood Marshall became the NAACP's Assistant Special Counsel.[58]

With the addition of Marshall to the staff, the Missouri Supreme Court's denial of the NAACP appeal for Gaines was simply viewed as the right challenge at the right time. Houston, Marshall, Andy Ransom, and Eddie Lovett were going to take this case to the U.S. Supreme Court to prove just how clear a violation of the Constitution it really was. It was an opportunity to vindicate the NAACP position regarding equal protection and the rights of black Americans.[59] But one thing worried them all and it was no small matter. Garland's American Fund for Public Service had no more to give the NAACP. Those resources had been exhausted by November. (See Appendix 5.) *Gaines* would be carried on through a contingent fund, but other projects seemed doomed unless the appeals to the National Negro Congress, the National Bar Association, NAACP members, fraternities, sororities, students, and parents throughout the nation met a more enthusiastic response than mass appeals of previous years. In one special appeal published in the *Crisis*, Houston warned of the grave danger of suppression if blacks could not make educational opportunities equal. Then he stressed the importance of mass involvement in and support of the struggle, insisting that "essentially leadership must develop from the aspirations, determinations, sacrifices and needs of the group itself."[60]

By the end of 1937, despite funding difficulties, Houston faced the problems that besieged the legal program he had guided from infancy with a new vitality and clarity. Rearrangements in his personal life had almost everything to do with this. He and Gladys had been separated for so long that the love which had brought them together in 1924 was difficult to recall, and when it was recalled it was with a great deal of pain. Conversations during Charles's visits home from New York never led to any reconciliation of their differences. Gladys had no desire to be a wife to Charles, and Charles had no intention of forcing his company on Gladys. The thirteen-year marriage was dead. They did not really think of themselves as married, since only a legal document and shared experiences from the past held them together in any way. Actually, Gladys tried to be gracious but was increasingly uncomfortable with Charles's visits. In contrast, a new woman, a secretary in the Houston firm, had made a point of greeting Charles with great enthusiasm whenever he returned to the office. After the work load of the NAACP headquarters, Charles came to look forward to the pleasant smile and inquiries regarding his health and work with which Henrietta Williams always met him. By the summer of 1936, Gladys and Charles had become a couple completely unresponsive to each other, while Henrietta and Charles had become friends. Charles wanted a divorce. It was not too late to remarry and start a family. Most important, Henrietta seemed genuinely to care about him and every aspect of his work. Gladys, being Catholic, had a difficult decision to make. The church frowned on divorce, but did she have the right to hold on to Charles when she knew they could never be happy together again? She talked with Charles, his father, and his mother. Eventually Gladys agreed that Charles would file for divorce. This he did in Reno, Nevada, in the summer of 1937. On 13 September of the same year, Charles Houston married the beautiful and vivacious Henrietta Williams, daughter of Mr. and Mrs. Henry Theodore Williams of Washington, D.C., and former secretary to William Houston. The bride, about ten years younger than Charles (who had turned forty-two a few days before the ceremony), wanted to live with her new husband in New York or wherever he was. Henrietta also wanted, as much as Charles, a family.[61]

Henrietta was a good listener, and little did she know how important that quality was. Almost every day Charles returned to the Harlem apartment (in the Dunbar on West 149th Street) he had some news to tell her. The NAACP's legal campaign had been under way for two years and had given him insight he had lacked when he arrived in New York. He had understood the interrelationship of the legal campaign against discrimination with extralegal activities in 1935. But it was now—after two years of seeking black support for the civil rights struggle—that Houston saw most clearly the impact of white suppression, intimidation, and racism on black people who were most affected by the legal fight. The economic depression continued for so many blacks who were barely able to make ends meet. The problems of teachers, students, and their families (who would suffer severe economic consequences if they were greatly financially supportive or vocal on behalf of the NAACP and rights of black citizens) and the fears of black people, who believed they would be risking their lives or their families if they participated in the fight in their own localities, were very real. Many were convinced that anonymity could and should be maintained. Not only were these problems and fears real, they were also obstacles that had to be overcome if there were to be any ultimate success in the overall struggle for freedom and equality.[62]

Despite this understanding of the problems and the importance of the NAACP's legal struggle, and his continuing desire to be involved in it, Charles Houston felt compelled to change his base of operations from the New York office to Washington, D.C. before the end of 1938. He had come to grips with the probability earlier in 1937 but did not advise officers of his decision until the new year. To Houston's mind, two personal—though not selfish—considerations necessitated his departure from the NAACP national office. First, the Houston firm was in need of a senior partner to do more than intermittent legal work. In 1937, William Hastie, of the firm, had been appointed to a federal judgeship in the Virgin Islands, and in that same year, William L. Houston was appointed Special Assistant to the Attorney General of the United States. It had not been an exciting practice for Charles Houston in his earlier years, but he felt an obligation to the firm and to his father. Later he told his friend Thurgood that the veterans of the civil rights struggle needed some place to retreat anyway; it might as well be the firm of Charles and William Houston.[63] (See Appendix 2.)

Although his father had complained about and criticized various NAACP and civil rights activities, Charles was well aware that his father had never interfered or attempted to make his son feel that the survival of the firm was in jeopardy. The simple truth was that William was more business-oriented than his son (or his son's "civil rights law" students) and he saw nothing wrong with becoming a successful private practitioner. But knowing his "Charlie" (and some of the students) and realizing that these younger lawyers had minds of their own, William chose to voice his opinion in a humorous manner. At the beginning of the NAACP educational discrimination campaign, William Houston wrote to Edward Lovett, Charles's former student and friend of the Houston family, while Lovett was in Cambridge studying at Harvard for an LL.M. Fearing that Lovett might be following in "Charlie's footsteps," William wrote,

Give my love to the Treasurer of Harvard Law School and tell him that although I have never met him personally, he bankrupted me by cashing the checks I sent when my son was up there taking a course which he now is applying to the saving of the "brother." If the Treasurer's conscience worries him for having taken all of my money under false pretenses (because he was pretending to me that he was educating Charlie for the practice of law and not to do the Abe Lincoln and John Brown stunts) then he can return me part of the cash he received and I will execute a release under oath and send it by air mail. I think he ought to do something like this before he dies if he expects to meet his maker with a clean conscience. And you might suggest to him that my own thought is as you dump your money in there he ought to send it by next mail to [your wife,] Lou. It is the only way he can square his conscience and look St. Peter in the face when he crashes the Heavenly gate.[64]

While William was proud of his son's accomplishments, he did not "bite his tongue" when discussing various volunteer or semivolunteer activities in civil rights. From time to time he chided his son, face-to-face, about spending all his time "saving the race" instead of building a private practice and saving money. William had dubbed him "Don Quixote . . . sheathed in the armour of his race interest . . . mak[ing] charges upon windmills."[65] Nevertheless, William had shown a father's love and demonstrated his concern for his son's well-being in tangible ways when ventures proved taxing—financially or otherwise—for his son. These were certainly men of vast differences which came to the fore sometimes in the heat of argument, other times in the wit of an anecdote. Yet after the storm or the laughter there remained a deep and abiding love. William did not choose to live his life as his son, but Charles was his son.[66]

A second consideration in the decision to leave New York and his NAACP position involved an obligation to the struggle for rights and to himself. The NAACP was willing to continue his salary. He also had received a lucrative offer from Howard University. Mordecai Johnson wanted Houston to take the deanship of Howard Law School for $6,000 a year (his father reported that Johnson was willing to increase the figure to $7,500). This in no way could be looked down on in comparison with an average yearly NAACP salary of $4,000, or the income from a practice which was always dependent on the number of clients brought in and disbursements made for the firm.[67] However, Charles Houston believed he could best render service if he were not confined. Evidently money was not a determining factor for him. He was not interested in returning to the institutional setting when the national struggle was so demanding and promised so much. Neither, however, by 1938, was he satisfied with the restrictions placed on his activities in the nation by virtue of his NAACP position. Even when money ceased to be an issue because the board of directors decided on 13 December 1937 that the work of Houston and Marshall was so "vital" that it would be continued "at all costs" and supported through the legal defense fund and general fund, Houston could not be persuaded to remain in New York.[68]

Charles Houston decided by the spring of 1938 that he would leave in July. He told his father, "I have had the feeling all along that I am much more of an outside man than an inside man." "I usually break down under too much routine," he explained to his father, who already understood. "Certainly, for the present, I will grow much faster and be of much more service if I keep free to hit and fight wherever the circumstances call for action."[69] This time Charles wanted his father to understand his son's plans. For that reason Charles spoke of a life that was more than a career and his spirit that was not the same as his body or his mind.

Charles had had a bout with tuberculosis and an inguinal hernia some years ago, and anyone who knew him could tell he worked too hard. What his wife, parents, and close friends knew was that he really felt hemmed in, insufficiently challenged, and unnaturally limited when he had the same routine for too long. His father could not convince him to concentrate on building the private practice, in part because of that restlessness, energy, and zeal for taking on just causes at will. Charles was meticulous, an organized, systematic planner, but he felt stifled by regularity that became monotonous or bureaucracy that became fixed. In the final analysis, Charles Houston, to be "Charlie," had to be more of an "outside man" than the NAACP could permit.[70]

After 15 July, Houston continued as Special Counsel but no longer worked full-time in New York. He transferred his base from the headquarters of the NAACP to his own firm in Washington, D.C. From 615 F Street, Northwest, he carried on both a private legal practice and activities on behalf of the legal campaign of the NAACP. In his Washington office he reviewed the matter of segregated schools, shared an article he had written on the subject with NAACP colleagues, and prepared for what would prove to be one of the most significant cases of the early NAACP legal campaign for equality of educational opportunity.[71]

A day before *Missouri ex rel. Gaines* v. *Canada* was to be heard by the U.S. Supreme Court, Charles Houston reread the record in the case, made notes on questions to pose and issues he needed to stress, refined his arguments, and walked from his F Street office to Fifth Street, the location of Howard's Law School. There students and professors listened attentively as Charles Houston rehearsed his oral argument. Robert Carter and Spottswood Robinson, both of whom would graduate from Howard and become highly respected federal judges, recalled that the former dean addressed "everyone in the audience including law students." Following the presentation, Houston received a "critique by the audience." However informal, it was one of the first in a long line of dry runs in which black civil rights lawyers presented their various legal positions to Howardites for scrutiny.[72]

On 9 November 1938, *Missouri ex rel. Gaines* v. *Canada* was argued before the U.S. Supreme Court. On trial was not simply the claim of Lloyd Gaines but also the convictions of a cadre of black lawyers who had made immeasurable personal sacrifices to bring a case supporting equality of educational opportunity for black Americans to this tribunal. Moreover, on trial were timeworn myths and social customs that had long overshadowed the black American's bid for equal protection and due process. In the brief and argument for the petitioner, counsel held that the state of Missouri had denied Gaines equal protection by excluding him from the law school of the tax-supported state university for no other reason than his race and that the university had failed to prove that the state provided equal protection through out-of-state scholarships. For these reasons, counsel sought a reversal of the state Supreme Court's decision. Countering Houston and his co-counsel, the University of Missouri's counsel, William Hogsett and Fred Williams, held that the state of Missouri had not denied Gaines equal protection by excluding him from the law school of the university and that the case did not present a federal question legitimately reviewable by the U.S. Supreme Court.[73]

The Court handed down its decision on 12 December 1938. It held that the Missouri Supreme Court had erred in its ruling, denying the petitioner his federal right. It reversed the decision and remanded it for further proceedings. In this historic opinion, Chief Justice Charles E. Hughes wrote:

> The question here is not of a duty of the State to supply legal training, or of the quality of the training which it does supply, but of its duty when it provides such training to furnish it to the residents of the State upon the basis of an equality of right. By the operation of the laws of Missouri a privilege has been created for white law students which is denied to negroes by reason of their race. . . . That is a denial of the equality of legal right to the enjoyment of the privilege which the State has set up, and the provision for the payment of tuition fees in another State does not remove the discrimination.
>
> The equal protection of the laws is a pledge of the protection of equal laws. Manifestly, the obligation of the State to give the protection of equal laws can be performed only where its laws operate, that is, within

its own jurisdiction. That obligation is imposed by the Constitution upon the States severally as governmental entities—each responsible for its own laws establishing the rights and duties of persons within its border. . . .

The essence of the constitutional right is that it is a personal one. . . . It was as an individual that he was entitled to the equal protection of the laws, and the State was bound to furnish him within its borders facilities for legal education substantially equal to those which the State afforded for persons of the white race, whether or not other negroes sought the same opportunity.[74]

The NAACP victory in *Gaines* provided an essential precedent on which a subsequent determination regarding the unconstitutionality of a state to require separation of the races in tax-supported educational institutions could be based. The *Gaines* decision denied the state's unconditional right to exclude a black applicant from a state-supported white law school. Thus, based on *Gaines*, a state must either admit black applicants to the established institutions supported by the state or provide equal facilities for their professional or graduate training. The implications were enormous. Using *Gaines*, any southern state could be brought to court for failure to provide educational opportunities, particularly graduate and professional training, for all its citizens on the basis of equality. Equal protection, as newly defined by the Court, became a broad, flexible concept touching on many areas. Moreover, in holding that the Fourteenth Amendment required equal protection of the laws within the state borders insofar as a state professes to compel any black student—with or without scholarship—to go outside the state for the same education offered to white students within the state, that state was guilty of violating that individual's right to equal protection. Furthermore, to some extent *Gaines* destroyed the idea of regional universities for blacks as a means by which states might maintain segregation and avoid their obligations to black citizens of their respective states.[75]

The perennial problem of adequate funding for the NAACP and its legal campaign took on another dimension as it became apparent to proponents of segregation that the NAACP intended to push the *Plessy* principle to the limit. Defending a way of life, southerners became more determined and the opposition to the NAACP grew. To meet this opposition the NAACP needed more money than remained available from the original Garland Fund grant. For some time the NAACP had been largely supporting the educational campaign. The administrative and leadership abilities of Thurgood Marshall and Charles Houston provided Walter White with the opportunity to establish a better mechanism for fund-raising. Application was made and received for a nonprofit educational and legal aid agency. In 1939 the NAACP Legal Defense and Educational Fund was incorporated. The "Inc. Fund," as it came to be called, was separated from the propaganda activities of the NAACP and Inc. Fund purposes were so defined that it was eligible to receive tax-deductible contributions. From that year on, the interpersonal skills of Houston and the close relationship between Marshall and Houston kept the lawyers of the Inc. Fund and the NAACP's National Legal Committee working in complete cooperation, a cadre dedicated to the purposes of the parent organization. All worked to topple the edifice of segregation, and the child was nurtured and sustained by direct contributions, supplemented when necessary by salary contributions and loans from the NAACP. However long the Inc. Fund could operate for educational purposes with staff members independent of the NAACP, it qualified for the tax advantage initially granted it by the Internal Revenue Service. More confident about funds coming in, co-Special Counsel Houston and Marshall pressed other higher education and teachers' salaries cases, with Houston handling a second Missouri case representing Lucile Bluford, who was seeking registration in the University of Missouri's School of Journalism. The NAACP and its Inc. Fund continued to press cases against state-supported educational institutions but no case involving segregated education was heard by the Supreme Court of the United States until 1948.[76]

Concurrent with the university cases, litigation for the equalization of teachers' salaries was begun. Although initially Houston developed the legal procedures for the Joint NAACP–Garland Fund campaign against discrimination and brought Thurgood Marshall into the program to assist him, Houston worked closely with lawyers in early teacher salary cases and later turned over the cases to Marshall, who primarily carried on this phase of the educational equalization fight. Houston considered the teachers' salaries cases also fundamental to the struggle of black Americans for freedom and equal rights. The chief aim was not simply to raise the pay scale for teachers. Houston intended to improve the education of blacks, to set a model of non-differentials and comparable worth by establishing the same pay for the same service and to foster a less racially prejudiced white public. Actually he believed that where the standards of wages were equal between blacks and whites, the level of education in the community followed.[77]

Charles Houston, Thurgood Marshall, and Edward Lovett, for the NAACP, with W. A. C. Hughes, a local attorney, argued successfully the Joint Committee's first suit to equalize teachers' salaries. This suit, in 1936, was brought against Montgomery County, Maryland's Board of Education. William B. Gibbs, Jr., an elementary school principal at Rockville Colored Elementary in Montgomery County, filed an action to compel the Montgomery County board to equalize his salary. The Board of Education attempted to have the suit dismissed, but the court, after taking the matter under advisement, ruled that the petition did state a cause of action which warranted a hearing on its merits. With little defense for its action regarding salaries, the board voluntarily entered into a stipulation agreeing to equalize salaries by 1938.[78]

As early as the fall of 1937, black teachers in Maryland were raising funds to take care of those in their ranks who suffered reprisals or loss of jobs because of participation in the equalization fight, and a number of local groups in North Carolina, Virginia, Florida, and Alabama resolved to initiate suits or otherwise pressure authorities for equal salaries. Success in Montgomery County, Maryland, became more of a beginning than a victory. Houston and Marshall hammered away at the equalization problem in other counties where teachers were ready to unite and fight the inequity.[79] With other Howardites, Howard Thurman, a man possessed of a brilliant, trenchant mind in addition to spiritual depth, which would make him one of the leading philosopher-theologians of the twentieth century, then dean of Howard University's chapel, took advantage of informal conversations with Houston to ask why he kept pushing the same issue in the same way in any county with willing teachers. Charles Houston smiled, and then the smile was replaced with an absolutely serious expression. No teachers' salary case would be won without significant mass support, and mass support could be generated only if he and the NAACP cared about mass education. How could one use a hostile or indifferent press to educate the masses to a sympathetic understanding of the constitutional rights of Negroes? He answered his own question: Make the civil rights struggle news by proceeding with meeting after meeting and case after case that the media would have to cover because it involved elected or appointed officials. Maximum exposure would work on the public and create a new sensitivity, a new apperceptive mass. Effective legal strategy was more than courtroom technique and knowing the law. After the Gibb's Montgomery case during the remainder of Houston's Special Counselship he served as co-counsel in cases in Prince George's County and Anne Arundel County, Maryland; Louisville, Kentucky; and Norfolk, Virginia. A significant precedent was set in *Alston* v. *Board of Education* of Norfolk. When the U.S. Supreme Court decided to let the Circuit Court of Appeals judgment stand, the principle was established that a differential in teachers' salaries based solely on race constituted a denial of equal protection of the laws.[80]

In addition to major cases in the areas of teacher salary equalization and desegregation of state university graduate and professional schools, the NAACP–Garland Fund campaign gave rise to a number of varied antidiscrimination drives. Few of these resulted in NAACP-supported litigation between 1935 and 1940. Nonetheless, they affected the conditions under which black people lived throughout the nation and provided an atmosphere for future action. Relative to elementary and secondary education, the NAACP investigated discrimination in public schools in Muskogee, Oklahoma; Port Huron and Muskegon, Michigan; Wise and Loudoun Counties, Virginia; Prentiss, Mississippi; York and Chester County, South Carolina; and Eastern Shore, Maryland. The NAACP fought—with the Permanent Committee for Better Schools in Harlem—problems of the education of black youth in New York City. Thurgood Marshall with Leon Ransom and Edward Lovett also conducted in 1937 a test case designed to compel the Baltimore County Board of Education to provide high school facilities within the county for black youth, *Margaret Williams* v. *David Zimmerman*. Although the suit was lost, it led to the liberalizing of provisions for black high school education and legislation for the equalization of school terms for black and white children throughout the state of Maryland.[81]

The major emphasis under the Joint NAACP–Garland Fund antidiscrimination campaign was education. Nevertheless, because the grant mandated activities in education and transportation, Special Counsel began some work in the latter area. Protests were made to bus companies regarding discriminatory treatment. Two cases were litigated in West Virginia and Virginia. The NAACP investigated racially restricted accommodations on the Seaboard Lines, Southern, Illinois Central, and Missouri Pacific railroads; the NAACP found abuses of separate car laws and made protests to the companies. In a case against the Nashville, Chattanooga, and St. Louis Railway, the NAACP forced the railroad company to provide Pullman accommodations for a black traveling between Nashville and Memphis, Tennessee.[82]

Planning and waging a battle against racial discrimination and for civil rights, Houston had served in the capacity of Special Counsel for the NAACP for five years when he decided to resign. His interests and concerns had broadened so extensively after his return to Washington, D.C., that he believed remaining an executive officer of the NAACP would be too confining.[83]

There were political campaigns pending and crucial matters revolving around fundamental rights for black people. Houston had his own ideas about changes that should be made to secure for black people in America freedom and first-class citizenship. Not wishing to sever ties with the NAACP or leave the fight for desegregated schools after having charted the course, Houston requested that he be discontinued as Special Counsel but restored to his "original place on the National Legal Committee." On 24 September 1940 the Committee on Administration recommended that the resignation be accepted and reinstatement on the National Legal Committee be approved. Subsequently the recommendation was accepted by the full board of directors.[84]

CHAPTER XI

Protecting the Right to Work

When Charles Houston changed his base of operations to Washington, D.C., his father, William, wanted to hope that this meant the winding down of his son's nonprofit activities. After all, the New Deal had affected the expectations more than the lives of most black Americans, and as a result there was still the need to work for a modicum of economic security. Yet Charles's prestige as the NAACP's chief civil rights lawyer made him a prime candidate for the leadership of innumerable causes. His return to the F Street offices did not deter individuals or groups from seeking to retain Houston as their lawyer in civil rights matters. He had hardly settled down to handle the affairs of local clients, following the *Gaines* victory, when he found himself faced with an extraordinary challenge. Samuel H. Clark, a yard brakeman with Norfolk & Western since 1913 and president of the Association of Colored Railway Trainmen and Locomotive Firemen's Local No. 5 with his fellow railroad worker, J. A. Reynolds, a member of Local No. 35 and staunch NAACP supporter, explained the nature of their 1939 visit. They had come from Roanoke, Virginia, to find "any body that . . . could find out what [they] should do to protect their rights."[1] Houston had become interested in discrimination against black workers when the NAACP campaign against discrimination in transportation led him to see unfair labor practices affecting black transportation workers.[2] But he was by no means a labor law expert. He did, however, have some idea about unions and black labor, and here was a chance to see what he could do. As Clark and Reynolds piled on Houston's desk "all the papers [they] could possibly find on the Railway Trainmen organization," Charles Houston admitted his lack of familiarity with recent labor law developments but took the materials promising to "study them and . . . come down to Roanoke and discuss them with [the] . . . local[s]."[3] He would try to fight for the operative workers as A. Philip Randolph did for the nonoperative porters, maids, and dining car workers.[4]

Houston called on a new member of the firm, Joseph C. Waddy, to assist with the legal fight "to protect the rights of Negroes in the railway industry."[5] The commitment of Houston and Waddy became a national one when in July 1939 Samuel Clark was elected to the office of grand president for the twenty-seven-year-old Association of Colored Railway Trainmen and Locomotive Firemen. "The organization was in financial straits," recalled Clark.

> They didn't have but around one hundred fifty members, paying a dollar and a half monthly dues, and they owed around twenty-five hundred dollars—they owed that salary to the officers. . . . So I, as the new President, . . . tried to work to improve the financial condition of the organization. . . . We had a ladies' auxiliary and I enlisted help from them and I paid that indebtment off in another year. . . . Mr. Houston began to work with us for twenty-five dollars a day. . . . If he argued the case in one day we only owed him twenty-five dollars and paid his way down here and back and his expenses. . . . Mr. Waddy was put on a ten-dollars-a-day salary.[6]

Charles Houston continued his private practice and involved himself in public protests of the barring of Marian Anderson from Constitution Hall by the Daughters of the American Revolution (DAR).[7] He met with other community leaders on the treatment of black registrants and black soldiers fighting in World War II. Also, he was consistently at work with the Citizens' Committee on Race Relations in the District. Once settled in Washington, D.C., again, Charles Houston was determined to make the living conditions for black people better. When ad hoc committees came together in emergencies to address discrimination in employment of blacks by public utilities or large chains of grocery stores with stores in the black community, Houston attended meetings, sent out written protests, and participated in direct action against companies. In discussing Houston's full commitment to civil rights, Anna Arnold Hedgeman (who once served as the executive for the National Council for a Permanent Fair Employment Practices Commission and assistant to Mayor Robert Wagner of New York) remarked, "Contrary to public opinion, picket lines are not new. We—Charles Houston and I and others—held them in Washington, D.C., for every conceivable need including the opportunity to eat in the restaurants of the city and to be able to secure a taxi cab out of Union Station."[8]

From 1939 to 1944, however, Houston focused primary attention on black workers and racism in the area of railway labor. With the war against Japan and Germany, so much was at stake that it was easy to argue the importance of railroads and full utilization of workers. Houston was "convinced [he had] the key to that."[9] Actually *persuading* white Americans was the problem. The railroad labor world, which included many black workers, had boasted racist practices and policies since the nineteenth century. Four brotherhoods that had always restricted their membership to whites—the Brotherhood of Locomotive Engineers, the Order of Railway Conductors, the Brotherhood of Locomotive Firemen and Enginemen, and the Brotherhood of Railroad Trainmen founded in 1863, 1868, 1873, and 1883, respectively—dominated railroad labor. Unable to bar blacks entirely from the crafts, however, they traditionally wielded their power—substantiated by their numbers—to eliminate blacks from the operating department of the industry and to better the working conditions, wages, and positions of their members. Moreover, it was clear to Houston that the amended Railway Labor Act, under which the National Mediation Board was authorized to certify a majority exclusive bargaining agent, was being used by the white unions to economically disfranchise blacks (the minority). Thus blacks in the railroad industry suffered serious discrimination not only by employers but also by railway labor organizations and the provisions and administration of the Railway Labor Act. The partisan National Railway Adjustment Board often denied aggrieved black workers a hearing. Moreover, since the right of review belonged to the victorious party, the adjustment board, more often than not in cases involving disputes between black workers and the "Big Four" brotherhoods, had become a labor court enforcing inequitable decisions.[10]

In 1940, with Joseph Waddy, Houston began a program of litigation for the Association of Colored Railway Trainmen and Locomotive Firemen. Houston was confident as he assured the association's members, "You don't have any laws to protect you, but I'm going to make some laws that will protect you. I'm going to make them." The first case concerned the nonunion car-riders on the Virginia line at the Norfolk piers. Black car-riders did the same dangerous work as white brakemen, but the car-riders had no contract and made less money. Houston, on hearing the grievances, secured permission from the general manager of the Virginia Railroad to visit the piers. "He climbed all up over those piers everywhere," Clark recalled, "[to] find out how the work was, what they had to do." Meetings were held with the management in an effort to avoid a suit. Negotiations failing, however, Houston represented the car-riders through the black trainmen's union in the case. It was decided favorably in the lower courts of the state. The car-riders were brought into the black trainmen's and locomotive fire-men's union, and a contract for better pay, better hours, and benefits was negotiated. No law was written from this case, but it was an important first step for the association and the black workers employed by the Virginia Railroad. The suit forced many members out of their complacency. It taught members and nonmembers a vital lesson about strength in organization and the effectiveness of collective bargaining. It bettered the working conditions of the car-riders.[11]

The Association of Colored Railway Trainmen and Locomotive Fire-men with a new general railroad workers organization, the International Association of Railway Employees (founded in 1934) litigated a second case, *Ed Teague* v. *Gulf, Mobile & Northern Railroad Company* (later *Gulf, Mobile & Ohio) and the Brotherhood of Locomotive Fire-men and Enginemen.* The Teague case grew out of the displacement of Ed Teague, a black fireman with seniority from the date of 5 March 1917, by a junior white fireman. The suit focused on discriminatory effects of a January 1938 secret agreement negotiated by the Brother-hood of Locomotive Firemen and Enginemen, the union that was act-ing as bargaining representative under the amended Railway Labor Act for all firemen on Gulf, Mobile & Northern. In contravention of a Chi-cago agreement of 15 March 1937, which stipulated that a locomotive fireman should be used in the cab of every locomotive regardless of how it was powered, the brotherhood made a deal with management. The white union relieved Gulf, Mobile & Northern of the obligation of the 1937 agreement on the condition that white firemen were given prefer-ence on mechanically stoked engines. The railroad company would thereby give the best jobs to white firemen and also be in a position to save thousands of payroll dollars by dismissing black firemen.[12]

This secret agreement had fatal implications for the employment of black firemen. In 1937 the Interstate Commerce Commission had ruled that all coal-burning locomotives built on or subsequent to 1 July 1938 weighing 160,000 pounds or more on driving wheels and in-tended for heavy or fast passenger service, and all such locomotives weighing 175,000 pounds or more intended for heavy or fast freight, and all engines of the same weights or more in service 1 July 1938 should be equipped with mechanical stokers by 1 July 1948. Thus the Teague suit challenging the validity of the January 1938 secret agree-ment between the brotherhood and Gulf, Mobile & Northern con-cerned a class of black railroad workers who either were or would be likewise displaced. The complaint for the injunction—damages for fraud, breach of contract, breach of trust, and violation of the Railway

Labor Act—and for a declaratory judgment called for relief not only for
Teague but also "for the other Negro locomotive firemen on the G, M &
N RR and/or the G, M & O RR, as a class" and was taken to the District
Court of the United States in Memphis, Tennessee, by Houston, Waddy,
Joseph Settle of Memphis, and F. O. Turnage of Washington, D.C.[13]

For Houston, the crux of the issue was the federal question, that is,
violation of the Railway Labor Act by the railroad company and the
brotherhood. Attorneys for the defendant railroads and union argued
that the U.S. District Court had no jurisdiction, first because there was
no federal question but rather a claim predicated on the contract between the railroad and the brotherhood. Second, they argued that even
if the judge were to view the matter as involving a federal question, the
only federal remedy would be the administrative one. Relief would
have to be granted by the Railroad Adjustment Board. Houston's points
were equally straightforward claims. First, the secret compromise
agreement between Gulf, Mobile & Northern, and the Brotherhood of
Locomotive Firemen and Enginemen broke the railroad's uniform individual contracts with the plaintiff and the other Negro Locomotive
firemen and violated or destroyed their vested seniority rights. Second,
the secret agreement of 1938 constituted, on the part of the brotherhood, a violation of its "statutory and fiduciary duty" and unlawful
"abuse [of] its authority under the Railway Labor Act." Unpersuaded
by Houston's arguments, the presiding U.S. district judge dismissed
the case as to the brotherhood. The right claimed by Houston's clients
was not specifically given in the Railway Labor Act, therefore, the
complaint did not present a federal question over which the court had
jurisdiction. Proceedings against the railroad company were stayed
pending determination of appeal.[14]

In March 1941, immediately after the decision was handed down,
the attorneys for Teague gave notice of appeal and prepared to take
their case to the Circuit Court of Appeals with jurisdiction over the
U.S. District Court for the eastern division of western Tennessee.
However, the Circuit Court of Appeals affirmed the ruling of the U.S.
District Court. In the matter of *Ed Teague* v. *Brotherhood of Locomotive Firemen and Enginemen* the rights claimed were contractual and
therefore relief was properly sought by the plaintiff-in-error in the
state courts. Houston, as did the black railroad workers supporting the
court action, "thought the decision was wrong, [but] . . . decided not to
seek certiorari."[15] Neither Houston nor Waddy nor Settle wanted to
run the risk of an adverse decision from the U.S. Supreme Court. They
thought seriously about pressing the case in the state courts but, with
further consideration of the amended complaint, the appeal record,

and Teague's personal situation, came to believe *Teague* v. *Brotherhood of Locomotive Firemen and Enginemen* was not the best vehicle for a clear presentation of the issue of fiduciary (good faith) duty of the majority-chosen representatives to the minority under the Railway Labor Act. The publicity given Teague and the national support of the case by black railroad workers made the decision difficult, but the attorneys subsequently advised the supporting unions that they believed it best to abandon *Teague* v. *Brotherhood* and prepare another case for the U.S. Supreme Court.[16]

Houston, Waddy, Settle, and an Alabama attorney, Arthur Shores, continued a program of litigation for the Association of Colored Railway Trainmen and Locomotive Firemen and the International Association of Railway Employees, concentrating on the cases of *Pearl Pyles* v. *Illinois Central Railroad et al.*, *Bester William Steele* v. *Louisville and Nashville, Brotherhood of Locomotive Firemen and Enginemen et al.*, and *Tom Tunstall* v. *Brotherhood of Locomotive Firemen and Enginemen et al.* Based on the experience of *Teague*, counsel decided to press *Steele*, which had been filed in the State Court of Alabama, and *Tunstall*, which had been filed in the U.S. District Court, Fourth Circuit, through their respective state and federal courts to the U.S. Supreme Court. Houston was convinced that even though there was no specific provision in the Railway Labor Act against racial discrimination, nonrepresentation, or misrepresentation of the minority members of the craft or union by union officials and statutory representatives, there was certainly a constitutionally implied protection against such conduct.[17]

Houston, with co-counsel, sought to spell out not only the right of fair and impartial representation under the Railway Labor Act (RLA), but also the unconstitutionality of denial of the right to work by virtue of abuse of exclusive bargaining rights under the RLA. In Houston's opinion two major issues were involved in the cases of Bester William Steele, a black locomotive fireman employed by the Louisville and Nashville Railroad Company (a member of the International Association of Railway Employees), and Tom Tunstall, a black locomotive fireman employed by the Norfolk Southern Railway (a member of the Association of Colored Railway Trainmen and Locomotive Firemen). One issue was the denial on the grounds of race and color of the right of the black firemen to work. A second was the abuse of the right to be the statutory exclusive bargaining agent.[18]

A number of subsidiary issues arose out of the primary complaints in each case. These included four that Houston would stress: (1) the general power of a statutory bargaining representative in relation to individual employees and the provisions under which they worked; (2) the duty of a majority-selected representative to represent the interest of all members of the craft or union under the RLA; (3) the rights of minority workers seeking protection when faced with an improper or racially discriminatory collective bargaining agreement; and (4) the enforcement of unfair or improper collective bargaining agreements. In the lower state and federal courts, both Bester Steele and Tom Tunstall were denied relief relative to loss of wages, destruction of seniority rights, and the brotherhood's breach of duty under the RLA. In addition, neither court would enjoin the defendant railroad companies and brotherhood from enforcing the "secret, fraudulent" agreements between each carrier and the brotherhood. The losses in trial court were appealed. When Charles Houston appeared before the Alabama Supreme Court for Bester Steele, it was the first time a black lawyer had argued before that court in twenty-nine years. However historically impressive this might have been, the Alabama court affirmed the lower court's decision in *Steele* and the U.S. Court of Appeals for the Fourth Circuit did the same in *Tunstall*.[19]

Houston and co-counsel applied for writs of certiorari and on receiving them prepared to argue before the U.S. Supreme Court. Houston told a Chicago attorney handling a similar case:

> I think most of the cases will be governed by the decision of the United States Supreme Court in the *Tunstall* case and its companion case, *Steele* v. *Brotherhood of Locomotive Firemen and Enginemen and Louisville and Nashville Railroad Company*. These cases raise the fundamental question as to the duty of the bargaining agent and grievance representative to the minority. If we are successful in establishing in the United States Supreme Court the principle that the bargaining agent has a fiduciary duty to the minority to represent them equally with the majority and to seek no profit for its members over against the minority, I think that most of the other cases will either be settled out of court or else the precedent will be controlling.[20]

Houston was well aware that "agitation . . . over the plight of the Negro firemen" and "the work of the President's Committee on Fair Employment Practices . . . served as a background preparing the way" for the court's decisions in *Steele* and *Tunstall*.[21] The International Association and Samuel Clark's Association of Trainmen and Locomotive Firemen were joined by A. Philip Randolph's Sleeping Car Porters Union in agitation about and protest of the conditions under which black operatives labored. The Porters' organization under Benjamin McLaurin, field organizer for a "Provisional Committee for the Organization of Colored Locomotive Firemen and Engineers," made efforts across the nation to unify black firemen "into a national labor union [to] wage an aggressive and militant organization campaign . . . to battle for their interests and rights."[22]

Randolph, who was a recognized leader of black workers, and his assistant, McLaurin, were vocal regarding the racist practices of the Brotherhood of Locomotive Firemen and Enginemen. Through attorneys Harold Stevens and Joseph Rauh, the Provisional Committee of the Brotherhood of Sleeping Car Porters initiated its own litigation program. Although officers of the International Association of Railway Employees and the Association of Colored Railway Trainmen and Locomotive Firemen looked on Randolph's organization's work as competition in most instances and in some situations an attempt to undercut the work of the International and the Association, Houston and Waddy believed their cases would speak for themselves and consequently attempted to cooperate with the provisional committee's lawyers.[23] Writing Arthur Lewis, the auditor of the International, Houston reminded him that the Brotherhood of Sleeping Car Porters did not begin a litigation program for firemen until after *Teague* was filed. "The Brotherhood is like the caboose and the international and association are the double heater engines. . . . Randolph's lawyers came down . . . and we gave them all possible aid."[24] Despite the suspicions of the International and the Association, Houston believed McLaurin and Randolph had a genuine desire to bring all black operatives together, and he cooperated in conferences and cases out of his desire "to help in shaping the programs that would benefit the majority of these men without regard to railroads."[25] For this reason Randolph had no animosity toward Houston; both had important roles to play if the black railroad workers were to free themselves from exploitative management and racially oppressive white unions. "I found . . . Houston . . . immensely valuable. . . . [H]e had . . . experience with some of the firemen," Randolph recalled, and then added as more than an afterthought that Houston "was racially oriented; . . . he wasn't ashamed to fight for black people."[26]

As for the President's Committee on Fair Employment Practices (FEPC), everyone connected with the cases, and especially Samuel Clark, J. A. Reynolds, Bester Steele, Tom Tunstall, and Charles Houston, knew how important it was as a beginning in the protection of black working-class people and how important A. Philip Randolph was in that drama. The FEPC was originally established by an executive order. That order, No. 8802, was a response to Randolph's threatened march of ten thousand black people on Washington, D.C. to exact their rights in defense industries and the armed forces. After the FEPC had been functioning for a time, blacks adversely affected by discrimination in the railway industry were invited to file or have their lawyers file complaints for a hearing scheduled first for June 1942 and second for January 1943. An indefinite postponement changed the nature of the FEPC's immediate impact on workers, but even this kept the problems before the people in power. Both Harold Stevens and Charles Houston resigned as counsel for the FEPC when the FEPC chairman failed to set a new date for an investigation into the workers' complaints.[27] Houston sent a copy of his resignation to President Roosevelt. It stated, in part: "The time when Negro issues can be disposed of without first conferring with Negroes themselves has passed, and it is important that government officials begin to realize that Negroes are citizens not wards."[28]

Charles Houston's ideas about the respect for the office of the U.S. President, the nation, patriotism, and the legal process were consistent. Years ago he had dared to believe and state that laws and federal authorities were not always supreme because they failed to protect all people regardless of race, religion, wealth, class, or power. Now the external struggle, the length of it, and the persistence of racism and the regular indignities, such as meted out by white officials, made a distinct statement about the place *still* reserved for blacks in America. But that place was not acceptable. Even the government was cognizant of a changing mood and attempted an antedote for declining morale. Several appointments including Ted Poston as special racial adviser in the Office of War Information and William Hastie as civilian aide to the secretary of war were gratuitously made to appease blacks and raise their morale. But blacks could not forget how General MacArthur seemed to think blacks were easily fooled when he claimed there was no discrimination in the armed forces. (Houston's reply contradicting MacArthur was carried by the Associated Negro Press under the headline "Houston Has Polite Way of Calling U.S. Army Chief . . . a Liar.") Then came the riot in Detroit, Michigan, that was stopped only after thirty-four deaths and a declaration of a state of emergency. So many blacks had moved to cities in the Midwest that racial tensions had heightened, and the riot in June 1943 made things worse. The *Pittsburgh Courier*, which had earlier published Houston's series on the experience of being a black officer in World War I, was waging a "Double-V" (victory at home and abroad) campaign and black people were no longer remaining silent about discrimination at home or in the armed services during wartime. No black Americans supported Nazism or condoned the Japanese attack on Americans at Pearl Harbor. It was difficult, however, for blacks to fight in defense of the "four freedoms" with which they had little to no acquaintance. Freedom of speech, freedom of worship, freedom from want, and freedom from fear were to white Americans part of a war slogan, but for black Americans freedom was the final purpose of a struggle still being waged at home. Mothers and fathers buried their dead from that war and America's wars while segregation and racial discrimination continued. White army officers placed most blacks at the front or behind the lines doing menial work. Few white civilians in private industry had any real desire to employ large numbers of blacks and treat them equally, even in the face of a long war, during which Americans would be called on to sacrifice much.[29]

Charles Houston decided to try once again with the FEPC for the sake of the black workers he had been working to protect. After reorganization of the FEPC and the scheduling of railway industry hearings for September 1943, he reassociated himself as an assistant special counsel to the FEPC for the hearings in Washington, D.C. These hearings brought to the attention of the public complaint after complaint about violence and unfair labor practices of fourteen unions and twenty-three railroads. The FEPC directed twenty companies and seven unions to abrogate all their racially discriminatory agreements between companies and unions, such as the Southeastern Carrier's Conference Agreement, and to eliminate quotas detrimental to black workers. By January 1944, however, only six railroad companies had even attempted to comply with the directives of the committee.[30]

President Roosevelt created the Stacey Committee to work out some agreement between the unions, the companies, and the FEPC. Led by Howard Smith of Virginia, however, the House of Representatives challenged the executive branch's interference in the management of railroad companies. The Smith Committee investigated acts of executive agencies beyond the scope of their authority. Specifically, the committee asked if the FEPC had power to issue directives. On this, Charles Houston offered testimony.

> This much is true, that the FEPC is the first Government body to deal with the problem, which like slavery, just is not going to be put off and just is not going to be solved by a "know nothing" attitude, . . . this right of persons to bargain and organize collectively and to be represented through representatives of their own choosing. . . . [T]o say that [N]egroes may not work on the railroads and that you are threatened with paralysis of transportation [if] the railroads attempt to enforce [N]egro employment . . . is a challenge . . . to every American.[31]

Charles Houston's activities on behalf of black workers and for the promotion of fair employment practices were noted by high-ranking officials in the executive branch of the federal government well before the *Steele* and *Tunstall* arguments. Following the resignation from the FEPC of Samuel Zemurray (president of the United Fruit Company) and P. B. Young (editor and publisher of the *Norfolk Journal and Guide*), Charles Horn (president of the Federal Cartridge Corporation), Percival L. Prattis (of the Associated Negro Press and *Pittsburgh Courier*), Virginius Dabney (editor of the *Richmond Times-Dispatch*), and Charles Houston were recommended by White House aide Jonathan Daniels to fill the two vacancies on the President's Fair Employment Practices Committee. In reply, President Roosevelt noted that he was "inclined to think that [they] might put in Charles Horn and Virginius Dabney. Or, if [Daniels thought] it better, [they] could put in Dabney and Charles Houston in order to have one negro [sic] on the Board."[32]

On 28 February 1944, Daniels reported that Houston and Horn had agreed to serve as members of the President's Fair Employment Practices Committee and letters of appointment were dispatched. Writing to the President, Houston replied, "I appreciate the appointment and hope that my service will justify the trust you have reposed in me." On 6 March the official announcement was made by Presidential Secretary Stephen Early.[33] Houston's appointment seemed to meet with general approval. Blacks and liberals were pleased because of Charles Houston's "militancy and ability."[34]

These qualities helped save Charles Houston from paralyzing disillusionment. He understood well the limitations of this temporary agency that could only recommend appropriate steps for the elimination of discrimination.[35] In reply to Roy Wilkins's congratulatory letter, Houston remarked, "Thanks about FEPC, I have no illusions about it, but the job appears to be a spot which may be important on account of future implications; and it will put me on the inside of many problems which otherwise I would not reach."[36] Charles Houston joined Malcolm Ross (former director of information for the National Labor Relations Board), John Brophy (director of the Industrial Union Councils for the Congress of Industrial Organizations), Charles Horn (president of Federal Cartridge), Boris Shishkin (economist for the American Federation of Labor), Sara Southall (supervisor of employment and service of the International Harvester Company), and Milton P. Webster (vice-president of the Brotherhood of Sleeping Car Porters) to "challenge . . . existing practices inside and outside of government." The committee handled complaints of three classifications from across the nation: those against federal government agencies, those against employers and unions with companies or corporations having federal government contracts, and those against employers and the union connected with war industries. To do its work, the FEPC depended not only on the extensive headquarter's staff of lawyers, examiners, field investigators, and information officers, but also in large measure on the regional offices in which "[much of] the effective work of the FEPC was accomplished."[37]

For Houston, March 1944 was the most incredible and exciting month of his entire life. *Steele* and *Tunstall*, the firm, and the FEPC kept him busy, but what gave him joy was his home. Every day he checked on Henrietta, his wife, who was pregnant, and he spent the first nineteen days of the month expecting her to deliver any minute. On March 20, a son arrived. The healthy boy of about seven pounds was named after his father, becoming Charles Hamilton Houston, Jr. For Mary it was an answer to prayer. She had not been very strong and had occasionally wondered if she would ever see her first grandchild. William was absolutely ecstatic about a male heir, while his sister Clotill saw the birth of a child to her nephew as a singular blessing. They all knew how Charles had felt about his childless first marriage. The threesome was a wonderful sight: Henrietta weary but smiling, Charles fussing over the baby even if he did not quite know what to do, and Charlie Jr., first in one set of arms and then in another. After very little discussion, Joseph Waddy was named Charlie Jr.'s first godparent.[38]

Since all work had to continue as usual, it took Charles months to adjust to being a father and having another "Charlie" in the house. But he wouldn't have traded those times for anything in the world. This part of Charles Houston's life, his son, became the new center. The birth of Charles Jr. could be compared with nothing else in its significance to Charles Houston. He continued to devote enormous amounts of time to civil rights litigation, FEPC work, and various civil liberties matters raised by black and biracial groups for presentation to Congress or the wider public. Yet to Henrietta, Charles seemed even more driven at times. More important, the greater zeal evident to his wife, friends, relatives, and colleagues emanated from a modified view of his role.[39] In the early years of the black railroad workers' fight, Houston frequently spoke of the inspiration provided by his family. Sam Clark, on one occasion, recalled Houston reminiscing about time spent with his grandmother Katherine Houston: "I've heard her sit and tell how the white people treated her when she was a slave, and I said if God lets me live long enough to become a man I was going to try to protect Negroes."[40] Now with Charlie Jr.—who had acquired the nickname "Bo"—a child in the immediate family, Charles Houston labored under greater obligations. As a father he owed his son time, love, and attention with some consistency, while also owing him a less hostile, less oppressive, less stifling environment outside the home. Any abstractions and theories that might have earlier informed the decisions of the Vice-Dean and the Special Counsel tended to recede as the faces and hopes of people who had grown close to him loomed larger in his thinking and his son became the special point of reference. Houston had counseled others' children against permitting ceilings on their ambitions and aspirations, and the issues stood in stark relief now.[41] What about opportunities to get a good education, to find a job to match one's skills and talents, to fulfill one's potential, to be safe and secure, to speak one's mind about societal injustice, to enjoy public accommodations during a family outing, to vote without fear, to be free and assured of one's rights under the law? Houston's dependent, innocent child, with more future than past, was enough of a reason for the continuing sacrifice; Houston's relation to all other black children and their parents was ample authentication of the necessity for sacrifice and struggle. With Henrietta, his wife and the mother of Bo, Houston shared such thoughts and added—perhaps unaware of the discomfort it caused her—"I would give my life fighting day and night."[42]

Concerned about principles and opportunities both in general and in particular, Houston exhibited extraordinary energy and fervor during the final stages of litigation for Bester Steele and Tom Tunstall. Houston presented oral arguments in *Tunstall* on 14 November and in *Steele* on 14 and 15 November 1944. Houston was determined that Joseph Waddy's being called to the army would not adversely affect the cases of the black railroad workers. The team of lawyers and black workers had come too far to make less than persuasive arguments to the U.S. Supreme Court. Houston had prepared for the back-to-back oral arguments. There was to Houston's mind only one constitutionally sound position: Any union representing a craft had a duty to represent equally white and black employees. The effort of Houston was remarkable. William O. Douglas, one of the justices before whom Houston pleaded, noted that "one of [Houston's] best was *Steele* v. *Louisville & Nashville*. . . . He was a veritable dynamo of energy guided by a mind that had as sharp a cutting edge as any I have known."[43] The court handed down its decisions, in both cases reversing the lower courts and remanding each for further proceedings consistent with the high court's opinion on 18 December 1944. Chief Justice Harlan Fiske Stone delivered the opinions of the court in the companion cases.[44]

In the *Steele* opinion, the court held that the representative selected by the majority of the craft to be exclusive bargaining representatives had a fiduciary duty to protect the minority. Justice Stone stated that "the language of the [Railway Labor] Act . . . expresses the aim of Congress to impose on the bargaining representative of a craft or class of employees the duty to exercise fully the power conferred upon it in behalf of all those for whom it acts, without hostile discrimination against them." Further, it was emphasized that the power to represent the craft or class of employees as to contracts, wages, and working conditions was statutory, but there was no statutory authority granted "to make among members of the craft discriminations not based on . . . relevant differences" and in the case before the high court discriminations were "based on race alone" and "obviously irrelevant and invidious." Given the nature of the discrimination, the court further held that the representative "may be enjoined" from such racial discrimination and the members also "may be enjoined from taking the benefit of such discriminatory action." Although the statute did not speak to the issues of eligibility and membership in unions which acted as collective bargaining agents, the court declared that "in collective bargaining and in making contracts with the carrier, to represent non-union or minority union members of the craft [the union is required to act] without hostile discrimination, fairly, impartially, and in good faith."[45]

In a separate concurring opinion, Justice Frank Murphy spoke more emphatically about what seemed to him the crucial constitutional issue raised by the economic discrimination practiced against the black railroad workers:

> Congress, through the Railway Labor Act, has conferred upon the union selected by a majority of a craft or class of railway workers the power to represent the entire craft or class in all collective bargaining matters. While such a union is essentially a private organization, its power to represent and bind all members of a class or craft is derived solely from Congress. . . . But it cannot be assumed that Congress meant to authorize the representative to act so as to ignore rights guaranteed by the Constitution.
> A sound democracy cannot allow such discrimination to go unchallenged. Racism is far too virulent today to permit the slightest refusal, in the light of a Constitution that abhors it, to expose and condemn it wherever it appears in the course of a statutory interpretation.[46]

This victory for the Association of Colored Railway Trainmen and Locomotive Firemen and the International Association of Railway Employees was the vindication of Houston's faith expressed through five years of struggle on behalf of the black railroad workers. With joy and satisfaction—even though he was aware of the numerous battles still to be fought—Houston wrote to the Association, the International, Arthur Shores, Bester Steele, Tom Tunstall, and Thurgood Marshall.

In a lengthy memorandum, Houston explained that through "the

Steele case . . . every single proposition we have advocated for five years was adopted by the United States Supreme Court." He added that he believed the decision would do a great deal to justify a permanent FEPC, because all the questions simply could not "be fought out in the courts because the courts are too slow and litigation is too expensive. What is needed now is some sort of administrative body which can move quickly." Houston further stressed that the principles would have to be developed in order to "make sure that they give our people real protection." The next move would be to "challenge the right of railroads to represent the craft or class at all as long as it excludes Negroes from membership." Finally he congratulated the black railroad workers: "The proof of effective work is the fact that the International and the A.C.R.T.&L.F. worked out an effective plan for aiding Negro firemen which is going to . . . have behind it the sanction of law which can be enforced by either putting those who disobey the law in jail, taking away representation rights, and/or awarding damages."[47]

Few were more thrilled to see Charles Houston prevail in *Steele* and in *Tunstall* than the executive director of the National Council for a Permanent Fair Employment Practices Commission, Anna Arnold Hedgeman. She had first come to know Houston as the Amherst- and Harvard-educated lawyer who "recognized that persuasion was not producing significant change in United States society" and who therefore "initiated the idea of *legal process as* a useful *weapon* toward necessary change." When, immediately after his Supreme Court victories for the black workers, Houston expressed the view that a permanent administrative body was a necessity for fair employment practices, Anna Hedgeman was not at all surprised. Supreme Court victories had never meant an end to struggle, for they always required enforcement. Even before Houston knew Steele and Tunstall, "when Fair Employment Practices legislation was discussed by A. Philip Randolph and the National Council for a Permanent F.E.P.C., it was Charles Houston who aided me," Hedgeman recalled. Houston did so "in the development of a group of lawyers who studied legislation, aided in securing congressional support and advised . . . continually. Charles Houston conferred with such political leaders as William Dawson (Democrat) and Robert Church (Republican) on general legislative strategies. Loved by the community, he was able to interpret to the local leaders and the local and national press." Charles H. Houston was, Anna Hedgeman added with definiteness, "an authentic African American citizen of the United States. Above all, his integrity was unquestioned."[48]

Houston recognized the obvious limitation of the legal approach and the limits of the *Steele* and *Tunstall* decisions. The greatest limitation may have been that the cases directly affected the rights of black people only after gainful employment had been obtained. *Steele* and *Tunstall* did not speak to those discriminatory practices, policies, or customs that barred blacks from employment. Houston, however, never believed that resort to the courts alone would solve the problem of the right of black Americans to work in the land of their birth. He believed the continuing task was to "sweep aside the discrimination against employing the Negro" in addition to "sav[ing] the jobs of those Negroes who were already employed." As his good friend and colleague James Nabrit, Jr., put it, "Houston conceived of the Negro railway labor fight as being two-pronged: (1) elimination of discrimination practiced against persons already employed . . . , (2) opening the doors of railroad employment to additional Negroes." As he moved throughout the nation, he was consistently open and forthright in his position of advocacy of fair employment practices, a permanent FEPC, and the right to work.[49]

As a presidential appointee to the FEPC, Houston attended and participated in regular committee meetings. Also, he handled his share of routine complaints and investigations of corporate hiring and promotion practices, dismissals, and union irregularities in St. Louis, Missouri, and on the West Coast. Yet he focused on the movement for a permanent postwar FEPC and the Capital Transit dispute in Washington, D.C., because the interrelated activities underscored the urgent need for enforceable laws. Being a parent provided Houston with a standpoint from which he would view the need for opportunities and fairness in the workplace as so critical that it placed an immediate obligation on his generation. For that reason he was almost always available to assist Anna Hedgeman with the review of legislative drafts. Because Capital Transit was the major case before the FEPC and the company's base of operations was his home, however, Charles was particularly persistent. At least in Washington, D.C., the seat of government, fair and nondiscriminatory employment practices should prevail.[50] Directives could never be equivalent to enforceable orders or laws, but the "FEPC's public hearings and . . . publication of its investigations did touch a 'raw nerve' in many employees," as the director of the Legal Division, general counsel, and deputy chairman, George M. Johnson, noted.[51] Some even altered their employment practices, and this was precisely what Houston sought in the matter of Capital Transit.

This was to be the last matter he would hear as an FEPC appointee, for on this matter he would reach an impasse with President Harry Truman and his staff. The Capital Transit Company of Washington,

D.C., deemed a war industry within the meaning of the executive order establishing FEPC, was requested to appear on 15 and 16 January 1945 to answer charges of discriminatory practices lodged against it by "fourteen Negro men and women applicants [who] were refused employment by the company." Houston, Southall, Shishkin, Webster, Brophy, and Ross were present in the courtroom of the U.S. Circuit Court of Appeals for the District of Columbia to hear the response of Capital Transit. The company's "refusal fully to utilize available manpower," according to the FEPC, "ha[d] resulted in inadequate transportation service to government and District war workers' to the detriment of the prosecution of the war, the workers' morale and national unity." During the course of the hearing, facts relative to the company's failure and refusal to hire blacks or upgrade them to positions as bus operators, checkers, motormen, or streetcar conductors from 15 July 1942 up to and including the time of the hearing were presented to the FEPC. Through experts' testimony and questions carefully phrased, Houston deliberately presented for his fellow committee members two central issues obstructing fair employment practices at Capital Transit: the view that platform positions were white men's jobs, and whites' fear of economic competition from black workers.[52]

The FEPC was cautious. Initially it sought to eliminate discrimination through *suggestions* of amicable adjustment. A proposed decision was submitted to the company in June 1945. The company filed exceptions. The relaxation of wartime controls after the war served to erode the strength of the FEPC's recommendations. Nevertheless, when a strike by employees of Capital Transit led the federal government to seize the transit line under the War Labor Dispute Act, the committee voted to issue its official directive calling for the elimination of racially discriminatory practices. Notice of this decision was given to the White House on 23 November 1945. In conversation with Phileo Nash of the White House staff and Guy A. Richardson, federal manager of Capital Transit under the executive order of 21 November 1945, it became clear that the executive branch might be opposed to the issuance of the final directive at that time. On orders from President Truman, a John Steelman telephoned Houston and instructed him not to issue the directive. Houston informed Steelman that contrary instructions had come from FEPC and that to hold the directive would therefore require written orders from the White House. Steelman stated that instructions would be requested. Then he told Houston that someone should remain in the FEPC office during the afternoon to receive the written instructions. The President had plans for Capital Transit with which a directive might "interfere," Steelman added.[53] On that basis Charles Houston intercepted the mailing of the directive pending receipt of the instructions from the White House and advised the deputy chairman to remain in the office. There were subsequent telephone calls but no written orders. Steelman, in fact, claimed he had made no promise to Houston. A Mr. Hassett of the White House staff, who had been present when the President called for the halting of the directive, informed the deputy chairman of Steelman's position. Before the end of the working day, Houston was unable to elicit from Steelman any confirmation of their previous conversation. Rather, Steelman told him that the FEPC "had received an order from the President and in his opinion it was advisable to obey it."[54]

Houston reluctantly held the committee's directive for the weekend and addressed a letter to the President recounting the events and stating in conclusion,

> It is my position that the order to hold up the Capital Transit decision involves grave public responsibility which must be properly established. In view of the urgency and gravity of this matter, and in accord with the position of certain committee members taken when the committee decided to issue the directive, that the committee should withhold the same only upon direct orders from you to be followed by an immediate conference with you, I herewith on behalf of the committee request such a committee conference with you. We sincerely trust that the conference can be held within the next twenty-four hours.[55]

By 3 December 1945, having received no reply to the letter, which according to the registry receipt was delivered to the White House on 26 November 1945, Houston resigned as a member of the President's Committee on Fair Employment Practices.

Showing little of the deference generally accorded the President of the United States, Houston reminded Truman that the FEPC was created as an independent agency by executive orders and was charged with bringing about nondiscriminatory full utilization of the country's manpower in war industries, government service, and government contract operations. "Since the effect of your intervention in the Capital Transit case is not to eliminate the discrimination but to condone it, to that extent," Houston told Truman, "you not only repudiate the committee, but more important you nullify the Executive Orders themselves." Houston went on to advise the President that there was no validity in the opinion "floating around the White House" that the executive order of 21 November 1945 did not allow for implementation of a nondiscriminatory hiring, promotion, and tenure policy after the seizure of the company.[56] In fact, continued Houston, a memorandum was prepared by the legal staff of the FEPC in which it was demonstrated that the federal manager of Capital Transit, as long as the company is under his control, is obligated to enforce the federal non-discriminatory employment policy. Finally Houston contended,

> Your action in the Capital Transit case means that you do not hesitate to seize Capital Transit when employees strike in violation of a private collective bargaining agreement, but will not move, or permit the Committee to move to effectuate the national discriminatory employment policy declared in Presidential Executive Orders.
>
> The issue of the Capital Transit case far transcends the question whether a few Negro workers shall be placed on the platform of street cars and buses and as traffic checkers on the Capital Transit system. It raises the fundamental question of the basic government attitude toward minorities. The failure of the Government to enforce democratic practices and to protect minorities in its own capital makes its expressed concern for national minorities abroad somewhat specious, and its interference in the domestic affairs of other countries very premature.[57]

This time Truman did respond to Houston. Truman's letter of 7 December 1945 read:

> Dear Mr. Houston:
>
> Your letter of December third has been received.
>
> When it was found necessary under the wartime powers conferred upon the President by the Congress, to seize the Capital Transit property, the conditions under which the property was to be operated were the same as those of any other property so seized. The law requires that when the Government seizes a property under such circumstances, it shall be operated under the terms and conditions of employment which were in effect at the time possession of such plant, mine, or facility was so taken.
>
> In view of this apparent contradiction between the law and the order which the Fair Employment Practice Committee proposed to issue, it was thought best to suggest that the order be temporarily postponed. The property was not seized for the purpose of enforcing the aims of the Fair Employment Practices Committee, laudable as these aims are, but to guarantee transportation for the citizens of Washington and vicinity.
>
> As anxious as I am for Congress to pass legislation for a permanent Fair Employment Practice Committee, I cannot contravene an Act of Congress in order to carry out the present Committee's aims. Under the circumstances it was felt that issuance of the proposed order would prove injurious to the accomplishments desired by all of us who are honestly interested in promoting the welfare of minority groups.
>
> I regret that you were unwilling to approach the problem from this viewpoint. As suggested in your letter, your resignation is accepted, to be effective immediately.
>
> Very sincerely yours,
/s/ Harry Truman[58]

Houston prepared and distributed copies of his letter of resignation to various foreign embassies, for he believed that the action of the

White House had serious international implications.[59] To domestic organizations, Houston distributed a three-point memorandum that responded directly to Truman's letter. In this memorandum he noted, first, that "the President does not touch the basic points of the Houston resignation letter," which included the affirmative duty of the government to enforce a nondiscriminatory employment policy so that it is not operating Capital Transit contrary to law (particularly in the clear absence of any clause, term, or condition of employment in the documents of the union requiring exclusion of blacks); second, that "the President does not explain why he ordered the FEPC not to issue the decision without previous consultation with the Committee or why he still refuses . . . a conference"; and third, that the President cannot seize Capital Transit "subject to applicable provisions of existing law" and then claim to have done it for reasons having nothing to do with the "aims of the present FEPC" since the executive orders creating the FEPC are part of existing law.[60]

There were those who believed that although Houston's resignation was dramatic it did not have any truly significant effect on the matter of fair employment practices, the work of the FEPC. Others believed it was a wise and courageous move. Houston was placed on the "Honor Roll of Race Relations" as a result of a nationwide poll conducted yearly by the Schomburg Collection of the New York Public Library. This revealed considerable public support for his action.[61] Yet the significant issue for Houston was not anyone's opinion of his action. He was concerned about his ability to promote and further the rights of minorities. For that same reason he had taken time, from 1944 through December 1945, to handle with W. A. C. Hughes of Maryland an NAACP case, *Louise Kerr* v. *Enoch Pratt Free Library*. In *Kerr* they secured a decision that barring the plaintiff, a young black woman, from the training school of Pratt Free Library, a state institution, was a violation of the Fourteenth Amendment.[62] Providing Louise Kerr and other blacks with an opportunity to train for librarianship was another victory under the equal protection clause of the Fourteenth Amendment. It had the effect of opening one more door and increasing the options for the children of black people in the United States. Despite the threat that the sharing of knowledge and the sharing of legal protection posed to white Americans, and despite their reactions, the important enterprise was to struggle against racial oppression. As a black man, a lawyer, a social engineer, a father, and a husband, there were countless unambiguous tasks, and to accomplish them Houston voiced and supported black aspirations while trying to keep faith with his family's hopes.[63]

CHAPTER XII

"Racism Must Go"

Houston's impressive record of victories in courts of the nation and his dramatic resignation from the FEPC because of the "failure of the federal government to enforce democratic practices . . . in its own capital" thrust him into a role of greater leadership and accountability.[1] People both inside and outside the District of Columbia approached Houston with almost every conceivable civil rights cause. The problem was time. By 1945, blacks had observed Houston's consistent advocacy for his people, and many were of the opinion that his competence was matched by his utter seriousness and zeal. Regardless of class or resources, black people came to expect that Houston would continue his private practice, teach occasionally at Howard's Law School, engage in jousts with the federal government, and argue civil rights issues. One of the lasting ironies of Charles Houston's life was how he struggled with the urgency of a man who refused to count on tomorrow so that he could improve conditions and opportunities for black people yet in struggling found less time to spend with his own family. (See Appendix 2.)

Jobs in defense industries and companies with war-related products or functions enabled urban blacks to find work, hold positions, and make a little more money. Working-class and middle-class blacks desired to move out of ghettos, especially when the housing was substandard. Some purchased homes in areas considered either "white" or "changing" neighborhoods and discovered that there were restrictive covenants attached to the contracts of sellers and others in the neighborhoods. Black couples began to retain Charles Houston and he more vigorously fought "the blanket national policy and standard . . . opposed to giving [black] people decent housing opportunities and committed to confining them to segregated ghettos." In particular, he handled District racially restrictive covenant cases. As part of his private practice, Houston "whittled away" at *Corrigan* v. *Buckley*, the 1926 Supreme Court decision declaring racially restrictive covenants enforceable by the courts, prosecuting after 1940 such District cases as *Arthur Bishop et al.* v. *Mabel Chamberlain et al.*, *Sallie Broadway et al.* v. *Arthur Bishop et al.*, *Arthur Bishop et al.* v. *Raphael G. Urciolo et al.* in the U.S. District Court, and *Hundley et ux.* v. *Gorewitz et al.* in the District Court and the U.S. Court of Appeals.[2]

With so many restrictive covenant cases, Houston decided he needed some assistance. He had heard of an extremely bright young Howard graduate who had done a civil rights seminar paper on restrictive covenants. Houston called Spottswood Robinson III to inquire about his availability. Robinson, quite shocked that *the* Charles H. Houston was asking for the assistance of a recent law school graduate, asked, "What makes you think I could do this?" Houston reassured Robinson but simultaneously explained the difficulty of the task before them. Robinson remembers being given a brief to write. He did a thorough job of research and then drafted the brief for presentation to the court. At that point, a lunch hour, Robinson advised Houston that he was ready for his review of the brief. They ate lunch and went back to the room at the end of the hall of the Houston firm offices. At 2:00 P.M. Houston gathered several large crayonlike black pencils, placed a green eyeshade around his forehead, and began to read the draft line by line. They took a dinner break—ordering sandwiches from a takeout restaurant—and continued until 1:00 A.M. Houston looked up and asked Robinson if he wanted to take a break and start again at about 7:00 A.M. This being a rather unattractive offer to Robinson, he insisted that they go on with the review. At 4:00 A.M. Houston completed reading the brief and making his notes and returned it to Robinson for a rewrite. Even after forty years had passed, Robinson still remembered and summed it up by saying, "Thoroughness was Charlie."[3] They continued to work together on cases fighting restrictive covenants and at both the trial level and the appellate level sought to build a record to invalidate the principle of *Corrigan*.

In the nationwide battle against restrictive covenants, Houston joined NAACP attorneys and civil libertarians from the several states and the District to reverse the principles of enforcement of such discriminatory clauses.[4] In light of the restrictive covenant case, *Mays v. Burgess*, such lawyers as Willis Graves and Francis Dent of Detroit; George Vaughn of St. Louis; Loren Miller of Los Angeles; Sidney Jones, Irvin Mollison, and Loring Moore of Chicago; Thurgood Marshall, Andrew Weinberger, Robert L. Carter, and Constance Motley of

New York; James Nabrit, Jr., Leon Ransom, Phineas Indritz, Raphael Urciolo, Edward Lovett, and Charles Houston of Washington, D.C., and William Hastie, Jr. of Washington, D.C., and the Virgin Islands agreed that it would be to their advantage to share their experiences and information on covenants if they wanted to take the matter to the Supreme Court. Some in 1945 and others later in 1947, attended "Meeting[s] of N.A.A.C.P. Lawyers and Consultants on Methods of Attacking Restrictive Covenants" to delineate clearly a strategy for the legal campaign. In Chicago for the first meeting, Houston, "undoubtedly the most respected lawyer present," expressed his views freely and suggested legal methods based on his litigation experience.[5]

Following the Chicago NAACP meeting, Houston argued *Hodge et al.* v. *Hurd et ux.* In this case he employed tactics revealed to his fellow lawyers during the Chicago conference. He broadened the issues, disputed assumptions—including the determination of race—whenever possible, and called among his witnesses scholars qualified to testify on matters of race. The court was not persuaded by Houston's defense of the Hurds. Judge F. Dickinson Letts ruled for the plaintiff, declaring "null and void" the deeds to James and Mary Hurd and revested the title to the premises in question on Bryant Street, Northwest. Raphael Urciolo, the real estate agent, Francis X. Ryan, the former owner, and all people participating with them were permanently enjoined "from renting, leasing, selling, transferring or conveying any of the . . . seven lots to any Negro or colored persons." The Hurds were ordered "to remove themselves and all of their personal belongings from the land and premises now occupied by them." Houston appealed the injunctions ordered by Judge Letts to the U.S. Court of Appeals for the District of Columbia. Raphael Urciolo, also a lawyer, appealed also a second Hodge case, *Urciolo* v. *Hodge*.[6]

Judge Letts had ruled as he did primarily because precedent required it; the Court of Appeals, in May 1947, affirmed the District Court's decisions largely on the basis of precedent in seven cases regarding racially restrictive covenants. Houston publicly condemned the court's decision upholding the private racially discriminatory agreements, declaring it "worse than legislation because a private covenant has no limit and can cover anything and everything to the end of time." As a consequence, Houston maintained, "in every city and every area" where the black population "has any significance" is encirclement by an "invisible wall" which crowds black people "into a ghetto." Further, Houston carefully noted that judicial enforcement of the private agreements throughout the nation revealed the problem to be "not simply the conspiratorious efforts of a few prejudiced individuals but a national policy." As almost a peroration, he affirmed that he was not discouraged by this "temporary defeat." The history of black people was "a record of doing the impossible." Of course he would "fight on."[7] After all, even the Court of Appeals' decision constituted a reason to continue. It could be distinguished from other decisions on such racially restrictive covenants by the dissent of Judge Henry Edgerton on grounds reflecting his persuasion by the briefs and arguments of counsel for the petitioners. Judge Edgerton dissented maintaining generally that "The covenants are void as unreasonable restraints on alienation; they are void because [they are] contrary to public policy; their enforcement by injunction violates the Civil Rights Act." Two special grounds on which Edgerton disssented were, first, "Enforcement of the covenant would defeat its original purpose since Negroes will pay much more than whites for the property and since the neighborhood is no longer white; and [second], the injunctions, against both transfer and occupancy, are broader than the covenant, since the covenant did not forbid use and occupancy."[8]

Seeing that his arguments had been heard by at least one judge, Houston quickly filed a petition for rehearing. It was denied less than a month after the Court of Appeals decision. Out of his obligation to his clients, who were involved in litigation because their need for better shelter and their combined resources compelled them to buy a covenanted home, Houston had filed for the rehearing. It was his duty to "exhaust every effort to win where [he] was and save [his clients] the anxiety and further expense of litigation." Yet the denial of the rehearing meant that Houston could seek certiorari and possibly be heard by the Supreme Court of the United States. Because of the larger issue, the principle at stake, Houston had mixed emotions about the Court of Appeals' denial of this motion. The timing also was an important and favorable factor. *Sipes* v. *McGhee* and *Shelley* v. *Kraemer*, covenant cases from Michigan and Missouri, were to be argued in the U.S. Supreme Court, and there existed now the possibility of argument against both state and federally enforced racially restrictive covenants.[9]

At this stage, Robinson and Houston concentrated on preparation for their most important restrictive covenant argument. After consulting with Raphael Urciolo, a local attorney and realtor, Houston worked in his usual intensive way to prepare *Hurd* v. *Hodge* and *Urciolo* v. *Hodge* as a consolidated case for presentation to the U.S. Supreme Court. "Long hours, incessant toil and meticulous attention to each element of the problem were part of each step." Seeking a writ of certiorari, Houston and Robinson reacquainted themselves with the record in the case and decided what needed to be done, who would do it, and

how to go about doing it. Next came the independent research, analyzing, synthesizing facts, rules, and applicable law, meeting together, and
finally writing. They "worked night and day, weekends, and weekdays."[10] In October 1947 the Supreme Court granted certiorari.

As they began to research, compile data, and examine issues of law
for the brief to be filed in the U.S. Supreme Court, Phineas Indritz, a
white attorney who worked at the Department of the Interior, contacted Houston. Indritz had read Edgerton's dissent in *Hurd* and
wanted to volunteer his services during evening hours. The two met
and talked. Finding themselves in agreement on matters of importance
with respect to the right claimed in the case, Houston enthusiastically
accepted Indritz's offer of assistance. Thereafter, on any weekday until
November 1947, Indritz could be found writing from 6:00 or 6:30 until
midnight so that he would have drafts of portions of the brief ready for
Houston's review the following morning. All three—Houston, Robinson, and Indritz—agreed that *Hurd* v. *Hodge* (and its companion case,
Urciolo v. *Hodge*) required the presentation of substantial social scientific data. Thus, a cadre of social scientists and lawyers came together
to cooperate in the preparation of a "Brandeis brief" for the Supreme
Court. The inclusion of nonlegal material (an approach Louis Brandeis
initiated early in the twentieth century) necessitated collaboration
with economists and sociologists for the development of an appendix
of pertinent scholarly articles. Then, with some attention to docu-
mentary evidence, Houston, Indritz, and Robinson refined their legal
arguments.[11]

Before completing the brief for the Supreme Court, Houston, Indritz, Robinson, and Urciolo joined forty other lawyers, civil libertarians, and social scientists for the second NAACP meeting on "Methods
of Attacking Restrictive Covenants" in New York City on 6 September
1947. Charles Houston chaired this meeting, which had as its central
concerns the clear presentation of issues and anticipation of probable
arguments. Given precedents favoring whites, conferees indicated
that issues of law were being refined in the various states and the District of Columbia, while matters of fact were receiving strict attention,
particularly where there were distinctions to be made. The meeting
eventually came to focus on the sociological data in support of the position of the NAACP lawyers. Thereafter, a special committee was constituted to coordinate the development of the sociological memorandum for use as an appendix to the brief in each covenant case.[12]

In November 1947, Houston, Robinson, Indritz, and Urciolo filed a
consolidated brief for appellees in *Hurd* v. *Hodge* and *Urciolo* v. *Hodge*.
It was a remarkable document containing numerous social scientific

data and an improved, polished legal argument.[13] Conrad Harper has observed that "Hurd, in which Houston's richly comprehensive presentation drew on constitutional, statutory, common law, public policy and social science materials, was [Houston's] most extensively prepared case."[14] The legal argument was clear and direct. Counsel for *Hurd* and *Urciolo* contended that enforcement of racially restrictive covenants in the District of Columbia constituted a violation of public policy, federal law, and the due process clause of the Fifth Amendment to the U.S. Constitution. Houston, with co-counsel, asked the court to address itself to one fundamental issue:

> Shall we in the United States have ghettoes for racial, religious and other minorities, or even exclude such minorities entirely from white areas of our country, by a system of judicially enforced restrictions based on private prejudices and made effective through the use of government authority and power?[15]

Since repeatedly it had been stressed by their opponents that the matter of racially restrictive covenant enforcement in the District had been settled by *Corrigan* v. *Buckley*, the attorneys were deliberate in their attempt to meet this contention head on. The lower court decisions and decisions since 1926 in state courts were based on erroneous assumptions relative to *Corrigan*, they maintained. In *Corrigan* the defendants claimed that the covenant was void. The question of statutory or constitutional propriety of judicial enforcement of a racially restrictive covenant was not raised. Thus, Houston and his co-counsel argued that the court adjudicated with these issues in mind. In response to the brief of the respondents, another brief was filed in January to rebut arguments that enforcement of racially restrictive covenants was consistent with public policy and the constitution.[16]

One of the most important factors in the cases was the cooperation of black lawyers and civil libertarians throughout the nation. The significant result was the filing of *amici curiae* briefs by over twenty organizations, including the American Civil Liberties Union, the American Council on Race Relations, the American Veterans Committee, the American Jewish Committee, the Civil Rights Congress, the National Association for the Advancement of Colored People, and the National Bar Association. Moreover, the weight of the federal government was thrown against the racially restrictive covenants when Attorney General Tom Clark and Solicitor General Philip Perlman filed a 123-page brief that called on the Supreme Court to strike down such agreements. In addition, it was exhilarating to Houston to be the beneficiary of the efforts of lawyers of the National Bar Association, the National

Legal Committee of the NAACP, the NAACP Legal Defense Fund, Inc., and Howard Law School, who had persevered and coordinated their efforts to abolish judicial enforcement of racially restrictive covenants. The cooperation and dedication they displayed was not altogether new. Black lawyers had begun joint civil rights efforts under the impetus of Houston's NAACP–American Fund for Public Service campaign against discrimination in education and found Howard Law School to be a center for serious concentration on civil rights law and precourt analysis of arguments. Therefore, as was customary prior to appearances in the U.S. Supreme Court, the dean of Howard University Law School made the facilities of the law school available to attorneys for the appellants. In this instance, Dean George Marion Johnson arranged a rehearsal. Professors assumed the roles of the nine justices; law school students were participant-observers. During this particular dry run, it is reported that a second-year law student asked a question that was actually raised by Felix Frankfurter when the court heard the oral arguments.[17]

Oral arguments were scheduled for 15 and 16 January 1948. Finally, the Supreme Court was to hear Charles Houston and Phineas Indritz for the District appellants, George Vaughn and Herman Miller for the St. Louis appellants, and Thurgood Marshall and Loren Miller for the Detroit appellants argue against Gerald Seegers, Henry Gilligan, and James Crook for "the right to live anywhere." Three and a half hours before the scheduled noon opening at the court, Mrs. Leon Ransom, wife of Charles Houston's friend, "entered the white marbeled corridor of the Supreme Court building with her crocheting and took up a position outside the door to the main courtroom which seat[ed] 268 persons. By 10:30 A.M., twenty-five others were in line. From then on the line grew steadily until one hundred, mostly [blacks] were in line." Only six justices—Frank Murphy, Felix Frankfurter, Hugo Black, William O. Douglas, Harold Burton, and Chief Justice Fred M. Vinson—filed in to hear the arguments. The chairs of Justice Stanley Reed, Robert Jackson, and Wiley Rutledge remained empty; they had disqualified themselves because of their personal connections with covenanted properties. For Houston "it show[ed] how deep the case cut when one-third of the nation's highest court disqualified itself."[18]

Presenting the first oral argument, U.S. Solicitor General Perlman asked the court to ensure American minorities the freedom to own and live in any subdivision, city, or county of the United States. The government believed it was time to destroy racially restrictive covenants by declaring them contrary to the Constitution and public policy and therefore unenforceable by the judicial branch of the government, whether state or federal. Following Perlman's opening argument on behalf of all the appellants the attorneys of record took the floor. In *Shelley* v. *Kraemer* and *Sipes* v. *McGhee* the appellants' lawyers directed the court's attention to the Fourteenth Amendment and the sociological data on the effect of segregation, while the opposition stressed the rights of private citizens. On behalf of Urciolo and Hurd, Houston and Indritz shared the oral argument. Houston discussed the legal propositions regarding constitutional and statutory violations, first. Thereafter he turned to facts and related information directing the Court's attention to the record. He documented the absence of violence and tension in the neighborhood under discussion and presented sociological data revelant to an understanding of the inequalities and illustrative of the racism inherent in the "right" claimed by the respondents. Phineas Indritz further elucidated the legal position of the petitioners, stressing the meaninglessness of the right to own property without the right to be free from judicially enforced discrimination. Representing the District respondents, Gilligan and Crooks confidently referred the Court to its own precedents and reminded the body that it was not Congress and therefore had no legislative policymaking function or duty. In rebuttal, Houston made a lasting impression on Justice Douglas as, with tremendous energy and incisiveness, Houston stressed that the judicial enforcement of racially discriminatory covenants was incompatible with the rationale for U.S. participation in World War II.[19] (From one perspective it could not be denied that war with Nazi Germany had placed the United States in opposition to fascism and racism abroad.) Putting the weight of the federal government behind the racially discriminatory covenants between private citizens would make racial unity in the United States impossible, Houston warned. He added that the danger to national security was also clear. Then a forthright Houston told the court, "Racism *must* go."[20]

On 3 May 1948 the Supreme Court in unanimous decisions (6–0) ruled against judicial enforcement of racially restrictive covenants. In the opinion for the Court, Chief Justice Vinson declared that the courts could not be used to deny rights of occupancy or ownership on the grounds of race. In the state cases, the Court held that the chief concern of framers of the Fourteenth Amendment to the Constitution was the prevention of deprivation of basic civil and political rights. When the courts of any state function so as to enforce a racially restrictive covenant, they are being used unconstitutionally to the detriment of individual private citizens who are suffering discrimination. In its holdings relative to the District of Columbia cases, the justices did not reach the constitutional issue that Houston, Indritz, Robinson, and

Urciolo had advanced on behalf of appellants. The justices found judicial enforcement of such covenants was improper on statutory grounds and was contrary to public policy. According to the Court, the Civil Rights Act of 1866 (Sec. 1978 of the Revised Statutes), which provides that "all citizens of the United States shall have the same right, in every State and Territory, as is enjoyed by white citizens thereof to inherit, purchase, lease, sell, hold and convey real and personal property," prohibited judicial enforcement of the discriminatory agreements. Furthermore, the Court held that enforcement of the covenants was violative of public policy of the United States as expressed in the Constitution, treaties, federal statutes, and relevant legal precedents.[21] Reversing the decision of the lower Court of Appeals, in conclusion, the Court declared:

> It is not consistent with the public policy of the United States to permit federal courts in the Nation's capital to exercise general equitable powers to compel action denied the state courts where such state action has been held to be violative of the guaranty of the equal protection of the laws. We cannot presume that the public policy of the United States manifests a lesser concern for the protection of such basic rights against discriminatory action of federal courts than against such action taken by the courts of the States.[22]

In a separate concurring opinion, Felix Frankfurter emphasized that Court issuance of injunctions to uphold racially restrictive covenants was primarily a constitutional question. He maintained:

> It cannot be "the exercise of sound judicial discretion" by a federal court to grant relief here asked for when the authorization of such an injunction by the States of the Union violates the Constitution—and violates it, not for any narrow technical reason, but for considerations that touch rights so basic to our society that, after the Civil War, their protection against invasion by the States was safeguarded by the Constitution.[23]

The unanimous rejection of the lower court decisions was a major victory for blacks and civil libertarians in the states and the District of Columbia.[24] For both Houston and Robinson, who had been challenging enforcement of the racially discriminatory covenants throughout the 1940s, the decision reenforced their vision and hopeful struggling. From the outset they had felt certain there would be an eventual victory. Another attack on racist deprivation of the rights of black people was successful, and they could claim another right due them.

The National Bar Association (NBA) paused to recognize Houston's more than a decade of struggle at its twenty-third annual convention:

> In recognition of his scholarly presentation of the issues before the Supreme Court of the United States of America, in the covenant cases

which resulted in a decision marking a notable landmark in the perennial struggle to eradicate every badge and indicium of second class
citizenship, based on race, color or creed. His efforts have added another
rung to the ladder which leads to the recognition of the basic dignity of
man consonant with our democratic ideals.

He has earned the blessings of those who believe in "Equal Justice
Under the Law."[25]

Houston could not be present to receive the citation personally. He
wrote the NBA president, Thurman L. Dodson, to explain that he
would be tied up with litigation and to express his gratitude and regrets. There was no time to stop for praise when so many rights remained unsecured. "The fight for human freedom," Houston knew
well, "[was] interminable."[26]

Since Charles Houston could never find it in himself to be confined
to just one cause or civil rights grievance, while he was pressing the
restrictive covenant cases he became more aggressive in his activities
against segregated recreational activities. He made his antisegregation position no secret. He wrote about the problem in his regular
Afro-American column and spoke about it when he appeared with David Brinkley on an NBC talk show, "America United." It was nothing
less than an indictment of the nation, Houston remarked to Brinkley,
that "on . . . playgrounds which are under the jurisdiction of the Board
of Recreation, the children are separated so long as they are open officially and just as soon as the flag goes down, then all the children of
the neighborhood come together and play."[27] Houston was not alone in
his disgust about segregated recreational facilities, and so with little
difficulty he enlisted the support of friends and civil libertarians in a
test of the Interior Department's policy for the District. On one occasion, Houston—with the help of Gardner L. Bishop, a black barber,
Mae Thompson, wife of Howard University professor of education,
Charles Thompson, and members of the District's interracial clubs—
shocked the Department of Interior and District authorities. They
staged an interracial swim in the department's Anacostia Pool. One
policeman on horseback broke the foot of one of the white young ladies
who had been in the pool with Howard men. When, in response, the
Interior Department ordered the pool closed, Houston asked how the
United States could consider governing a defeated Japan if it couldn't
keep down the commotion around a swimming pool without suspend-
ing operations.[28]

Although Charles Houston, as a result of his own earlier efforts and
those of other District blacks, could sit down and eat a meal in the
downtown Union train station, he found the widespread segregation of
public accommodations particularly galling.[29] White law students and

clerks at lunch recesses could eat anywhere. Houston and his black associates could go from the office or court to the carryout stand of a nearby restaurant, where they could wait for lunch to be prepared and bagged. Benjamin Amos, Houston's former neighbor, then a young lawyer in the Houston firm, vividly recalled lunch on one particular day:

> At that time they had the Executive . . . at the corner of Fifth and F, and we had to go in there and stand by the fountain and watch clerks [of various judges], judges, and other whites belong[ing] to the court go in there, sit down, and eat. We'd have to stand there and take it out. This . . . day, Charlie, I, and a third person . . . got the lunch. We went up to the office, and he got inside and he couldn't stand it. . . . He stood in front of Gloria Young [who was at the switchboard]. . . . She was there with Lucretia Jackson [one of the secretaries] and said, "I just can't take it any longer," and threw the stuff on the floor in the center of the office . . . and burst into tears. [In that] very emotional moment for him he said, "one day, we'll see these streets open and Negroes . . . go anywhere and eat."[30]

Shortly thereafter Houston joined the research team of the National Committee on Segregation in the nation's capital, which had as its task preparation of a report on segregation in Washington, D.C. When completed, the 1948 report of the committee, "Segregation in Washington," attracted attention to heretofore "lost" antidiscrimination statutes of 1872 and 1873. In 1949 a Coordinating Committee for the Enforcement of the District Antidiscrimination Laws was created and the campaign against segregated public accommodations was under way. Houston worked with several lawyers, including a bright young lawyer actively associated with the National Lawyers Guild but formerly associated with his firm, Margaret Haywood. During what developed into six months of work in the Supreme Court library, they researched the question of the validity of nineteenth-century statutes. The final report, which was submitted to the District commissioners in September 1949, was accepted by the District's corporation counsel.[31]

Demanding enforcement was absolutely essential to all who had devoted months to checking the District's statutes. For Charles Houston enforcement was urgent. Time and again personal affronts came simply because of race, and bitterness welled up inside of him. When racism caused dislocations in the life of his child, Houston's bitterness and pain could be almost intolerable. One day Henrietta left little Charlie Jr. with his father while she went for an appointment. Joseph Waddy, little Charlie's godfather and Houston's partner in the firm, recalled

> Charlie had to go to the drugstore for something and he took the boy along. While Charlie was being taken care of, the boy climbed up on a

stool by the soda fountain and the man behind the fountain said to him "Get down from there, you little nigger—you got no business here." When they got back to the office, we had to take Charlie into the back room and give him a sedative.[32]

Pushing enforcement of the antisegregation statutes was one response to this kind of vicious and insipid racism, while direct action was one of the most appealing means.

Mary Church Terrell, a nationally respected leader of civil rights causes and wife of Judge Robert Terrell, as titular head of the Coordinating Committee for the Enforcement of the District Antidiscrimination Laws arranged and led an organized protest, while Houston, Haywood, and James Cobb of the Lawyers Guild District Affairs Committee developed a legal strategy. This was most gratifying work for Charles Houston, who, seeing the mass-supported movement and the cooperation of lawyers, knew victory was at hand.[33]

As Charles Houston went about the performance of his duties relative to creating a nondiscriminatory Washington, D.C., he maintained his association with the nation's important training ground for black lawyers, Howard Law School. After James Nabrit, Jr. developed the first formal civil rights course, Houston occasionally taught that subject, and "Code Pleading." In his lectures, informal conferences, and through an academic scholarship offered in his father's honor, Houston continued to encourage students to aspire to be social engineers.[34] His service to Howard was appreciatively noted in a letter from President Mordecai Johnson to Charles Houston later in his career.

> The assembled guests at the Charter Day Dinner voted unanimously to have me write, expressing to you their esteem and affection for the great service you have rendered to Howard . . . in building up the new School of Law— . . . reference had been made in one of the addresses to your pioneer efforts in this regard—and for the rich fruitage of gain in the field of Civil Rights which has come through the Law School and through your own personal efforts. . . . The vote asking me to convey this message was not only unanimous but was given with standing enthusiasm.[35]

Not only the Howard University community held Charles Houston in high esteem for his civil rights work. This was made clear time after time in the 1940s. In 1947, when Charles S. Johnson was inaugurated the first black president of the celebrated Fisk University, Houston was awarded an honorary doctor of laws. It was a moving experience for Houston personally. Yet on this occasion he stressed the struggle, not his accomplishments. "To me the most significant thing in Fisk awarding me an honorary degree for the fight on civil rights," declared Houston, "is the notice that it serves on the country that we are determined to get our rights."[36] Other honors came to Houston between 1942 and 1949. Charles Houston was endorsed by influential District Democrats for appointment to one of the judgeships on the bench of the newly created District court, supported by various citizens groups for appointment to the U.S. Supreme Court vacancy created by the death of Frank Murphy, and twice drafted by District residents who sought Truman's consideration of a black nominee for a District commissioner.[37]

Ironically, it was in a sense because of the 1947 abortive attempt to have Houston named District commissioner that the voices of numbers of District citizens came to be heard not only in Washington, D.C., but also throughout the nation. The citizens who would seek out Houston would ultimately pursue their cause until segregation in the schools of the District was ruled illegal in May 1954. These voices were the voices of "little people" who were black and cared desperately about the future of their children but were not very "well-fixed" economically. They were black people of the community who "work[ed] two jobs and [went] to church on Sunday." Under the leadership of Gardner L. Bishop, barber and father of fourteen-year-old Judine, these parents came to be known as the Consolidated Parent Group, Incorporated. But when they sought out Charles Houston that December 1947 they were simply very concerned parents whose children were in the Browne Junior High School district.[38] In early December they had begun a protest strike against "parttime education [of their children] at Browne Junior High, a 'colored' school in Northeast, built for 800 students, but jammed with 1,800 while nearby 'white' schools had empty seats in their classrooms."[39] The strike was waning. Discussions with the superintendent of schools, Hobart Corning, and the president of the Board of Education, Mrs. Henry Grattan Doyle, had accomplished nothing. There was still no relief for the children.

Gardner Bishop was as suspicious of "upperclass Negroes" as were the other parents of Browne Junior High students who had gone on strike. Most immediately the parents recalled the beginning of the Browne Junior High fight and the class divisions among parents of children attending and parents who comprised the Browne Junior High PTA. The "handpicked" Browne PTA, according to Bishop, had a membership of property owners in the area, various civic association representatives, parents, and even nonparents. The bulk of the parents whose children actually attended the school felt "passed over," since in most meetings they were ignored when they attended. The Browne PTA litigated *Carr* v. *[Superintendent] Corning* (decided for the defendants in 1948) but it was not "the people's case." The parents of the striking students objected strenuously to the double shift devised by Garnet Wilkinson, first assistant superintendent in charge of the black schools and protested the use of Blow and Webb elementary schools as annexes. Objections were of two types: (1) The elementary school equipment was too small for the junior high students, and there were no labs, shops, libraries, gyms, or auditoriums; and (2) the junior high students from Browne would have to travel excessive distances in areas of considerable traffic. The parents therefore met together in Jones Memorial Church and voted to keep their children out of school until appropriate relief was granted. It was not easy for the parents to turn to Houston for aid, because to their minds he was part and parcel of the upper class of blacks who had shown no understanding of, interest in, or sympathy for blacks less fortunate. He was one of the "big people" who as a class, in general, had "hurt" the "little people." Yet Bishop hated to see them carry on the strike so long, "lose the fight and not gain anything." He had heard that Charles Houston supported the cause of full and equal educational opportunities for all children. Bishop was voted permission, by the group, to ask for Houston's assistance. One December evening, Bishop attended a Houston-for-Commissioner rally in a local church and afterward went up to Houston and introduced himself. Houston seemed glad, almost "elated," to meet a representative of the strikers. He asked Bishop to bring the group to his home at 3611 New Hampshire Avenue, Northwest, to discuss the strike. Bishop and nine others gathered at Houston's home and explained the situation. Despite the lack of funds, the forces against them, and the unpopularity of the strike, Bishop recalled that Houston had a simple, straightforward response: "You got yourself a lawyer."[40]

Houston took the position that school officials were guilty of not providing adequate educational facilities for black children, and further of defrauding the people of the District since the administration claimed black children received the same education in one-half day as whites received in a full day. He and Bishop prepared letters and press releases stating their position and announcing that the Board of Education would be sued for damages. The parents became the Consolidated Parent Group and adopted as their motto "To Give the Child a Fair Chance." In the years following, Houston pressed cases for the parents—*Bishop et al.* v. *Doyle et al.*, *Gregg et al.* v. *Sharpe et al.* and *Haley et al.* v. *Sharpe et al.*—in the U.S. District Court for the District of Columbia. Houston worked without compensation and alone, preparing what he believed to be the argument most apt to bring a favorable ruling as quickly as possible for the parents—that is, a finding of the denial of equality of educational facilities and opportunities—while simultaneously expressing a preference for a forthright fight for desegregation.[41] When the work became too much for Houston alone,

Harry Merican (whom Houston had met during his work on the restrictive covenant cases) was retained on Houston's recommendation by the Parent Group. Together they refined briefs, amended complaints, took depositions, and researched the many facets of the District's dual school system in order to assure that the Consolidated Parent Group's position could be clearly and accurately presented. In preparing depositions ordered by the courts, the Parent Group had the professional assistance of members of the Howard University community who for some time had been participating in civil rights activities. Among these Howardites were Dean Joseph Johnson of the Medical School, Dean Charles Thompson of the School of Education, Professors James Nabrit, Jr., and Ellis Knox. Houston's firm aided the younger Houston whenever possible. This team gathered data to support and improve arguments of law.[42]

Houston "never let up; . . . never backed down; . . . never ceased working and . . . never accepted a penny."[43] Bishop recalled that Houston "personally paid the filing fee for all the cases."[44] He did this because "the fight for equal education concerns me as a citizen and as a parent," Houston told the Browne Junior High School parents. "I want nothing for my services, but I am in it to the end."[45] It was as if he and the Consolidated Parent Group were one; there was more than an attorney–client relationship.

Nearly consumed by this struggle, in every available moment he sought new ways to draw attention to the inequalities and injustices of segregated schools and recreational areas in the District and to gain support for the Parent Group's fight. In 1948 Houston, with the Consolidated Parent Group leadership—Gardner Bishop (president), Marie W. Smith and Burma Whitted (vice-presidents), Unity T. Macklin (secretary), and James Haley, Sr. (treasurer)—conducted a campaign for desegregation of recreational areas, held open hearings on depositions regarding the black schools, and through mass complaints compelled the administration to reduce the teachers' loads and survey the District public schools. Finally, the Consolidated Parent Group filed suits for relief of black children excluded from kindergarten, overcrowded in Cardozo High School, and suffering from inadequate facilities and unequal opportunities in the dual system. Support came from Houston's friends who were economically better off than the parents of Consolidated Parent Group. Edward and Jewel Mazique, Kline and Charlotte Price, James and Dorothy Porter, Charles and Mae Thompson (District physicians and professors at Howard University and their wives). They not only made financial contributions to the Consolidated Parent Group's cases, but also encouraged organizations to which they belonged or with which they had contact—Jack and Jill, the Oldest Inhabitants, Alpha Phi Alpha, National Council of Negro Women, and Omega Psi Phi—to support the parents. Despite class differences Gardner Bishop viewed as so divisive, the worthiness of the cause created a certain unity in this struggle.[46]

The Report of a Survey of the Public Schools of the District of Columbia, by George D. Strayer, for which the parents and other citizens had pressured the District Board of Education, appeared in February 1949. It admitted the inequalities but offered no immediate relief or solutions to be effected before 1952. Bishop and Houston discussed the report and the entire situation. They were both fathers and had lived through some difficult times because of racial discrimination. Were the parents ready to deal with getting rid of segregated schools? Bishop's reply to Houston was direct: "We are ready." The families could handle "integration" of the schools, and would, because they wanted a "fair chance" for their children.[47] A special article for the local press, "Suffer Little Tots Don't Come Near Me," assailed the evils of the dual system as exposed by the Strayer Report. Houston declared that the black child never has a fair chance in the segregated system. Citing gross inequities in the areas of kindergarten opportunities, classroom space and facilities, and teacher-student ratios, Houston condemned school officials who have made and make no "vigorous fight" to see that the black child "gets an equal chance for education" and accused them of being more concerned with saving their jobs in the dual setup than building community support for at least "an equal start" for black children.[48]

Throughout all this Henrietta Houston could not help but be deeply disturbed and wonder how her husband could be so consumed by this fight for the District's black children and for people he hardly knew or would never know personally; it even intruded into his time for Bo, his son. It frequently left him little time for her. The office, the court, the library—work seemed never to end. So often she heard him say, "The test of character is the amount of strain it can bear." She understood that her husband had defined personal integrity in terms related to the struggle for freedom of his people and in terms of promoting a morality higher than America's existing laws. From Henrietta Houston's standpoint there seemed to be a "force" that compelled her "Charlie" to "champion . . . human rights." She understood also that he did what he did and all that he did to ensure equitable changes and to improve the conditions under which black people lived.[49] Despite having given up her work as a legal secretary to be a wife and mother, Henrietta felt she was coping well. Besides, it was not as if they had no time together.

There were parades and special outings for Bo. Occasionally getting away to Ben Amos's cottage in Pleasantville, New Jersey, or to Hampton, Virginia, became the only moments for the three Houstons. Henrietta pondered these things during evenings when she sat alone in her New Hampshire Avenue home waiting for her husband to return from 615 F Street, the Supreme Court library, or Howard. Appropriating all her changing fortunes, she accepted quietly the necessity of watching their son at the dining room table restlessly draw a figure and then inquire about his father's return so that he could look at Bo's art work from Georgetown Day School and an evening of drawing. She could not help but have mixed emotions.[50] Nevertheless, emotions would not change her having a husband who absolutely believed there was "No tea for the feeble, No crepe for the dead."[51] It was an uneasy reality because Henrietta's life revolved around her two men, but her husband refused to stop pushing himself. He was straining to his limit constantly. And all this was related to his refusal to give up the right to assert his human dignity and that of all other black Americans. There were inalienable rights, and by definition they could not be yielded; there was, then, as he argued it, at the center, struggle where there could be no compromise.[52]

Yet human beings can bear up under only so much strain. Charles Houston knew this: "Rest is what I need, but there is too much to do in such a short time," he told his wife.[53] Charles Houston continued to work his normal fourteen- to eighteen-hour days. Ordering out for sandwiches instead of eating balanced meals had become customary. Going back and forth between New York City and Washington, D.C., to meet with Marshall and the NAACP lawyers, traveling to try cases for which he was chief counsel, maintaining the ordinary paperwork of his private practice, going out on picket lines in Washington, strategizing with the black railroad workers and the Consolidated Parent Group, writing his *Afro-American* column, teaching at Howard and trying to fulfill professional obligations to the Washington Bar Association, National Bar Association, and the National Lawyers Guild, while still being concerned about being a reasonably attentive husband, father, and son took an enormous toll on Houston.[54] In addition, there always seemed to be one more important matter to which he must attend. It is ironic that one concern was health services for black people of the District of Columbia. If there were a problem touching on the welfare of black Washingtonians and their health, Houston would get out of even his sickbed to perform a needed service. Anna Hedgeman remembered that on one occasion she called Houston, unaware that he was not well. In her capacity as assistant to Oscar Ewing of the Department of Health, Education, and Welfare, she had run into a problem with aid for Freedmen's Hospital. Houston "was half-ill and it was a rainy day." Nevertheless, for a meeting with the surgeon general and his staff regarding congressional appropriations for Freedmen's, Houston "came out" and spoke so cogently and forcefully that he "turned the tide in favor of Freedmen's Hospital."[55]

During the fall of 1949 Houston was doing more but feeling less energetic. His resistance was low and he was not as strong as he once had been or wished to be. Nevertheless there was, after all, "no tea for the feeble." He just kept going. In October, pains in his chest sometimes caught him off guard and made him sit down. However sharp they were, they soon subsided, and he would return to his meeting schedule, his work with clients, or his fifty-word-per-minute "pecking" at the typewriter to ensure that a complaint got to its destination on time. Yet it was not long before one sharp pain stopped his routine altogether and, after a short drive home, sent Charles Houston back to bed, asking that Henrietta call "Eddie" Mazique, the family's physician. "I was called in my office," Dr. Mazique remembered. "I went to visit him in his home on New Hampshire Avenue. . . . I got there. He had symptoms of heart disease." The electrocardiogram substantiated a diagnosis of acute myocardial infarction once Charles was in the hospital. Dr. Mazique ordered that Charles Houston be confined to Freedmen's Hospital and Charles—who so adamantly believed in strength and struggle—lay helpless in his hospital bed.[56]

CHAPTER XIII

"In Any Fight, Some Fall"

Although Charles Houston's activities between 1945 and 1949 on behalf of black Americans in the District of Columbia were many and demanding, the grueling pace that led to his heart attack and hospitalization was not the result of these activities alone. As a lawyer-publicist, Houston concerned himself with and addressed himself to the major civil rights issues throughout the nation. Affiliating himself with professional, race betterment, and race relations organizations, ad hoc committees, and the black press, Charles Houston fought against racial discrimination.

As early as 1934 he had assailed forces responsible for segregation in the armed services, and as late as April 1949 he was agitating for more than "token" integration. Having reminded the President's Committee on Civil Rights in 1947 that "if any fight comes between this nation and another, . . . we [blacks] have moved beyond the point where we are going to fight for our own chains," Houston believed it unwise to let the matter rest with the Executive Order of 1948 for desegregation of the armed forces.[1] His past experience with President Truman had taught him an important lesson about persistence and public agitation. With equal zeal he also fought against racially discriminatory treatment of soldiers and minority veterans.[2]

Houston's participation in professional organizations such as the National Bar Association (NBA) and the National Lawyers Guild had greatly increased during the 1940s. Highly respected by his colleagues, Houston served on a number of NBA committees and was chosen to succeed William H. Hastie, Jr., as a vice-president of the National Lawyers Guild in 1949.[3] Houston made a major contribution to the guild when he and W. E. B. Du Bois presented to the national convention papers on the interpretation and enforcement of the Thirteenth,

Fourteenth, and Fifteenth Amendments. Because guild lawyers considered Charles Houston "one of the leading constitutional lawyers in the century," Houston had been selected to supplement Du Bois's study with a reexamination of the amendments in light of recent decisions.[4] Prior to his hospitalization, Houston also accepted membership on the demanding National Lawyers Guild's Committee on Labor Law.[5]

Houston's interest in the guild's labor law committee was in large measure a reflection of his continued concern about protection of the right to work for blacks. Federal protection through an executive agency such as a permanent Fair Employment Practices Commission (FEPC) was crucial, and Houston supported Anna Hedgeman's work with the Council for a Permanent FEPC. In the absence of the executive branch's order for such a commission, however, the redress of grievances through the judicial branch remained an indispensable approach to equal rights and fair treatment in the field of labor. Houston had emphasized in a speech for Charles S. Johnson's Race Relations Institute at Fisk University in 1947 that there existed limited federal protection for black workers. *Smith* v. *Texas* (1914) and *Meyer* v. *Nebraska* (1923) provided that no one could establish a privileged class and give said class a monopoly of work, and also that "liberty" protected by the Fourteenth Amendment included "the right to engage in any of the common occupations of life." As a result of *Hodges* v. *United States* (1906), however, when black workers wanted to register complaints regarding suspected conspiracies by or malicious interference of private citizens, they still had to look to states with no tradition of legal protection, on the one hand, and a history of racism, on the other.[6] This meant, in Houston's view, that there were severe limits on free choice in labor, a fundamental aspect of the rights to "liberty and the pursuit of happiness." In fact, Houston believed, "keeping a man down to certain limited jobs in restricted places is nothing but a refined form of involuntary servitude and . . . lawyers must keep digging until they find a way to make the United States Supreme Court change [the] view [held in *Hodges* v. *United States*]."[7]

Joseph Waddy and Charles Houston, as part of their fight for minority rights in the nation, had accepted the challenge of *Hodges* after *Steele* and *Tunstall*. From 1947 to 1949 they had worked together on behalf of the Association of Colored Railway Trainmen and the International Association of Railway Employees to move beyond the 1944 decision of the Supreme Court. In *James Tillman* v. *St. Louis–San Francisco Railways et al.* they sought to establish the principle that "it is against the law and public policy of the United States to bar employment of an entire group of citizens from a public utility like a railroad, solely because of race, creed, or color."[8] On 25 April 1949 the black unions forced the four brotherhoods to come to court and cancel a 1928 contract in which they compelled the railroad to agree never to hire any more black brakemen or firemen.[9]

In another case against the same railroad, *Simon L. Howard* v. *St. Louis–San Francisco Railway Company*, Houston and Waddy with Victor Packman and Henry Espy pursued subtle questions of law raised by the insufficient notice given train porters relative to the abolition of their positions with the San Francisco Railway Company. They also examined the courts' jurisdiction in regard to agreements between railroads and unions and the relation of court opinions to Railway Adjustment Board decisions. Consistent with Houston's practice of setting precedents in order to create law of fundamental import, the attorneys worked with particular diligence for a favorable opinion.[10]

Following the initiation of the St. Louis–San Francisco Railway cases, Houston and Waddy handled cases for black locomotive firemen in *George Palmer et al.* v. *The Brotherhood of Locomotive Firemen* and *David H. Hinton et al.* v. *Seaboard Air Line Railroad Company et al.* The chief issues were displacement of black workers and conduct of collective bargaining agents hostile to the minority. In these cases and others of the International Association of Railway Employees and the Association of Colored Railway Trainmen and Locomotive Firemen, the principle Houston and Waddy sought to establish was a further extension of *Steele* and *Tunstall*. That principle was "that a railroad union has no right to represent a non-member minority worker unless it gives [him] a chance to elect the officials to conduct the collective bargaining process, to censure and remove them." Houston completed an article for *Crisis* in the fall of 1949 to publicize this legal position and the series of abuses he and Waddy sought to address.[11]

Finally, prior to his hospitalization, Houston argued that it was essential to establish the principle that it was illegal and against public policy to bar the employment of any group on an interstate carrier railroad because of race, color, creed, or national origin because "every principle which they could establish for railroads [could] be applied to every other public utility." Public utilities, he reasoned, were owned privately, but dedicated to the public use and with the knowledge and blessings of the government were virtually monopolistic. Thus, gas, electricity, telephone, telegraph, in addition to airlines and buslines— all industries affecting the public interest—should be compelled by law to operate under the purview of federal nondiscriminatory employment policies.[12]

Houston struggled against the unjust laws and discriminatory interpretations in the courts, but he knew that a pressing need was to have some significant input with respect to law making and some control over lawmakers. For this reason he had supported home rule for the District of Columbia and enlarged educational opportunities for minorities and had vigorously fought disfranchisement.[13]

From his assistance with the Texas white primary cases since the 1930s, to his greater participation in the anti-poll-tax drive of the early 1940s, Charles Houston had sought to involve himself in the battle against black disfranchisement. The right to vote without prohibitive restrictions or stipulations was in Houston's view a fundamental civil liberty. Houston felt so strongly about this that by the 1940s it figured prominently in his thinking when he advocated the commutation of the death sentence given Odell Waller, a black sharecropper convicted of the murder of a white farmer whom he had shot in self-defense. The case had received national attention because of the efforts of the Workers Defense League to appeal the decision of the court. When the appeal was not secured, Waller's case became a *cause célèbre* as a result of the skillful and dedicated work of the league's field secretary, Pauli Murray (a black civil rights and labor activist who would become a nationally known lawyer-writer-educator-priest), and the league's national secretary, Morris Milgram. Waller's case was one that few could ignore. He had not been given a trial by a jury of his peers, because in Virginia the poll tax and its discriminatory use with respect to the formulation of jury lists resulted in unconstitutional exclusion of blacks from juries. Houston supported the letter-writing campaign of the league. Writing to the Governor of Virginia, Colgate W. Darden, Jr., Houston declared, "The issues of civil liberties involved in the Waller case are so fundamental to American democracy that they call for commutation for their own vindication, regardless of the merits of Waller's case as an individual." In the presence of injustice occasioned by disfranchisement of blacks, respect for the legal process could not be unconditionally required or expected.[14]

An investigation by Congressman Charles M. LaFollette of Indiana had encouraged Houston, as chairman of the NAACP's National Legal Committee, to push forward the movement for the expulsion of Mississippi Senator Theodore G. Bilbo, a rabid opponent of the vote for blacks. The campaign against "Bilboism," that is, the "spreading fascist philosophy of racial superiority," had thrust to the fore weighty socioeconomic and political issues of national and international significance. Shortly after the hearings, the National Negro Congress filed with the U.N.'s Economic and Social Council a petition on behalf of black Americans, seeking the assistance of the United Nations "in the struggle to eliminate political, economic, and social discrimination imposed on them in the United States [of America]."[15] The petition was no sooner filed than opponents declared that the treatment of blacks in America was a purely domestic issue and as such not within the purview of the United Nations as presently chartered. Houston felt compelled to expose this fallacious position. In his column "The Highway," Houston wrote regarding the U.N. charter and racism in the United States:

> Article 1 states that one of the purposes of the United Nations is "to achieve international cooperation in solving international problems of an economic, social, cultural or humanitarian character, and in promoting and encouraging respect for human rights and . . . fundamental freedoms for all. . . .
>
> The Economic and Social Council of the United Nations . . . has specifically authorized the Commission on Human Rights to establish a Sub-Commission on the prevention of discrimination on the grounds of race, sex, language or religion." *It may be true that the UN does not have jurisdiction to investigate every lynching . . or denial of the ballot. . . .*
>
> *But where the discrimination and denial of human and civil rights reach a national level, or where the national government either cannot or will not afford protection and redress for local aggressions against colored people, the national policy of the United States . . . becomes involved, and at the national policy level the UN can take jurisdiction and receive the complaints presented by national organizations. A national policy of the United States which permits disfranchisement of colored people in the South is just as much an international issue as the question of free elections in Poland, or the denial of democratic rights in Franco Spain.*[16]

Part of the discrimination on a national level that disturbed Charles Houston most was discrimination that interfered with the education of blacks. He still maintained that exploitation and oppression were directly related to the denial of education and equal opportunities. He continued the battle for enlarged educational opportunities in conjunction with the NAACP and the NAACP Legal Defense and Educational Fund, Inc. (the Inc. Fund). Houston was chairman of the National Legal Committee and a member of the NAACP's board of directors.[17] His most satisfying work, however, was advising the lawyers of the NAACP's Legal Defense Fund as they built on the foundation of *Gaines*.[18]

The NAACP's lawyers and the Inc. Fund lawyers were "one and the same."[19] The Inc. Fund had been separately incorporated to facilitate tax-exempt contributions as of 1939. The NAACP, however, sometimes paid the salaries of Inc. Fund lawyers, especially Marshall's (who was occasionally needed to represent the NAACP) and the two organizations "spoke with one voice."[20] (In fact, there was virtually "no separation until 1956," when the tax-exempt status of the Inc. Fund was in jeopardy.[21]) Charles Houston wrote and talked with Marshall frequently. He also "met . . . fairly regularly" with the [NAACP's] Board."[22] After Houston successfully argued *Steele* in the U.S. Supreme Court, he met on weekends with Marshall and sometimes the entire staff to discuss matters of tactics and strategy, such as what to include in complaints, cases on which to focus, and witnesses to be used in cases. Houston was looked to for the best advice (as was Hastie, when there was no conflict of interest growing out of his positions in the government), and if it could be avoided, "Thurgood . . . didn't make any moves without [either] Houston [or] Hastie."[23] During most New York trips Houston was too busy and too serious about problems presented by the cases to spend any time socializing, but once Houston brought Henrietta and Charlie Jr. to the Inc. Fund and NAACP offices and took time out from his consultations to introduce his family to staff members. Houston had to earn an independent living by means of his private practice, but he was as anxious as Marshall and his first assistant, Robert L. Carter, to push the NAACP's legal campaign to achieve its original goal—the elimination of legal segregation. Despite the eventually prohibitive costs of separate and equal facilities, racist southerners were determined to resist at all costs. It seemed the better part of wisdom to take full advantage of the *Gaines* decision and the increasing militancy of the post–World War II black population. Marshall, Carter, and other staff members saw no compelling reason to wait for segregation to topple under its own weight.[24] Carter regularly argued that it was time to attack the *Plessy* doctrine of "separate but equal." Charles Houston looked at how far the NAACP had come since 1935 and heartily supported a direct attack on segregation both in the NAACP–Inc. Fund meetings and in public.[25] A 1947 article in the *Afro-American* included Houston's affirmation of the escalated struggle. "The NAACP lawyers in order to get the campaign underway accepted the doctrine that the state could segregate . . . provided equal accommodations were afforded. . . . Now the NAACP is making a direct, open, all-out fight against segregation. . . . There is no such thing as 'separate but equal.' Segregation itself imports inequality."[26]

Thurgood Marshall depended on Houston not only for advice and counsel. Sometimes the demands of the Inc. Fund's caseload were such that Houston was needed to litigate at the trial level and teach by example. *McCready* v. *Byrd*, the suit of Esther McCready for admission to the University of Maryland's school of nursing, was a case in point. Constance Baker Motley, Chief Judge of the United States District Court in New York, recalls that she came in 1945 to the Inc. Fund to work as a clerk but found the work and the cause so much to her liking that she stayed on as a staff lawyer. Before she was permitted to argue an Inc. Fund case, however, Marshall directed her to go to Baltimore, where "Charlie Houston" was chief counsel in *McCready*, and "watch the case being tried." This man who "could design strategy" and whom "everyone regarded as a legal scholar" was considered by most the "best trial lawyer—white or black." "Forceful but not . . . flamboyant," Charles Houston handled this case so that it could be readily appealed. As was his custom, he had a notebook in hand "with every question written out."[27] When his heart condition forced him to turn the case over to Marshall, Houston left an impeccable record, and all that remained was for Marshall to handle what black lawyers always encountered, any racist chicanery of opposing counsel.

By 1948 a more solid foundation was laid when the U.S. Supreme Court handed down its opinion that Oklahoma must not only provide Ada Sipuel with a legal education but also "provide it as soon as it does for applicants of any other group."[28] Charles Houston was also available to advise on and participate in cases concerning other matters of racial discrimination such as voting rights (*Rice* v. *Elmore*) and public transportation (*Morgan* v. *Virginia* and *Boynton* v. *Virginia*). After the restrictive covenant cases and the *Sipuel* victory against Oklahoma, however, Houston participated primarily in the higher education cases, such as *McCready*, *Sweatt* v. *Painter*, and *McLaurin* v. *Oklahoma State Regents*, as time and energy permitted.[29]

By August 1949, when Houston had first begun to feel that something other than fatigue was a problem, he had not confided in Henrietta but he had made a firm decision. He had coordinated programs and assisted with NAACP litigation for nearly fifteen years. Houston knew that he had dangerously overextended himself. With no regrets, Houston wrote to assure Robert L. Carter, First Assistant Special Counsel: "These education cases are now tight sufficiently so that anyone familiar with the course of the decisions should be able to guide the cases through. You and Thurgood can proceed without any fear of crossing any plans I might have."[30] (By mid-1950 the NAACP and its Inc. Fund won two more Supreme Court victories in *Sweatt* v. *Painter* and *McLaurin* v. *Oklahoma State Regents*, providing—as Houston had planned—a foundation of precedents beginning with *Missouri ex rel Gaines* v. *Canada* to eviscerate the "separate but equal" doctrine of *Plessy* v. *Ferguson* and to "re-interpret equal protection under the fourteenth amendment." The NAACP's victory of 1954 in *Brown* v.

Board of Education was simultaneously the culmination of the legal campaign based on Charles Houston's modified strategy carried forward by the NAACP's cadre of lawyers and a watershed decision in constitutional law with respect to equal protection of the laws.)[31]

Charles Houston's concept of the larger struggle for human rights and freedom was not limited to African Americans in the United States any more than his efforts were limited to NAACP work. Stress and strain that led to his heart disease were also the result of his saying "yes" to involvement in international causes. His affiliation with the Council on Inter-American Relations and the American Continental Congress for World Peace reflected his strong interest in pan-American affairs. Regarding Latin America, for example, Charles Houston in 1941 was a member of the advisory board of the Council on Inter-American Relations. In 1946 he wrote an open letter protesting U.S. economic imperialism in Bolivia as part of his constant criticism of U.S. policies in Bolivia, Cuba, Mexico, and Panama. In addition, by the late 1940s Houston was in correspondence with leaders of the American Continental Congress for World Peace. Maintaining an active interest in African affairs during the 1930s, Houston called on the NAACP to picket the Italian embassy in protest of the war against Ethiopia, and he challenged the National Education Association to include in its manual a discussion of the realities of African colonization. In the 1940s he condemned the use of black troops in Africa and the imperialist roles of European nations and the United States on the continent of Africa. Houston held membership in various African support organizations, including American Aid for Ethiopia, the Committee for the American Celebration of the One Hundredth Anniversary of Liberia, and the African Affairs Council. Through his *Afro-American* column he called for self-determination in the colonized areas of Africa. These associations and political preferences were indicative of a persistent, pro-African liberation and independence activism.[32]

Similarly, Houston's *Afro-American* column became a vehicle for relentless protest against racism, economic exploitation, and oppression not only in America but also in Africa and Asia. With regularity he focused on the relationships among the struggles for liberation on these continents for, as he revealed later in 1949, "the important thing" he wanted to stress was "the international aspect of the struggle for freedom."[33] Thus, under the column titles "The Highway," "Along the Highway," and "Our Civil Rights" he discussed such issues as the elimination of all segregation, anti-Semitism, and racism, the success of Asian movements against Western imperialism with its implications for "white supremacy," and U.S. alignment with colonial powers against the legitimate aspirations of Africans and a growing bloc of non-white nations intent upon shifting the balance of power in the world and bringing freedom to greater numbers of people.[34]

When Houston emphasized the international nature of the struggle, he also proposed a role of leadership for African American people. On one occasion he had written, "We have to save the United States to save ourselves" and "the present American leadership is . . . incapable of leading the United States toward [the] brotherhood" necessary for a democratic society. Moreover, he called for leadership in the world because "our three hundred years of suffering and trials have purged us of arrogance, given a patience and taught us how to get along with peoples of every race and every land."[35] In Houston's view, black people in the United States had a "spiritual responsibility to lead . . . white United States brethren into the real fellowship of nations." Addressing the black readers of his column, he reminded them, "We have suffered and are still suffering so much that we are instinctively sympathetic with any person or nation . . . faced with oppression. We do not come with armies, navies or planes; we look for footholds rather than beach-heads. . . . Because our past is clean we can carry it into our future."[36] Indispensable to that future, according to Houston, was freedom. Thus, an inevitable part of the future of black people was the "fight for freedom" since, as Langston Hughes poetically admonished, "Freedom ain't freedom if a man ain't free."[37]

Spending himself in the outward struggle did not by itself lead to Charles Houston's confinement in Freedmen's Hospital. Both a personal tragedy and the stress and strain of an inward struggle he waged took their toll. Restricted to his bed, Charles reflected on the death of his mother and the issues he had been compelled to confront as the government's Red-baiting and surveillance of its critics worsened with dangerous consequences.[38]

In May 1947, Charles Houston's mother had died. In some ways it was a desolating event, and Charles suffered an enormous sense of loss. Although she had been losing strength for nearly seven years, Charles had not really prepared himself to let go. He was devoted to his mother. She had always been intimately acquainted with every aspect of his being no matter how pedestrian or crucial. And because of her all-encompassing love she was also part of his becoming. Almost as difficult to handle had been Charles's father's reaction. When Mary Houston died, her husband felt that "the light went out of [his] life." This ambitious man, energetic beyond his seventy-six years, had, he insisted, "little or no interest in life."[39] He was troubled (because he had not always demonstrated his deep feeling) and grieving. Charles suffered too, from William's grief. Charles considered himself responsible for a wife, a son, and a seventy-six-year-old father. For that reason and his position of greater responsibility in the Houston law firm, Charles Houston was forced to weigh more carefully all decisions relative to the use of his time and energies for causes.[40]

Charles Houston had an impressive record of support of the civil liberties of citizens who criticized the government of the United States. Houston and Abraham Isserman for the National Federation for Constitutional Liberties had filed in 1941 an amicus curiae brief urging that "in the interest of protecting democratic rights as guaranteed in the first, fourth and fifth amendments of the Constitution, the indictments against Albert Blumberg, Thomas O'Dea and Philip Frankeld, Communist Party officials charged with contempt of the Dies Committee, be dismissed.[41] The concern in *United States* v. *Albert Blumberg* was "the protection of . . . constitutional rights whenever and wherever they are properly asserted."[42] The denial of constitutional liberties was the issue when Charles Houston, in 1943, volunteered his services to William Pickens and Mary McLeod Bethune in defense against the Dies Committee's charges of subversive activities and worked particularly in Mrs. Bethune's behalf. He advised the press that he wanted to do all he could "to head off the apparent drive to frighten all colored leaders into silence." He insisted, "One should not have to denounce the Communist Party just to clear [oneself] of unfounded charges . . . because we cannot deny that the Communists have done us great service."[43]

His efforts against congressional committees and for radical spokespersons led him to reflect on the role of Communists in the United States and the Party's relationship to blacks. In the same year, 1943, Houston refused to endorse an American Civil Liberties Union resolution that was unfair, from his perspective, in its condemnation of the Communist Party. His response was revealing:

> I must say in fairness that the Communists are working in many fields of special interest to me: anti-lynching, anti-poll tax, anti-segregation, integration of Negroes in the labor movement, etc. I appreciate their activities, and I believe that in many ways their work will bring about a broader base of democratic participation by the common people, although the pattern which our economic structure may take may be foreign to their design.[44]

In July 1943, following Doxey Wilkerson's decision to join the Communist Party, Houston wrote Etta Moten Barnett:

> Doxey's move was entirely logical. He was marked as a progressive. . . . There [was] only one thing to do; keep going forward. . . . I think it will

do much good because it shows that some Negroes regardless of position are willing to stake all for principle. He has not lost any of his friends . . . and he has made a lot of people re-examine their own convictions and position to find out whether they are cowardly for material advantages. . . . Maybe he is very smart, just a little ahead of his time as all true leaders are.[45]

In April 1947, Charles Houston with W. E. B. Du Bois, Benjamin Mays, Paul Robeson, Mary Church Terrell, and others had come out forthrightly against Secretary of Labor Lewis B. Schwellenbach's proposal to outlaw the Communist Party in the United States. "Conditions must be much worse internationally than the President has told us or else a large part of his tub thumping against Communism is an attempt on the part of the federal government to divert attention from its own lack of program," Houston wrote in his *Afro-American* column.[46]

Having strong convictions about civil liberties for all citizens, Houston had been pleased to be retained in the "Hollywood contempt trial" of Dalton Trumbo, novelist, editor, and Hollywood director, in 1948. When several Hollywood authors, directors, producers, and stars were commanded to appear before the House Un-American Activities Committee in Washington on 23 September 1947, Houston was familiar with the issues. In a November *Afro-American* column, he condemned the "smear campaign to . . . drive all independence of thought from the screen" conducted by the House Un-American Activities Committee.

> If the Committee is able to stifle independence on the screen, it will move on to radio, to newspapers, and periodicals, to books, to the Sunday pulpit, and even to private conversations in the home. . . . I do not trust the House Committee on Un-American Activities Committee and will not trust it until it investigates lynching, disfranchisement, segregation and discrimination.

He praised the Communist Party for its litigation challenging the legality of the House Un-American Activities Committee, and despite attacks on his position he called for an NAACP amicus curiae brief in the cases of John Lawson, an author and first president of the Screen Writers Guild, and Dalton Trumbo.[47] As a consequence of this and his continued activism in the civil rights struggle, Houston, for a time, seemed to be under surveillance. According to a friend and colleague in the firm, Houston was followed by police. Both the Communist Party and the NAACP were considered "subversive" by authorities.[48] As another consequence of Houston's representation of Trumbo and Lawson, Houston was asked to consider being an attorney for the Party. There were no written communications or negotiations. The matter never went very far. Houston refused to become counsel for the Party because he did not "advocate the overthrow of the United States government." "We first," he believed, "must learn how to reverse the laws that are directed against us in the name of law and order."[49]

Despite a courageous record of independent activity on behalf of radicals and radical or minority rights' causes, later in 1948 when Charles Houston was asked to assist other lawyers without fee in the defense of Communist Party leaders, he felt unable to volunteer his services to the twelve indicted under the Smith Act. It was a difficult decision, but he wrote Cedric Dover,

> I shall not be associated in the trial of the 12 communists as the Civil Rights Congress had decided that it cannot meet the fee which I asked. I was compelled to ask a fee because the trial would mean being out of the office for about 4 months and there are, presently, 3 persons . . . and after January there will be 4, whose living is dependent upon my work. If I were so situated I would donate my services, but I cannot.[50]

Charles Houston had agonized over the letter to Dover. He had not been accustomed to turning his back on just causes or respected colleagues. William Patterson was a leader of the Civil Rights Congress and Benjamin J. Davis, Jr., prominent New York City politician and black Communist, was among those indicted. Indictments under the Smith Act for conspiracy to overthrow or advocate overthrow of the U.S. government represented clear violations of the civil liberties of the twelve communists. Although he could not find it within his capabilities to work on the case without compensation, Houston wrote a strong statement for the press prior to mailing the Dover letter. In it he explained that he believed the indicted members of the Communist Party were coming to trial merely for being members. As he saw it, the trial "involves fundamental rights of freedom of political association, freedom of speech, the right to a free ballot, and . . . the right to agitate for a change in the form of government itself, if the people so will." He continued his statement, insisting that the government was engaging in political prosecution and that "if the government can prosecute Communists not because of what they have actually done, but because of what the government is afraid they may do at some future, indefinite date, the government can also prosecute us for fighting against segregation . . . or agitating for mixed schools." He stressed, in conclusion, "The only way I can make sure of my own liberty of action and freedom to agitate for what I believe to be right, is to fight for the liberty of action and freedom to agitate for every man."[51]

In the same vein, despite U.S. paranoia about Communists—"Reds"—in 1948, Houston was outspoken in defense of others who criticized the United States and were consequently labeled "unAmerican." Houston restated and affirmed the position of Paul Robeson, re-nowned singer, actor, and opponent of racism and injustice, when he was under attack for his testimony before the Senate Judiciary Committee. In his testimony he emphasized the lack of progress for blacks in the United States with respect to freedom and equality and made an unfavorable comparison of the United States with the Union of the Soviet Socialist Republics, to which he had traveled. Houston wrote in the *Afro-American*: "For [Blacks] there is no liberty in the United States. . . . [They] have to fight bitterly for all those rights which white Americans take for granted. . . . Segregation has to go the way chattel slavery went and go soon."[52]

In 1949, Charles Houston's father's assumption of more duties as senior member of the firm and the work of young lawyers there freed Houston to do more than just publicize the injustice involved in the case against the Communist Party members. During the October term of the Supreme Court, with attorneys George W. Crockett, Jr., Richard Gladstein, Abraham Isserman, Louis F. McCabe, Harry Sacher, Paul Kern, and Walter F. Dodd, Charles Houston filed a petition for writ of certiorari on behalf of Gus Hall and Henry Winston.[53] In that same year, less than a month before his heart attack, Houston joined other members of the National Lawyers Guild, Clifford Durr, Herbert Thatcher, Belford V. Lawson, and Martin Popper, to confer with Attorney General Tom Clark regarding the survey instituted by Clark to check subversive influences on lawyers and evaluate their fitness to practice law. These lawyers declared in a prepared statement for the attorney general,

> By no conceivable constitutional or statutory authority does it come within the purview of the functions of the Department of Justice to make policy as to permissible political views and opinions of attorneys as such. The right of a lawyer to hold such views as he sees fit on political, economic and social subjects, is as absolute as that of any American.

Prompted by concerns relative to thought-control, confidentiality, liberty, and due process, Houston and the others "earnestly urged that [Clark] . . . discontinue any investigation that may have been instituted under . . . [his] directions."[54]

With litigation pending and restriction of the freedom of attorneys being threatened, it was difficult for Houston to rest, even in the hospital. Yet Charles Houston's confinement to Freedmen's did provide the atmosphere and opportunity for his winding down. Unfortunately his hospitalization had the opposite effect on his family. As a result of the "strain of his illness and the increased burden it threw on his wife," Henrietta Houston was hospitalized in November.[55] Little Charlie spent the remaining days of 1949 moving from place to place. He lived for the greatest periods of time with Dr. and Mrs. Mazique ("Uncle" Eddie and "Aunt" Jewell) and Dr. and Mrs. Ulysses Houston, his father's brother and sister-in-law. Meanwhile Dr. Mazique treated Charles Houston's heart condition.[56]

As for Charles, the seriousness of the illness and his wife's hospitalization made him apprehensive about his son's future. At five years of age little Charlie was so vulnerable and dependent. Charles decided he must recuperate as quickly as possible, and through sheer strength of will and careful attention to Dr. Mazique, "Charlie did well."[57] In December 1949, Charles Houston was released from the hospital. He moved into the Maziques' home. Edward Mazique, friend, second godfather to Bo (Charlie's only child), and a doctor in whom Charles had complete confidence, could more easily see that his discharged patient followed medication and rest orders with the two Charles Houstons living in his home. Charles and his son spent an extraordinary Christmas season together at the Maziques. There were few presents. Charles had neither energy nor opportunity to select and purchase any gifts from the District stores. But he had something for his friends and his son. He presented to Edward and Jewell Mazique, and asked them to save for his son, a large poster of an open-air Scottsboro protest meeting in Amsterdam. The Maziques were so touched that it was difficult to respond. The poster had been one of Charles's most important possessions. Edward Mazique simply asked Charles if there were thoughts or recollections he wanted to share with them and Bo. Charles Houston decided that he wanted to have a tape recorder so he could leave a message for his son and others to hear in later years. Jewell and Edward Mazique found their recorder and Edward introduced the tape: "Charlie, I know there are things on your mind that you would like to interpret . . . begin please . . . your interpretation [of the] significance of this."

"There's a long history . . . ," Houston began what became a lengthy message. He told the Scottsboro story and expressed his views about Scottsboro—its domestic and international significance. He recounted experiences and spoke of meanings in broad terms. "[Since Scottsboro] you have seen . . . the movement of the great masses of the people. And . . . it is necessary to establish the principle of the indivisibility of liberty so that the masses recognize that no matter where liberty is challenged, no matter where oppression lifts its head, it becomes the business of all the masses." He went on to discuss appeals to foreign countries, pan-Africanism, and the liberation of Africa. He touched on the struggle of Native Americans ("Indians"), Mexican-Americans, and migrant workers. He spoke also of the struggle for civil rights and asserted that with respect to written law, he was not worried about black Americans winning civil rights.[58] He was admittedly apprehensive, however, about the future of his people and the conditions under which they would be living even when civil rights became laws on the books under the existing system of government in the United States. He ended his message with some sobering thoughts.

> I am . . . concerned about . . . the fact that the Negro shall not be content simply with demanding an equal share in the existing system. It seems to me that his fundamental responsibility and his historical challenge is to use his weight, since he has less to lose in the present system than anybody else or any other group, to make sure that the system which shall survive in the United States of America—I don't care what system you call it—shall be a system which guarantees justice and freedom for everyone. The way I usually put it is, "Sure we're being invited now in to take a front seat, but there's no particular honor in being invited now in to take a front seat at one's own funeral. . . . When things go wrong, I look up at this picture and then realize . . . that we are fighting a system, that we are trying to remove the lid off of the oppressed peoples everywhere. And also I regard what I am doing and my work as a lawyer not as an end in itself, but simply as the means of a technician probing in the courts, which are products of the existing system, how far the existing system will permit the exercise of freedom before it clamps down. And I have seen several instances as to the limitations on which the existing system as represented by its courts will go. . . . Some day, if things get worse—and I don't see how they can avoid getting worse because we are in a situation where we have got to have an expanding economy and our markets are contracting and we are losing our markets; we are losing the power to exploit colored and other peoples—the struggle for freedom having accomplished itself politically in Asia will soon shift to Africa. So I can't see how we can avoid a crisis. And we've seen enough in the present days to know that the first reaction of the powers that be is going to be silence and oppression, censorship, and others things. They are going to try to cut off the intellectuals from the masses. So that in this day, while there is still little time, the primary task is to probe, to struggle, . . . to teach the masses to think for themselves . . . to know their place and to recognize their power and to apply it intelligently.[59]

After Christmas, Charles Houston returned to his home on New Hampshire Avenue. Shortly thereafter, Charles "got out of bed and went back to work."[60] Charles and his friend Ben Amos worked out a system. Ben took Charlie Jr. to Georgetown Day School and Charles Sr. to the Houston firm every day. There Charles worked on cases for his regular clients and the Consolidated Parent Group for a few hours. (He had asked Thurgood Marshall to take over *McCready* and Marshall had agreed to do so.) Yet even by the time his wife came home, Charles Houston was pessimistic about his recovery. He told his wife that he would prefer that she and Bo go visit her sister in Louisiana. Henrietta wanted to be with her husband, and Charlie Jr. was hoping that the family could be together again. Charles, however, was adamant. He wanted them to go to Louisiana and among other things insisted that "he wanted his son to remember his father as vigorous, impressive, and strong," when he spoke with Henrietta. Yet his close friends knew how much "Charlie" wished he were able to work and have his son with him. Henrietta was going through a terrible ordeal herself, and it seemed that mother and son ought to be together. Perhaps the least selfish thing to do was to let Bo and his mother provide each other with love and comfort. Charles Houston's chest pains came and went, but with time became more constant. He telephoned as often as he could to be in communication with his son and his wife. He knew he would not be at home very long. Eventually, Dr. Mazique had to hospitalize his friend.[61]

As a veteran, Houston was entitled to hospitalization benefits, and Mazique thought that Houston should be in the quietest possible place. Houston was admitted to Bethesda Naval Hospital. Nevertheless, Charles Houston suffered a second heart attack. Although Henrietta was called at her sister's home and told, because of Henrietta's health no one encouraged her to return to Washington, D.C., immediately. In March, at Houston's request, he was moved to Freedmen's Hospital where he could more easily be visited by his partners, friends, colleagues, and his father. Great damage had been done to the heart muscle, but Charles was feeling better.[62] This news made his family and friends less anxious. However much better Charles felt, Dr. Mazique suspected that there were entirely too many visitors because of Freedmen's Hospital's proximity. Charles could disobey his doctor's orders and his father's wishes by having people from the office bring work in for him to do and receiving visitors with business concerns. On one occasion Houston called in Gardner Bishop of the Consolidated Parent Group, Inc. The children must have the fair chance for which the organization had been formed and this was not possible in the dual system of the District of Columbia's public schools, Houston stressed. Although he had maintained this since his term as a Board of Education member in the 1930s, in recent years the inequity had been conclusively demonstrated and the parents had definitely come too far to lose. Houston explained that this period of hospitalization was the result of his second heart attack and, if he survived, he doubted he would practice law. This would affect the education cases. He then came directly to the point of the meeting. Few matters were of greater concern than the future of the children in Washington, D.C. "Ask

Hayes [George E. C. Hayes] to take full charge . . . and ask Nabrit [James M. Nabrit, Jr.] . . . to help him."[63] Go tell "Hayes and Jim Nabrit [that] they owe me and take your case."[64] The meeting had been too strenuous, but Charles Houston rested better after giving Gardner Bishop instructions for the Parent Group.

After Bishop left, Houston returned to a book, which he had gotten from his Aunt Clotill, *Peace of Mind* by Joshua Liebman. Clotill Houston, a devout Christian and member of the Nineteenth Street Baptist Church, had prayed for and with her nephew. His spiritual welfare, however, was something to which she could not entirely attend. Perhaps he thought *Peace of Mind* would help him find exactly that. Charles read it and digested its teachings. When his Aunt Clotill visited him she was delighted that they could talk about the book and other concerns Charles had. He made her promise that if he did not survive this illness she would give *Peace of Mind* to his son Bo. On page forty-eight, Charles Houston had written words he had left unsaid and could not communicate to his son, who was in Louisiana. Just in case, Houston wrote something in the form of an explanation about his life and work—almost epitaphic—for his young son.[65]

With Charles's wife and son in Baton Rouge at the home of Eva Williams Taylor, Henrietta's sister, and Thomas Taylor, Eva's husband, Dr. Mazique decided it best to limit Houston's visitors. Dr. Mazique advised Charles's friends that because of his heart condition Houston could not afford to take lightly any of his physician's orders. Dr. Mazique permitted regular visits from only a few people, primarily William Houston and Joseph Waddy. Numerous cards and bed rest, in addition to the regular visits of Charles's father and his partner, seemed to have a restorative effect. Dr. Mazique was more than pleased to report to Henrietta, Bo, William and Clotill Houston, Joseph Waddy, William Hastie, Jr., and other friends and relatives by early April 1950 that "Charlie [is] doing well." Even Charles felt somewhat optimistic and began to talk about his plans for his future. Some of his most intimate thoughts and concerns he shared with his physician and friend, Eddie Mazique. Then one "beautiful spring day," 22 April, Dr. Mazique went to Ward 3, Room 3, to check on his friend and patient, "Charlie." It was early in the afternoon, one o'clock or close to two. Before his doctor even had a chance to inquire about his patient's health, Charles Houston greeted Mazique, "Hi, Eddie," and asked about his wife, "How's Jewell?" The nurse had just given Charles a bath; he was freshly shaven. Dr. Mazique responded warmly to the greeting and asked Charles how he was feeling. "Oh, I feel fine," Charles replied, "except I just feel like I'm a little bit nauseated. I ate a good breakfast this morning. It'll pass." "Well, let me check it out and fix [some] medication," Mazique told his patient. At that moment, Joseph Waddy appeared at the door of the room. He opened it, took one step in and held up his hand to greet both "Charlie" and "Eddie." As Dr. Mazique recalls, "Charlie saw him come in and he said, 'Hi, Joe.' Those were the last words [Charles Houston] spoke. . . . [H]is hand slumped and he took a deep breath and he was gone as quickly and as suddenly as that."[66]

On 22 April 1950, at 2:15 P.M., Charles Hamilton Houston died of acute coronary thrombosis.[67] Henrietta and their only child, Charles Jr., were called home. Still somewhat in shock, Henrietta took Charles's personal effects. William, close friends, and relatives assisted Henrietta with the funeral arrangements. Cards, calls, and telegrams of condolence and tribute came from such well-known people as Mary McLeod Bethune, Arthur Garfield Hays, Arthur Spingarn, Channing Tobias, and Hubert Humphrey, and people whose names meant little to Henrietta, for they were among the hundreds of clients and District citizens with whom Charles had worked over the years. Even the President— with whom Charles had had such conflict—sent a personal note to Mrs. Charles Houston. Houston would be remembered for his "strength of conviction and strict integrity," wrote Harry Truman.[68]

On 26 April 1950 services to celebrate the life and work of Charles Hamilton Houston were held at Howard University's Rankin Chapel.[69] In death as in life, among those paying respect were scores of people whose names the widow and the son did not know but who came because of what "Charlie" Houston had meant to their lives. The press took note of the presence of Supreme Court Justices Tom Clark and Hugo Black, Secretary of the Interior Oscar Chapman, Judges Henry Edgerton, Armond W. Scott, and Nathan Cayton, civil rights activists, Howard University professors, attorneys and friends including Lester Granger, Walter White, Clarence Mitchell, Roy Wilkins, Campbell Johnson, Emmett Scott, Charles H. Thompson, Spottswood W. Robinson, III, Leon Ransom, and Louis T. Wright. Other close friends, former students, and colleagues—Benjamin F. Amos, Joseph Waddy, George Marion Johnson, Thurgood Marshall, Edward P. Lovett, Phineas Indritz, and Oliver W. Hill—served as active pallbearers. The Rev. Mr. A. F. Elmes, who had preached at Mary Houston's funeral, delivered the eulogy at Charles Houston's funeral. William Henry Hastie Jr. read the obituary.[70] Hastie spoke of a life dedicated to "unremitting struggle to win for the Negro full status without discrimination." He described years of civil rights work in which Charles Houston "stopp[ed] only when his body could no longer keep pace with his will and his spirit." Finally he spoke of mourning:

As we grieve, we cannot forget that he believed, perhaps above all else in strength; strength to do and to bear what lesser men would regard as impossible or unbearable. He counted nothing, no physical weakness and not even death itself as an obstacle to the onward sweep of strong men and women in the accomplishment of worthwhile ends. . . . I know he would wish all of us to carry on in that spirit.[71]

The family tried to work off its grief. The book from Charles's hospital bedside, Joshua Liebman's *Peace of Mind*, was set aside. The message for Charles Jr. would be read to him in time.

Tell Bo I did not run out on him but went down fighting that he might have better and broader opportunities than I had without prejudice or bias operating against him, and in any fight some fall.[72]

CONCLUSIONS

Charles Hamilton Houston's commitment to the struggle of African Americans for freedom, justice, and equality presupposed the validity of moral values as determinants in matters of social enterprise both for individuals and for groups. He believed that moral values could overlap with but were distinguishable from legal imperatives. In his sharp rebuke to a staff assistant of President Franklin D. Roosevelt regarding an ill-fated attempt to arrange a meeting on lynching, Houston disclosed a moral posture that informed his civil rights activity and set the tone for his advocacy on behalf of his people.

> We protest that the lives and physical protection of American citizens are just as important as any N[ational] R[ecovery] A[dministration] program ever can be; and that . . . the traditional policy of temporizing with injustice and disrespect of law is to a great extent responsible for the moral collapse and selfishness exhibited in so many quarters today.[1]

When Charles Houston emerged as a man seriously committed to struggle for black people and mingled his intellect, time, and energies with the sacrifices of a host of warrior-ancestors to affect history, he did so on the basis of three moral-jurisprudential principles. One was expressed in his letter to Roosevelt's assistant, namely, that "the law and constituted authority [were] supreme only as they cover[ed] the most humble and forgotten citizen."[2] Two others were infrequently enunciated but consistently revealed in Charles Houston's actions: Human beings, regardless of their differences, were "each equally entitled to life, liberty and the pursuit of happiness";[3] and in a good society, its system of government "guarantees justice and freedom for everyone" while providing for succeeding generations "better and broader opportunities . . . without prejudice or bias operating against [them]."[4]

Charles Houston lived as if a total, irrevocable commitment to the African-American struggle was required by the obvious truth of a racist United States of America. The nation's social structure was, he declared, one in which the place reserved for blacks was "the bottom."[5]

Clearly, "they [we]re not included in the department [of Justice's] slogan 'Justice for all.'"[6] Furthermore, blacks were "economically exploited, politically ignored and socially ostr[a]cized" as a function of private prejudice and public laws, while ruling whites, by design, discriminated against young blacks in education so that they w[ould] be prepare[d] . . . to accept an inferior position in American life."[7] "The discriminations practiced against [blacks were] no accident."[8] What historian Mary Frances Berry persuasively demonstrated in her 1971 study of constitutional racism Houston saw in the 1940s: "The national policy of the United States [was] to deny human and civil rights or not afford protection and redress for local aggressions against [black] people."[9] Houston therefore did not find it shocking that Paul Robeson suggested that the United States compared unfavorably with the Soviet Union in programs for equality and, in defense of Robeson, Houston emphasized that for blacks "there [was] no liberty in the United States," since they had to "fight bitterly for all those rights which white Americans t[ook] for granted."[10]

Charles Houston never considered it sufficient merely to recognize that "the race problem [was] one of the most fundamental . . . in American life."[11] Early in his career he determined that struggle against racial oppression was a necessary response. Houston's life and work demonstrated that he grappled with at least two fundamental questions. First, could a higher standard of living for all people be provided within the framework of capitalism and a constitutional federal republican form of government? Second, could the laws and legal process of the United States be used effectively by black people to aid in promoting and securing fundamental social change to end their oppression and to achieve their rightful places as free and equally protected citizens in the nation? To each question Charles Houston initially gave an affirmative answer. A life of struggle prompted serious questions about black rights in the context of reformist solutions.

Although Houston never hesitated to criticize the economic exploitation of the American capitalist system and called on poor people—black and white—to resist such exploitation, Houston did not see his primary struggle as one against the capitalist system. The more pressing and basic reason to assume a posture of lifelong struggle was the racism of the United States. Throughout his career of public service, Houston refused to be a captive of labels or organizational lines, but sought to identify himself with progressive, antiracist forces to the end that the United States become a better society. Houston was affiliated with the NAACP for most of his adult life, but on matters of importance to blacks he did not indiscriminately reject cooperative struggle with the political Left or succumb to Red-baiting. Vocal and forthright on the issue of the advisability of teaching communism as a philosophy in public schools, he protested the Red-scare tactics of the government. His aversion to the violent overthrow of the government prevented Houston from becoming a salaried lawyer for the Communist Party, but he assisted with cases supported by the political Left and occasionally praised the International Labor Defense (ILD) and Communist Party for their leadership in areas of common interest, such as lynchings, the poll tax, segregation, and defense of indigent blacks accused of crimes. Despite the advice of liberals and the surveillance to which he was subjected, Houston joined other intrepid lawyers to petition the U.S. Supreme Court in *Gus Hall and Henry Winston* v. *United States.* Although his distaste for receiving strategies for the black American struggle by "remote control" from the Soviet Union kept Houston out of the Party, he made a matter of public record his support of the civil liberties of Communists with respect to free speech, the right of political association, and the freedom to agitate for a change in the form of government if so willed by the people.[12]

After his heart attack in the fall of 1949, Houston's remarks to friends and family—some of which he clearly intended to be heard by a larger audience—revealed a willingness to concede that an alternative to the system of government in the United States might more satisfactorily both improve the conditions under which black people lived and provide the legal basis for a good society free of oppression. However, he was not as concerned with a specific alternative system—for example, socialist, socialist-democratic, or communist—as he was with encouraging black people to continue to struggle for a society in which there was no operative policy of racial segregation and discrimination. He wanted a system of government that assured all black people freedom with guarantees of equality and justice and broader opportunities for fulfilled lives. The irony of Charles Houston's life of struggle was the irony of the lives of so many blacks. Because of the expressed fundamental laws and principles of the United States, he was within the reform tradition, but because of the racist past and practices of the United States, his protest and his demands were radical. He favored extreme, fundamental change for the nation, to uproot racism—particularly in its promotion of white supremacy—and to replace it with a legal-moral system that truly recognized the equal entitlement of all people to life, liberty, and the pursuit of happiness.

Whether struggling for reform of the system or fighting the system, Charles Houston never questioned the propriety of black self-determination. Having come from a long line of black people who decided what was best for themselves and their families and who then proceeded to work for its accomplishment, it was evident to Houston that Americans of African descent should lead their own struggle. They would develop their own strategies and tactics in the fight, make their own decisions about goals, ideologies, allies, causes, sacrifices, and resources, explain their own positions, interpret their own aspirations, and set their own priorities. He, as most blacks, did not view this as an abstract theory; it was a constant concern. When he spoke to the NAACP's annual convention, he suggested the tactical wisdom of attempting to unite with poor whites on issues of common oppression, but he was careful to emphasize that the NAACP as a black rights organization with branches throughout the nation must be "for its greatest effectiveness . . . of the Negroes, by the Negroes, . . . and for all the Negroes," being equally committed to a program of "intelligent leadership plus intelligent mass action."[13] Two postulates were enunciated during and reflected in the NAACP campaign and his subsequent work with black communities: "The inspirational value of a struggle is always greater when it springs from the soil than when it is a foreign growth"[14] and "essentially leadership must develop from the aspirations, determinations and sacrifices and needs of the group itself."[15] Neither malicious disregard nor benign neglect could be silently condoned, and some level of control for blacks was mandatory. Houston reminded President Roosevelt of this in a letter of 1943, which made up for in truth what it lacked in tact. "The time when Negro issues can be disposed of without first conferring with Negroes themselves has passed and it is important that government officials begin to realize that Negroes are citizens, not wards."[16]

Challenging the government to give credence to constitutional guarantees of full citizenship, Charles Houston's contribution to civil rights advocacy, in particular, and the black struggle against oppression, in general, was theoretical and practical. He was a legal scholar-teacher-practitioner who became so involved in struggle that he wrote neither treatises nor lengthy law review articles. He, however, expounded a theory of "social engineering" to the black bar and black law students. The term fell into disuse, but his concepts of social engineering continued beyond his lifetime, as they became part of the legal training for Howard University students and the NAACP's lawyers of the National Legal Committee and the Legal Defense and Educational Fund, Inc.

Charles Houston understood from his law school education that the principal professional task was knowing the law and understanding the legal process, so that one could capably advise and represent lay people in "legal matters revolving around [their] . . . problems with family or community."[17] As a law professor he was called everything from "insensitive" to "a machine" because of his unyielding attachment to the goal of graduating *only* first-rate lawyers from Howard, no matter how many students began the three-year course of study.[18] Beyond this, however, Houston felt a social-moral obligation to produce cadres of socially alert black lawyers for the struggle. The values transmitted from one oppressed generation to the next, in combination with Houston's liberal arts educational background and his Harvard encounter with Roscoe Pound's sociological jurisprudence, were evident in the premises of the theory that Houston posited about law, lawyers, and the United States. He accepted as givens that "every group must justify and interpret itself in terms of the general welfare . . . [i.e.,] doing a distinct, necessary work for the social good"[19] and that "lawyers serve as reinforcement units in the social structure."[20] In light of this, Houston insisted that black lawyers could not afford the luxury of merely being capable lawyers handling ordinary professional tasks. "The [black] lawyer must be trained as a social engineer," Houston argued, in contrast to the traditionalists' view of the lawyer's role.[21] Thereafter he variously described between 1929 and 1948 the role and the functions of the social engineer. Houstonian social engineering entailed five obligations for black lawyers: (1) to be "prepared to anticipate, guide and interpret group advancement";[22] (2) to be the "mouthpiece of the weak and a sentinel guarding against wrong";[23] (3) to ensure that "the course of change is . . . orderly with a minimum of human loss and suffering," when possible "guid[ing] . . . antagonistic and group forces into channels where they w[ould] not clash";[24] (4) to recognize that the written constitution and inertia against its amendment give lawyers room for social experimentation and therefore, to "use . . . the law as an instrument available to [the] minority unable to adopt direct action to achieve its place in the community and nation";[25] (5) to engage in "a carefully planned [program] to secure decisions, rulings and public opinion on . . . broad principle[s]"[26] while "arousing and strengthening the local will to struggle."[27] Of these obligations, Houston taught that the second and third were basic, regardless of race. This also distinguished Howard's legal education from legal education elsewhere.

Undoubtedly, Pound's view that judicial and legislative functions, while separate, at times ran together in the "judicial ascertainment of the common law by analogical application of decided cases" was a catalyst as Houston urged black social engineers to prepare for arguments in the U.S. Supreme Court.[28] In the Court a black man could "compel a white man to listen," and reforms could be forced when blacks had no chance through politics.[29] So convinced was Charles Houston of the correctness of his theory of social engineering and its potential with respect to prompting a nondiscriminatory interpretation of the Constitution or federal statutes that he taught students a lawyer was "either a social engineer or a parasite on society."[30] Moreover, in a 1935 article, he declared that "the primary social justification" for the black lawyer in the United States was "the social service he c[ould] render the race as an interpreter and proponent of its rights and aspirations."[31]

In its reliance on resort to courts for gaining recognition of their constitutional rights, social engineering was consistent with the traditional faith of African Americans in the possibility of changing their subordinate status not only through resistance but also through protests and appeals based on the expressed fundamental principles of the U.S. government. The influence of social engineering on the black jurisprudential matrix was significant and novel in its exposition of the duties of black American lawyers and its presentation of the rationale for use of the law by blacks. Finally, Houston's emphasis on experimentation with the constitution and on planning and affinity with the local community of blacks in struggle provided the basis both for black law studies and for action on behalf of the masses of black people.

Charles Houston's entire career as a civil rights lawyer exemplified the belief that the law could be used to promote fundamental social change and that it was an instrument available to a minority even when that minority was without access to the ordinary weapons of democracy. His reputation is indelibly linked with the NAACP and its Legal Defense Fund, which were one and the same, and with his initiation of the litigation campaign of the NAACP against racial discrimination in education that ultimately led to the watershed public school segregation decisions of 1954, *Brown* v. *Board of Education* and *Bolling* v. *Sharpe*.[32] His place of significance in history has been principally established by his role as either chief counsel and key strategist or adviser-strategist for precedent-setting cases in three areas of law: education, labor, and housing. As a constitutional lawyer and litigator—in the graduate public education "equal protection" case of *Missouri ex rel. Gaines* v. *Canada* (1938), the fair-representation cases of *Steele* v. *Louisville & Nashville Railroad Company* and *Tunstall* v. *Brotherhood of Locomotive Firemen and Enginemen* (1944), and the anti-restrictive-covenant cases of *Hurd* v. *Hodge* and *Shelley* v. *Kraemer* (1948)—Charles Houston demonstrated that demands could be made on the system's courts with the result being changes in the common law.[33] The U.S. Supreme Court in *Gaines, Steele, Tunstall, Hurd,* and *Shelley* rendered decisions supportive of the protection of the civil rights of African Americans, sometimes relying on constitutional interpretations of federal statutes, and other times reaching adjudication of constitutional issues per se. Houston's work underscored that resort to the courts, while an insufficient remedy for fully combating and eliminating racism in the United States was an appropriate means for blacks to use in the struggle to alter the conditions under which they lived in America.

Houston engaged in planned litigation campaigns with what Brazilian social theorist Paulo Freire has described as "critical consciousness."[34] This critical consciousness incorporated both understanding and rejecting the oppressor's ideology and explanations, rejecting the oppressor's models and behavioral traits, identifying the system (or aspects of the system) that was the cause of oppressive conditions, and approaching transformation of the system (or those aspects of the system) as a collective endeavor, the strategies of which were to be developed through dialogue across class lines.[35] Although after the defenses of George Crawford and Bernard Ades, Houston exhibited a naiveté about the dominant majority and the legal process, his consciousness was raised as he confronted leftist condemnations and reflected both on the criticisms and on the black experience in the United States. Even when they were overzealous, Communists, socialists, and ILD members influenced Houston by directing his attention to the analysis that assumed class antagonism, while stressing not only mass resistance and militant struggle but also the class ties of the judiciary. For all three litigation programs—education, labor, and housing—in addition to voting, jury exclusion, and transportation cases in which Houston was involved, Houston's assumption was that "public officials . . . [were] servants of the class which place[d] them there" and blacks could "not depend upon judges to fight . . . [their] battles."[36] A critical consciousness also prompted Houston to extract from his legal training those aspects of the judicial process that were likely to have the greatest impact on the black struggle. In planning his activity, he took into account *stare decisis*, judicial self-restraint, the step-by-step process and the requirement of reasonable predictability of legal consequences. The result was a three-pronged strategy: selecting cases that presented clear legal issues and building strong records in those cases; overturning negative legal decisions by invalidating gradually or attacking directly the controlling precedents; and developing a sustaining community or mass interest in each case.

The relation between Houston's critical consciousness and planning effectiveness has been examined by Jesse McNeil, Jr., in a study of the Houston-directed NAACP campaign against discrimination in education.[37] Characteristic of each program of litigation handled by Charles Houston was a well-conceived and well-executed plan of preparation and litigation. Houston's high level of competence in planning was indicated by his consistent pattern of defining the problem, setting a goal, analyzing the situation, assessing the available options, developing the appropriate strategy and tactics, and implementing the planned strategy. In addition, the legal campaign was characterized by collaborative activity among lawyers, scholars, and concerned lay people, responsive leadership with communication across traditional class and social boundaries and the use of the media and public forums to raise community consciousness and to mobilize community support.[38]

During the early 1930s, Charles Houston criticized the NAACP—as did Du Bois. In contrast to Du Bois, who at the time counseled "voluntary segregation," Houston stressed another criticism of the NAACP's leadership and its relationship to the masses. In his view, an effective assault on racial discrimination was essential during this era. Such an attack on racism required black self-determination and consciousness-raising appeals to blacks and whites of the society. Although the NAACP never had the mass support of the Garvey movement, substantial numbers of blacks were branch members. They knew and articulated their local concerns and identified with such general issues as the right to vote, the right to have blacks serve on trial juries, equal schools, and equal pay for teachers' equal work. Houston devoted resources to such clearly relevant issues with the hope that even greater interest would arise, and when necessary he slowed down the litigation campaign until factors generating mass support were developed.

Outside the NAACP structure, Houston consistently planned civil rights litigation in response to client-identified grievances, while assessing and then implementing appropriate strategies and tactics. Effective work in the areas of labor, housing, and public education resulted in the precedent-setting *Steele* doctrine, the *Hurd* ruling, and predecessor cases of the District of Columbia's 1954 decision against segregated public education. Collaboration and cooperation across class, social, and racial boundaries again proved indispensable to court victories, while Houston's concurrent warnings about the limitations of the judicial system proved indispensable to the larger civil rights struggle.

Charles Houston held a respected position of leadership among blacks during the 1930s and 1940s. His ability to educate and inspire lawyers and lay people, respectively, to work as social engineers and to pool their resources to seek enforcement of rights through the courts was of particular historical significance. His legal successes, especially in the U.S. Supreme Court, were key collective victories that laid the groundwork for subsequent civil rights laws supporting equality of educational opportunity, fair housing, and fair representation. These

Court victories had far-reaching significance for the future progress of blacks, while most of Houston's efforts in the African-American struggle had an immediate impact on opportunities for blacks to exercise rights in some areas of American life. His work was also instrumental in creating a climate for more militant direct action.

Houston's commitment to the use of the law for social change was prudent because blacks, even if a "subordinate minority," had rights through the "thirteenth, fourteenth and fifteenth amendments . . . in theory and in law" and one "problem [was] enforcement."[39] However, there were other systemic problems that required Houston to maintain a flexible posture toward the American legal process, and despite his Supreme Court victories, realism dictated that he perceive himself as "a technician probing in the courts . . . how far the existing system w[ould] permit the exercise of freedom before it clamp[ed] down."[40] In 1935, while some cheered his saving of Jess Hollins from execution as a triumph for the NAACP's first black appellate team, Houston wrote about being struck by the relationship between miscarriages of justice, race, and poverty.[41] A few years later, when Odell Waller (the sharecropper convicted of first-degree murder after fatally shooting a white farmer in self-defense) had not sufficiently able counsel to defend him and was scheduled for execution in spite of a conviction by an unconstitutional jury, Houston gave short shrift to the legal process. In response to the request of Pauli Murray and Morris Milgram of the Workers Defense League, Houston communicated with the governor of Virginia: The violation of fundamental American civil liberties required commutation "regardless of the merits of . . . [the] case."[42]

Rejection of any position that might hold the legal code absolutely sacred also marked Houston's approach to the American legal process in general. Flawed in its ability to protect a subordinate racial minority and hold in check the immoral conduct of the majority, Houston sometimes found the legal system and its enumerated civil liberties inadequate as a basis for protest. Whereas he acted within the system to prepare and have published a brief condemning the Tuscaloosa lynchings and the complicity of officials, he immediately advised an NAACP official that it was "not a matter of free speech and free press . . . but a fundamental matter of human life and orderly government."[43] For Houston it was evident that a government's obligation to protect its citizens' lives, regardless of race, took priority over arguments for free speech and press. This belief had a simple origin: Houston never questioned the moral superiority of a society governed by laws that guaranteed basic human rights. Repeated incidents of blatant disregard for the lives of black people pushed Houston away from the standpoint that the "goodwill of the dominant majority" might be a determining factor in devising civil rights protest tactics. By 1935 he asserted that "real amicable race relations c[ould] not be purchased by the surrender of . . . rights."[44]

As an NAACP official, political appointee, publicist, and concerned black American, Houston regularly attempted to use the legislative and executive branches to direct attention to pervasive racism with respect to lynchings, jury exclusion, "railroading" of blacks to jail, the need for a federal agency with power to enforce fair employment policies, discrimination in the armed forces, racially segregated public accommodations, and black disfranchisement. Regarding the latter, Houston was adamant that, in the United States, voting—the ability to put in and take out of office particular officials in relationship to their representation of one's interests—was of paramount importance. However, the disfranchisement of overwhelming numbers of blacks in the South—where the majority lived—rendered the race virtually ineffectual in the political-legal process. Moral suasion seemed to fail consistently when presidents, senators, and members of the House weighed support of the rights of nonvoting blacks against other political considerations.

Logically, Houston refused to place his faith entirely in the three branches of the American legal system, but encouraged and participated in direct action to secure African Americans' rights. Peaceful assembly, petitioning, and extralegal demonstrations as well escalated the black struggle that could not achieve all its aims within the legal process. Participating in and organizing extralegal marches and demonstrations, in addition to publicizing injustice and pressing for mass resistance, were not the principal sources of Charles Houston's significance. They were, however, indicative of his recognition that some radical analyses must be translated into concrete action. Not only did he conclude that law had value always within its limitations, he also joined other black people whom he had challenged to "do [their] own fighting and more of it by extra-legal means."[45] As he promoted this extensive fight against oppression, he realistically urged that some grievances not be presented as special pleading for blacks alone, but when possible as propositions for the relief of the oppressed masses to support a greater public good. As a racial minority in the United States, blacks needed allies among the citizens of the nation. Simultaneously, he stressed the potential alliance of blacks in the United States with the nonwhite majority of the rest of the world. He was certain that the struggle against oppression was indivisible.

From 1935 to 1950, Charles Hamilton Houston played a principal role in defining and pacing the legal phase of the struggle of African Americans for freedom, justice, equality, and a right to the pursuit of happiness. His role was definitive because, in the context of this struggle, he operated primarily within the arena of the courts. This constituted a limitation of the legal thrust, because it placed major emphasis on litigation and obtaining favorable Supreme Court judgments, rather than on legislation or executive orders and their enforcement. Houston did recognize that use of the other branches of the legal system might result in more speedy remedies, but with little power to compel congressional or presidential concessions and with violent racism ever a possible consequence of direct action, blacks were in a better position to seek redress of grievances through the courts, Houston reasoned. The usually high chances for reversals of court decisions favorably affecting the legal status of African Americans were minimized by the strategy of Charles Houston. His own legal accomplishments were the consequence of carefully considered, well-developed legal strategies and skillful arguments. More important, many civil rights lawyers throughout the nation accepted Houston's philosophy of social engineering. Their use of the law to secure fundamental social change for the protection of African Americans and the improvement of society placed pressure on the judicial system, to which it yielded. Supreme Court decisions handed down and civil rights statutes enacted after Houston's death in 1950 specify rights for which he effectively argued in courts, and black lawyers continue to use the law as a weapon in the struggle against racial discrimination. As Derrick Bell concluded in *Race, Racism, and American Law*, "decisions, particularly since World War II . . . seem[ed] to support an argument that reliance by blacks on courts [was] not misplaced."[46]

Nonetheless, in a nation where wealth, privilege, and power were vested in the dominant majority of a different race, where racism was the prevailing attitude, and where a racist, exploitative ruling class governed with discriminatory laws so pervasive as to have established apartheid in the United States, the adoption of legalism could neither eradicate oppression nor guarantee freedom, justice, and equality. This understanding—reached after years of struggle within the framework of the American system—obliged Charles Houston to see himself in the late 1940s as a technician probing *not if* the system would clamp down on the exercise of freedom, *but when* it would.

Charles Houston's groundwork extends beyond contributions to American law and the improvement of African Americans' legal status. In historical perspective, it becomes clear that Houston's life is especially instructive because of his open-mindedness and ideological integrity. Houston always struggled so that his people might have freedom, self-determination, justice, equality of rights, and equality of opportunity. Yet in struggling, he openly entertained a wide range of views pertaining to the means to create a society in which such conditions were guaranteed by law. As most blacks of his era, Houston sought to exhaust every option within the existing system. He was, however, so fundamentally opposed to injustice and laws that contravened morality that, when moved to criticism of the existing system, he did not equivocate. His concern and his commitment to struggle were so great that—at the time he felt he might not survive his first heart attack—he decided to cheat death of any opportunity to obscure his most highly developed critical views. The tape-recorded message that resulted from this resolve (and his desire to have his son more clearly understand his father's sacrifice) stands as Charles Houston's final word on the struggle. His paramount concern was "that the Negro shall not be content simply with demanding an equal share in the existing system." (It is significant that this was not the first time he had expressed this position, as is evident in his tape-recorded message.) Thus, Houston's groundwork was also the grim reminder that "there's no particular honor in being invited to take a front seat at one's own funeral."[47] In the final analysis, Houston believed that it was the task of all black people in the United States "to make sure that the system, which shall survive in the United States of America, . . . guarantees justice and freedom for everyone."[48]

Charles Hamilton Houston cut through the bitterness that racism and the absence of authentic freedom in the United States might have made a permanent malady for African Americans and affirmed his own values. The price exacted by American society was great. Relentless struggle brought him to his death at the age of fifty-four. Yet, as he told his son, "in any fight some fall."[49] Charles Houston laid the groundwork for part of the continuing black struggle in an effort to keep faith with his ancestors, to create a better society, and to offer hope to the children. The cost was not nearly as important as the cause. He emerged in history insisting that the United States must use the Constitution and its laws to reform itself and to assure black people human rights. He turned the Constitution, the laws, and the legal process into weapons in the cause of his people, but finally, he challenged black people to fight for their rights even as the system threatened to "clamp down."[50] This too was Charles Houston's legacy: that there should be no end to struggling, no immobilizing weariness until full human rights were won.

Children don't get weary
Children don't get weary
Children don't get weary
'Til your work is done.[51]

APPENDIXES

---

1. Houston Genealogy

2. The Private Case Load of Charles H. Houston, 1924–1950

3. Charles Hamilton Houston—Houston & Houston, Washington, D.C. Earnings and Expenditures After Two Years of Private Practice

4. Legal Defense and Legal Aid Inquiries Handled by the Office of the Special Counsel of the NAACP, 1935–1938

5. American Fund for Public Service Support of Educational Campaign of the Joint Committee (NAACP/AFPS) During Period of Houston's New York NAACP Special Counselship

Figure 1. Genealogy of Charles Hamilton Houston

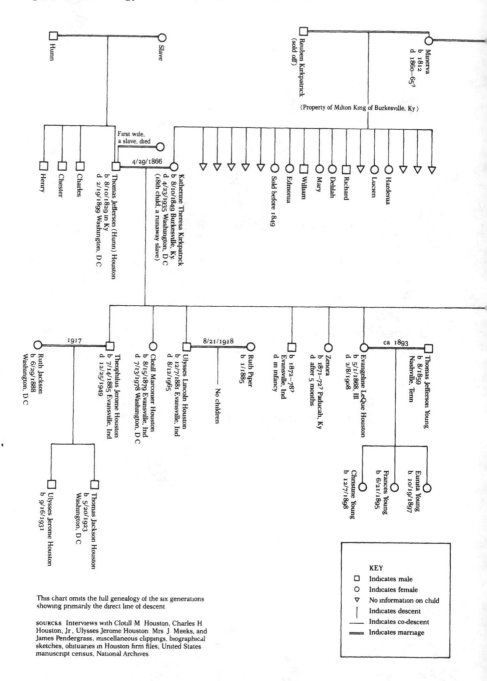

This chart omits the full genealogy of the six generations showing primarily the direct line of descent

SOURCES Interviews with Clotill M Houston, Charles H Houston, Jr , Ulysses Jerome Houston Mrs J Meeks, and James Pendergrass, miscellaneous clippings, biographical sketches, obituaries in Houston firm files, United States manuscript census, National Archives

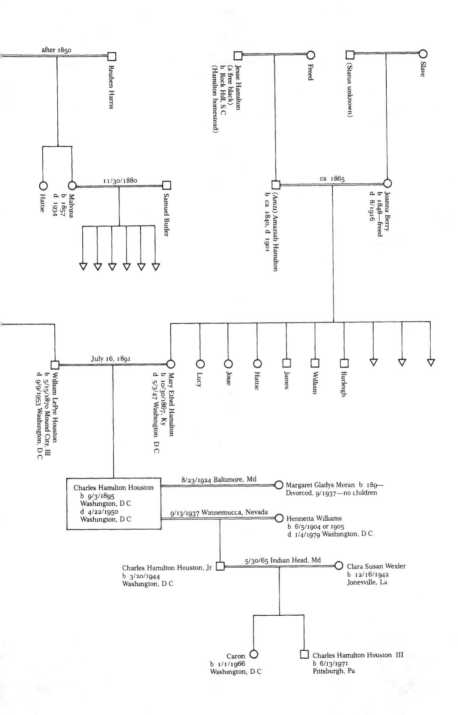

2. The Private Case Load of Charles Hamilton Houston, 1924–1950

Type and Cause of Action	1924 to 1935	1936 to 1939	1940 to 1950
CIVIL	97.60%	97.80%	90.50%
Civil liberties/civil rights—racial discrimination	0.80	1.10	9.60
Contracts	2.40	7.90	1.20
Debt	23.00	7.90	5.60
Domestic relations	4.10	9.00	18.80
Incompetence	1.65	2.25	0.90
Insurance	1.65	2.25	1.20
Legal partnerships and corporations	3.30		1.20
Real property	16.40	4.56	11.70
Tax			0.30
Torts (wrongs—excluding breach of contract—for which civil suits for damages may be brought, e.g., negligence or malicious prosecution)	18.90	51.70	29.20
Trusts and estates	23.80	11.20	9.60
Miscellaneous			
Disbarment	0.80		
Job security and/or classification dispute	0.80		1.20

Type and Cause of Action	1924 to 1935	1936 to 1939	1940 to 1950
CRIMINAL	2.40%	2.20%	9.50%
Assault and battery			0.30
Assault and rape			0.30
Assault with a deadly weapon			0.90
Attempt to commit carnal knowledge			0.30
Attempt to do bodily harm			0.30
Bigamy			0.30
Conspiracy to obstruct justice			0.60
Contempt of court			0.30
Criminal negligence			0.30
Drunk and disorderly conduct			0.30
Forcible entry			0.30
Grand larceny	0.80		0.30
Illegal abortion			0.30
Murder	0.80		2.20
Operating rooming house without permit			0.30
Perjury	0.80		0.30
Reckless driving	0.80		0.60
Refusal to give up seat on bus in alleged violation of Virginia statute			0.30
Robbery			0.30
Tampering with the mails			0.30
Transporting goods across state lines for compensation without proper license			0.30
Using the mails to defraud		1.10	
Violation of narcotics act		1.10	0.30

Source: Compiled from private files of the Houston firm that were originally divided into several alphabetical series. Extant files did not include a complete run of all alphabetical series. Nevertheless, the general character of the practice from 1924 to 1950 is ascertainable from records examined (536 civil and criminal actions).

3. Charles Hamilton Houston—Houston &
Houston, Washington, D.C.
Earnings and Expenditures After Two Years of
Private Practice

GROSS EARNINGS, January–September 1927

Gross Cash Income

January 1927	$ 607.43
February	242.44
March	458.13
April	367.88
May	206.25
June	275.42
July	659.83
August	1,065.85
September	220.48
Total	$4,103.71

Accounts Receivable

June 1927	$ 325.00
July	210.00
August	188.60
September	231.15
Total	$ 954.75
Gross Earnings	$5,058.46
Average Monthly Gross Cash Income	455.97

EXPENDITURES, January–September 1927

Average Fixed Monthly Office Expenses

Check	$	80.00
Lawyers Co-operative Publishing Company (A.L.R., U.S., L.ed. Rptrs.)		22.50
The Dictaphone Corporation		17.22
G.O.E.C., Sundstrand (Adding Machine)		12.00
Chesapeake & Potomac Telephone Company (Charles Houston's Share of firm bill)		12.00
Miscellaneous		20.00
Total	$	163.72
Estimated average fixed monthly office expenses		160.00
For nine months		$1,440.00

NET CASH INCOME, January–September 1927

Net earnings from office during period	$3,618.46
Accounts receivable from office	954.75
Net cash income from office during period	2,663.71

Source: Data extracted from Report on Total Income and Expenditures, 1927, Charles H. Houston Correspondence and Reports, Houston Survey, Negro Legal Status, Laura Spelman Rockefeller Memorial, Rockefeller Archive Center.

4. Legal Defense and Legal Aid Inquiries Handled by the Office of the Special Counsel of the NAACP, 1935–1938

		Houston	Marshall
	CRIMINAL		
(1)	Larceny[a]	3	7
	Robbery	10	5
	Burglary	2	4
	Attempted rape or rape	9	10
(5)	Assault (including assault with a deadly weapon)	8	20
	Murder (including in self-defense and accidental)	36	24
	Arson	1	—
	Counterfeiting		1
	Embezzlement	1	1
(10)	Participation in riot	1	—
	Disturbing the peace	1	—
	Riding in a stolen vehicle	—	1
	Receipt of stolen goods	1	—
	Forgery	1	—
(15)	Fraud	1	—
	Illegal manufacture of liquor or possession of illegal or untaxed liquor	2	—
	Vagrancy	2	2
	Violating parole	—	1
	Selling or possession of narcotics	1	
(20)	Selling of medicine without a license	—	1
	Unspecified[b]	45	63
	Assault or assault with deadly weapon[c]	3	—
	Rape or attempted rape	1	1
	Abduction	1	—
(25)	Illegal detention	1	1
	Assault or assault with a deadly weapon of relative of complainant	1	1
	Murder (includes lynching of relative or of someone known to the complainant)	4	6

CIVIL
(1)	Wills, trusts, or estates[d]	3	2
	Debt and recovery	2	8
	Compensation, pension or insurance	12	10
	Real property	14	8
(5)	Damages for: invasion of privacy	1	—
	Negligence-personal injury	6	4
	Assault	1	1
	Wrongful death	8	2
	False arrest or illegal imprisonment	2	3
(10)	Fraud	2	1
	Unfair labor practices	—	1
	Unspecified tort	4	3
	Unspecified	1	—

Source: Data extracted from extant general legal files of the National Association for the Advancement of Colored People.

[a] Categories (1)–(21) (criminal) refer either to the crime the person inquiring has been accused of, charged with, or convicted and incarcerated because of, or to the crime against which the person inquiring desires to have a second party defended.

[b] Inquiries reveal a decided reluctance of inmates to discuss details of their crimes through censored mails. In addition, the large number of unspecified crimes is due to the volume of letters in which solely the subject of parole is discussed.

[c] Categories (22)–(27) (criminal), unless otherwise indicated, refer to crimes committed against a nonincarcerated complainant.

[d] Categories (1)–(13) (civil) refer to the subject of the inquiry.

5. American Fund for Public Service Support of Educational
Campaign of the Joint Committee (NAACP/AFPS) During Period of
Houston's New York NAACP Special Counselship

	November 1934 to July 1936	July 1936 to April 1937	May 1937 to May 1938
Receipts			
American Fund	$10,000.00	$6,500.00	$ 700.00
Interest on back deposits	208.86	28.58	
Balance of AFPS appropriation		1,394.55	612.81
Total	10,208.86	8,123.13	
Disbursements			
Allocation not indicated			612.81
University cases			
Maryland	1,616.91		
Virginia	80.00*		
Missouri	710.50	527.50	700.00
Tennessee	510.00	1,230.44	
Teachers' salaries and school cases			
Baltimore County High School	315.00	1,213.81	
Virginia County Schools	70.11		
South Carolina School reports	50.00		
Misc.: Education—Related: Richmond, Virginia, library case		105.69	
Salaries	2,251.14	3,199.84	
Publicity	722.15	44.00	
Traveling	2,125.06	673.98	
Miscellaneous—postage, books, etc.	353.44	391.83	
Total	$ 8,814.31	$7,387.09	$1,312.81

Sources: Charles H. Houston, "Memorandum for the Joint Committee of the [NAACP] and [AF for PS]," 24 July 1936 [p. 8] (financial statement), Joint Committee, 1936–37 folder, AFPS, Administrative files, C200, NAACP Papers; [Charles H. Houston], "Report to the Joint Committee . . . ," 4 May 1937 [p. 10] (Receipts and Disbursements), Educational Campaign, 1937 folder, AFPS, Administrative files, C198, NAACP Papers; AFPS, *Applications Favorably Acted Upon—Gifts and Loans*, vols. 8, 9.
* Case not pressed because of weakness of test litigant's scholastic record, according to Houston.

SELECTED BIBLIOGRAPHY

PRIMARY SOURCES

American Fund for Public Service Records, Manuscripts Division, New York Public Library, New York, N.Y.

Records of the Adjutant General's Office, Record Group No. 407, National Archives and Records Service, Washington, D.C.

Records of the American Expeditionary Forces, 1917–21, Record Group No. 120, National Archives and Records Service, Washington, D.C.

Marian Anderson Collection, Manuscripts Division, Moorland-Spingarn Research Center, Howard University, Washington, D.C.

Records of Army Commands, 1813–1942, Record Group No. 98, National Archives and Records Service, Washington, D.C.

Claude A. Barnett Papers, Manuscript Division, Chicago Historical Society, Chicago, Ill.

Records of the Brotherhood of Sleeping Car Porters, Manuscript Division, Library of Congress, Washington, D.C.

Samuel H. Clark, Private Papers, Residence of S. H. Clark, Christianburg, Va.

Consolidated Parent Group Papers (uncataloged collection), Manuscripts Division, Moorland-Spingarn Research Center, Howard University, Washington, D.C.

A. Mercer Daniel Collection, Manuscripts Division, Moorland-Spingarn Research Center, Howard University, Washington, D.C.

Records of the Department of Interior, 1849–1943, Record Group No. 48, National Archives and Records Service, Washington, D.C.

Records of the Department of Justice, Record Group No. 60, National Archives and Records Service, Washington, D.C.

Felix Frankfurter Papers, Manuscript Division, Langdell Library, Harvard University Law School, Cambridge, Mass.

Felix Frankfurter Papers, Manuscript Division, Library of Congress, Washington, D.C.

Thomas M. Gregory Papers, Manuscript Division, Moorland-Spingarn Research Center, Howard University, Washington, D.C.

Margaret Haywood Private Files (in re Thompson Restaurant cases), Washington, D.C.

Charles H. Houston Letters, Papers and firm case files, Houston & Gardner, Washington, D.C. (part of collection donated to Moorland-Spingarn Research Center, Howard University).

Charles H. Houston Family Collection, Houston Residence, Washington, D.C.

William L. Houston Letters, Papers and firm case files, Houston & Gardner, Washington, D.C.

William L. Houston Family Papers, Library of Congress, Washington, D.C.

Records of Howard University School of Law, Howard University, Washington, D.C.

Campbell C. Johnson Papers, Manuscripts Division, Moorland-Spingarn Research Center, Howard University, Washington, D.C.

Charles S. Johnson Papers, Special Collections, Fisk University Library, Fisk University, Nashville, Tenn.

Phileo Nash Papers, Truman Library, Independence, Mo.

National Association for the Advancement of Colored People Records, Manuscript Division, Library of Congress, Washington, D.C.

National Association for the Advancement of Colored People, District of Columbia Branch Records, Moorland-Spingarn Research Center, Howard University, Washington, D.C.

Roscoe Pound Papers, Manuscript Division, Langdell Library, Harvard University Law School, Cambridge, Mass.

Records of the President's Fair Employment Practice Committee, Record Group No. 228, National Archives and Records Service, Washington, D.C.

Laura Spelman Rockefeller Memorial, Rockefeller Estate, Tarrytown, N.Y.

Franklin Delano Roosevelt Papers, Roosevelt Presidential Library, Hyde Park, N.Y.

Julius Rosenwald Fund Collection, Special Collections, Fisk University Library, Fisk University, Nashville, Tenn.

Joel E. Spingarn Collection, Manuscripts Division, Moorland-Spingarn Research Center, Howard University, Washington, D.C.

Harry S. Truman Papers, Truman Presidential Library, Independence, Mo.

James G. Tyson Papers, Manuscripts Division, Moorland-Spingarn Research Center, Howard University, Washington, D.C.

Records of the U.S. Senate, Record Group No. 46, National Archives and Records Service, Washington, D.C.

Urban League Records, Manuscript Division, Library of Congress, Washington, D.C.

Published Articles of Charles Hamilton Houston

"Commonwealth v. William Brown." *Opportunity* 11 (April 1933): 109–11.

"The George Crawford Case: An Experiment in Social Statesmanship." *The Nation*, 4 July 1934, pp. 17–19. (Co-author, Edward Lovett.)

"TVA: Lily White Reconstruction." *Crisis* 41 (October 1934): 209–31, 311. (Co-author John P. Davis.)

"The Need for Negro Lawyers." *Journal of Negro Education* 4 (January 1935): 49–52.

"Educational Inequalities Must Go." *Crisis* 42 (October 1935): 300–301, 316.

"Cracking Closed University Doors." *Crisis* 42 (December 1935): 364, 370, 372.

"Glass Aided School Inequalities." *Crisis* 43 (January 1936): 15, 27.

"How to Fight for Better Schools." *Crisis* 43 (February 1936): 52, 59.

"Don't Shout Too Soon." *Crisis* 43 (March 1936): 79, 91.

"A Challenge to Negro College Youth." *Crisis* 45 (January 1938): 14–15.

"Future Policies and Practices Which Should Govern the Relationship of the Federal Government to Negro Separate Schools." *Journal of Negro Education* 7 (July 1938): 460–62.

"Critical Summary: The Negro in the U.S. Armed Forces in World War I and II." *Journal of Negro Education* 12 (Summer 1943): 364–66.

"Foul Employment Practice on the Rails." *Crisis* 56 (October 1949): 269–71, 284–85.

Personal Interviews

Raymond Pace Alexander, Philadelphia, Pa., 18 September 1972.

Benjamin Amos, Washington, D.C., 17 January 1973.

Melvin Banks, Dallas, Tex., 14 August 1972.

Gardner Bishop, Washington, D.C., 2 March 1972.

Lucille Black, New York, N.Y., 7 December 1972.

St. Clair Bourne, New York, N.Y., 16 January 1974.

Charles K. Brown, Washington, D.C., 9 January 1973.

Sterling Brown, Washington, D.C., 12 January 1974.

William Bryant, Washington, D.C., 4 June 1982.

Robert L. Carter, New York, N.Y., 5 May 1982.

Elwood Chisolm, Washington, D.C., 5 December 1972.

Samuel H. Clark, Christianburg, Va., 26 July 1972.

William Colden, Detroit, Mich., 15 August 1974.

Ollie Cooper, Washington, D.C., 21 December 1972.

George W. Crockett, Detroit, Mich., 1 August 1974.

A. Mercer Daniel, Washington, D.C., 18 October 1971.

Earl R. Dickerson, Chicago, Ill., 2 and 9 March 1972.

Herbert Dudley, Detroit, Mich., 1 August 1974.

John Ellison, Washington, D.C., 25 July 1972.

Jack Greenberg, New York, N.Y., 24 August 1972.

William H. Hastie, Jr., Philadelphia, Pa., 19 September 1972.

Margaret Haywood, Washington, D.C., 2 January 1973.

Anna Arnold Hedgeman, New York, N.Y., 8 July 1982.

Oliver Hill, Richmond, Va., 8 December 1972.

Charles H. Houston, Jr., Washington, D.C., 3 and 4 January 1974, 17 September 1974, 7 April and 18 July 1978.

Clotill M. Houston, Washington, D.C., 21 January 1972, 20 April 1972, 21 June 1972, 24 July 1972, 1 January 1973, 19 November 1973.

Margaret Gladys Moran Houston, Washington, D.C., 22 January 1973.
Ulysses Jerome Houston, Washington, D.C., 18 July 1978.
Maceo Hubbard, Washington, D.C., 26 January 1974.
Phineas Indritz, Washington, D.C., 23 April 1973.
James Jackson, New York, N.Y., 8 July 1974.
Joseph L. Johnson, Washington, D.C., 26 October 1972.
Mordecai Johnson, Washington, D.C., 16 January 1975.
Belford V. Lawson, Jr., Washington, D.C., 23 December 1972.
Rayford W. Logan, Washington, D.C., 18 October 1971.
Edward Lovett, Washington, D.C., 18 January 1973.
Edward Mazique, Washington, D.C., 8 January 1973, 23 September 1978.
Ernest R. McKinney, Chapel Hill, N.C., 17 October 1974.
Benjamin McLaurin, New York, N.Y., 17 July 1973.
Bertha McNeill, Washington, D.C., 13 March 1972.
Harry Merican, Washington, D.C., 19 April 1972.
Henry Lee Moon, New York, N.Y., 18 January 1974.
Constance Baker Motley, New York, N.Y., 23 June 1982.
George B. Murphy, Jr., Washington, D.C., 19 April 1974.
Phileo Nash, Washington, D.C., 23 October 1972.
William L. Patterson, New York, N.Y., 15 July 1973.
James Pendergrass, Washington, D.C., 18 July 1978 and 1 May 1982.
Dorothy Porter, Washington, D.C., 2 March 1972.
Charlotte Price, Washington, D.C., 11 February 1972.
Asa Philip Randolph, New York, N.Y., 16 July 1973.
Spottswood Robinson III, Washington, D.C., 4 June 1982.
Juanita Kidd Stout, Philadelphia, Pa., 21 August 1972.
Charles H. Thompson, Washington, D.C., 28 December 1974.
Howard Thurman, Durham, N.C., 25 January 1979.
Joseph Waddy, Washington, D.C., 25 June 1971.
Burma Whitted, Washington, D.C., 28 March 1972.
Roy Wilkins, New York, N.Y., 6 December 1972.

Public Documents

EXECUTIVE DEPARTMENT

U.S. Department of Interior, *Annual Reports*, 1921–1938.
U.S. Department of Interior, *Official Register of the United States*, vols. 1 and 2.
U.S. Department of Interior, Bureau of Census, 6th, 7th, 10th, 11th, and 12th Censuses of the United States.

U.S. STATUTES

District of Columbia Instruction Act. *Statutes at Large*, vol. 13, chap. 156, 1864.
District of Columbia Government Act. *Statutes at Large*, vol. 20, chap. 180, 1878.

U.S. SUPREME COURT RECORDS AND BRIEFS

Case No. 193, *Bountiful Brick Company* v. *Elizabeth Giles*, 276 U.S. 154 (1927).

Case No. 686, *Hollins* v. *Oklahoma*, 295 U.S. 394 (1935).

Case No. 680, *Hale* v. *Commonwealth of Kentucky*, 303 U.S. 613 (1937).

Case No. 57, *Missouri ex rel Gaines* v. *Canada*, 305 U.S. 337 (1938).

Case No. 37, *Tunstall* v. *Brotherhood of Locomotive Firemen and Enginemen et al.*, 323 U.S. 210 (1944).

Case No. 45, *Steele* v. *Louisville & Nashville Railroad Company et al.*, 323 U.S. 192 (1944).

Case No. 72, *Shelley* v. *Kraemer*, 334 U.S. 1 (1948).

Case No. 87, *Sipes* v. *McGhee*, 334 U.S. 1 (1948).

Case No. 290, *Hurd* v. *Hodge*, 334 U.S. 24 (1948).

Case No. 291, *Urciolo* v. *Hodge*, 334 U.S. 24 (1948).

Legal Digests and Reports

American Law Reports—Annotated, 1927–54.

Atlantic Reporter, 1925–37.

Atlantic Reporter (2d series), 1938–50.

Federal Digest, Table of Cases, pre-1940.

Federal Reporter (2d series), 1927–52.

Federal Supplement, 1927–52.

Maryland Reports, 1935–36, 1940–50.

Modern Federal Practice Digest, post-1939.

Northwestern Reporter (2d series), 1942–49.

Shepard's Atlantic Reporter Citations, vol. 1.

Shepard's Federal Citations, vol. 1.

Shepard's Southwestern Citations, vol. 1, Supplement (1950–71).

Shepard's United States Citations, Case Edition, vol. 1, Supplement (1943–71).

Southwestern Reporter (2d series), 1938–52.

Supreme Court Reporter, 1927–54.

United States Law Week: Section 3—Supreme Court, 1944, 1948.

United States Reports, 1927–54.

United States Supreme Court Reports—Lawyers' Edition, 1927–54.

Vertical Clipping and Pamphlet Files

Charles Abrams, Schomburg Center for Research in Black Culture (hereafter, Schomburg Center) New York Public Library, New York, N.Y.

Benjamin J. Davis, Schomburg Center New York Public Library, New York, N.Y.

Housing, Schomburg Center, New York Public Library, New York, N.Y.

Charles Hamilton Houston, Moorland-Spingarn Research Center, Howard University, Washington, D.C.

242   SELECTED BIBLIOGRAPHY

Charles Hamilton Houston, Schomburg Center, New York Public Library, New York, N.Y.

Charles H. and William L. Houston, Washingtoniana Collection, District of Columbia Public Library, Washington, D.C.

International Labor Defense, Schomburg Center, New York Public Library, New York, N.Y.

League for Industrial Democracy, Schomburg Center, New York Public Library, New York, N.Y.

Vito Marcantonio, Schomburg Center, New York Public Library, New York, N.Y.

Clarence Mitchell, Schomburg Center, New York Public Library, New York, N.Y.

James M. Nabrit, Jr., Schomburg Center, New York Public Library, New York, N.Y.

NAACP, Schomburg Center, New York Public Library, New York, N.Y.

Adam Clayton Powell, Jr., Schomburg Center, New York Public Library, New York, N.Y.

Asa Philip Randolph, Schomburg Center, New York Public Library, New York, N.Y.

Roy Wilkins, Schomburg Center, New York Public Library, New York, N.Y.

Workers Defense League, Schomburg Center, New York Public Library, New York, N.Y.

Newspapers and Periodicals

Afro-American (Baltimore; Washington, D.C.), 1931–50, 1954.

Amsterdam News (New York), 1933.

Boyd's Directory of the District of Columbia, 1895–1911.

Chicago Defender, 1950.

The Colored American (Washington, D.C.), 1899.

Crisis, 1915, 1932–40, 1949–50.

Current Biography, 1948.

The Daily Worker (New York), 1947, 1948, 1950.

The Guild Lawyer, 1949, 1950.

The Hilltop (Howard University, Washington, D.C.), 1924.

Howard University Catalogue, 1915–17, 1924–49.

Journal of Negro Education, 1935–50.

Nation, 1934.

National Bar Journal, 1941, 1944–48.

Negro History Bulletin, 1935–50.

Negro Liberator (New York), 1933–34.

New York Times, 1939, 1945–46, 1950, 1954.

Norfolk Journal and Guide, 1933, 1935, 1944.

Opportunity, 1923, 1933.

Pittsburgh Courier, 1940, 1949, 1950.

Washington Post, 1942, 1949, 1950, 1954.

Minutes, Proceedings, Reports, Resolutions, and Speeches

Association for the Study of Negro Life and History, *Annual Report*, 1927–28.
Association of American Law Schools, *Handbook of the Association of American Law Schools and Proceedings of the Twenty-ninth Annual Meeting*. December 1931.
District of Columbia Board of Education, *Minutes*, 1933–35, 1939–48.
Houston, Charles H. "An Approach to Better Race Relations," Address delivered May 5, 1934, Thirteenth National Convention of the Young Women's Christian Associations of America (microfilm publication, YWCA, New York, N.Y.).
National Association for the Advancement of Colored People, *Annual Report*, 1911–50.
"The Proceedings of America United," 19 December 1948. Washington, D.C.: Congress of Industrial Organization, 1948.
"Resolutions of the Communist International on the Negro Question in the United States." In *The Communist Position on the Negro Question*. New York: New Century Publishers, 1947, pp. 41–63.

Miscellaneous

Certification of Incorporation of Consolidated Parent Group, Incorporation Records, Office of the Recorder of Deeds, Washington, D.C.
"Record of Charles Hamilton Houston . . . from September 1919 to . . . June 1923," Law School of Harvard University, Cambridge, Mass.
"The 'Standard Guide' Ready Reference Map of Washington." Washington, D.C.: Foster & Reynolds, 1901, 1906.
Transcript of Charles H. Houston, M Street High School, 10 February 1908, to 11 June 1911, Washington, D.C.
Transcript of Charles H. Houston, Amherst College, 1911–15, Amherst, Mass.

SECONDARY SOURCES

Books

Abraham, Henry J. *Freedom and the Court: Civil Rights and Liberties in the United States*. New York: Oxford University Press, 1977.
Abrams, Charles. *Forbidden Neighbors*. New York: Harper & Bros., 1955.
Anderson, Jervis. *A. Philip Randolph: A Biographical Portrait*. New York: Harcourt Brace Jovanovich, 1972.
Auerbach, Jerold. *Unequal Justice: Lawyers and Social Change in Modern America*. New York: Oxford University Press, 1976.
Bell, Derrick A. *Race, Racism, and American Law*. Boston: Little, Brown & Co., 1973.
Berry, Mary F. *Black Resistance/White Law: A History of Constitutional Racism in America*. Englewood Cliffs, N.J.: Prentice-Hall, 1974.

————. *Military Necessity and Civil Rights Policy: Black Citizenship and the Constitution, 1861–1868.* Port Washington, N.Y.: Kennikat Press, 1977.

————. *Stability, Security, and Continuity: Mr. Justice Burton and Decision-making in the Supreme Court, 1945–1956.* Westport, Conn.: Greenwood Press, 1978.

Blassingame, John W. *The Slave Community: Plantation Life in the Antebellum South.* Rev. ed. New York: Oxford University Press, 1979.

Blaustein, Albert, and Ferguson, Clarence C., Jr. *Desegregation and the Law.* Rev. ed. New York: Vintage Books, 1962.

Bogle, Donald. *Toms, Coons, Mulattoes, Mammies, and Bucks: An Interpretative History of Blacks in American Films.* New York: Viking Press, 1973.

Brown, Sterling. *Negro Caravan.* New York: Dryden Press, 1941.

Bunche, Ralph J. *The Political Status of the Negro in the Age of FDR.* Chicago: University of Chicago Press, 1973.

Carter, Dan T. *Scottsboro: A Tragedy of the American South.* New York: Oxford University Press, 1971.

Dalfiume, Richard. *Desegregation of the U.S. Armed Forces.* Columbia, Mo.: University of Missouri Press, 1960.

Douglas, William O. *The Court Years, 1939–1975: The Autobiography of William O. Douglas.* New York: Random House, 1980.

Dyson, Walter. *Howard University, the Capstone of Negro Education, A History: 1867–1940.* Washington, D.C.: Graduate School of Howard University, 1941.

Emilio, Luis. *A Brave Black Regiment.* Boston: Boston Book Co., 1891.

Foner, Philip S. *Organized Labor and the Black Worker.* New York: Praeger, 1974.

Foster, William. *The Negro People in American History.* New York: International Publishers, 1954.

Franklin, John Hope. *From Slavery to Freedom.* 3rd, 4th, and 5th rev. eds. New York: Alfred A. Knopf, 1967, 1974, 1980.

Franklin, John Hope and Meier, August, eds. *Black Leaders of the Twentieth Century.* Urbana, Ill.: University of Illinois Press, 1982.

Franklin, Vincent P. and Anderson, James, eds. *New Perspectives on Black Educational History.* Boston: G. K. Hall, 1978.

Freire, Paulo. *Education for Critical Consciousness.* New York: Continuum Books, 1980.

————. *Pedagogy of the Oppressed.* New York: Herder & Herder, 1970.

Green, Constance. *The Secret City.* Princeton: Princeton University Press, 1967.

Greenberg, Jack. *Race Relations and American Law.* New York: Columbia University Press, 1959.

Gutman, Herbert G. *The Black Family in Slavery and Freedom, 1750–1925.* New York: Random House, 1976.

Harding, Vincent. *There Is a River: The Black Struggle for Freedom in America.* New York: Harcourt Brace Jovanovich, 1981.

Harper, Michael S., ed. *The Collected Poems of Sterling A. Brown*. New York: Harper & Row, 1980.

Historical Statistics of the United States, Colonial Times to 1957. Washington, D.C.: Government Printing Office, 1960.

Horowitz, Harold, and Karst, Kenneth. *Law, Lawyers, and Social Change*. Indianapolis: Bobbs-Merrill Co., 1969.

Huggins, Nathan. *Harlem Renaissance*. New York: Oxford University Press, 1971.

Hughes, Langston. *Fight for Freedom*. New York: W. W. Norton & Co., 1967.

Hundley, Mary G. *The Dunbar Story, 1870–1955*. New York: Vantage Press, 1965.

Ingle, Edward. *The Negro in the District of Columbia*. Johns Hopkins University Studies in Historical and Political Sciences 11. Baltimore: Johns Hopkins University Press, 1893.

Johnson, James Weldon. *Negro American, What Now?* New York: Viking Press, 1934.

Kellogg, Charles Flint. *NAACP: A History of the National Association for the Advancement of Colored People, 1909–1920*. Vol. 1. Baltimore: Johns Hopkins University Press, 1967.

Kesselman, Louis C. *The Social Politics of FEPC: A Study in Reform Pressure Movements*. Chapel Hill: University of North Carolina Press, 1948.

Kluger, Richard. *Simple Justice: The History of Brown v. Board of Education and Black America's Struggle for Equality*. New York: Alfred A. Knopf, 1976.

Konvitz, Milton R. *A Century of Civil Rights*. New York: Columbia University Press, 1961.

———. *The Constitution and Civil Rights*. New York: Columbia University Press, 1947.

Kurland, Philip B. *Mr. Justice Frankfurter and the Constitution*. Chicago: University of Chicago Press, 1971.

———. *Politics, the Constitution, and the Warren Court*. Chicago: University of Chicago Press, 1970.

Levy, Eugene. *James Weldon Johnson: Black Leader, Black Voice*. Chicago: University of Chicago Press, 1973.

Lewis, David L. *District of Columbia: A Bicentennial History*. New York: W. W. Norton & Co., 1976.

———. *When Harlem Was in Vogue*. New York: Alfred A. Knopf, 1981.

Logan, Rayford W. *Howard University: The First Hundred Years 1867–1967*. New York: New York University Press, 1969.

Logan, Rayford W. and Winston, Michael, eds., *Dictionary of American Negro Biography*. New York: W. W. Norton & Co., 1982.

Martin, Tony. *Race First: The Ideological and Organizational Struggles of Marcus Garvey and the Universal Negro Improvement Association*. Westport, Conn.: Greenwood Press, 1976.

Mason, Alpheus T. *The Supreme Court from Taft to Warren*. Rev. ed. Baton Rouge: Louisiana State University Press, 1968.

Meltzer, Bernard. *Labor Law: Cases, Materials, and Problems.* Boston: Little Brown & Co., 1970.

Miller, Charles A. *Supreme Court and the Uses of History.* Cambridge: Harvard University Press, 1969.

Miller, Loren. *The Petitioners: The Story of the United States Supreme Court and the Negro.* New York: Random House, 1966.

Moss, Alfred. *The American Negro Academy.* Baton Rouge: Louisiana State University Press, 1981.

Ovington, Mary W. *The Walls Came Tumbling Down.* New York: Harcourt, Brace, 1947.

Patterson, Haywood, and Conrad, Earl. *Scottsboro Boy.* Garden City, N.Y.: Doubleday & Co., 1950.

Patterson, William L. *The Man Who Cried Genocide.* New York: International Pub. Co., 1971.

Raboteau, Albert. *Slave Religion.* New York: Oxford University Press, 1978.

Record, Wilson. *The Negro and the Communist Party.* Chapel Hill: University of North Carolina Press, 1951.

————. *Race and Radicalism: The NAACP and the Communist Party in Conflict.* Ithaca, N.Y.: Cornell University Press, 1963.

Redding, J. Saunders. *The Lonesome Road.* Garden City, N.Y.: Doubleday & Co., 1958.

Ross, Barbara Joyce. *J. E. Spingarn and the Rise of the NAACP, 1911–1939.* New York: Atheneum, 1972.

Rudwick, Elliott. *W. E. B. Du Bois: A Study in Minority Group Leadership.* Philadelphia: University of Pennsylvania Press, 1960.

Segal, Geraldine. *In Any Fight Some Fall.* Rockville, Md.: Mercury Press, 1975.

Spero, Sterling, and Harris, Abram. *The Black Worker.* New York: Atheneum, 1969.

Synnott, Marcia. *The Half-opened Door: Discrimination and Admissions at Harvard, Yale, and Princeton, 1900–1970.* Westport, Conn.: Greenwood Press, 1979.

Thirty Years of Law Which Changed America. Special Pre-publication edition. New York: NAACP Legal Defense and Educational Fund, 1970.

Vose, Clement. *Caucasians Only: The Supreme Court, the NAACP, and the Restrictive Covenant Cases.* Berkeley: University of California Press, 1959.

Ware, Gilbert, ed. *From the Black Bar.* New York: G. Putnam, 1976.

Weaver, Robert. *The Negro Ghetto.* New York: Harcourt, Brace, 1948.

Weinstein, Allan, and Gatell, Frank O., eds. *The Segregation Era, 1863–1954.* New York: Oxford University Press, 1970.

Wolters, Raymond. *Negroes and the Great Depression: The Problems of Economic Recovery.* Westport, Conn.: Greenwood Press, 1970.

Articles

Bornet, Vaughn D. "Historical Scholarship, Communism, and the Negro." *Journal of Negro History* 27 (July 1952): 304–24.

Dalfiume, Richard M. "The 'Forgotten Years' of the Negro Revolution." *Journal of American History* 55 (June 1968): 90–106.

Daniel, Allen Mercer. "The Law Library of Howard University, 1867–1956." *Law Library Journal* 51 (1958): 203.

Diamond, K. Norman. "Exclusion of Negroes from State Supported Professional Schools." *Yale Law Journal* 45 (1936): 1296–1301.

Hill, Adelaid Cromwell. "Black Education in the Seventies: A Lesson from the Past." In *The Black Seventies*, edited by Floyd Barbour. Boston: Porter Sargent, 1970. Pp. 55–67.

Hine, Darlene Clark. "Blacks and the Destruction of the Democratic White Primary, 1935–1944." *Journal of Negro History* 62 (January 1977).

Mann, Arthur. "The Progressive Tradition." In *The Reconstruction of America*, edited by John Higham. New York: Harper & Row, 1962. Pp. 157–79.

Mathews, John. "School Integration: 20 Years Later." *Washington Star News*, 12 May 1974.

McLean, Hector. "Four Years of Legal Work End in Victory for Two Colored Lawyers." *Washington Evening Star*, 18 May 1954.

McNeil, Genna Rae. "Charles Hamilton Houston." *Black Law Journal* 3 (Spring 1974): 123–31.

Meier, August, and Rudwick, Elliott. "Attorneys Black and White: A Case Study of Race Relations Within the NAACP." *Journal of American History* 62 (1976): 913–46.

Murray, Hugh T. "The NAACP Versus the Communist Party: The Scottsboro Rape Cases, 1931–1932." In *The Negro in Depression and War*, edited by Bernard Sternsher. Chicago: Quadrangle Books, 1969. Pp. 267–81. (Originally published in *Phylon* 28 [3d Quarter, 1967]).

Naison, Mark. "Harlem Communists and the Politics of Black Protest." In *Community Organization for Urban Social Change: A Historical Perspective*, edited by Robert Fisher and Peter Romonofsky. Westport, Conn.: Greenwood Press, 1979.

Robinson, Spottswood W., III. "No Tea for the Feeble: Two Perspectives on Charles Hamilton Houston." *Howard Law Journal* 20 (1977): 1–9.

Sowell, Thomas. "Black Excellence—The Case of Dunbar High School," *The Public Interest* 15 (Spring 1974): 3–20.

Stratford, Mary. "How Our Lawyers Changed Washington," *Afro-American* (Washington, D.C.), 25 April 1964.

Synnott, Marcia. "The Half-opened Door: Researching Admissions Discrimination at Harvard, Yale, and Princeton," *American Archivist* 45 (Spring 1982): 175–87.

Ulmer, Sidney. "Supreme Court Behavior in Racial Exclusion Cases, 1935–1960." In *The Negro in Depression and War*, edited by Bernard Sternsher. Chicago: Quadrangle Books, 1969. Pp. 93–103. (Originally published in *American Political Science Review* 56 [June 1962]).

Waite, Edward F. "The Negro in the Supreme Court," *Minnesota Law Review* 30 (March 1946): 219–304.

———. "The Negro in the Supreme Court—Five Years More," *Minnesota Law Review* 35 (June 1951): 625–39.

Winkler, Allan M. "The Philadelphia Transit Strike of 1944," *Journal of American History* 59 (June 1972): 73–89.

Zangrando, Robert L. "The NAACP and a Federal Anti-lynching Bill, 1934–1940," *Journal of Negro History* 50 (April 1965): 106–17.

Unpublished Theses, Dissertations, and Manuscripts

Anliot, Mary. "A Study of the Dual School System in the District of Columbia." M.A. thesis, American University, 1954.

Avery, Sheldon B. "Up from Washington: William Pickens and the Negro Struggle for Equality, 1900–1954." Ph.D. dissertation, University of Oregon, 1970.

Daniel, Allen Mercer. "History of Howard University School of Law, 1869–1970." Manuscript, Law School, Howard University, n.d. (c. 1973).

Hamby, Alonzo L. "Harry S. Truman and American Liberalism, 1945–1948." Ph.D. dissertation, University of Missouri, 1965.

Kellogg, Peter J. "Northern Liberals and Black America: A History of White Attitudes, 1936–1952." Ph.D. dissertation, Northwestern University, 1971.

Mann, Kenneth E. "Black Leaders in National Politics, 1873–1943: A Study of Legislative Persuasion." Ph.D. dissertation, Indiana University, 1971.

McGuire, Philip. "Black Civilian Aides and the Problems of Racism in the United States." Ph.D. dissertation, Howard University, 1975.

McNeil, Genna R. "Charles Hamilton Houston (1895–1950) and the Struggle for Civil Rights." Ph.D. dissertation, University of Chicago, 1975.

McNeil, Jesse J. "A Critical Analysis of Planning for Social Change." Ed.D. dissertation, University of Massachusetts, 1975.

Segal, Geraldine R. "A Sketch of the Life of Charles Houston." M.A. thesis, University of Pennsylvania, 1963.

A NOTE ON SOURCES
AND ABBREVIATIONS

The following notes are intended not only to acquaint the readers with the varied published and unpublished materials that comprise the sources for the life and times of Charles Hamilton Houston, but also to direct those who have an interest in pursuing any particular matters to the sources used for this study. To avoid distracting readers from the text, all citations have been placed at the end. In a selected bibliography that precedes this section, principal published and unpublished sources are cited. Collections from which unpublished sources primarily have been drawn are identified by the following abbreviations.

AEF/RG120   Records of the American Expeditionary Forces, 1917–23 Record Group No. 120, National Archives and Records Service, Washington, D.C.

AFPS Records   American Fund for Public Service, Inc., Records, Rare Books, and Manuscripts Division, New York Public Library, Astor, Lenox, and Tilden Foundations, New York, N.Y.

AGO/RG407   Records of the Adjutant General's Office, Record Group No. 407, National Archives and Records Service, Washington, D.C.

AMD Papers   A. Mercer Daniel Papers, Manuscript Division, Moorland-Spingarn Research Center, Howard University, Washington, D.C.

CAB Papers   Claude A. Barnett Papers, Manuscript Division, Chicago Historical Society, Chicago, Ill.

CHH Fam.   Charles Hamilton Houston Family Collection, Houston Residence, Washington, D.C.

CHH/H&G firm files   Charles Hamilton Houston Letters, Papers and firm case files, Houston & Gardner Law Firm, Washington, D.C. (Some of the papers have been donated to the Moorland-Spingarn Research Center by Charles Houston, Jr.)

CPG Records   Consolidated Parent Group Records, Manuscript Division, Moorland-Spingarn Research Center, Howard University, Washington, D.C.

CSJ Papers   Charles S. Johnson Papers, Special Collections, Fisk University Library, Fisk University, Nashville, Tenn.

DC/NAACP   District of Columbia NAACP Branch Papers, Moorland-Spingarn Research Center, Howard University, Washington, D.C.

FDR Papers   Franklin Delano Roosevelt Papers, F. D. Roosevelt Presidential Library, Hyde Park, N.Y.

FEPC/RG228   Records of the President's Fair Employment Practice Committee, Record Group No. 228, National Archives and Record Service, Washington, D.C.

FF Papers   Felix Frankfurter Papers, Manuscript Division, Library of Congress, Washington, D.C.

HST Papers   Harry S. Truman Papers, Truman Presidential Library, Independence, Mo.

HULS Archives   Archives of the Howard University School of Law, Moorland-Spingarn Research Center, Washington, D.C.

ID/RG48   Records of the Department of Interior, 1849–1943, Record Group No. 48, National Archives and Records Service, Washington, D.C.

JD/RG60   Records of the Department of Justice, Record Group No. 60, National Archives and Records Service, Washington, D.C.

JR Papers   Julius Rosenwald Fund Collection, Special Collections, Fisk University Library, Fisk University, Nashville, Tenn.

JS Papers   Joel E. Spingarn Collection, Manuscript Division, Moorland-Spingarn Research Center, Howard University, Washington, D.C.

MH Papers   Margaret Haywood Private Files, Washington, D.C.

NAACP Records   National Association for the Advancement of Colored People Records, Manuscripts Division, Library of Congress, Washington, D.C.

PN Papers   Phileo Nash Papers, Harry S. Truman Presidential Library, Independence, Mo.

SHC Papers   Private Papers of Samuel H. Clark, Residence of Samuel H. Clark, Christiansburg, Va.

TG Papers   Thomas M. Gregory Collection, Manuscript Division, Moorland-Spingarn Research Center, Howard University, Washington, D.C.

UL Records   Urban League Records, Manuscripts Division, Library of Congress, Washington, D.C.

WLH Fam.   William LePre Houston Family Papers, Library of Congress, Washington, D.C.

WLH/H&G firm files   William LePre Houston Letters, Papers and firm case files, Houston & Gardner Law Firm, Washington, D.C.

The following initials are used in place of full names of Charles Houston, members of his family, and associates on whose letters and papers I frequently relied.

CHH   Charles Hamilton Houston
CHH Jr.   Charles Hamilton Houston, Jr.
CMH   Clotill Marconier Houston
HWH   Henrietta Williams Houston
KTH   Katherine Theresa Kirkpatrick Houston
MGH   Margaret Gladys Moran Houston
MHH   Mary Ethel Hamilton Houston
WLH   William LePre Houston
WH   William Henry Hastie, Jr.
TM   Thurgood Marshall
WW   Walter White

NOTES

PREFACE

1. CHH, "An Approach to Better Race Relations" (Address before the YWCA Convention, New York, N.Y., 5 May 1934). (Courtesy of Dr. Charles Wesley.)

2. CHH, Inscription to son in Joshua Liebman, *Peace of Mind* (New York: Simon & Schuster, 1946), p. 48.

3. Interview with WH, Philadelphia, Pa., 19 September 1972.

4. CHH to WLH, 14 April 1938, Charles H. Houston folder, Personal Correspondence, Administrative Files, C82, NAACP Records.

5. *Return to the Source: Selected Works of Amilcar Cabral* (New York: Africa Information Servcice, 1973), pp. 88–89.

6. Rayford W. Logan, *Howard University: The First Hundred Years, 1867–1967* (New York: New York University Press, 1969), p. 140.

7. See [J. Clay Smith, Jr., comp.,] "The Fiftieth Year Commenoration Law Day Dinner and Inaugural Presentation of the Charles Hamilton Houston Medallion of Merit—The Washington Bar Association, 1925–1976" (Washington, D.C., 1976); and "College Honors Charles Houston '15," *Amherst Magazine*, Spring 1978, pp. 12–14. See also Richard Kluger, *Simple Justice: The History of Brown v. Board of Education and Black America's Struggle for Equality* (New York: Alfred A. Knopf, 1976); Spottswood W. Robinson [and William H. Hastie, Jr., "No Tea for the Feeble: Two Perspectives on Charles Hamilton Houston," *Howard Law Journal* 20 (1977): 1–9; and Geraldine Segal, *In Any Fight Some Fall* (Rockville, Md.: Mercury Press, 1975), with a foreword by William H. Hastie, Jr.

8. On Houston's philosophy of law, see J. Clay Smith, Jr., "In Memoriam: Professor Frank D. Reeves—Toward a Houstonian School of Jurisprudence and the Study of Pure Legal Existence," *Howard Law Journal* 18 (1973): 1; on the Spingarn Medal, see Erwin N. Griswold, "Charles Hamilton Houston," *Negro History Bulletin* 13 (June 1950): 206, 210, 212–13.

9. Text of Spingarn Medal citation, *Negro History Bulletin* 13 (June 1950): 213.

10. See Robinson, "No Tea for the Feeble."

INTRODUCTION

1. "College Honors Charles Houston '15," *Amherst Magazine*, Spring 1978, p. 14.

2. Ibid., pp. 12, 14.

3. William O. Douglas to J. Clay Smith, 19 April 1974 (copy in possession of author, courtesy of Mr. Smith). See also 347 U.S. 483 (1954) and 347 U.S. 497 (1954).

4. William O. Douglas, *The Court Years, 1939–1975: The Autobiography of William O. Douglas* (New York: Random House, 1980), p. 185.

5. Kenneth S. Tollett, "Black Lawyers, Their Education, and Their Community," *Howard Law Journal* 17 (1972): 326–27.

6. Derrick A. Bell, Jr., "Black Faith in a Racist Land," in *From the Black Bar*, ed. Gilbert Ware (New York: G. P. Putnam's Sons, 1976), pp. 11–12.

7. 19 Howard 393 (1857).

8. A. Leon Higginbotham, Jr., "Racism and the Early American Legal Process, 1619–1896," *Annals of the American Academy of Political and Social Science* 407 (May 1973): 15.

9. 14 Stat. 27 (1866).

10. Bell, "Black Faith in a Racist Land," p. 12.

11. 109 U.S. 3 (1883) and 163 U.S. 537 (1896).

12. See Mary Frances Berry, *Black Resistance/White Law: A History of Constitutional Racism in America* (Englewood Cliffs, N.J.: Prentice-Hall, 1971), pp. 100, 103–239 passim. See also John Hope Franklin, *From Slavery to Freedom*, 5th ed. (New York: Alfred A. Knopf, 1980), pp. 263–69.

13. William H. Hastie, Jr., "Toward an Equalitarian Legal Order," *Annals of the American Academy of Political and Social Science* 407 (May 1973): 19–20 passim.

14. Jerold Auerbach, *Unequal Justice: Lawyers and Social Change in Modern America* (New York: Oxford University Press, 1976), p. 102.

15. Berry, *Black Resistance/White Law*, p. 236.

16. Oliver Wendell Holmes, *The Common Law*, as quoted in A. Leon Higginbotham, Jr., *In the Matter of Color—Race and the American Legal Process: The Colonial Period* (New York: Oxford University Press, 1978), p. 14.

17. Howard Thurman, *With Head and Heart* (New York: Harcourt Brace Jovanovich, 1979), pp. 10, 2–29 passim.

18. *The Complete Poems of Paul Laurence Dunbar* (1913; reprint. New York: Dodd, Mead & Co., 1962), p. 479.

19. Charles H. Houston, "An Approach to Better Race Relations" (Address before the YWCA Convention, New York, N.Y.), 5 May 1934.

20. Langston Hughes, ed., "The Negro Speaks of Rivers," in Langston Hughes and Arna Bontemps, *The Poetry of the Negro, 1746–1970* (Garden City, N.Y.: Anchor Press/Doubleday & Co., Inc.), p. 187.

21. Lawrence W. Levine, *Black Culture and Black Consciousness from Slavery to Freedom* (New York: Oxford University Press, 1977), p. xi.

22. See Donald Bogle, *Toms, Coons, Mulattoes, Mammies, and Bucks: An Interpretative History of Blacks in American Films* (New York: Viking Press, 1973).

23. W. E. B. Du Bois, "The Souls of Black Folk," in *Three Negro Classics* (New York: Avon Books, 1965), p. 215.

24. Pauli Murray, "Dark Testament," in *Dark Testament and Other Poems* (Comstock Hill, Conn.: Silvermine Publishers, 1970), p. 24.

25. See Chinweizu, *The West and the Rest of Us* (New York: Vintage Books, 1975), pp. 431–57 passim.

26. Carolyn Rodgers, "For H. W. Fuller," in C. Rodgers, *Songs of a Black Bird* (Chicago: Third World Press, 1969), p. 30.

CHAPTER ONE
The Inheritance

1. [WLH & CHH,] "Obituary [of MHH]," typescript, n.d. [c. May 1947], p. 3, General Correspondence, CHH, CSJ Papers; interview with CMH, 21 June 1972 and 16 January 1973.

2. [WLH & CHH,] "Obituary [of MHH]," typescript, n.d. [c. May 1947], p. 3, General Correspondence, CHH, CSJ; telephone conversation with J. Pendergrass, 1 May 1982.

3. [WLH & CHH,] "Obituary [of MHH]," typescript, n.d. [c. May 1947], p. 3, General Correspondence, CHH, CSJ Papers.

4. Ibid.; interview with CMH, 21 June 1972 and 16 January 1973; KTH, "Autobiography—Mrs. T. J. Houston," manuscript, pp. 1–25 passim, WLH/H&G firm files; *The Colored American*, 4 March 1899, p. 1; conversation with James Pendergrass and Ulysses J. Houston, 18 July 1978.

5. Luis Emilio, *A Brave Black Regiment* (Boston: Boston Book Co., 1891).

6. *The Colored American*, 4 March 1899, p. 1; KTH, "Autobiography," p. 25; [WLH,] "Obituary [of KTH]," typescript, n.d. [c. May 1935], WLH/H&G firm files; interveiw with CMH, 26 December 1972; Population Schedule of the Seventh Census of the united States, Slave Inhabitants in Cumberland County Kentucky, 1850, s.v. "Owner: Milton King," microfilm, National Archives and Records Service, Washington, D.C. See John W. Blassingame, *The Slave Community: Plantation Life in the Antebellum South*, rev. ed. (New York: Oxford University Press, 1979); Herbert G. Gutman, *The Black Family in Salvery and Freedom, 1750–1925* (New York: Random House, 1976); and Albert Raboteau, *Slave Religion* (New York: Oxford University Press, 1978).

7. KTH, "Autobiography," p. 1. Blassingame, *The Slave Community*, pp. 249–83.

8. KTH, "Autobiography," pp. 14–22 passim.

9. Ibid., p. 23.

10. Ibid., pp. 25–26; [WLH,] "Obituary [of KTH]," p. 1.

11. KTH, "Autobiography," pp. 26–27.

12. Ibid., pp. 29, 31, 43: Two children, a daughter Zenora and a son, died in infancy; interview with CMH, 21 June 1972, 19 November 1973, and 8 December 1973; *Afro-American*, 31 December 1949, pp. 1, 2. See Appendix 1, Houston genealogy.

13. KTH, "Autobiography," pp. 32, 35.

14. [WLH & CHH,] "Obituary [of MHH]," p. 2.

15. KTH, "Autobiography," pp. 6, 30, 36; interview with CMH, 21 June 1972.

16. [WLH & CHH,] "Obituary [of MHH]," p. 2; and "Biographical Sketch of William L. Houston," second draft, n.d. [c. 1942], p. 1, WLH/H&G firm files; *Boyd's Directory of the District of Columbia, 1891*, p. 528.

17. 20 Stat. 102–108 (1878); David L. Lewis, *District of Columbia: A Bicentennial History* (New York: W. W. Norton & Co., 1976), pp. 40–70 passim; U.S. Department of Interior, Census Office, *Compendium of the Eleventh Cen-*

sus, 1890, I: Population (Washington, D.C.: Government Printing Office, 1892), pp. 2, 473.

18. Lewis, *District of Columbia*, pp. 66–71 passim; Rayford W. Logan, *Betrayal of the Negro* (New York: Collier Books, 1965), pp. 26, 320.

19. "The Nation's Capital: How Can It Achieve More Democracy?" transcript, 19 December 1948, p. 3, CHH folder, Board of Directors file, NAACP Records.

20. U.S. Department of Interior, Census Office, *Report on Population, 1890*, pt. 2 (Washington, D.C.: Government Printing Office, 1892), p. 544; Lewis, *District of Columbia*, pp. 66–73 passim; Edward Ingle, *The Negro in the District of Columbia* (Baltimore: Johns Hopkins University Press, 1893), pp. 48–49; U.S. Department of Commerce, Bureau of Census, *Historical Statistics of the United States: Colonial Times to 1957* (Washington, D.C.: Government Printing Office, 1960), p. 710; U.S. Department of Interior, *Official Register of the United States, II & III*, Washington, D.C.: 1892, NA; Rayford W. Logan, *Howard University: The First Hundred Years, 18671967* (New York: New York University Press, 1969).

21. Interview with CMH, 24 July 1972 and 19 November 1973; *Washington Post*, 21 December 1952, clipping, CHH vertical file, Washington, D.C. (hereafter Washingtoniana); "Biographical Sketch of William L. Houston," second draft, n.d. [c. 1942], pp. 1–2, WLH/H&G firm files; "Biographical Sketch of William LePre Houston," n.d. [c. 1933–35], p. 1, CHH/H&G firm case files.

22. [WLH & CHH,] "Obituary [of MHH]," pp. 1–3.

23. Ibid.; CHH to WLH, 20 November 1934, WLH/H&G firm files; see Blassingame, *The Slave Community*, pp. 249–83.

24. [WLH & CHH,] "Obituary [of MHH], p. 1; Population Schedule for the Ninth Census of the United States, Cedarville, Green County, Ohio, s.v. "Hamilton, Amzi," microfilm, NA; population schedule for Tenth Census of the United States, Cedarville, Green County, Ohio, s.v. "Hamilton, Amziah," microfilm, NA. See Houston genealogy, Appendix 1, and interview with CMH, 21 June 1972. For discussion of black views on the Fugitive Slave Law of 1850 and the *Dred Scott* decision, see Vincent Harding, *There Is a River: The Black Struggle for Freedom in America* (New York: Harcourt Brace Jovanovich, 1981), pp. 200–203.

25. [WLH & CHH,] "Obituary [of MHH]," p. 1.

26. Ibid., p. 3; "Biographical Sketch of William L. Houston," second draft.

27. Interview with CMH, 21 June 1972 and 24 July 1972.

CHAPTER TWO
Charles Hamilton Houston

1. Interview with CMH, 24 July 1972; *Boyd's Directory of the District of Columbia, 1895* (Washington, D.C.: William H. Boyd, 1895), p. 519; *Boyd's Directory of the District of Columbia, 1896* (Washington, D.C.: William H. Boyd, 1896), p. 516; *Washington Post*, 21 December 1952, clipping, CHH verticle file, Washingtoniana. See Appendix 1, Houston genealogy.

2. [WLH & CHH] "Obituary [of MHH]," typescript copy n.d. [c. May 1947], p. 2, General Correspondence - CHH, CSJ Papers; cf. *Boyd's Directory of the District of Columbia, 1895*, p. 519, with *Boyd's Directory of the District*

of Columbia, 1897, p. 512, and *Boyd's Directory of the District of Columbia, 1898*, p. 538; *Afro-American* (Washington, D.C.) n.d. [c. December 1952], clipping, CHH verticle file, Washingtoniana; interview with CMH, 24 July 1972.

3. *The Colored American* (Washington, D.C.) 4 March 1899, pp. 1, 2.

4. Interview with CMH, 24 July 1972 and 7 December 1973; conversation with Ulysses J. Houston and James Pendergrass, 18 July 1978; Christine Young Perry to author, 26 October 1972.

5. Interview with CMH, 24 July 1972 and 7 December 1973, Christine Young Perry to author, 26 October 1972; "The Nation's Capital: How Can It Achieve More Democracy?" CHH, Board of Directors file, NNACP Papers.

6. 13 Stat. 191 (1864); 12 Stat. 402, 407, 537–538 (1862); Constance M. Green, *The Secret City* (Princeton: Princeton University Press, 1967), p. 138; Mary G. Hundley, *The Dunbar Story, 1870–1955* (New York: Vantage Press, 1965), pp. 62–63.

7. Jacobeth P. Novak, Director of School Attendance and Work Permits, Public Schools of Washington, D.C., to author, 5 December 1973; Official transcript of CHH (copy), M Street (presently Dunbar) High School, 10 February 1908 [–11 June 1911]; interview with CMH, 24 July 1972.

8. *Boyd's Directory of the District of Columbia, 1908*, p. 675; *Boyd's Directory of the District of Columbia, 1909*, p. 700; *Boyd's Directory of the District of Columbia, 1910*, p. 728; *Boyd's Directory of the District of Columbia, 1911*, p. 777; *Washington Post*, 21 December 1952, clipping, CHH verticle file, Washingtoniana; "William L. Houston," typewritten resumé, n.d. [c. 1952], [WLH,] Excelsior Diary, 1909, and [WLH,] Standard Diary, 1910, WLH/ H&G firm files.

9. "William L. Houston," typewritten resumé, n.d. [c. 1952], [WLH,] Standard Diary, 1910, 1911, WLH/H&G firm files.

10. *Washington Post*, 21 December 1952; [WLH & CHH] "Obituary of [MHH]," p. 4; interview with CMH, 26 July 1972.

11. [WLH & CHH,] "Obituary of [MHH]," p. 5; [WLH,] "Biographical Sketch of William L. Houston," second draft, n.d. [c. 1942], pp 1, 2; *Afro-American*, 24 December 1949; interview with CMH, 21 June 1972 and 24 July 1972; KTH, "Autobiography," p. 1, WLH/H&G firm files; interview with Samuel Clark, 26 July 1972; CHH, "Saving the World for Democracy" *Pittsburgh Courier*, 20 July 1940–12 October 1940, clippings, CHH/H&G firm files.

12. [Campbell C. Johnson,] "Autobiography," draft, n.d., p. 7, Biographical Material, Campbell C. Johnson Papers, Manuscript Division, Moorland-Spingarn Research Center, Howard University, Washington, D.C.

13. Thomas Sowell, "Black Excellence—The Case of Dunbar High School," *The Public Interest* 35 (Spring 1974): 5.

14. Hundley, *Dunbar Story*, p. 30; interview with Bertha McNeill, 13 March 1972; Bertha McNeill to author, 22 March 1973.

15. Bertha McNeill to author, 22 March 1973.

16. Hundley, *Dunbar Story*, p. 31; T. Sowell, "Black Excellence," *The Public Interest* 35 (Spring 1974): 5.

17. Interview with Sterling Brown, 12 January 1974. See interview with Bertha McNeill, 13 March 1972; *Washington Star-News*, 25 March 1974, p. C7.

18. Sowell, "Black Excellence," p. 6. Hundley, *Dunbar Story*, pp. 30–31 passim.

19. David L. Lewis, *District of Columbia: A Bicentennial History* (New York: W. W. Norton & Co., 1976), pp. 70–78 passim; Green, *Secret City*, pp. 126, 150–54 passim.

20. See Alfred Moss, *The American Negro Academy* (Baton Rouge: Louisiana State University Press, 1981).

21. Hundley, *Dunbar Story*, pp. 30–31; Adelaid C. Hill, "Black Education in the Seventies: A Lesson from the Past," in Floyd Barbour, ed., *The Black Seventies* (Boston: Porter Sargent, 1970), p. 59; Sowell, "Black Excellence," p. 9.

22. Interview with Bertha McNeill, 13 March 1972.

23. Bertha McNeill to author, 22 March 1972.

24. Interview with Bertha McNeill, 13 March 1972.

25. Jessica Fauset to Mary Houston, 29 April 1910, Cont. 7, WLH Fam.

26. Interview with Bertha McNeill, 13 March 1972.

27. Official transcript of CHH (copy), M Street (presently Dunbar) High School, 10 February 1908 [–11 June 1911]; WH, "Charles Hamilton Houston," *Negro History Bulletin* 13 (June 1950): 208; [WLH], Standard Diary, 11 June 1911, WLH/H&G firm files.

28. Sowell, "Black Excellence"; interview with Sterling Brown, 12 January 1974; conversation with Ernest McKinney, 17 October 1974. See Marcia Synnott, "The Half-opened Door: Researching Admissions Discrimination at Harvard, Yale, and Princeton," *American Archivist* 45 (Spring 1982): 176–77.

29. Interview with Edward Lovett, 18 January 1973. See [WLH,] Standard Diary 11, 25, 26, 28, 30 June 1911; 1, 11, 18 July 1911; 11, 13, 14, 26, 27 September 1911, WLH/H&G firm files. See also [WLH,] Standard Diary June & July 1914.

30. Interview with CMH, 24 July 1972. See CHH to "Dad" [WLH], 10 July 1938, CHH/H&G firm files.

31. [CHH,] Untitled Recollections of Amherst and World War I, n.d., p. 1, CHH/H&G firm files.

32. CHH to WLH, 27 January 1913, Cont. 7, WLH Fam.; see also correspondence of this period with mother and father.

33. CHH to WLH, 26 April 1914, Cont. 7, WLH Fam.

34. Ibid.

35. [CHH,] Untitled Recollections of Amherst and World War I, n.d., p. 1, CHH/H&G firm files.

36. Interview with CMH, 24 July 1972.

37. CHH to WLH, 27 January 1913, Cont. 7, WLH Fam.

38. Ibid.

39. Robert F. Grose, registrar, Amherst College to author, 10 March 1972 with enclosures, excerpt from *Olio* 1915 re CHH.

40. Official Transcript of CHH (copy), Amherst College, 1911–15.

41. Interview with CMH, 24 July 1972. See Darlene M. Holdsworth, Assistant Archivist of Special Collections, Amherst College, to author, 24 August 1973; *Crisis* 10 (May 1915: 8; "Ninety-fourth Commencement," Amherst College, 30 June 1915 (program), CHH Fam.

42. Robert F. Gross to author, 10 March 1972, with enclosurs, excerpts from Amherst College Catalogue, 1910–11, 1915–16; "Ninety-fourth Commencement," Amherst College, 30 June 1915 (program); official transcript of CHH (copy), Amherst College, 1911–15. (On an undated postcard [CHH/

H&G firm files], Houston discussed climbing to the top of the chapel and carving his initials. A visit of 24 April 1978 to Amherst and Johnson Chapel Tower with Charles Houston, Jr., confirmed Houston Sr.'s report.)

43. [WLH,] Standard Diary, 30 June 1915; "Ninety-fourth Commencement," Amherst College, 30 June 1915 (program), CHH Fam.; interview with CMH, 21 November 1973.

44. Gordon Hall to CHH, 17 April 1945; CHH to Gordon Hall 25 April 1945; Louis Eaton to CHH 2 July 1946; CHH to "Dad" [WLH] 10 July 1938; CHH/H&G firm files.

45. [WLH & CHH,] "Obituary [of MHH]," p. 1, and [WLH] Standard Diary, 18 May, 1 June 1915 WLH/H&G firm files; interview with CMH, 24 July 1972.

46. Interview with CMH, 24 July 1972; [WLH,] Standard Diary, 1 June 1915 and 2 August 1916; interview with MGH, 22 January 1973.

CHAPTER THREE
"Army Justice"

1. [WLH,] Standard Diary, 1 June 1915. See [WLH,] Standard Diary, 14 January, 5 February, 1 March and 18 May; Rayford W. Logan, *Howard University: The First Hundred Years, 1867–1967* (New York: New York University Press, 1969), p. 169.

2. Logan, *Howard University*, p. 169.

3. Walter Dyson, *Howard University, the Capstone of Negro Education, A History: 1867–1940* (Washington, D.C.: Graduate School of Howard University, 1941), pp. 119–22, 336, 369; Logan, *Howard University*, pp. 142–44.

4. "Bro. Charles Hamilton Houston," *The Sphinx* (publication of Alpha Phi Alpha), October 1923, p. 5, CHH/H&G firm files.

5. CHH, "Saving the World for Democracy" *Pittsburgh Courier*, 14 September 1940, clipping, CHH/H&G firm files. See CHH, "Saving the World for Democracy," *Pittsburgh Courier* (Chicago edition) 20 July 1940, clipping, CHH/H&G firm files.

6. See Barbara Joyce Ross, *J. E. Spingarn and the Rise of the NAACP* (New York: Atheneum, 1972), and Charles Flint Kellogg, *NAACP: A History of the National Association for the Advancement of Colored People, 1909–1920*, vol. 1. (Baltimore: Johns Hopkins University Press, 1967).

7. CHH, "Saving the World for Democracy," *Pittsburgh Courier*, 20 July 1940.

8. Ibid.

9. Ross, *Spingarn and the Rise of the NAACP*, p. 90.

10. CHH, "Saving the World for Democracy," *Pittsburgh Courier*, 20 July 1940; [Campbell C. Johnson,] "Howard University and the Two Wars," unpublished speech, March 1943, pp. 1–2, Speeches, Box 3, Campbell C. Johnson Papers, Manuscript Division, Moorland-Spingarn Research Center, Howard University, Washington, D.C. (hereafter MSRC).

11. Central Committee of Negro College Men to "Dear Brother," 14 May 1917, Cont. 26, WLH Fam.

12. CHH, "Saving the World for Democracy," *Pittsburgh Courier* 20 July 1940; Emmett Scott, *Scott's Official History of the American Negro in the World War* (New York: Arno Press and New York Times, 1969), pp. 84–89 passim.

13. CHH, "Saving the World for Democracy," *Pittsburgh Courier*, 14 September 1940.

14. CHH, "Saving the World for Democracy," *Pittsburgh Courier* 20 July 1940.

15. Ibid.

16. Seventeenth Provisional Training Regiment Commanding Officer to AGO [Adjutant General's Office], 10 July 1917, AGO/RG407; *Leslie's Illustrated Weekly*, 13 October 1917, clipping, Newspaper Clippings, Fort Des Moines Officers; Training Camp for Negro Officers—World War I, Military Box 1, Thomas Montgomery Gregory Collection, Manuscript Division, MSRC (hereafter TG papers); CHH, "Saving the World for Democracy," Pittsburgh Courier, 27 July 1940, clipping, CHH/H&G firm files; interview with Earl B. Dickerson, 29 March 1973.

17. Seventeenth Provisional Regiment Commanding Officer, to AGO, 10 July 1917. See *Leslie's Illustrated Weekly*, 13 October 1917.

18. Seventeenth Provisional Regiment Commanding Officer to AGO, 10 July 1917.

19. AGO to Commanding General, Central Department, Chicago, Ill., 19 July 1919 (War Department Memo on Fort Des Moines) AGO/RG407.

20. CHH, "Saving the World for Democracy" *Pittsburgh Courier*, 27 July 1940.

21. "Welcome Reception for Officers of the Seventeenth Provisional Training Regiment," program, Central Committee of Negro College Men file, Box 1, TG Papers; [WLH,] Standard Diary, 17–30 October 1917; interview with MGH, 22 January 1973.

22. Return of Company G, 368th Infantry, Camp Meade, November 1917, 369th Inf. 1917–19 Officers Returns and Rosters, AEF (1917–23) RG120; *Afro-American* (Baltimore) 9 April 1938, clipping, CHH vertical file, MSRC: [WLH,] Standard Diary, November–December 1917 and [WLH,] Liberty War Diary, January–June 1918; interview with Rayford W. Logan, 18 October 1917; CHH to Donald G. Lathrop, 21 November 1940, CHH/H&G firm files.

23. CHH to Thomas MacDonald, 12 June 1942, CHH/H&G firm files.

24. CHH, "Saving the World for Democracy," *Pittsburgh Courier*, 24 August 1940, clipping, CHH/H&G firm files.

25. CHH, 'Saving the World for Democracy," ms., 2 August 1940, p. 2, CHH/H&G firm files.

26. [WLH,] Liberty War Diary, 24 February–26 May 1918; interview with WH, 19 September 1972; interview with CMH, 24 July 1972.

27. CHH to Continental Casualty Company, 7 January 1918, Cont. 20, WLH Fam.

28. CHH, "Saving the World for Democracy," *Pittsburgh Courier*, 24 August 1940.

29. Ibid.

30. CHH, "Saving the World for Democracy," *Pittsburgh Courier*, 31 August 1940, clipping, CHH/H&G firm files. See CHH, "Saving the World for Democracy," *Pittsburgh Courier*, 9 August 1940 and 7 September 1940, clippings; [WLH,] Liberty War Diary, 16–18 September 1918. See also Return of Company G, 368th Infantry, June 1918, Camp Meade and "Condition of the Regiment at Midnight the last day of June, 1918" Returns of 368th Infantry, 1917–1918–1919, AEF (1917–23) RG120; "Fifty Years of Progress in the

Armed Forces," ms., 7 June 1950, p. 11, Box 4, Campbell C. Johnson Papers, Manuscript Division, MSRC.

31. CHH, "Saving the World for Democracy," *Pittsburgh Courier*, 7 September 1940, clipping, CHH/H&G firm files.

32. CHH, "Saving the World for Democracy," *Pittsburgh Courier*, 9 August 1940, clipping, CHH/H&G firm files.

33. CHH, "Saving the World for Democracy," *Pittsburgh Courier*, 7 & 14 September 1940, clippings, CHH/H&G firm files; interview with Joseph L. Johnson, 26 October 1972; interview with Rayford W. Logan, 18 October 1971; Jetta Norris Jones to author, 3 October 1978; CHH, "Saving the World for Democracy," *Pittsburgh Courier*, 21 September 1940, clipping, CHH/H&G firm files.

34. CHH to MHH, 27 December 1918, Cont. 21, WLH Fam.

35. CHH to MHH, 5 January 1919, and Diary of CHH, 1919, 1 & 3 January Cont. 19, WLH Fam.

36. Diary of CHH, 3 January 1919, Cont. 19, WLH Fam.

37. Diary of CHH, 21 January 1919, Cont. 19, WLH Fam.; and see CHH to MHH, 24 November 1918, Cont. 21, WLH Fam.

38. Diary of CHH, 16 Janruary 1919, Cont. 19, WLH Fam.

39. Ibid.

40. CHH, "Saving the World for Democracy," *Pittsburgh Courier*, 5 October 1940, clipping, CHH/H&G firm files; field return of the 3rd Battalion, 351st Field Artillery, 22 February 1919, 351st Field Artillery Regument Field and Strength Returns, 92nd Division, AEF/RG120.

41. CHH to MHH, 5 January 1919, Cont. 21, WLH Fam.

42. CHH, "Saving the World for Democracy," *Pittsburgh Courier*, 5 October 1940.

43. [WLH,] Excelsior Diary, 25 February 1919; 7, 11, & 12 March 1919; 3 April 1919; interview with WH, 19 September 1972; "Saving the World for Democracy," *Pittsburgh Courier*, 12 October 1940, clipping, CHH/H&G firm files.

CHAPTER FOUR
Studying Law at Home and Abroad

1. John Hope Franklin, *From Slavery to Freedom*, 4th ed. rev. (New York; Alfred A. Knopf, 1974), p. 355.

2. CHH to U.S. Veterans Bureau, 19 January 192[2], Cont. 4, WLH Fam.

3. CHH, "Saving the World for Democracy," *Pittsburgh Courier*, 14 September 1940, clipping, [WLH,] Excelsior Diary, 17 April 1919, interview MGH, 22 January 1973.

4. Franklin, *From Slavery to Freedom*, p. 357. See Eugene Levy, *James Weldon Johnson: Black Leader, Black Voice* (Chicago: University of Chicago Press, 1973), pp. 200–202.

5. Franklin, *From Slavery to Freedom*, p. 357 and pp. 349–50 passim.

6. Ibid., p. 358 and pp. 348–61 passim.

7. Application for executive clemency, October 1926, CHH/H&G firm files: After Charles Houston began law school he assisted with this case, and when he had completed school he worked for clemency for "T.S. Jones," who

was convicted of manslaughter. Charles Houston corresponded with Jones until 1929, when he was released. With Charles's help he sought and found gainful employment by 1930. (The client's name is not used here for reasons of the privileged nature of the files and the former client's wish to live in anonymity.)

8. Marcia Synnott, "The Half-opened Door: Researching Admissions Discrimination at Harvard, Yale, and Princeton," *American Archivist* 45 (Spring 1982): 176–77.

9. See Chapter 11; see also Mrs. W. L. Stark "To Whom It May Concern" 1903, Cont. 7, WLH Fam.

10. Erwin Griswold, "Charles Hamilton Houston," *Negro History Bulletin* 13 (June 1950): 216. See "Record of Charles Hamilton Houston . . . from September 19, 1919 to . . . June 21, 1923," Harvard Law School; CHH, "Liabilities," blue book, 3 January 1920 enclosure of J. H. Beale to CHH, 13 June 1923, CHH/H&G firm files. See also interview with CMH, 24 July 1972.

11. Interview with Raymond Pace Alexander, 18 September 1972. See [WLH,] Standard Diary, 23 December 1920; "Bro. Charles H. Houston," *Sphinx* (October 1923): 5.

12. Interviews with MGH, 22 January 1973; Edward Mazique, 8 January 1973; and R. P. Alexander, 18 September 1972. See CHH's series "Saving the World for Democracy," CHH/H&G firm files.

13. List of subscribers to Garvey Luncheon, 17 January 1921, WLH Fam.

14. Report of Agent C. H. Houston in re 19 January 1921 luncheon for Garvey, WLH Fam.

15. Ibid.

16. See CHH, "An Approach to Better Race Relations," Address delivered during the 13th national convention of the Young Women's Christian Association (YWCA) of America, 5 May 1934 (courtesy of Dr. Charles Wesley; and National Board of YWCA, New York). See also Chapter 8.

17. Roscoe Pound to "My dear Sir," 27 September 1921, enclosed in CHH to U.S. Veterans Bureau, 19 January 192[2].

18. Interview with R. P. Alexander, 18 September 1972. See *Harvard Law Review* 35 (1921–22).

19. Interview with R. P. Alexander, 18 September 1972. See Roscoe Pound to CHH, 27 September 1921; "Record of Charles Hamilton Houston . . . September 19, 1919 to . . . June 21, 1923"; Griswold, "Charles Hamilton Houston," p. 210.

20. Pound to "My dear Sir," 27 September 1921.

21. CHH to "Folks," 8 January 1922, Cont. 7, WLH Fam.

22. Interview with R. P. Alexander, 18 September 1972.

23. CHH to U.S. Veterans Bureau, 19 January 192[2].

24. Pound to "My dear Sir," 27 September 1921.

25. "Record of Charles Hamilton Houston . . . September 19, 1919 to . . . June 21, 1923."

26. John H. Muller, Jr. (of the Harvard Law School Alumni Center) to author, 7 December 1973; CHH, Preliminary Reports on "Functional Study of the Requirements of Notice and Hearing in Governmental Action in the United States," prepared for Felix Frankfurter (copies) April and June, 1923, in possession of CHH Jr. See Roscoe Pound to Fenton Booth, 3 December 1923 (copy) in possession of author. (Librarians have not been able to locate the dis-

sertation.) See also interview with R. P. Alexander, 18 September 1972, and Raymond Pace Alexander, "Voices from Harvard's Negroes," *Opportunity* 1 (March 1923): 29–31. See also Roscoe Pound, *An Introduction to the Philosophy of Law* (New Haven: Yale University Press, 1922).

27. CHH, "Report Under the Sheldon Travelling Fellowship in Law, 1923–24" (copy), CHH correspondence and reports, Survey, Houston, Negro legal Status, Laura Spelman Rockefeller Memorial, Rockefeller Archive Center. (I wish to thank Professor August Meier for making copies of materials on Charles Houston from this collection available to me.). Also: Interview with CMH, 21 June and 24 July 1972; interview with WH, 19 September 1972; [WLH,] Standard Diary, 4 September 1923.

28. CHH, "Report Under the Sheldon Travelling Fellowship in Law, 1923–24," pp. 1–11 passim. See CHH to Roscoe Pound, 9 October 1923, CHH, Additional Correspondence, Roscoe Pound Papers, Manuscripts Division, Langdell Library, Harvard Law School, Cambridge, Massachusetts (hereinafter RP Papers) (courtesy Manuscripts Librarian).

29. CHH to Roscoe Pound, 9 October 1923, CHH, Additional Correspondence RP Papers; CHH, "Report Under the Sheldon Travelling Fellowship in Law, 1923–4," pp. 8–22 passim. See CHH to Roscoe Pound, 11 December 1923, and Roscoe Pound to CHH, 31 December 1923, CHH, Additional Correspondence RP Papers.

30. CHH to Cervera Little, 20 June 1942, CHH/H&G firm files. See CHH to R. C. Bruce, 20 May 1943, CHH/H&G firm files; interview with WH, 19 September 1972; interview with CMH, 24 July 1972; CHH, "Report Under the Sheldon Travelling Fellowship in Law, 1923–24," pp. 15–22 passim.

31. Interview with CMH, 24 July 1972. See [CHH,] Biographical Statement, ms., n.d. [c. 1947], CHH/H&G firm files.

32. See Tony Martin, *Race First: The Ideological and Organizational Struggles of Marcus Garvey and the Universal Negro Improvement Association* (Westport, Conn.: Greenwood Press, 1976), David L. Lewis, *When Harlem Was in Vogue* (New York: Alfred A. Knopf, 1981); and Nathan Huggins, *Harlem Renaissance* (New York: Oxford University Press, 1971).

33. [WLH,] Standard Diary, 1 June, 10 August, 23 August 1924; interview with MGH, 22 January 1973; certificate of admission to practice, District Court, District of Columbia, 9 June 1924, CHH/H&G firm files.

CHAPTER FIVE
Houston & Houston

1. See the Statutes at Large of the Supreme Order of Helpers (Washington, D.C., 1915), WLH/H&G firm files; [WLH,] Standard Diary, entries for 9 June–31 December 1924; interview with CMH, 24 July 1972.

2. See WLH firm case files, 1908–24, WLH/H&G firm files; interview with CMH, 24 July 1972, 12 February 1974; interview with WH, 19 September 1972.

3. Interviews with WH, 19 September 1972; Margaret Haywood, 2 January 1973; Juanita Kidd Stout, 21 August 1972; and Benjamn Amos, 17 January 1973. Conversation with Thurgood Marshall, 6 April 1978.

4. Interview with CMH, 24 July 1972. See also interviews with Judges

M. Haywood and J. Stout and conversation with Justice Marshall. See [WLH,] Biographical Sketch, ms., n.d. [c. 1933–35], CHH/H&G firm case files: William L. Houston served as Professor of Law at Howard from 1921 to 1936, lecturing on insurance, office management, and legal ethics.

5. Interview with Juanita Kidd Stout, 21 August 1972. See HWH, untitled notes on CHH, CHH Fam.

6. *Washington Post*, 21 December 1952, clipping, CHH vertical file, Washingtoniana, District of Columbia Public Library, Washington, D.C.; "William L. Houston," resumé, n.d. [c. 1952], WLH/H&G firm files.

7. Interview with Benjamin Amos, 17 January 1973.

8. See also my "Charles Hamilton Houston (1895–1950) and the Struggle for Civil Rights" (Ph.D. diss. University of Chicago, 1975), Appendix C, Table 6, pp. 485–89.

9. See my "Charles Hamilton Houston," Appendix C, Table 7, pp. 490–510.

10. See "Charles Hamilton Houston" p. 83, note 2 for information on the estates of CHH and WLH. See also below, p. 79, regarding CHH's law school income. (Data in Table 2 on CHH's earnings and expenditures extracted from sources in the Laura Spelman Rockefeller Memorial made available courtesy of Professor August Meier.)

11. 276 U.S. 154 (1927); see 72 L.Ed. 506–508.

CHAPTER SIX
The Transformation of Howard University Law School

1. Interview with Sterling Brown, 12 January 1974. See, e.g., Sterling Brown, *Negro Caravan* (New York: Dryden Press, 1941); see also Michael Harper, ed., *The Collected Poems of Sterling A. Brown* (New York: Harper & Row, 1980).

2. CHH to Joseph H. Beale, 14 April 1932, HULS Archives; J[oseph] H. Beale to CHH, 13 June 1923, CHH/H&G firm files; Roscoe Pound to Fenton W. Booth, 31 December 1923 (copy), in my possession; Felix Frankfurter to CHH, 3 January 1924, CHH/H&G firm files; interview with Edward Lovett, 18 January 1973. See CHH to U.S. Veterans Bureau, 19 January 1922, Cont. 4, WLH Fam.

3. Roscoe Pound to Fenton W. Booth, 31 December 1923.

4. WW to Roger N. Baldwin, 8 July 1933, American Fund for Public Service, *Applications Favorably Acted Upon* 8:135, AFPS; Felix Frankfurter to CHH, 3 January 1924, CHH/H&G firm files.

5. See my "'To Meet the Group Needs': The Transformation of Howard University School of Law, 1920–1935," in Vincent P. Franklin and James Anderson, eds., *New Perspectives on Black Educational History* (Boston: G. K. Hall, 1978), pp. 149–71.

6. Rayford W. Logan, *Howard University: The First Hundred Years 1867–1967* (New York: New York University Press, 1969), p. 225; see McNeil "'To Meet the Group Needs'"; see also Jerold Auerbach, *Unequal Justice: Lawyers and Social Change in Modern America* (New York: Oxford University Press, 1976), pp. 95–99 passim.

7. Felix Frankfurter to CHH, 3 January 1924, CHH/H&G firm files.

8. Notes of CHH for Agency, Surety, Administrative Law, and Jurispru-

dence courses, AMD Papers; *Howard University Record* 19 (November 1924): 31–32. See Howard University catalogs for 192526, pp. 22, 267, 272–73.

9. Interview with WH, 19 September 1972, and Thurgood Marshall, "Homage to Charles Houston," Address delivered at Amherst College, Amherst, Massachusetts, 6 April 1978.

10. A. Mercer Daniel, "History–School of Law–Howard University," ms., n.d. [c. 1972], chap. 2, pp. 22–23, 26 HULS Archives.

11. Interview with Joseph L. Johnson, 26 October 1972.

12. Interview with WH, 19 September 1972.

13. Daniel, "History–School of Law–Howard University," p. 23.

14. Spottswood W. Robinson III, "No Tea for the Feeble: Two Perspectives on Charles Hamilton Houston," *Howard Law Journal* 20 (1977): 5.

15. Ibid., p. 7.

16. Interview with WH, 19 September 1972.

17. CHH, "Lecture 1, Jurisprudence" and "Notes," typescript and handwritten notes, n.d. [c. 1924], AMD Papers.

18. [CHH,] "Jurisprudence Examination," 20 November 1924, AMD Papers.

19. Ibid., 18 December 1924, AMD Papers.

20. CHH, Administrative Law notes, n.d., AMD Papers.

21. CHH, Jurisprudence examination, 21 May 1926, AMD papers.

22. See CHH, "The Need for Negro Lawyers," *Journal of Negro Education* 4 (January 1935): 49–52.

23. Charter of the Washington Bar Association (copy), enclosed in J. Clay Smith, Jr., to author, 10 February 1975.

24. CHH to Felix Frankfurter, 29 December 1925, General Correspondence—CHH, Box 67, Felix Frankfurter Papers, Library of Congress, Washington, D.C.

25. "Howard University Law School Announces Legal Survey," press release, n.d. [c. 1927], CHH/H&G firm files; [WLH,] Standard Diary, 15 November 1927.

26. Ibid.

27. [WLH,] Standard Diary, 15 November 1927; Association for the Study of Negro Life and History, "Annual Report of Director," 1 July 1927–30 June 1928, p. 5; correspondence and reports of CHH to Leonard Outhwaite, November 1927–May 1928, Survey, Houston Negro Legal Status, Laura Spelman Rockefeller Memorial, Tarrytown, New York (hereafter LSR Collection).

28. CHH, "Survey of Howard University Law Students," 1927, CHH/H&G firm files.

29. Interview with MGH, 22 January 1973.

30. CHH to Leonard Outhwaite, 13 June 1928, LSR Collection.

31. CHH to Leonard Outhwaite, 11 July 1928, LSR Collection.

33. Emmett Scott to CHH, 27 September 1928, AMD Papers; interview with MGH, 22 January 1973; CHH to Senior Class, Howard University Law School, 18 January 1928, AMD Papers.

34. Logan, *Howard University*, pp. 226–27, 248, 266–67; Benjamin E. Mays, "The Relevance of Mordecai Wyatt Johnson," *New Directions* 5 (April 1978): 16–19.

35. CHH, "Personal Observations on the Summary of Studies in Legal Education as Applied to the Howard University School of Law," ms., 28 May 1929, CHH/H&G firm files; Logan, *Howard University*, p. 267.

36. CHH, "Personal Observations," pp. 1–2.

37. Ibid., pp. 6–8. For a further discussion of Houstonian "social engineering," see Chapter 7.

38. Ibid., pp. 9–11 passim.

39. Interview with Mordecai W. Johnson, 16 January 1975; Logan, *Howard University*, pp. 266–67; see McNeil, "'To Meet the Group Needs.'"

40. Logan, *Howard University*, pp. 266–67, 285; "Alumni Protest Abolition of the Night Classes,"*Washington Tribune*, 6 June 1930, clipping, Howard University Correspondence and Clippings, AMD Papers. See U.S. Department of Interior, *Annual Report, 1929*, p. 86; U.S. Department of Interior, *Annual Report, 1930*, pp. 118–19.

41. "Alumni Protest Abolition of Night Law Classes."

42. Ibid.

43. Interview with Belford V. Lawson, Jr., 23 December 1972.

44. "Dissatisfaction Disrupts Law School Faculty," *Washington World*, 8 August 1930, clipping, Howard University Correspondence and Clippings, AMD Papers; interview with Charles Thompson, 28 December 1974; interview with Mordecai W. Johnson, 16 January 1975.

45. Fenton Booth to CHH, 6 April 1933, and CHH to Fenton Booth, 14 January 1933, HULS Archives.

46. "Howard Law School," *Washington Tribune*, 15 August 1930, clipping, Howard University Correspondence and Clippings, AMD Papers.

47. "Day Classes to Cut Attendance at Law School," and "Dr. Johnson's Predicament," *Washington World*, 15 August 1930, clipping, Howard University Correspondence and Clippings, AMD Papers.

48. "The Howard Law School," *The Palmetto Leader*, 23 August 1930, clipping, Howard University Correspondence and Clippings, AMD Papers.

49. CHH to Charles A. Brown, 16 March 1934, HULS Archives.

50. See McNeil, "'To Meet the Group Needs,'" pp. 160–65.

51. "Law School Quizzed by Bar Association," *Afro-American* (Capital edition), 18 October 1930, clipping, Howard University Correspondence and Clippings, AMD Papers; U.S. Department of Interior, *Annual Report, 1931*, p. 149.

52. *Handbook of the Association of American Law Schools and Proceedings of the Twenty-ninth Annual Meeting* (December 1931), pp. 197–205 passim.

53. U.S. Department of Interior, *Annual Report, 1931*, p. 149. See Judy Kirkendall, American Bar Association staff assistant, to author, 9 December 1974. See also CHH, untitled statement on accreditation, 6 Juen 1932, HULS Archives.

54. U.S. Department of Interior, *Annual Report, 1931*, "Howard University," p. 149; ibid., 1932, p. 150; Rayford W. Logan, *Howard University*, pp. 267, 314; *Handbook of [A.A.L.S.], pp. 197–205, passim; "Law Schools in the United States and Canada," in *Directory of Law Teachers* (1973), p. 865.

CHAPTER SEVEN
"Dean" Houston's School for Social Engineers

1. William H. Hastie, Jr., quoted in Spottswood W. Robinson III, "No Tea for the Feeble: Two Perspectives on Charles Hamilton Houston," *Howard Law Journal* 20 (1977): 3–4.

2. CHH to Mordecai Johnson, 17 December 1931, HULS Archives. See [CHH,] "Activities of . . . Law Faculty . . . 1933," and CHH to Paul Annes, 14 February 1934, HULS Archives. See also WLH to Edward Lovett, 14 October 1935, WLH/H&G firm files.

3. Robinson, "No Tea for the Feeble," p. 5; interview with Juanita Kidd Stout, 21 August 1972.

4. Thurgood Marshall quoted in Geraldine Segal, *In Any Fight Some Fall* (Rockville, Md.: Mercury Press, 1975), pp. 33–34. See correspondence between CHH and Ruby and/or Clarence Darrow, September 1930, HULS Archives.

5. Announcement of lecture series by Clarence Darrow; transcripts of lectures and correspondence between CHH and Ruby Darrow, February 1931, HULS Archives. (It is interesting to note that the Darrow lectures were in part transcribed by a Woolsey Hall, who earlier had used this skill in the service of the federal government while it sought evidence to discredit Marcus Garvey [Tony Martin, *Race First* (Westport, Conn.: Greenwood Press, 1976), p. 206, n. 18].) See *Washington Tribune*, 16 January 1931.

6. CHH, "Personal Observations," 28 May 1929, p. 15, CHH/H&G firm files.

7. CHH to Faculty of Howard Law School, 5 February 1931, CHH/H&G firm files.

8. "Howard Academic Year Is Increased Bulletin Reveals," *Washington Post*, 31 March 1931, clipping, Howard University Correspondence and Clippings, AMD Papers. See Howard University Catalog for 1931–32 (pp. 332ff.), which stipulated that the term would be thirty-three weeks beginning 19 September 1931, with courses offered from 8:30 A.M. to 12:30 P.M.

9. "Appointments Criticized by Alumni," *Washington Times*, 31 March 1931, clipping, Howard University Correspondence and Clippings, AMD Papers.

10. "Inside Strife May Disrupt School of Law," *Washington World*, 3 April 1931, clipping, Howard University Correspondence and Clippings, AMD Papers.

11. CHH to Faculty and Administrative Staff of Howard Law School, 29 June 1931, WLH/H&G firm files. See Howard University Catalog, 1931–32.

12. "Inside Strife May Disrupt School of Law"; Rayford W. Logan, *Howard University: The First Hundred Years 1867–1967* (New York: New York University Press, 1969), pp. 248–321; interview with Mordecai Johnson, 16 January 1975.

13. Robinson, "No Tea for the Feeble," p. 4.

14. Interviews with Mordecai Johnson, 16 January 1975; Ollie M. Cooper, 21 December 1972; A. Mercer Daniel, 18 October 1971; and William Hastie, 19 September 1972; A. Mercer Daniel, "History–School of Law–Howard University," ms., n.d. [c. 1972], chapter 3, HULS Archives. (According to his first wife, Charles Houston also hoped to see his friend Leon "Andy" Ransom appointed to the deanship [interview with MGH, 22 January 1973].)

15. CHH to Faculty and Administrative Staff of Howard Law School, 29 June 1931, p. 2.

16. Interview with Elwood Chisolm, 5 December 1972; CHH to Paul Annes, 14 February 1934; and CHH, "Objectives of the School of Law," 1932, 27 January 1932, HULS Archives; Logan, *Howard University*, p. 267.

17. Interview with Ollie M. Cooper, 21 December 1972. See Ollie M. Coo-

per, comp., untitled scrapbook. See also Logan, *Howard University*, p. 227, and J. Clay Smith, Jr., "The Black Bar Association and Civil Rights," *Creighton Law Review* 15 (1981–82): 651–79.

18. Interview with A. Mercer Daniel, 18 October 1971.

19. Interview with Ollie Cooper, 21 December 1972.

20. CHH, untitled statement on Law School and Student Body, 6 Juen 1932, HULS Archives; see CHH to Faculty and Administrative Staff of Howard Law School, 20 June 1931, p. 1.

21. U.S. Department of Interior, *Annual Report, 1933*, pp. 304–306, 317, 318 passim; U.S. Department of Interior, *Annual Report, 1934*, pp. 382, 384, 397–98 passim; "Minutes of Meetings of Committee on Law School Budget, 1933–34," 9 February 1933, AMD Papers.

22. "Minutes of Meeting of Committee on Law School Budget, 1933–34," p. 2.

23. CHH to Nathan Cayton, 19 March 1933, AMD Papers.

24. "Minutes of Meeting of Committee on Law School Budget, 1933–34," pp. 1–2.

25. See *Handbook of the Association of American Law Schools*, December 1931, and Articles of the Assoication of American Law Schools. See also U.S. Department of Interior, *Annual Report, 1934*, p. 397.

26. CHH to George W. Crawford, 20 July 1934, CHH/H&G firm files. See U.S. Department of Interior, *Annual Report, 1933*, pp. 317–18.

27. CHH to George Crawford, 20 July 1934, CHH/H&G firm files; [WLH,] Standard Diary, 11, 13, 14, 15, 16, and 20 April 1934, WLH/H&G firm files.

28. WLH to J. C. Napier, 20 October 1934, WLH/H&G firm files.

29. See class roster and class record books of CHH, AMD Papers.

30. See, e.g., class roster for Criminal Law Laboratory and Evidence, 1931–32; Legal bibliography, Conflict of Laws, 1932–33, AMD Papers.

31. William Bryant quoted in *Washington Post*, 15 April 1976, clipping (courtesy of J. C. Smith); interview with Oliver Hill, 8 December 1972.

32. Interview with WH, 19 September 1972; interview with Edward Lovett, 18 January 1973.

33. TM, "Homage to Charles Houston," 6 April 1978.

34. TM, quoted in Segal, *In Any Fight Some Fall*, p. 34. See TM quoted in Richard Kluger, *Simple Justice: The History of Brown v. Board of Education and Black America's Struggle for Equality* (New York: Alfred A. Knopf, 1976), pp. 127–28.

35. Robinson, "No Tea for the Feeble," p. 4.

36. Interview with Oliver Hill, 8 December 1972.

37. CHH, "Special Caveat to First Year Class," 23 November 1933, HULS Archives.

38. CHH, Caveat to Student Body, 23 November 1933, HULS Archives.

39. WH, quoted in Robinson, "No Tea for the Feeble," p. 4.

40. CHH, quoted in ibid., p. 5; see interview with Juanita Kidd Stout, 21 August 1972, and CHH to Walullah, n.d. [c. 1946] (courtesy of Judge Stout).

41. Interview with William Bryant, 4 Juen 1982.

42. *Washington Post*, 15 April 1976, clipping.

43. WH, quoted in Robinson, "No Tea for the Feeble," p. 5.

44. Interview with MGH, 22 January 1973.

45. TM, quoted in Kluger, *Simple Justice*, p. 128; cf. with TM, "Homage to Charles Houston," 6 April 1978.

46. Interviews with Edward Lovett, 18 January 1973; Oliver Hill, 8 December 1972; TM, "Homage to Charles Houston." Houston's "social engineering" is to be distinguished from earlier Progressive era notions regarding "correction" of society. See, for example, Paul Violas, "Progressive Social Philosophy: Charles Horton Cooley and Edward Alsworth Ross," in Clarence Karier, Paul Violas, and Joel Springer, eds., *Roots of Crisis: Essays in Twentieth Century Education* (Chicago: Rand McNally, 1973), pp. 40–65.

47. Interview with Edward Lovett, 18 January 1973.

48. TM, in Segal, *In Any Fight Some Fall*, p. 34. See WH in Robinson, "No Tea for the Feeble," p. 4.

49. Interview with Edward Lovett, 18 January 1973. See J. Clay Smith, Jr., "Toward a School of Houstonian Jurisprudence and the Study of Pure Legal Existence," *Howard Law Journal* 18 (1973): 1ff., for a further interpretation.

50. CHH to Monroe Berger, 10 February 1948, CHH/H&G firm files.

51. CHH, "Law as a Career," 27 July 1932, CHH/H&G firm files.

52. Ibid.

53. CHH, "Outline of Lecture, New School," 12 December 1946, CHH/H&G firm files. See my "'To Meet the Group Needs': The Transformation of Howard University School of Law, 1920–1935," in Vincent P. Franklin and James Anderson, eds., *New Perspectives on Black Educational History* (Boston: G. K. Hall, 1978), p. 171, n. 58. See also Chapter 10, pp. 132–53.

54. Interview with CMH, 24 July 1972, and compare interviews with M. Haywood, 2 January 1973 and Juanita Stout, 21 August 1973. See conversation with TM, 6 April 1978.

CHAPTER EIGHT
The Limitations of American Law

1. Roosevelt quoted in R. Hofstadter, W. Miller, D. Aaron, L. Litwack, *The United States: A World Power*, 4th rev. ed. (Englewood Cliffs, N.J.: Prentice-Hall, 1976), p. 564.

2. Charles Flint Kellogg, *NAACP: A History of the National Association for the Advancement of Colored People, 1909–1920*, vol. 1 (Baltimore: Johns Hopkins University Press, 1967); Eugene Levy, *James Weldon Johnson: Black Leader, Black Voice* (Chicago: University of Chicago Press, 1973); and Tony Martin, *Race First: The Ideological and Organizational Struggle of Marcus Garvey and the Universal Negro Improvement Association* (Westport, Conn.: Greenwood Press, 1976).

3. See, e.g., Marjorie Paschkiss to author, 7 February 1973; NAACP, *Annual Report, 1932* (New York, 1933), pp. 12, 14; CHH and John P. Davis, "TVA: Lily White Reconstruction," *Crisis* 41 (October 1934): 290–91, 311.

4. CHH, "Law as a Career," 27 July 1932, CHH/H&G firm files.

5. Interview with CHH Jr., 24 July 1972.

6. Sheldon B. Avery, "Up from Washington: William Pickens and the Negro Struggle for Equality, 1900–1954" (Ph.D. diss., University of Oregon, 1970), pp. 195–96; Amenia Conference Press Release, 1 September 1933, Adm. files, C229, NAACP Records. See Barbara Joyce Ross, *J. E. Spingarn and the Rise of the NAACP, 1911–1939* (New York: Atheneum, 1972), p. 179.

7. See [W. E. B. Du Bois,] "Youth and Age at Amenia," *Crisis* 40 (October 1933): 226–27 and Avery, "Up from Washington," pp. 195–96, 198–99 passim.

8. CHH, "An Approach to Better Race Relations," Address delivered during the thirteenth national convention of the Young Women's Christian Association (YWCA) of America, 5 May 1934 (courtesy of Dr. Charles Wesley and the National Board of the YWCA, New York, N.Y.). See correspondence and papers, Amenia Conference, September–December 1933, Amenia Conference Folder, Adm. files, C229, NNACP Records.

9. Amenia Conference Press Release, 1 September 1933, p. 2. Adm. files, NAACP Records.

10. CHH to Stephen T. Early, 16 August 1933, CHH/H&G firm files. See interview with George B. Murphy, 19 April 1974. Note the number of people lynched between 1922 and 1932. (Source: CHH, Leon Ransom, Edward Lovett, *Memorandum Brief for the Attorney General of the United States* [New York: NAACP, 1933], NAACP Postscript, CHH/H&G firm files.)

"1922, 61 (5 white)   1928, 11
1923, 28 (2 white; 1 woman)   1929, 12 (4 white)
1924, 16   1930, 25 (1 white)
1925, 18   1931, 14
1926, 34 (5 white; 2 women)   1932, 10 (2 white)"
1927, 21 (2 white)

11. "Smart Aleck a White House Secretary," *Afro-American*, 2 September 1933, clipping, CHH/H&G firm files.

12. See Afreda M. Duster, ed., *Crusade for Justice: The Autobiography of Ida B. Wells* (Chicago: University of Chicago Press, 1970), and "Democracy Escapes," in John Hope Franklin, *From Slavery to Freedom* (New York: Alfred A. Knopf, 1974).

13. "Federal Action Urged," *Pittsburgh Courier*, 9 September 1933, clipping; "Little Used Federal Law Cited to Punish Lynchers," *Afro-American*, 16 September 1933, clipping and Memorandum Report from CHH, Andy Ransom, and Edward Lovett to International Labor Defense (ILD), American Civil Liberties Union (ACLU) and National Association for the Advancement of Colored People (NAACP), 13 October 1933, CHH/H&G firm files. See Southern Commission on the Study of Lynching, *The Plight of Tuscaloosa* (Atlanta, 1933).

14. Memorandum Report from CHH, Andy Ransom, and Edward Lovett to ILD, ACLU, and NAACP, 13 October 1933, CHH/H&G firm files. See CHH, Ransom, and Lovett, *Memorandum Brief for the Attorney General of the United States*, pp. 1–47 passim, CHH/H&G firm files.

15. CHH to WW, 18 October 1933, Legal files—cases supported—George Crawford, D52, NAACP Records and CHH to Stephen Early, 16 August 1933, CHH/H&G firm files, respectively.

16. CHH et al., *Memorandum Brief*, pp. 41–47 passim.

17. CHH to Homer S. Cummings, 19 February 1934, CHH/H&G firm files; Assistant Attorney General William Stanley to Frank M. Parrish, 24 February 1934; Assistant Attorney General Joseph B. Keenan to Assistant Attorney General Stanley, 2 March 1934; and Assistant Attorney General Stanley to CHH, 5 March 1934, file no. 158260, JC/RG60.

18. See NAACP, *Annual Report, 1933*, pp. 12, 13, 16–18, 20–21; [WW,] "George Crawford—Symbol," n.d., p. 2, D52, NAACP Records; Nannie H.

Burroughs to WW, 2 February 1933, "Boston N.A.A.C.P. Attorneys Fighting Extradition of Man to Virginia," press release, 27 January 1933, Legal files— cases supported—George Crawford, D51, NAACP Records; CHH to WW, 20 July 1934 (with enclosure CHH to Richard Hale, 19 July 1934), Adm. files— Special Correspondence (hereafter Sp. Corr.)—CHH, C64, NAACP Records; WW to Roy Wilkins, 24 April 1933, "Findings of Court," typescript copy, 2 May 1933; WW to editor of *The Nation*, 4 May 1933; Butler Wilson to CHH, 25 April 1933; and CHH to WW, 17 October 1933.

19. CHH to WW, 11 June 1933, with attached "Memorandum of the George Crawford Case—Significance," n.d. [c. 1–10 June 1933], D52, NAACP Records.

20. CHH and Leon A. Ransom, "The George Crawford Case: An Experiment in Social Statesmanship," *The Nation* 139 (4 July 1934): 17.

21. CHH to WW, 16 October 1933, D52, NAACP Records.

22. Ibid.

23. WW to CHH, 20 October 1933; WW to J. Weston Allen; see 20 October 1933, WW to Butler Wilson, 20 October 1933, D52, NAACP Records.

24. WW, "Special Letter to Editors of Weekly Press: Colored," 20 October 1933, D52, NAACP Records. See memorandum of WW re long-distance conversation with CHH, 1 November 1933, CHH, Sp. Corr., C64, NAACP Records. See also "Crawford to Have All Negro Defense Counsel," press release, 10 November 1933, D52 NAACP Records.

25. CHH, "Motion to Quash," 26 October 1933 (filing date), *Commonwealth of Virginia* v. *George Crawford* (Circuit Court of Loudoun County, Virginia October Term 1933), CHH/H&G firm files. See CHH and L. A. Ransom, "Suggestive Unconstitutional Exclusions of Negroes from the Grand Jury" (copy in CHH/H&G firm files and NAACP Records).

26. "Crawford Case Called Test of Negro Service on Juries," press release, 17 November 1933, D52, NAACP Records.

27. Ibid. See "Commonwealth of Virginia v. George Crawford . . . History," n.d., CHH/H&G firm files. See also *Washington Post* 7 and 8 November 1933; *Times Mirror* (Loudoun County, Va., 2, 9, 16, 23 November 1933.

28. CHH to editor of *News Leader* (Richmond, Va., 9 November 1933, D52, NAACP Records.

29. *Commonwealth of Virginia* v. *George Crawford*, transcript, Legal files— class supported—George Crawford, D54, NAACP Records; Helen Boardman and Martha Gruening, "Is the NAACP Retreating?" *The Nation* 138 (27 June 1934): 730–32 passim; CHH and Ransom, "The George Crawford Case," pp. 17–19 passim.

30. CHH and L. A. Ransom, "The George Crawford Case," pp. 17–18.

31. Ibid.

32. Interview with Edward Lovett, 18 January 1973; interview with M. Gladys Houston, 22 January 1973; CHH and Ransom, "The George Crawford Case," p. 19.

33. *Commonwealth of Virginia* v. *George Crawford*, transcript, D54, NAACP Records: "Crawford Accuser Sensationally Unmasked in . . . Courtroom," press release, 15 December 1933, D52, NAACP Records; CHH and Ransom, "The George Crawford Case," p. 18.

34. *Commonwealth of Virginia* v. *George Crawford*, transcript (closing arguments of CHH, 16 December 1933, pp. 603ff.) D54, NAACP Records.

35. Interview with MGH, 22 January 1973; interview with Edward Lovett,

18 January 1973; CHH and Ransom, "The George Crawford Case," p. 18. See Richard Kluger, *Simple Justice* (New York: Alfred A. Knopf, 1976), pp. 152–54. See also Boardman and Gruening, "Is the NAACP Retreating?" p. 732.

36. CHH and Ransom, "The Crawford Case," p. 19; Boardman and Gruening, "Is the NAACP Retreating?" p. 731; "Hearing on the indictiment Charging George Crawford with the Murder of Mina Buckner," 12 February 1934, *Commonwealth of Virginia* v. *George Crawford*, CHH/H&G firm files.

37. [WW,] "Report of the Secretary," 8 January 1934, pp. 4–6 passim, Board of Directors file, A24, NAACP Records. See CHH and Ransom, "The George Crawford Case," p. 18; interview with John M. Ellison, 25 January 1972. See also Frank Getty, "The Dramatic Leesburg Murder Trial," *Washington Post Magazine*, 31 December 1933, clipping, CHH Fam. (Existing records examined do not provide further information on whether or not Crawford served the life sentence.)

38. CHH and Ransom, "The George Crawford Case," p. 18.

39. CHH to Bernard Ades, 7 December 1933, CHH/H&G firm files. (The ILD was composed of workers, labor sympathizers, lawyers, and others who were political radicals. [This included Communists and non-Communist.] See William L. Patterson, *The Man Who Cried Genocide* (New York: International Pubs. Co., 1971).

40. CHH to Mordecai Johnson, 17 February 1934, CHH/H&G firm files.

41. "Ades Ousted as Lee Counsel in U.S. Court—Suspended by Judge Coleman on 'Evidence of Unethical Conduct,'" *Baltimore Sun*, 24 October 1934, clipping, CHH/H&G firm files.

42. CHH to Mordecai Johnson, 17 February 1934, CHH/H&G firm files.

43. [CHH,] "In re Bernard Ades: Summary of Charges and Answers," 5 March 1934, pp. 1–18, CHH/H&G firm files. (No transcript exists in the records of the District Court for case no. 291 or in the Houston firm files.) See CHH to editor of *Afro-American* (Baltimore), 14 May 1934, clipping, CHH/H&G firm files; and Order, 29 November 1933, *In re Bernard Ades*, case no. 291, District Court of the United States for the District of Maryland.

44. [CHH,] "In re Bernard Ades: Summary of Charges and Answers," pp. 19–20.

45. Ibid., p. 19.

46. "Houston Takes Issue with Governor on Race Problem in Virginia at Interracial Meet," *Norfolk Journal & Guide*, 3 February 1934, clipping, CHH vertical file, Moorland-Spingarn Research Center, Howard University, Washington, D.C.

47. Ibid.

48. CHH, "Statement . . . Before the Subcommittee of the United States Judiciary Committee in Hearings on the Costigan-Wagner Bill, S1978," 73d Congress, 2d Session, 20 February 1934, pp. 1, 2, Personal Correspondence—Thurgood Marshall—Administrative Files (hereafter Per. Corr., Adm.), C84, NAACP Records.

49. Ibid., p. 2.

50. Ibid., pp. 4–5.

51. Ibid., p. 5.

52. Ibid., p. 8.

53. Ibid., pp. 8–9.

54. Ibid., p. 11.

55. Opinion, 19 March 1934, pp. 15–18, 21 passim, *In re Bernard Ades*, District Court of the U.S. for the District of Maryland.

56. Statement of Reprimand, 19 March 1934, pp. 1–2 (filed 27 March 1934), *In re Bernard Ades*, District Court of the U.S. for the District of Maryland.

57. CHH to Charles A. Horsky, 2 April 1934, CHH/H&G firm files.

58. "Statement by the ILD on the Ades Case Decision," 2 April 1934, p. 203, enclosed in Lawrence Emery, "To All Attorneys," 4 April 1934, CHH/H&G firm files.

59. William Patterson to John P. Davis, 5 May 1934 (copy), CHH/H&G firm files. See CHH to William Patterson, 17 April 1934, CHH/H&G firm files.

60. William Patterson to Isadore Polier, 5 May 1934 (copy), CHH/H&G firm files.

61. CHH to Bernard Ades, 1 May 1934, CHH/H&G firm files.

62. Bernard Ades to CHH, 9 May 1934, CHH/H&G firm files. See CHH to editor of *Afro-American* (Baltimore), 14 May 1934, CHH/H&G firm files. See also CHH, "An Approach to Better Race Relations," Address delivered to National YWCA convention, 5 May 1934 (copy courtesy of Charles Wesley and YWCA of New York).

63. CHH, "An Approach to Better Race Relations," p. 4.

64. Ibid., p. 5.

65. Ibid., p. 6. See Martin, *Race First*.

66. Ibid., pp. 8–10 passim.

67. Ibid., p. 9.

68. See CHH to Ades, 16 June 1934, and Ades to Joseph Brodsky, 5 June 1934 (copy), CHH/H&G firm files.

69. Ades to J. Brodsky, 5 June 1934 (copy), CHH/H&G firm files.

70. CHH to Ades, 16 June 1934, CHH/H&G firm files.

71. CHH, Untitled address before the 24th Annual Conference of the NAACP, 2 July 1933, pp. 7, 8, Annual Conference files, B10, NAACP Records.

72. Ibid.

73. Jervis Anderson, *A. Philip Randolph: A Biographical Portrait* (New York: Harcourt Brace Jovanovich, 1972), pp. 211, 219.

74. Interview with William L. Patterson, 15 July 1973.

75. See W. E. B. Du Bois, "NAACP and Race Segregation," *Crisis* 41 (February 1934): 52–53; Du Bois, "Segregation and Self-Respect," *Crisis* 41 (February 1934): 85.

76. CHH to Roy Wilkins, 2 May 1934, and CHH to WW, 26 September 1934, CHH Sp. Corr., Adm. Files, C64, NAACP Records.

77. "Negro and Poor White Should Unite," clipping, n.d. [c. June 1934], CHH Fam.

78. Boardman and Gruening, "Is the NAACP Retreating?" p. 732.

79. CHH and Ransom, "The Crawford Case," pp. 18–19.

80. Ibid. See 100 U.S. 339 (1879).

81. CHH and Ransom, "The Crawford Case," p. 19.

82. Ibid.

83. "Houston Indicts NAACP Leadership in Statement," *Negro Liberator*, 7 July 1934, p. 8, Wayne State University Library, Detroit, Mich. (I would like to acknowledge the valuable assistance of Ernest Allen, scholar of the labor movement and the black "left," who located the *Negro Liberator* and shared primary sources on Houston and the League.)

84. "A Dirty Stab in the Back," *Negro Liberator*, 18 August 1934, p. 4, Wayne State University Library. See "Lynch Judge to Praise NAACP Lawyer at Fari, *Negro Liberator*, 18 August 1934, p. 1, Wayne State University Library.

85. "Trying to Crawl Back," *Negro Liberator*, 15 September 1934, p. 4, Wayne State University Library.

86. *Negro Liberator*, 29 December 1934, p. 8, Wayne State University Library.

87. Interview with George B. Murphy, Jr., 19 April 1974.

88. P. L. Prattis to CHH, 18 May 1934, and CHH to P. L. Prattis, 22 May 1934, with enclosure "Houston Discovers Reds Are Hot Potatoes in His Mouth," CHH/H&G firm files. See CHH to P. L. Prattis, 15 May 1934, CHH/H&G firm files.

89. Interview with William Patterson, 15 July 1973; CHH to P. L. Prattis, 18 May 1934, and Benjamin Davis to CHH, 12 June 1933, CHH/H&G firm files.

90. Interview with George B. Murphy, Jr., 19 April 1974.

CHAPTER NINE
Matters of Conscience

1. Wilson Record, *The Negro and the Communist Party* (Chapel Hill: University of North Carolina Prss, 1951), pp. 79–80 passim. See the *League's Equality, Land and Freedom: A Program for Negro Liberation* (New York: League of Struggle for Negro Rights, 1933) for a complete statement of its program. The League was an outgrowth of "the American Negro Labor Congress and also of the African Blood Brotherhood, the Equal Rights League, and the League of African Freedom." Until it was merged with the National Negro Congress in February 1936, it carried on its work in the North and South. Langston Hughes was its president and Richard B. Moore and Harry Haywood were its general secretaries. (William Z. Foster, *The Negro People in American History* [New York: International Publishers, 1954], p. 481.)

2. Foster, *Negro People*, pp. 460–61 passim.

3. Interview with William L. Patterson, 15 July 1973; Elliott Rudwick, *W. E. B. Du Bois: A Study in Minority Group Leadership* (Philadelphia: University of Pennsylvania Press, 1960).

4. "Resolution of Communist International, October 26, 1928," in *The Communist Position on the Negro Question* (n.p., n.d.), pp. 57–58.

5. Arthur Mann, "The Progressive Tradition," in *The Reconstruction of American History*, ed. John Higham (New York: Harper Torchbook, 1962).

6. Record, *The Negro and the Communist Party*, pp. 80, 55. See Sheldon B. Avery, "Up from Washington: William Pickens and the Negro Struggle for Equality, 1900–1954 (Ph.D. diss., University of Oregon, 1970), pp. 164–166, 200–202.

7. Record, *The Negro and the Communist Party*, p. 135.

8. Interview with William Patterson, 15 July 1973. The united front was again endorsed by the Party at the World Congress of the Communist International in 1935. After the congress the American Party and its related radical organizations engaged in more extensive and intensive cooperative efforts. With regard to African Americans, by 1936 the self-determination/independent nation theory was abandoned in favor of concentration of the struggle for freedom and equality by a united front of black people. (See Foster,

Negro People, p. 488. See also Jervis Anderson, *A. Philip Randolph: A Biographical Portrait* [New York: Harcourt Brace Jovanovich, 1972], pp. 229–40 *passim.*)

9. *CHH to F. M. Lemay (with enclosure), 30 March 1935, CHH/H&G firm files; interview with WH, 19 September 1972; interview with William Patterson, 15 July 1973.*

10. *Dan T. Carter, Scottsboro: A Tragedy of the American South* (New York: Oxford University press, 1971), p. 33.

11. P. L. Prattis to CHH, 18 May 1934, CHH/H&G firm files.

12. Interview with Edward Lovett, 18 Janaury 1973; W. Patterson to CHH, 13 September 1932; CHH to Patterson, 6 January 1933; Patterson to CHH, 2 May 1933, CHH/H&G firm files.

13. Patterson to CHH, 13 May 1933, CHH/H&G firm files. (The reference is probably to Harry Haywood [courtesy of Ernest Allen].)

14. CHH to editor, *Amsterdam News*, 27 May 1933, Scottsboro Correspondence, CHH/H&G firm files. See Benjamin Davis to CHH, 12 June 1933, Scottsboro Correspondence, CHH/H&G firm files. See also W. Pickens, "Reflections," *Amsterdam News*, 24 May 1933, clipping, CHH/H&G firm files.

15. Avery, "Up from Washington," pp. 184–89 passim; Clarence Darrow, "Scottsboro," clipping from unnamed source, n.d., CHH/H&G firm files.

16. CHH, "An Approach to Better Race Relations," 5 May 1934, p. 7.

17. Ibid.

18. CHH to editor, *Amsterdam News*, 27 May 1933.

19. Ibid.

20. Ibid., at n. 14.

21. CHH to WW, 10 November 1933, CHH/H&G firm files.

22. CHH to WW, 12 October 1934, CHH, Sp. Corr., Adm. files, C64, NAACP Records. See "Reds Told to Drop Scottsboro Case," *New York Times*, 11 October 1934, clipping, CHH/H&G firm files.

23. CHH to WW, 12 October 1934, C64, NAACP Records.

24. Interview with WH, 19 September 1972; Carter, *Scottsboro*, pp. 316–34 passim.

25. CHH, "Justice for All" 19 December 1934, pp. 1–7, C64, NAACP Records; interviews with E. Lovett, 18 January 1973, and W. Bryant, 4 June 1982.

26. TM to CHH, 18 December 1934, TM, Per. Corr., Adm. files, C87, NAACP Records.

27. CHH to Carol King, 20 December 1934, NAACP vertical file, Schomburg Center, New York Public Library. See CHH, "Justice for All." See also interviews with George B. Murphy, Jr., 19 April 1974, and Edward Lovett, 18 January 1973; and Robert L. Zangrando, "The Efforts of the National Association for the advancement of Colored People to Secure Passage of a Federal Anti-lynching Law, 1920–1940" (Ph.D. diss., University of Pennsylvania, 1963).

28. CHH, "Justice for All"; interview with Edward Lovett, 18 January 1973; unidentified clipping (on Houston and the Howard Law School strike), n.d. [c. December 1934]; CHH vertical file, Moorland-Spingarn Research Center, Howard University, Washington, D.C. (hereafter cited as MSRC); CHH, "Memorandum for the Joint Committee of the N.A.A.C.P. and the American Fund for Public Service, Inc.," pp. 1–2 passim, AFPS, C199, NAACP Records.

29. Charles Garland's letter of July 15, 1922 quoted in Memorandum to

Board, AFPS, *Board of Directors Correspondence, 1934–1941*, 2:48, AFPS Records and "Memorandum to the Directors of the American Fund for Public Service from Committee on Negro Work", n.d. [28 May 1930, date of action on memorandum], Committee on Negro Work, 1930–33 folder, AFPS, C197, NAACP Records.

30. AFPS, *Miscellaneous Correspondence, 1922–1941*, 2:9–10, 217–219; AFPS, *Board of Directors Correspondence, 1934–1941*, 2:4–21, 29–48, AFPS Records. Second memorandum of Committee on Negro work also in NAACP Records as cited above, note 29.

31. AFPS, Miscellaneous Reports, 1930–1938, pp. 3–27 and 29–195, AFPS Records and Nathan Margold, "Preliminary Report to the Joint Committee Supervising the Expenditure of the 1930 Appropriation by the American Fund for Public Service to the NAACP", n.d., Margold Reprot—1930 folder, AFPS, Adm. files, C200, NAACP Records.

32. Nathan Margold, Ibid. See also *Yick Wo* v. *Hopkins*, 118 U.S. 356 (1886).

33. "Memorandum to the Directors of the American Fund for Public Service from Committee on Negro Work," Committee on Negro Work, 1930–33 folder, AFPS, C197, NAACP REcords.

34. WW to CHH, 21 June 1933, C196, NAACP Records; Nathan Margold, "Preliminary Report. . ." as cited in note 31.

35. WW to Roger Baldwin, 8 July 1933, *Applications Favorably Acted Upon Gifts & Loans*, 8:135, AFPS Records.

36. Nathan R. Margold to WW, 22 October 1934, March–December, 1934 folder, AFPS, C 196, NAACP Records.

37. CHH, "Memorandum for the Joint Committee of the NAACP and the American Fund for Public Service, Inc.", AFPS-Joint Committee, 1933–35 folder, AFPS, C199, NAACP Records.

38. Ibid.

39. Ibid. See *Plessy* v. *Feruson*, 163 US 537 (1896). See also 1933 case of Thomas Hocutt (Durham, NC), discussed below, p. 277, note 33.

40. Ibid., p. 12.

41. NAACP, *Annual Report*, 1934 (New York, 1935), p. 22.

42. Interviews with WH, September 19, 1972, Robert Carter, May 5, 1982 and Constance Baker Motley, June 23, 1982. See Chapter 13 and accompanying notes. Compare Jack Greenberg, "Reflections on Leading Issues in Civil Rights, Then and Now", *Notre Dame Lawyer*, 57 (April 1982): 635.

43. CHH to Roy Wilkins, 31 December 1934, C64, NAACP Records.

44. Draft of Appeal for Funds (11 January 1935) enclosed in CHH to WW, 15 January 1935, C64, NAACP Records.

45. CHH to WW, 15 January 1935, C64, NAACP Records.

46. Ibid.

47. "Statement of Charles H. Houston, Representing the National Ass'n [sic] for the Advancement of Colored People," Economic Security Act Hearing before the Committee on Finance, United States Senate [74th Congress, 1st sess.], S1130 (pt. 8, 8 and 9 February 1935), p. 636 RG46, NA.

48. "Punishment for the Crime of Lynching," Hearing before the Subcommittee of the Judiciary Committee, U.S. Senate, 74th Congress on S.24, 14 February 1935 (Washington, D.C.: Government Printing Office, 1935), pp. 25–32 passim, CHH/H&G firm files.

49. Walter Pollack, George Chamlee, Osmond Fraenkel, and Samuel Liebo-witz to CHH, 30 January 1935, Carol King to CHH, 5 February 1935, CHH/H&G firm files; Claude Barnett to CHH, 7 February 1935, uncataloged Claude Barnett Collection, Chicago Historical Society.

50. CHH to Carol King, 6 February 1935, CHH/H&G firm files.

51. "Extracts from the Statement of Charles H. Houston in Debate with Bernard Ades, Before the Liberal Club of Howard University, on *The Scottsboro Case*," 28 March 1935, CHH/H&G firm files.

52. Ibid.

53. Ibid.

54. CHH, untitled tape recording [c. December 1949] CHH Fam.

55. Rayford W. Logan, *Howard University: The First Hundred Years, 1867–1967* (New York: New York University Press, 1969), p. 268; CHH to Mordecai Johnson, 22 May 1935, C64, NAACP Records.

56. *Norris* v. *Alabama*, 294 U.S. 599 (1935); *Patterson* v. *Alabama* 294 U.S. 601 (1935); *Jess Hollins* v. *State of Oklahoma*, 295 U.S. 394 (1935). See "High Court Hears Jury Issue Case," *Norfolk Journal and Guide*, 11 May 1935, clipping, CHH/H&G firm files. See also CHH to Roy Wilkins, 31 December 1934, C64, NAACP Records.

57. CHH, "Statement of Certain Legal Activities Carried on Behalf of the Association," 24 June 1935, p. 6, CHH/H&G Records.

58. WH, "Charles Hamilton Houston," *Crisis* 57 (July 1950): 365; interview with Ollie Cooper, 21 December 1972.

59. CHH, "The Need for Negro Lawyers," *Journal of Negro Education* 4 (January 1935): 49–50.

60. Ibid., pp. 49–52 passim.

61. CHH to WW, 21 May 1935, and Mordecai Johnson to CHH, 22 May 1935, CHH/H&G firm files.

62. [WLH,] "Biographical Sketch of William L. Houston," second draft, n.d. (c. 1942), p. 3, WLH/H&G firm files. Board of Education of the District of Columbia, "First Meeting of the Board of Education [July 1, 1933]," p. 1, *Minutes of the Board of Education of the District of Columbia*, July 1933 to June 1934, vol. 24, unpublished typescript, Office of the Executive Secretary of the Board of Education, Washington, D.C. (Board of Education of the District of Columbia hereafter cited "D.C. Bd. of Ed."; *Minutes of the Board of Education of the District of Columbia*, hereafter cited as "D.C. Bd. of Ed. Minutes"); "Charles Houston Succeeds Bennett on School Board," *Washington Tribune*, 1 July 1933, clipping, CHH, vertical file, MSRC.

63. See my "Charles Hamilton Houston (1895–1950) and the Struggle for Civil Rights" (Ph.D. diss., University of Chicago, 1975), p. 237, n. 1.

64. Ibid., p. 237, n. 2, for list of relevant meetings, D.C. Bd. of Ed.

65. Ibid.

66. Ibid., p. 238, n. 1, for list of relevant meetings, D.C. Bd. of Ed.

67. Ibid.

68. D.C. Bd. of Ed., Tenth (postponed) Meeting of the Board of Education (9 January 1935), pp. 25–26, D.C. Bd. of Ed. Minutes, vol. 25. See "Education Board Fights Dictation by District Heads," *Evening Star* (Washington, D.C.), 10 January 1935, clipping, CHH/H&G firm files.

69. D.C. Bd. of Ed., tenth (postponed) meeting, pp. 25–26.

70. Ibid., p. 26.

71. D.C. Bd. of Ed., "Seventeenth Meeting," 3 April 1935, pp. 4–7.

72. "Dr. Houston Protests Denial of School Building to Forum," *Afro-American*, 23 February 1935, clipping, CHH vertical file, MSRC.

73. D.C. Bd. of Ed., "Twenty-third (Special) Meeting of the Board of Education," 12 June 1935, pp. 23–24.

74. Ibid.

75. Interviews with MGH, 22 January 1973; CMH, 1972–73; William Bryant, 4 June 1982; and Edward Lovett, 18 January 1973.

76. CHH to "Houston Family," 11 July 1935, Cont. 7, WLH Fam.

CHAPTER TEN
"This Fight . . . Is Not an Isolated Struggle"

1. Interview with Lucille Black, 7 December 1972.

2. CHH to Harlan Miller, 21 November 1938, CHH/H&G firm files.

3. "Charles Houston Will Join NAACP Staff in July," *Crisis* 42 (July 1935): 208; "Report of the American Fund for Public Service, Inc. for the Two Years, July 1, 1934–June 30, 1936" (New York, 1936), pp. 2, 4, 6.

4. See NAACP, *Annual Report, 1911–1935*; Charles Flint Kellogg, *NAACP: A History of the National Association for the Advancement of Colored People, 1909–1920* (Baltimore: Johns Hopkins University Press, 1967), pp. 61–62.

5. NAACP, *Annual Report, 1935*, pp. 9, 12–13; ibid., *1936*, pp. 16, 29; ibid., *1937*, pp. 9, 16–17; ibid., *1938*, pp. 13–14, 16–17, 18; ibid., *1939*, pp. 12, 30; ibid., *1940*, p. 11; Charles S. Johnson (copy), n.d. [c. June or July 1935] folder of E. Franklin Frazier, Sp. Corr., Adm. files, C64, NAACP Records; CHH to WLH, 13 March 1936, WLH/H&G firm files; "Englewood Social Notes," *Bergen Record* (Hackensack, N.J.), 23 March 1938, clipping, CHH vertical file (Moorland-Spingarn Research Center, Howard University, Washington, D.C.). According to the Annual Reports, in 1935, Houston traveled 4,588 miles for the NAACP; in 1936, some 6,084 miles; and in 1937, some 14,589 (NAACP, *Annual Report, 1935*, p. 38; ibid., *1936*, p. 23; ibid., *1937*, p. 23). In 1938 he attended seven meetings at which he represented the NAACP; the mileage is not given (NAACP, *Annual Report, 1938*, p. 23).

6. Interview with Roy Wilkins, 6 December 1972.

7. CHH, "Tentative Statement Concerning Policy of NAACP in Its Program of Attacks on Educational Discrimination," 12 July 1935, p. 1, C197 NAACP Records.

8. WH, "Charles Hamilton Houston," *Negro History Bulletin* 13 (June 1950): 207.

9. CHH, "Law as a Career," 27 July 1932, CHH/H&G firm files. See Chapter 7, pp. 84–85.

10. Ibid. See interviews with Oliver Hill, 8 December 1972, and Edward Lovett, 18 January 1973. See also J. Clay Smith, Jr., in *Howard Law Journal* 18 (1973): 1ff.

11. [CHH,] "A Program Against Discrimination in Public Education," ms., n.d. [c. December 1935], p. 2, Fraternities and Sororities, 1935, AFPS, Adm. files, C199 NAACP Records.

12. CHH, "Memorandum Re Projected Pictures of Inequalities of Negro Education in South Carolina," 16 June 1935, p. 10, C64, NAACP Records.

13. Ibid.

14. "Segregated Educational System Hit," unidentified clipping, n.d., [c. 1935], CHH Fam.

15. CHH, "Proposed Legal Attacks on Educational Discrimination," typescript summary of address delivered to the National Bar Association, 1 August 1935, p. 2, CHH folder, Speeches, Adm. files C429, NAACP Records.

16. Ibid.

17. CHH and Leon Ransom, "The George Crawford Case: An Experiment in Social Statesmanship," *The Nation*, 4 July 1934, p. 18; and CHH, "Proposed Legal Attacks on Educational Discrimination," p. 3.

18. Interview with Earl B. Dickerson, 2 and 9 March 1973.

19. Nathan Margold, "Preliminary Report to the Joint Committee Supervising the Expenditure of the 1930 Appropriation by the American Fund for Public Service to the NAACP," n.d. [c. 1933], Margold Report—1930 folder, AFPS, Adm. files, C200 NAACP Records.

20. CHH, "Proposed Legal Attacks on Educational Discrimination," p. 8, C429, NAACP Records.

21. CHH, "Memorandum to the Joint Committee American Fund for Public Service, Inc.—NAACP," 14 November 1935, p. 4, C199, NAACP Records.

22. Ibid., p. 4.

23. CHH, "Proposed Legal Attacks on Educational Discrimination," pp. 2–3.

24. Ibid., pp. 3–4.

25. Ibid., p. 6.

26. CHH, "Tentative Statement Concerning Policy of N.A.A.C.P.," 12 July 1935, p. 11, AFPS, Adm. files, C197, NAACP Records. See *Plessy* v. *Ferguson*, 163 U.S. 537 (1896).

27. CHH, "Tentative Statement Concerning Policy of N.A.A.C.P.," p. 1; and CHH, "Proposed Legal Attacks on Educational Discrimination," pp. 6–7.

28. CHH, "Proposed Legal Attacks on Educational Discrimination," p. 7.

29. Lyonel Florant to CHH, 24 September 1935; CHH to Lyonel Florant, 26 September 1935, 1935 legal files, D7, NAACP Records.

30. CHH, "Tentative Statement Concerning Policy of N.A.A.C.P.," p. 2.

31. CHH, "Proposed Legal Attacks on Educational Discrimination," p. 7. See *Dameron* v. *Bayliss*, 14 Ariz. 180 (1912).

32. CHH, "Proposed Legal Attacks on Educational Discrimination," p. 5.

33. CHH to K. Norman Diamond, 1 April 1936, Educational Campaign (hereafter "Ed. C.") 1936, AFPS Adm. files, C198, NAACP Records. Before Houston's initiation of the campaign the first case involving exclusion of a black from a state university graduate or professional school in which the NAACP was involved arose in North Carolina during 1933, before Houston's special counselship. The case was begun independently by two black lawyers from Durham, Conrad Pearson and Cecil McCoy. After they pleaded they called on the NAACP for assistance in the trial. William Hastie, Jr. a new member of the National Legal Committee, member of the D.C. bar, and instructor on leave from Howard's Law School taking his S.J.D. at Harvard, went down to try the case. He did a good job, but the case was lost in part because North Carolina Central (the black college that Thomas Hocutt, the test-case litigant seeking admission to the university's School of Pharmacy, was attending) had refused to send Hocutt's transcript to the University of North Carolina without a request from the State University. There was no appeal. (John Hope Frank-

lin, *From Slavery to Freedom*, 4th rev. ed. [New York: Alfred A. Knopf, 1974], p. 419.)

34. Interview with Donald Gaines Murray, 10 April 1974. (Two blacks, Harry Cummins and W. Ashbie Hawkins, attended the university when it was a private corporation. The latter earned an LL.B. at Howard in 1892. After Maryland's law school came under state supervision in 1920, however, no blacks were admitted. (Courtesy of Bettye Collier Thomas and see "Court Upholds Negro as U. of M. Law Student," *Evening Sun*, 15 January 1936, clipping, CHH/H&G firm files.)

35. CHH, "Proposed Legal Attacks on Educational Discrimination," pp. 4–5.

36. CHH to K. Norman Diamond, 14 April 1936, Educational Campaign, 1936, AFPS, Adm. files, C194, NAACP Records.

37. *Pearson et al.* v. *Murray*, 169 Md. 478, K. Norman Diamond, "Exclusion of Negroes from State Supported Professional Schools," *Yale Law Journal* 45 (1936): 1226–1301. WW, "Report of Meeting of Joint Committee of the American Fund for Public Service, Inc., and the [NAACP]," 21 March 1935, p. 1. Joint Committees 1933–1935, AFPS, Adm. files, C199, NAACP Records; "Court Upholds Negro as U. of M. Law Student"; interview with Donald G. Murray, 10 April 1974; CHH to K. N. Diamond, 14 April 1936, C194, NAACP Records; see files of University of Maryland (Cases supported—legal files) D93, D94, NAACP Records. See also *Sweatt* v. *Painter*, 339 U.S. 629 (1950).

38. CHH, "Don't Shout too Soon," *Crisis* 43 (March 1936): 79.

39. Ibid., pp. 79, 91.

40. CHH to Edgar Dale, 27 May 1937, Ed. C., 1937 folder, AFPS, Adm. files, C198, NAACP Records. See Itinerary of CHH and Edward Lovett, 28 November 1934, pp. 1–6, Sp. Corr., C64, NAACP Records and "Memorandum . . . Re Projected Picture on Inequalities of Negro Education in South Carolina," 16 June 1935, C64, NAACP Records.

41. CHH to WW, 24 December 1935, Ed. C., 1934–35 folder AFPS, Adm. files, C197, NAACP Records (memorandum in which he reports on conversation with Roy Wilkins).

42. CHH, "Memorandum Report to Joint Committee, [AFPS, Inc.]—NAACP," 14 November 1935, p. 3; and CHH, Memorandum to Joint Committee, 14 November 1935, p. 4, AFPS, Adm. files, C199, NAACP Records; CHH, Memorandum to Joint Committee, 1936–37, AFPS, Adm. files, C200 NAACP Records; interview with Edward Lovett, 18 January 1973. See Requisition for Travel Advance to CHH, 1935, C196, NAACP Records.

43. Interview with MGH, 22 January 1973; interview with Oliver Hill, 8 December 1972.

44. CHH, "Memorandum Report to Joint Committee," p. 3, and CHH, "Educational Inequalities Must Go," *Crisis* 42 (October 1935): 300, 316.

45. CHH, "Educational Inequalities Must Go," p. 316.

46. Ibid.

47. Ibid.

48. CHH, "How to Fight for Better Schools," *Crisis* 43 (February 1936): 52, 59 (emphasis mine).

49. WW to Ed Lewis, 8 September 1937, Ed. C., 1937 folder, AFPS, Adm. files C198, NAACP Records.

50. See communications between Houston and officers of Zeta Phi Beta, Omega Psi Phi, Phi Beta Sigma, Alpha Kappa Alpha, etc., in Fraternities and

Sororities folder, AFPS, Adm. files, C100, NAACP Records and memorandum from CHH to WH, TM, Leon Ransom, Juanita Jackson, 23 December 1935, re speeches to Greek letter societies in same file. See also "Greek Letter Societies to Hear of NAACP Work," press release, 26 December 1935, Ed. C., C197, NAACP Records; CHH, "A Program Against Discrimination in Public Education," ms., n.d. (c. December 1935), pp. 2–3, Fraternities and Sororities, 1935 folders, AFPS, Adm. files, C199, NAACP Records; CHH to Joint Committee, 11 January 1936, pp. 1–2, Joint Committee, 1936–37 folder, AFPS, Adm. files, C200 NAACP Records.

51. See legal files D94–97 of NAACP Records for correspondence and briefs in University of Tennessee case, *State of Tennessee ex rel William B. Redmond II* v. *O. W. Hyman*; "To Appeal Ruling in Redmond Denial," *Pittsburgh Courier*, 24 April 1937, clipping; "Scholarship Bill to Aid Negro Students Passed in Tennessee," *New York Age*, 15 May 1937, clipping, CHH/H&G firm files; cf. CHH, "A Challenge to Negro College Youth," *Crisis* 45 (January 1938): 14–15. See also for University of Missouri Case, CHH, "Memorandum for Preliminary Investigation into Exclusion of Negroes from the University of Missouri," 15 July 1935, Ed. C. 1934–1935 folder, AFPS, Adm. files, C197, NAACP Records, and 305 U.S. 337, *Missouri ex rel Gaines* v. *Canada*.

52. CHH, "Memorandum for Preliminary Investigation into Exclusion of Negroes from the University of Missouri," 15 July 1935, and Fee Agreement between Charles H. Houston and Sidney R. Redmond, n.d. [c. Summer 1935], Ed. C. 1934–35 folder, AFPS files, C197, NAACP Records; 1936 folder, AFPS Adm. files, C197, NAACP Records; CHH to office staff of Houston firm, 5 June 1936, WLH/H&G firm files. Files of University of Missouri Case, D94–95, NAACP Records.

53. CHH, "Confidential Office Memorandum *Gaines* v. *U. Missouri*," 11 July 1936, p. 1, CHH, Per. Corr., Adm. files, C81, NAACP Records.

54. Ibid., pp. 1–3.

55. Ibid.

56. Ibid., p. 4; NAACP *Annual Report, 1937*, p. 10; CHH, "A Challenge to Negro College Youth," p. 14.

57. CHH to TM, 17 September 1936, Joint Committee, 1936–37 folder, AFPS, Adm. files, C200, NAACP Records.

58. CHH to WW, confidential memorandum, 17 September 1936, Ed. C. 1936 folder, AFPS, Adm. files, C198, NAACP Records; Charles H. Houston, "Memorandum for the Joint Committee, N.A.A.C.P., and the American Fund for Public Service, Inc.," 28 September 1936, Joint Committee, 1936–37 folder, AFPS, Adm. files, C200, NAACP Records; "Thurgood Marshall on NAACP Legal Staff," *New York Age*, 24 October 1936, clipping, CHH/H&G firm files; [CHH,] "Report to the Joint Committee American Fund for Public Service, Inc., and the N.A.A.C.P." n.n., 4 May 1937, Ed. C. 1937 folder, Adm. files, C198, NAACP Records. Minutes of Board of Directors meeting, 13 October 1936, p. 2, July–December 1936, Minutes folder, Board of Directors file, A3, NAACP Records.

59. "To Hear Univ. of Missouri Case May 18," *Pittsburgh Courier*, 3 April 1937, clipping, CHH/H&G firm files; CHH, "Memorandum for the Secretary, Joint Committee of the American Fund . . . and the N.A.A.C.P.," 25 October 1937, *Applications Favorably Acted Upon—Gifts and Loans*, 9:75–76, AFPS Records; 342 Mo. 121, *Gaines*.

60. CHH, "A Challenge to Negro College Youth," p. 15.

61. Interview with MGH, 22 January 1973; HWH, Biographical Statement on CHH (1st edited version) for *National Cyclopedia of American Biography*, 21 July 1952; and "Charles H. Houston Brings Bride to Dunbar Apt." unidentified clipping, n.d., CHH Fam.; see CHH–Personal Correspondence, 1936 & 1937, CHH/H&G firm files.

62. "Charles H. Houston Brings Bride to Dunbar Apt."; CHH, "Memorandum for Secretary, Joint Committee," 25 October 1937; *Applications Favorably Acted Upon—Gifts and Loans*, 9:75, AFPS Records; [CHH,] "Report to the Joint Committee," 4 May 1937, pp. 1, 5, Ed. C., 1937, AFPS, Adm. files, C198, NAACP Records.

63. Untitled Press Release, 15 July 1938, CHH Per. Corr., Adm. files, C82, NAACP Records; CHH to WLH, 1 October 1937, WLH/H&G firm files; TM, "Homage to Charles Houston," 6 April 1978. See "College Honors Charles Houston '15," *Amherst*, Spring 1978, pp. 12–14. See also Richard Kluger, *Simple Justice* (New York: Alfred A. Knopf, 1976), p. 205.

64. WLH to Edward Lovett, 14 October 1935, WLH/H&G firm files.

65. Ibid. See interviews with CMH, 24 July 1972; Ben Amos, 17 January 1973; Juanita Kidd Stout, 21 August 1972; and Margaret Haywood, 2 January 1973.

66. Interviews with Ben Amos, 17 January 1973; Juanita Kidd Stout, 21 August 1972; CMH, 24 July 1972; and MGH, 22 January 1973.

67. CHH to WLH, 14 April 1938, and CHH to George Johnson, 3 June 1938, CHH Per. Corr., Adm. files, C82, NAACP Records. See minutes of Board of Directors meetings, 14 November 1934, 6 January 1936, 11 May 1936, 14 December 1936, 14 June 1937, 13 December 1937, in Board of Directors files, A3, NAACP Records; also see Budget Committee Reports in A18, NAACP Records.

68. WLH to Samuel Horovitz, 10 June 1936, WLH/H&G firm files; Minutes of Meeting of Board of Directors, 13 December 1937, pp. 5, 6, Board of Directors file, A3, NAACP Records.

69. CHH to WLH, 14 April 1938, CHH, Per. Corr., Adm. files, C82, NAACP Records.

70. HWH, "Biographical Mat[erial]" (notes), 15 January 1969, CHH Fam., and CHH's application to Employers' Liability Assurance Corp. [31 May 1938], CHH Per. Corr., Adm. files, C82, NAACP Records; interview with Edward C. Mazique, M.D.; and HWH, "An Appeal to Whom It May Concern," 19 and 21 January 1967, CHH Fam. (compare Kluger, *Simple Justice*, pp. 204–5).

71. CHH, "Future Policies and Practices Which Should Govern the Relationship of the Federal Government to Negro Separate Schools," *Journal of Negro Education* 7 (July 1938): 460–62. See Appendix 5: The "Garland Fund" voted $700 for *Gaines*. See also CHH's private case load during his Special Counselship (Appendix 2).

72. Interviews with Robert Carter, 5 May 1982, and Spottswood W. Robinson III, 4 June 1982.

73. 305 U.S. 337–342, *Gaines*.

74. 305 U.S. 349–351.

75. Unfortunately, shortly after the Supreme Court decision, Gaines disappeared and the point of admission could not be immediately forced. The case went back to the state supreme court for a second hearing; Missouri amended state legislation by making it mandatory on the curators of Lincoln to provide equal facilities for the study of law. Some $200,000 was appropriated to imple-

ment the legislature mandate. The court in its second decision held that if there was not a separate-and-equal law school by September 1939, Gaines would have to be admitted to the law school of the University of Missouri. This further indicated that the maintenance of segregated school systems would depend on the actual existence of separate and equal educational facilities for black citizens (344 Mo. 1234; Charles H. Houston, untitled testimony, n.d. [1941], pp. 4–6, CHH/H&G firm files). See Conrad Harper, "Charles Hamilton Houston," in Rayford W. Logan and Michael Winston, eds., *Dictionary of American Negro Biography* (New York: W. W. Norton, 1982); see also Harold Horowitz and Kenneth Karst, *Law, Lawyers, and Social Change* (Indianapolis: Bobbs-Merrill Co., 1969), pp. 150–237, for further discussions of the significance of *Gaines.*)

76. Interviews with Robert Carter, 5 May 1982; Constance Baker Motley, 23 June 1982; Roy Wilkins, 6 December 1972; and William Hastie Jr., 19 September 1972.

77. 348 Mo. 298, Bluford, "NAACP to Appeal, Second University of Missouri Court Case," press release, 1 November 1940, CHH/H&G firm files. See Legal Committee 1938, 1939, Committee Correspondence, Board of Directors files A28, NAACP Records; "Memorandum for the Joint Committee," 20 October 1937, p. 4, Ed. C. 1937 folder, AFPS, Adm. files, C198, NAACP Records. See Maryland Teachers' Salary Cases, Legal files D89, D90 NAACP Records.

78. "Pay War Opens," *Afro-American*, 12 June 1937, clipping, CHH/H&G firm files. "Memorandum for the Joint Committee of the American Fund for Public Service, Inc., and the N.A.A.C.P.," 20 October 1937, p. 4, C198, NAACP Records; CHH, "Report to the Joint Committee . . ."; 12 November, 1937, *Applications Favorably Acted Upon—Gifts and Loans*, 9:70–71, AFPS Records; *William B. Gibbs, Jr. v. Edwin W. Broome . . .* [and] *Members of the Board of Education of Montgomery County*, Maryland Teachers Salary Cases, Cases Supported, D90 NAACP Records. The action of Maryland teachers in establishing the rehabilitation fund is probably also attributable to Houston's efforts in 1936 to contact and involve in the campaign the "colored parent-teachers associations" and "national associations of teachers in colored schools." (Letters from Charles Thompson to CHH, 7 January 1936; Garnet Wilkinson, 6 January 1936; CHH to Charles Thompson, 4 January 1936; Charles Houston to Garnet Wilkinson, 4 January 1936; CHH to Executive Secretary, National Federation of P.T.A., 11 January 1936, Ed. C., 1936, AFPS, Adm. files, C197, NAACP Records.

79. "Memorandum to WW and CHH Re: Garland Fund," 7 October 1936, p. 3, C197, NAACP Records; "Memorandum for the Joint Committee of the American Fund for Public Service, Inc., and the N.A.A.C.P.," 20 October 1937, p. 7, C198, NAACP Records; CHH, "Report to the Joint Committee," 12 November 1937, AFPS, *Applications Favorably Acted Upon—Gifts and Loans*, 9:71; NAACP, *Annual Report, 1939*, p. 6; "Memorandum to County Teachers; Associations: Re Procedure to Equalize Teachers' Salaries," n.d., Ed. C. Adm. files, C197, NAACP Records; CHH, untitled testimony, n.d. [c. 1941], pp. 10–12, CHH/H&G firm case files; interview with Oliver W. Hill, 8 December 1972; Maryland Teachers Salary Cases Supported, Legal files, D88–90, and Virginia Teachers Salary Cases Supported, Legal files, D91, NAACP Records.

80. Conversation with Howard Thurman, 25 January 1979. See, e.g., Memorandum to County Teachers' Associations: Re Procedure to Equalize Teachers' Salaries," C197, and Maryland Teachers Salary Cases Supported, Legal

files, D91, NAACP Records. See also my "Charles Hamilton Houston," pp. 303–304.

81. See, e.g., NAACP, *Annual Report, 1937; Margaret Williams v. David Zimmerman,* 172 Md. 563 (and Legal files, NAACP Records), CHH, "Report to the Joint Committee," 12 November 1937, AFPS, *Applications Favorably Acted Upon—Gifts and Loans,* 9:65–74; CHH, "Memorandum Concerning the Fight for Equality of Educational Opportunity," 19 December 1936, C198, NAACP Records. See my "Charles Hamilton Houston," pp. 304–306.

82. CHH, "Report to the Joint Committee," 12 November 1937, AFPS, *Applications Favorably Acted Upon—Gifts and Loans,* 9:73–74. See also my "Charles Hamilton Houston," p. 307.

83. In 1937 the board of the NAACP passed a resolution prohibiting paid executives from signing or issuing "statements in support of party candidates or . . . policies and programs" and speaking "at meetings called by partisan political groups." (NAACP Board of Directors, "Minutes of the Meeting of the Board of Directors," 11 October 1937, A3, NAACP Records.) By 1940 the prohibition was extended by interpretation of the committee on administration to include nonpartisan political activity (ibid., 14 October 1940, A3, NAACP Records).

84. NAACP Board of Directors, "Minutes of the Meeting of the Board of Directors," 14 October 1940, p. 3, A3, NAACP Records; NAACP, *Annual Report, 1940,* p. 38.

CHAPTER ELEVEN
Protecting the Right to Work

1. Interview with Samuel H. Clark, 26 July 1972. See files of Association of Colored Railway Trainmen and Locomotive Firemen (A.C.R.T. & L.F.), SHC Papers.

2. CHH, "Report to the Joint Committee of the American Fund for Public Service, Inc., and the NAACP," 4 May 1937, p. 1, American Fund for Public Service (AFPS) folders, Adm. files, C198, NAACP Records.

3. Interview with Samuel H. Clark, 26 July 1972.

4. See Jervis Anderson, *A. Philip Randolph: A Biographical Portrait* (New York: Harcourt Brace Jovanovich, 1972), pt. 4; see also Sterling Spero and Abram Harris, *The Black Worker* (1931; reprint ed., New York: Atheneum, 1969), p. 313, for an explanation of the two major classifications of workers on railroad, i.e., the operatives or operating workers (those who run the trains) and nonoperatives or nonoperating workers (those who work in other such capacities as pullman porters).

5. Interview with Samuel Clark, 26 July 1972.

6. Ibid.

7. See Appendix 2 for private practice, January 1936 to January 1939. See also Marian Anderson Collection, Moorland-Spingarn Research Center, Howard University, Washington, D.C. (hereafter MSRC); Minutes of the D.C. Board of Education, 1 and 3 March 1939, 5 April 1939; *New York Times,* 17 April 1939, p. 19. (Houston chaired the Marian Anderson Citizens Committee of Washington, D.C., which was formed to protest Marian Anderson's being denied permission to present a concert in both Central High School and the

D.A.R. Constitution Hall. Because of the work of the Committee, Anderson sang at Lincoln Memorial by special invitation of Secretary of the Interior, Harold Ickes, and after the concert an Anderson mural committee was organized by interested committee members. Some members pressed the constitutional issue with respect to Central High School and continued dialogue with the D.A.R. until exclusion on the basis of race was discontinued.)

8. Re Citizens Committee on Race Relations and other District civil rights activities, see Wilbur La Roe, Jr., to CHH, 18 August 1943, and other letters and papers in Houston's "Race Relations" file, CHH/H&G firm files; Genna R. McNeil, "Charles Hamilton Houston (1895–1950) and the Struggle for Civil Rights" (Ph.D. diss., University of Chicago, 1975), pp. 407–408; CHH, "Critical Summary: The Negro in the U.S. Armed Forces in World War I and II," *Journal of Negro Education* 12 (Summer 1943): 364–66; and interview with Anna Hedgeman, 8 July 1982.

9. CHH to WW, 22 May 1939, WLH/H&G firm files.

10. CHH, "Brief Record of Some Major Acts of Racial Hostility Toward Negroes by the Train, Engine, and Yard Service National Railway Labor Unions," July 1949, A.C.R.T. & L.F. files, SHC Papers; Railway Labor Act 44 Stat. 577 (chap. 347) and 48 Stat. 1185 (chap. 691). See Spero and Harris, *Black Worker*, p. 285 and Herbert R. Northrop, *Organized Labor and the Negro* (New York: Harper & Bros., 1944), p. 53. See also Phillip S. Foner, *Organized Labor and the Black Worker* (New York: Praeger, 1974).

11. Interview with Samuel Clark, 26 July 1972. See Association grievances and legal activities in A.C.R.T. & L.F., files, SHC Papers.

12. "A Hearing . . . Racial Discrimination in Employment . . . Railroads [U.S.]," [FEPC,] September 15–18, 1943, pp. 150–51, Hearing Box 305, Legal Division, FEPC RG228; "First Meeting of International Association of Railway Employees," n.d., n.p. (courtesy of Samuel H. Clark, Christianburg, Va.).

13. "Amended Complaint," n.d. [c. June 1940], p. 8, *Ed Teague v. Brotherhood of Locomotive Firemen & Enginemen and Gulf, Mobile & Northern Railroad Company*, Hearing Box 309; and "A Hearing . . . Racial Discrimination in Employment . . . Railroads [U.S.]," [FEPC,] September 15–18, 1943, pp. 151–56, Hearing Box 305, Legal Division, FEPC/RG228; Interview with Samuel H. Clark, 26 July 1972; CHH untitled notes in re U.S. District Court session on *Teague*, 27 June 1940, CHH/H&G firm files.

14. See sources cited in note 13. The National Railroad Adjustment Board refused to hear the complaint because the black union was not the RLA duly authorized representative.

15. CHH to Carol King, 29 June 1942, CHH/H&G firm files. See CHH, "Notice of Appeal" (draft), 13 March 1941; CHH to "Office," 28 September 1941; CHH to Samuel Clark and Frank Caldwell, 10 October 1941; CHH, Memorandum in re Ed Teague, 3–4 March 1942; 127 F 2d 53.

16. Joseph Settle to CHH, 4 April 1942, and S. H. Clark to CHH, 17 October 1942, CHH/H&G firm files; interview with Samuel Clark, 26 July 1972; "Report of Proceedings," Conference for Colored Locomotive Firemen, 28–29 March 1941, pp. 7–8, 19–20, 29–33, 48–55 passim, CHH/H&G firm files.

17. James Nabrit, Jr., "Late Lawyer Was Champion—Houston Sparked Fight for Labor," *Pittsburgh Courier* (national edition), 3 June 1950, p. 2. *Pyles* (1941–42) was not assessed as having the clarity of *Steele* (1941–44),

although *Pearl Pyles* v. *Illinois Central Railroad Company, Inc. et al.* received considerable attention during its first year from J. T. Settle and Houston. Apparently the issues were framed as in the *Teague* Amended Complaint, and there were concerns about proving conspiracy between the railroad and the brotherhood since the Southeastern Carriers Conference Agreement was not applicable, thus making *Pyles* less suitable for prosecution through to the Supreme Court. (CHH/H&G firm files).

18. See 16 So. 2d 416; 140 F. 2d 35. See also "Agreement Between the Southeastern Carriers' Conference Committee . . . and the Brotherhood of Locomotive Firemen and Enginemen," 21 February 1941, Hearing Box 309, Legal Division, FEPC/RG228.

19. "First Race Lawyer Presents Oral Argument in Alabama," *Philadelphia Independent*, 12 December 1943, clipping, CHH vertical file, MSRC; 16 So. 2d 416; 140 F. 2d 35.

20. CHH to Richard Westbrooks, 6 July 1944, CHH/H&G firm files. See 16 So. 2d 416; 140 F. 2d 35. See also *Steele*, 323 U.S. 192, 194–209, and *Tunstall* 323 U.S. 210–213.

21. CHH to M. S. Stuart, 26 December 1944, CHH/H&G firm files.

22. "Report of Proceedings," Conference for Colored Locomotive Firemen, 28–29 March 1941, pp. 46–47, CHH/H&G firm files; CHH to A. Philip Randolph, 1 November 1941, and A. Philip Randolph to CHH, 5 November 1941, CHH/H&G firm files; interviews with Samuel Clark, 26 July 1972; A. Philip Randolph, 16 July 1973; and Benjamin McLaurin, 17 July 1973.

23. Harold Stevens to CHH, 4 October 1941, CHH to Frank Caldwell and Samuel Clark, 10 October 1941, CHH to Jonathan Daniels, 3 December 1941, CHH/H&G firm files; CHH to A. Philip Randolph, 10 January 1942, CHH/H&G firm files. Interview with Benjamin McLaurin, 17 July 1973; interview with Samuel H. Clark, 26 July 1972; A. Philip Randolph to CHH, 10 January 1942, Correspondence Ha-Hu Container 14, Brotherhood of Sleeping Car Porters Collection, Library of Congress, Washington, D.C. See Brotherhood of Locomotive Firemen folders, Container 89, Brotherhood of Sleeping Car Porters, Library of Congress, for additional correspondence between the International and/or Association and the Brotherhood. See also CHH to A. Philip Randolph, 1 November 1941, in which issue of unified support for *Steele* is raised. (Correspondence Ha-Hu [Container 14], Brotherhood of Sleeping Car Porters Collection, Library of Congress.)

24. CHH to Arthur Lewis, 1 November 1941, CHH/H&G firm files.

25. Interview with Benjamin McLaurin, 17 July 1973; "Document X" (Short history of the Brotherhood of Sleeping Car Porters' Provisional Committee for the organization of "Colored Locomotive Firemen"), Brotherhood of Locomotive Firemen folder no. 3, Brotherhood of Sleeping Car Porters Collection, Library of Congress. See "To Colored Firemen," 5 March 1941, Brotherhood of Locomotive Firemen folder no. 2, Container 89, Brotherhood of Sleeping Car Porters Collection, Library of Congress, Washington, D.C.

26. Interview with A. Philip Randolph, 16 July 1973.

27. CHH to Malcolm McLean, 16 January 1943, 4245f in Official File, FDR Papers. "Chairman Resigns in Job Bias Group," *New York Post*, 19 January 1943, clipping, CHH vertical file, MSRC. See Anderson, *A. Philip Randolph*, pp. 247–61 passim.

28. CHH to Franklin D. Roosevelt, 18 January 1943, 4245g in Official File, FDR Papers.

29. "Houston Has Polite Way of Calling U.S. Army Chief of Staff a Liar," *Afro-American*, 15 September 1934, clipping, CHH/H&G firm files; CHH to Douglas MacArthur, 9 August 1934, enclosed in CHH to WW 10 August 1934, Sp. Cor., Adm. file, C64, NAACP Records; CHH to editor of *New York Times*, 9 March 1938, CHH/H&G firm files. See John Hope Franklin, *From Slavery to Freedom*, 5th rev. ed. (New York: Alfred A. Knopf, 1980), pp. 428–44 passim.

30. "Report of Proceedings [of] Hearings Held Before Select Committee of the House of Representatives to Investigate Acts of Executive Agencies Beyond the Scope of Their Authority," 11 January, 25 February, 1, 2, and 10 March, 1944, pp. 2798, 2799, 2807–8 passim, Box 335, Legal Division, FEPC/RG228.

31. Ibid.

32. Franklin D. Roosevelt to Jonathan Daniels, 22 February 1944, Official File, FDR Papers.

33. Jonathan Daniels to Franklin D. Roosevelt, 28 February 1944; Franklin D. Roosevelt to CHH, 28 February 1944; and CHH to Franklin D. Roosevelt, 2 March 1944, Official File, FDR Papers. "Houston New Member of FEPC," *Norfolk Journal and Guide* [c. March 1944], clipping, CHH vertical file, MSRC; "President's Committee on Fair Employment Practice," press release, Division of Review and Analyses, Headquarters Records, FEPC RG228.

34. "Houston New Member of FEPC."

35. George Johnson to author, 17 October 1972; interviews with St. Clair Bourne, 16 January 1974, Maceo Hubbard, 26 January 1974, Earl B. Dickerson, 2 and 9 March 1973.

36. CHH to Roy Wilkins, 8 March 1944, CHH, Board of Directors file, NAACP Records.

37. George Johnson to author, 17 October 1972; FEPC, "The President's Committee on Fair Employment Practice . . ." Reference file, July 1944–April 1946, Division of Review and Analyses, FEPC/RG228; See Headquarters and Regional Offices' Records, FEPC/RG228.

38. *Weekly News Digest*, March 24, 1944, p. 2, Division of Information and Public Relations, Headquarters Records, FEPC/RG228; CHH to "Old Master" (Ed Rogers of Reno, Nevada), CHH/H&G firm files; interviews with Benjamin Amos, 17 January 1973, and CMH, 24 July 1972 and 7 December 1973.

39. Interviews with CMH July 1972–December 1973 and Benjamin Amos 17 January 1973.

40. Interview with Samuel H. Clark, 26 July 1972.

41. Interview with Juanita Kidd Stout, 21 August 1972.

42. Henrietta Houston, "An Appeal to Whom It May Concern," January 1967, CHH Fam. See also Spottswood W. Robinson, "No Tea for the Feeble," *Howard Law Journal* 20 (1977): 1–9.

43. William O. Douglas, *The Court Years, 1939–1975* (New York: Random House, 1980), p. 185.

44. 323 U.S. 199, 201–204, 207; 323 U.S. 210–214; interview with Samuel Clark, 26 July 1972. (Within the context of a war effort and national concern with the FEPC, the U.S. Supreme Court noted the filing of amici curiae briefs for Bester William Steele and Tom Tunstall by the Department of Justice, the American Civil Liberties Union, and the NAACP when it heard the arguments of counsel for the petitioners and respondents in *Steele* v. *Louisville and Nashville et al.* and *Tunstall* v. *Brotherhood of Locomotive Firemen and Enginemen et al.*)

45. 323 U.S. 199, 201–204, 207. See 323 U.S. 210–214 for *Tunstall* opinion. In this opinion the court also held that Tom Tunstall's cause of action was indeed cognizable in the federal courts (323 U.S. 213). After being remanded to the lower court, plaintiff Tunstall was awarded one thousand dollars in compensatory damages against the Brotherhood of Locomotive Firemen and Enginemen for losses sustained because of the violation of his seniority rights and his displacement. (CHH to Mrs. Gifford Pinchot, 12 March 1946, CHH/ H&G firm files; "Firemen's Rights Restored by Court," *Afro-American* (Baltimore), 1 February 1947, pp. 1, 2; interview with Samuel H. Clark, 26 July 1972.

46. 323 U.S. 208–209.

47. CHH to Association of Colored Railway Trainmen & Locomotive Firemen, International Association of Railway Employees, Arthur D. Shores, Bester William Steele, Tom Tunstall, and Thurgood Marshall, 20 December 1944, CHH/H&G firm files. See 323 U.S. 198 for Houston's elected representative analogy. See also interview with Joseph Waddy, 25 June 1971.

48. Interview with Anna A. Hedgeman, 8 July 1982.

49. James Nabrit, Jr., "Late Lawyer Was Champion—Houston Sparked Fight for Labor," *Pittsburgh Courier* (national edition), 3 June 1950, p. 2. See Interview with A. A. Hedgeman, 8 July 1982.

50. CHH to Malcolm Ross, 1 December 1944, H-L. Office files of George M. Johnson (Director), Legal Division, Headquarters Records, FEPC/RG228; FEPC, *Final Report* (Washington, D.C.: Government Printing Office, 1947), pp. 15–16, in Reference File, Division of Review and Analyses, FEPC/RG228. See my "Charles Hamilton Houston," pp. 343–47. See also interview with A. A. Hedgeman, 8 July 1982, and Louis C. Kesselman, *The Social Politics of FEPC: A Study in Reform Pressure Movements* (Chapel Hill: University of North Carolina Press, 1948).

51. George M. Johnson to author, 17 October 1972; CHH to Harry S. Truman, 25 November 1972, CHH, Board of Directors file, NAACP Records.

52. Untitled press release re the action of the FEPC in the matter of Capital Transit Company of Washington, D.C., 2 January 1945, Official File, FDR Papers. "Capital Transit Company" (case no. 70), hearing, January 15–16, 1945, pp. 185–215, 219–21, pp. 206–9 passim, Hearings, Box 349, Legal Division, FEPC/RG228; "Talks with Transit Workers on Racial Views Described" *Evening Star* (Washington, D.C.), n.d., clipping, Capital Transit Company, Miscellaneous file, Hearings, Box 349, Legal Division, FEPC/RG228.

53. CHH to Harry S. Truman, 25 November 1945, CHH, Board of Directors file, NAACP Records. See FEPC, *Final Report*, p. 16, in Reference file, Division of Review and Analysis, FEPC/RG228.

54. CHH to Harry S. Truman, 25 November 1945, CHH, Board of Directors file, NAACP Records.

55. Ibid.

56. CHH to Harry S. Truman, 3 December 1945, CHH, Board of Directors file, NAACP Records.

57. Ibid.

58. Harry S. Truman to CHH, 7 December 1945, courtesy of CHH Jr.

59. See, e.g., letters to embassies of Costa Rica, Cuba, Mexico, the Netherlands, Panama, Switzerland, and Yugoslavia, FEPC file, CHH/H&G firm files.

60. "Memorandum of Charles H. Houston re President Truman's letter of

December 1945," n.d. [c. 11 December 1945], CHH, Board of Directors file, NAACP Records.

61. L. D. Reddick to CHH, 20 February 1946, CHH/H&G firm files. Regarding diversity of opinion, see interviews with Maceo Hubbard, 26 January 1974, St. Clair Bourne, 16 January 1974, Earl B. Dickerson, 2 and 9 1973, and George M. Johnson to author, 17 October 1972.

62. "Applicability of the Fourteenth Amendment to Private Organizations," *Harvard Law Review* 61 (January 1948): 344–47; *Kerr* v. *Pratt*, CHH/H&G firm files; 59 Fed. Supp. 514 (1944) and 149 F. 2d 212 (1945).

63. CHH, untitled handwritten note, 4 April 1950, in Joshua Loth Liebman, *Peace of Mind* (New York: Simon & Schuster, 1946), p. 48 of copy among possessions of Clotill M. Houston, Washington, D.C.

CHAPTER TWELVE
"Racism Must Go"

1. CHH to Harry S. Truman, 3 December 1945, CHH folder, Board of Directors file, NAACP Records.

2. *Afro-American* (Baltimore), 5 July 1947; private case files of CHH included data on these restrictive covenant cases in the District, CHH/H&G firm files.

3. Interview with Spottswood W. Robinson III, 4 June 1982.

4. *Corrigan*, 271 U.S. 323 (1926). In 1937 Charles Houston recommended that the national office of the NAACP give some financial support to E. B. Dickerson, C. F. Stradford, and I. Mollison in the *Hansberry* v. *Lee* case 372 Ill. 369 (1940). (See Memorandum from Charles Houston to W. White, R. Wilkins, T. Marshall, and A. Spingarn, 19 July 1937, WLH/H&G firm files; interview with Earl B. Dickerson, 2 and 9 March 1973.) For the background of this challenge to court enforcement of racially restrictive covenants and the prosecution of cases through the Supreme Court, see the excellent detailed and analytical account presented in Clement Vose, *Caucasians Only: The Supreme Court, the NAACP, and the Restrictive Covenant Cases* (Berkeley: University of California Press, 1959).

5. *Mays* v. *Burgess*, 325 U.S. 868, 896 (1945), 147 F. 2d 969 (1945); Vose, *Caucasians Only*, pp. 58–59, 60–61, 265–66, 274. Vose's chapters "Evolution of the NAACP Legal Strategy" and "Preparations for the U.S. Supreme Court" (chaps. 3 and 7) are especially instructive.

6. Consolidated petitions and supporting brief for writs of certiorari to the U.S. Court of Appeals for the District of Columbia, 22 August 1947, *Hurd* v. *Hodge* (no. 290), and *Urciolo* v. *Hodge* (no. 291), U.S. Supreme Court, p. 3, CHH Fam.; transcript of the record, *Hodge* v. *Hurd* (civil action no. 26192), U.S. District Court for the District of Columbia, Philadelphia Bar Association Library, Philadelphia, Pa. (courtesy of the Honorable Juanita Kidd Stout). See Vose, *Caucasians Only*, pp. 84–92 passim.

7. *Afro-American* (Baltimore), 21 June 1947, p. 4.

8. Consolidated petitions and supporting brief for writs of certiorari to the U.S. Court of Appeals for the District of Columbia, 22 August 1947, *Hurd* v. *Hodge* (no. 290), and *Urciolo* v. *Hodge* (no. 291), U.S. Supreme Court, pp. 3–4, CHH Fam.

9. *Afro-American* (Baltimore), 5 July 1947, p. 4, and 15 May 1948, p. 4.

10. Interview with Spottswood W. Robinson III, 4 June 1982. See Spotts-wood W. Robinson, "No Tea for the Feeble," *Howard Law Journal* 20 (1977): 5–6.

11. Interview with Phineas Indritz, 23 April 1973; consolidated petitions and supporting brief for writs of certiorari to the U.S. Court of Appeals for the District of Columbia; Robinson, "No Tea for the Feeble," pp. 5–6. See also *Muller* v. *Oregon*, 208 U.S. 412 (1908).

12. Minutes of meeting of NAACP lawyers and consultants on methods of attacking restrictive covenants, 6 September 1947, pp. 3–14, Box 363 (1 of 5) NAACP Records. Interview with Constance B. Motley, 23 June 1982.

13. Social scientists assisting with the appendix to the improved consoli-dated brief included Charles S. Johnson (with whom Houston had worked during Fisk University Race Relations Institutes), Louis Wirth, and Robert Weaver. Compare transcript of record in *Hodge* v. *Hurd* in U.S. District Court for the District of Columbia with *Hurd* v. *Hodge* (no. 290) and *Urciolo* v. *Hodge* (no. 291), U.S. Supreme Court. See consolidated brief for petitioners in *Shelley* v. *Kraemer* and *Sipes* v. *McGhee* (on which Charles Houston is listed "of counsel"), U.S. Supreme Court Library, Washington, D.C.

14. Conrad Harper, "Charles Hamilton Houston," in Rayford W. Logan and Michael Winston, eds., *Dictionary of American Negro Biography* (New York: W. W. Norton & Co., 1982).

15. Consolidated brief for petitioners in *Hurd* v. *Hodge* and *Uricolo* v. *Hodge* p. 71, U.S. Supreme Court Library.

16. Consolidated reply brief for petitioners in *Hurd* v. *Hodge* and *Urciolo* v. *Hodge*, U.S. Supreme Court Library.

17. See, e.g., Brief of United States as amicus curiae in *Shelley* v. *Kraemer*, *Sipes* v. *McGhee* (334 U.S. 1 [1948]); see also *Afro-American* (Baltimore), 13 December 1948, p. 1; WH to CHH, 28 November 1939, CHH/H&G firm files; interview with Robert Carter, 5 May 1982, and Spottswood Robinson III, 4 June 1982; and annual reports of Howard University's School of Law, 1938–39 to 1948–49, HULS Archives, and courtesy of JoAnne King, Registrar, HULS; Vose, *Caucasians Only*, p. 200.

18. *Afro-American* (Baltimore), 24 January 1948, pp. 1, 12.

19. William O. Douglas, *The Court Years 1939–1975* (New York: Random House, 1980), p. 185.

20. 16 Law Week 3219–24 passim. See *Afro-American* (Baltimore), 24 January 1948, p. 12.

21. *Shelley* and *Sipes*, 334 U.S. 1 (1948); *Hurd* and *Urciolo* 334 U.S. 24 (1948).

22. 334 U.S. 35–36 (1948).

23. 334 U.S. 36 (1948).

24. *Afro-American* (Baltimore), 12 February 1949, p. 4.

25. Citation for Charles Houston, 17 September 1948, "Done by the Au-thority of the National Bar Association in Its Twenty-third Annual Convention . . . ," CHH Fam.

26. Ibid.; CHH to Thurman L. Dodson, 14 September 1948, CHH/H&G firm files. Houston continued in his role of advocate for black residents fight-ing for occupancy of covenanted property after the U.S. Supreme Court ruling in the Hodge cases. With Donald G. Murray (the young man for whom Mar-

shall and Houston had argued in the University of Maryland Law School case [169 Md. 478]), Houston successfully argued *Phillips et al.* v. *Saunders et al.*, 336 U.S. 967 or 93 L. Ed. 1118 (1948).

27. "The Nation's Capital: How Can It Achieve More Democracy?" printed transcript, 19 December 1948, p. 8, CHH folder, Board of Directors file, NAACP Records. See *Afro-American* (Baltimore), 4 October 1947, p. 4. 25 June 1949, p. 4, and 16 July 1949, p. 4.

28. Interview with Gardner Bishop, 2 March 1972; "Annual Report of Consolidated Parent Group, Inc. [for December 1947–August 1949]," n.d., CPG Records.

29. Conversation with Howard Thurman, 25 January 1979, and CHH to Harlan Miller, 21 November 1938, CHH/H&G firm files.

30. Interview with Benjamin Amos, 17 January 1973.

31. James Forer, James A. Cobb, Daniel Crystal, Margaret A. Haywood, J. H. Krug, Herbert S. Thatcher, CHH, "Opinion on the Anti-discrimination Acts of the Legislative Assembly of the District of Columbia," typescript, n.d. [c. 20 May 1949], CHH/H&G firm files; interview with Margaret A. Haywood, 2 January 1973; National Committee on Segregation in the Nation's Capital membership roster (1948–49), Box 37, DC/NAACP; "How Our Lawyers Changed Washington," *Afro-American* (Washington, D.C.), clipping, 25 April 1964, CHH Fam.; Constance Green, *The Secret City* (Princeton: Princeton University Press, 1967), p. 296; interview with Bertha McNeill, 13 March 1972; CHH in *Afro-American* (Baltimore), 18 December 1948, p. 4.

32. Recollection of Joseph Waddy in Richard Kluger, *Simple Justice* (New York: Alfred A. Knopf, 1976), pp. 279–80.

33. The test case for desegregation of Washington's restaurants based on the status was filed after Houston's death, and the court did not render its historic decision upholding the nineteenth-century antidiscrimination statutes until 1953. (See *District of Columbia* v. *John R. Thompson Company, Inc.* [no. 967], Municipal Court of Appeals for the District of Columbia [decided 24 May 1951]; *John R. Thompson Company* v. *District of Columbia* [no. 11039], and *District of Columbia* v. *John R. Thompson Company* [no. 11044], U.S. Court of Appeals for the District of Columbia Circuit [decided 22 January 1953], "Briefs for Margaret Haywood," courtesy of the Honorable Margaret A. Haywood, Washington, D.C.).

34. CHH, Final Examination in Civil Rights, Howard University School of Law, 25 May 1940, WLH/H&G firm files; CHH, Final Examination in Civil Rights, Howard University School of Law, 19 May 1941, CHH/H&G firm files; Leon A. Ransom to CHH, 25 January 1941; CHH to Leon A. Ransom, 8 July 1942, CHH/H&G firm files; *Catalogue of Howard University, 1939–1940*, pp. 26, 221; George M. Johnson to CHH, 10 July 1946 and 9 February 1949; CHH to George M. Johnson, 1 September 1949, CHH/H&G firm files. See my "Charles Hamilton Houston" (Ph.D. diss., University of Chicago, 1975), pp. 385–86 re scholarship.

35. Mordecai Johnson to CHH, 20 March 1950, file 1196 (CHH/H&G firm files). During his lifetime, Howard University did not select Charles Houston for a public award or honor other than his selection for the Law School Visiting Committee (Rayford Logan, *Howard University* [New York: New York University Press, 1969], p. 399). It was not until 1966 that Charles Houston was selected for a major award or honor. On 11 November 1966 his aunt, Clotill M.

Houston, accepted for Charles Houston "The Centennial Lawyer Award as the Foremost Lawyer of the Century in the Struggle for Freedom for Citizens of the United States Within the Rule of Law and Under the Constitution" (see plaque located in the Howard University Law School). A secret ballot election was held during the time of James Nabrit's presidency and Clarence G. Ferguson, Jr.'s deanship.

36. CHH to James Atkins (Director of Racial Relations, Bureau of Community Facilities, Federal Works Agency) 14 November 1947, CHH/H&G firm files; *Afro-American* (Baltimore), 15 November 1947, pp. 1, 18.

37. See, e.g., Houston for Commissioner campaign leaflet, CHH vertical file, Moorland-Spingarn Research Center, Howard University (hereafter MSRC); interview with Joseph L. Johnson, 26 October 1972; Stephen G. Spottswood to Harry S. Truman, 19 September 1949, copy, CHH/H&G firm files. "Petition for Houston Given to White House," *Washington Post*, 20 April 1949, clipping, D.C., District of Columbia branch, NAACP Records, MSRC. See also my "Charles Hamilton Houston," pp. 388-96 and accompanying footnotes.

38. Interview with Gardner Bishop, 2 March 1972; "People's Champion to Valhalla," *Pittsburgh Courier*, 6 May 1950, clipping, CHH vertical file, MSRC. See Mary Anliot, "A Study of the Dual School System in the District of Columbia" (M.A. thesis, American University, 1954). See also Certificate of Incorporation of Consolidated Parent Group, 22 March 1950, certificate no. 34209, Liber no. 73, p. 254, incorporation records, Office of the Recorder of Deeds. Although the parents were not officially incorporated until 1950, they became a duly organized group with constitution, bylaws, and rules in September 1948. According to the constitution, the purpose of "the Consolidated Parent Group" was to "fight discrimination in the District of Columbia and vicinity; primarily in the District Schools and Recreation," and its activity was "to protect the civil rights of the members, the community in general and all persons regardless of race, color or religion." See "Constitution of the Consolidated Parent Group Papers," CPG Records; *J. C. Bishop et al.* v. *Doyle et al.*, Civil Action No. 290-48, U.S. District Court for the District of Columbia; *Eddie Gregg et al.* v. *Sharpe et al.*, Civil Action No. 4205-49, U.S. District Court for the District of Columbia; *Gloria Haley et al.* v. *Sharpe et al.*, Civil Action No. 4227, U.S. District Court for the District of Columbia, CHH/H&G firm files.

39. John Mathews, "School Integration: 20 Years Later," *Washington Star News*, 12 May 1974, p. 1; see interview with Gardner Bishop, 2 March 1972.

40. Interview with Gardner Bishop, 2 March 1972.

41. Interview with Burma Whitted, 28 March 1972; interview with Gardner Bishop, 2 March 1972; "Four Years of Legal Work End in Victory for Two Colored Lawyers," *Evening Star* (Washington, D.C.), 18 May 1954, p. A4; Gardner Bishop Scrapbook, CPG Records. See Complaint for Declaratory Judgment, *Bishop et al.* v. *Doyle*, Civil Action No. 290-48, U.S. District Court for D.C., CHH/H&G firm files.

42. Interview with Burma Whitted, 29 March 1972; interview with Charles Thompson, 23 December 1974, interview with Harry Merican, 19 April 1972. See, e.g., "Proposed Scope of Examination of Dr. Hobart M. Corning on Taking His Deposition," *Gloria Haley et al.* v. *Sharpe et al.*, Civil Action No. 4227-49, U.S. District Court for D.C., CHH/H&G firm files.

43. "The People's Champion to Valhalla," *Pittsburgh Courier*, 6 May 1950, clipping, CHH vertical file, MSRC.

44. Gardner Bishop's statement in "Annual Report of Consolidated Parent Group, Inc. [for December 1947–August 1949]," n.d., p. 7, CPG Records.

45. Interview with Gardner Bishop, 2 March 1972.

46. "Annual Report of Consolidated Parent Group, Inc. [for December 1947–August 1949]," n.d.; "Facts—A Statement of the Accomplishments of Consolidated Parent Group [from 1947 to 1951]," n.d. [c. September 1951] and miscellaneous papers re membership, proposals, resolutions, etc., CPG Records; interview with Dorothy Porter, 2 March 1972; interview with Charlotte Price, 11 February 1972; interview with Charles Thompson, 28 December 1974.

47. Interview with Gardner Bishop, 2 March 1972. See George D. Strayer, The Report of a Survey of the Public Schools of the District of Columbia (Washington, D.C.: Government Printing Office, 1949); "Gardner L. Bishops's Position Clarified," unidentified newspaper, 21 April 1949, clipping; "Suffer Little Tots Don't Come Near Me," unidentified newspaper, n.d. [c. April 1949], clipping, Gardner Bishop Scrapbook, CPG Records.

48. "Suffer Little Tots Don't Come Near Me," unidentified newspaper, n.d. [1949], clipping, Gardner Bishop Scrapbook, CPG Records.

49. HWH, "An Appeal to Whom It May Concern," typewritten notes, 19 and 21 January 1967, CHH Fam.

50. Interviews with CMH, July 1972–November 1973; interview with Edward Mazique, 8 January 1973. Conversations with CHH Jr., 3 and 4 January 1973, 17 September 1974; interview with Benjamin Amos, 7 January 1973; interview with Phileo Nash, 23 October 1972. See Edith Nash, "The Story of an Integrated School," The Independent School Bulletin (December 1967), pp. 18–23, for background on the school Charles Jr. attended 1949–50, Georgetown Day School, Washington, D.C.

51. HWH, "Biographical Mat[erial]," handwritten notes, 15 January 1969, CHH Fam. See interview with Edward Lovett, 18 January 1973. See also Robinson, "No Tea for the Feeble," pp. 1–9.

52. HWH, "An Appeal to Whom It May Concern," typewritten notes, 19 and 21 January 1967, CHH Fam.

53. HWII, "Biographical Mat[erial]," handwritten notes, 15 January 1969, CHH Fam.

54. Interview with Spottswood W. Robinson III, 4 June 1982, and William Bryant, 4 June 1984; interview with C. B. Motley, 23 June 1982.

55. Interview with Anna Arnold Hedgeman, 8 July 1982.

56. Interview with Edward Mazique, 8 January 1973; WLH to Collector of Taxes, D.C., 13 March 1950, file 1196, CHH/H&G firm files.

CHAPTER THIRTEEN
"In Any Fight, Some Fall"

1. "Statement of Mr. Charles H. Houston [before the President's Committee on Civil Rights]," typescript, n.d. [c. 15 May 1947], p. 9, Box 5, CSJ Papers.

2. See, e.g., CHH to General Douglas MacArthur, 9 August 1934, in CHH to WW 10 August 1934, Sp. Cor.—CHH, NAACP Records, with CHH, Statement for Senate Subcommittee on Appropriations, typescript, 11 May 1940, CHH/H&G firm files or CHH to Frank Knox, 12 December 1941 (with clip-

ping), Box 865, FDR Papers, and CHH, "Civil Rights," *Afro-American* (Baltimore), 16 April 1949, p. 4. See Jervis Anderson, *A. Philip Randolph* (New York: Harcourt Brace Jovanovich, 1972), p. 276. See also my "Charles Hamilton Houston" (Ph.D. diss., University of Chicago, 1975), pp. 403–15.

3. CHH to Sidney R. Redmond, 24 April 1940, CHH/H&G firm files; see *National Bar Journal*, vols. 1–6.

4. "Lawyers Guild Asks End to House Probers," *Washington Post*, 23 February 1949, clipping; and *The Guild Lawyer*, Spring 1949, CHH/H&G firm files.

5. Leonard Boudin to CHH, 2 May 1949, and CHH to Leonard B. Boudin, 16 May 1949, CHH/H&G firm files.

6. CHH, "Protecting the Right to Work," handwritten note, n.d. [p. 3], CHH/H&G firm files; *Afro-American* (Washington, D.C.), 15 April 1947, p. 4; *Smith* 233 U.S. 630 (1914), *Meyer* 262 U.S. 390 (1923), and *Hodges* 23 U.S. 81 (1906). See interview with A. A. Hedgeman, 8 July 1982.

7. *Afro-American* (Washington, D.C.), 15 April 1947, p. 4.

8. *Afro-American* (Baltimore), 4 September 1947, p. 4; interview with Samuel H. Clark, 26 July 1972.

9. CHH, "Foul Employment Practice on the Rails," *Crisis* 56 (October 1949): 4; interview with Samuel H. Clark, 26 July 1972.

10. Brief of Simon L. Howard, Sr., n.d. [c. July 1949], *Simon L. Howard Sr. v. St. Louis–San Francisco Railway Company*, CHH/H&G firm files. See 191 F. 2d 442 (1951) and 72 S. Ct. 1022 (1952).

11. CHH, "Foul Employment Practice on the Rails," p. 285; Brief of David H. Hinton, et al., *David H. Hinton et al. v. Seaboard Air Line Railroad Company et al.*, CHH/H&G firm files.

12. CHH, "Foul Employment Practice on the Rails," p. 286; *Afro-American* (Baltimore), 4 September 1947, p. 4.

13. See, e.g., "Houston for Commissioner Committee," campaign leaflet, n.d. [c. 1947], CHH vertical file, Moorland-Spingarn Research Center, Howard University (hereafter MSRC); and WH, "Charles Hamilton Houston," *Crisis* 57 (July 1950): 365. See also interview with Joseph L. Johnson, 26 October 1972.

14. A. Maceo Smith to HWH, 25 April 1950; Workers Defense League to CHH, 12 June 1942; CHH to Colgate W. Darden, 22 June 1942; CHH to Charles LaFollette, 8 December 1947; CHH/H&G firm files.

15. CHH, "The Highway—Appeal to U.N. by Minorities in Order," *Afro-American*, 1 February 1947, p. 8.

16. Ibid.

17. See my "Charles Hamilton Houston," p. 426, n. 1; see also boxes 49 and 380, Legal files (Post 1940) and Minutes, 1942–50, Board of Directors files, NAACP Records.

18. TM to Legal Committee, 3 December 1947, and TM, Legal Department Monthly Reports, 1948, CHH/H&G firm files; TM to CHH, 6 December 1948; TM to CHH, James Nabrit, Robert Ming, n.d. [c. 8 December 1948]; TM to CHH et al., 29 December 1948, Daily Mail Bulletin file, Box 49 (no. 1 of 6) post-1940 NAACP Records. See generally Legal Department Reports, post–1940 NAACP Records.

19. Interview with Robert Carter, 5 May 1982.

20. Interview with Constance B. Motley, 23 June 1982.

21. Interviews with Robert Carter, 5 May 1982, and Constance B. Motley, 23 June 1982.

22. Interview with Constance B. Motley, 23 June 1982.

23. Ibid.

24. Ibid.

25. Interview with Robert Carter, 5 May 1982.

26. CHH quoted in Genna McNeil, "Charles Hamilton Houston—Social Engineer for Civil Rights," in J. H. Franklin and A. Meier, eds., *Black Leaders of the Twentieth Century* (Urbana, Ill.: University of Illinois Press, 1982), p. 232.

27. Interview with Constance B. Motley, 23 June 1982, and *McCready*, 195 Md. 131 (1950).

28. *Sipuel*, 332 U.S. 631 (1948).

29. *Sweatt*, 339 U.S. 629 (1950); *McLaurin*, 339 U.S. 639 (1950); *McCready*, 195 Md. 131 (19); Roy Wilkins, Keynote Address to 41st Annual NAACP Conference, 20 June 1950, p. 11, Annual Conference File, NAACP Records.

30. CHH to Robert Carter, 27 August 1949, Box 380 (no. 2 of 5), NAACP Records.

31. *Brown,* 347 U.S. 483 (1954). See text of Spingarn Medal citation, *Negro History Bulletin* 13 (June 1950): 213, and Richard Kluger, *Simple Justice* (New York: Alfred A. Knopf, 1976). See also my "Charles Hamilton Houston," *Black Law Journal* 3 (Spring 1974): 123–31.

32. See, e.g., CHH to "All Those Concerned About American Democracy," 22 August 1946; CHH to Editor of *The People's Voice*, February 23, 1945; Paul Robeson and Max Yergan to CHH, 7 February 1947; CHH to Max Yergan, 17 March 1947; CHH/H&G firm files; and *Afro-American* (Washington, D.C.), 1 May 1940, p. 4, 28 February 1948; *Afro-American* (Baltimore), 13 March 1948, p. 4, 30 July 1949, p. 4. See also my "Charles Hamilton Houston," (Ph.D. diss., University of Chicago, 1975), pp. 427–28.

33. CHH, untitled tape recording, n.d. [c. December 1949], CHH Fam.

34. See, e.g., *Afro-American* (Baltimore), 7 June 1947, p. 4; 11 December 1948, p. 4 (re racism and anti-Semitism, etc.); 21 May 1949, p. 4; 18 June 1949, p. 4; 6 August 1949, p. 4 (re India, Pakistan, Mao Tse-tung, and China), p. 2; October 1948, p. 4; 1 January 1949, p. 4; 25 February 1949, p. 4; 21 May 1949, p. 4 (re colonized Africa, non-white people of the world, and the struggle against imperialism and colonialism). See also CHH's columns in capital edition.

35. *Afro-American* (Baltimore), 21 December 1946, p. 4.

36. Ibid., 11 June 1949, p. 4.

37. Ibid., 11 December 1948, p. 4.

38. Interviews with Benjamin Amos, 17 January 1973; WH, 19 September 1972; Edward Lovett, 18 January 1973; and Edrd Mazique, 8 January 1975. See interviews with George Crockett, 1 August 1974; George B. Murphy, Jr., 19 April 1974; and William Patterson, 15 July 1973.

39. WLH to Lucy [Baldwin], 13 June 1947, WLH/H&G firm files. Margaret Gladys Houston recalls that during a visit she and the nurse hired to stay with Mary Houston at home realized that Mary Houston had only a brief while to live. Margaret called Charles Houston at his home. William was with Mary when Charles arrived. Charles had an opportunity to see his mother before she died as did his father. William was so upset he collapsed by Mary's bedside when she died. (Interview with MGH, 22 January 1973.)

40. CHH to Cedric Dover, 13 November 1948, CHH/H&G firm files; interview with MGH, 22 January 1973.

41. Press release of National Federation for Constitutional Liberties, 28 March 1941, CHH/H&G firm files.

42. Brief of National Federation for Constitutional Liberties as amicus curiae in *United States* v. *Albert Blumberg*, CHH/H&G firm files. See 38 F. Supp. 1018 (1941).

43. "Houston Offers to Defend Dies Purge Victims," *Afro-American*, clipping, n.d. [c. 1943], CHH Fam.; CHH to "Friend[s] of Mary McLeod Bethune," 14 April 1943; folder for "Investigation of Mary McLeod Bethune by House under House Resolution 105, 78th Congress, 1st Session," CHH/H&G firm files.

44. CHH to George S. Counts, 25 March 1943, CHH/H&G firm files.

45. CHH to Etta Moten Barnett (Mrs. Claude), CHH/H&G firm files.

46. *Afro-American* (Washington, D.C.), 8 April 1947, p. 4.

47. *Afro-American* (Baltimore), 1 November 1947, p. 4, and 29 November 1947, p. 4; CHH to TM, 7 October 1948, CHH to Marjorie Penny, 18 October 1948, CHH/H&G firm files.

48. Interview with Benjamin Amos, 17 January 1973. See Gordon Kahn, *Hollywood on Trial* (New York: Boni & Gaer, 1948).

49. Interview with Benjamin Amos, 17 January 1973.

50. CHH to Cedric Dover, 13 November 1948, CHH/H&G firm files; *Afro-American* (Baltimore), 31 July 1948, p. 5. See 18 U.S.C. 10 (Smith Act).

51. *Afro-American* (Baltimore), 30 November 1948, p. 4.

52. *Afro-American* (national edition), 12 June 1948, p. 4.

53. Petition for writ of certiorari to the U.S. Court of Appeals for the second circuit in *Gus Hall and Henry Winston* v. *United States of America*, 11 August 1949, U.S. Supreme Court, CHH/H&G firm files. See 288 U.S. 851; see also 176 F. 2d 78, 163.

54. Clifford Durr, Herbert S. Thatcher, Belford V. Lawson, Martin Popper, CHH, "Statement of the Delegation of Lawyers Who Conferred with the Attorney General, September 26, 1949, Regarding the Survey Instituted by Tom Clark of the Fitness of Certain Attorneys to Practice Law," typescript, 26 September 1949, CHH/H&G firm files.

55. WLH to Collector of Internal Revenue, Maryland, 16 January 1950, file 1196 CHH/H&G firm files.

56. Interview with Edward Mazique, 8 January 1973; conversation with CHH Jr. (telephone), 17 September 1974; conversation with CHH Jr., 7 April 1978 and 18 July 1978.

57. CHH, untitled tape recording [c. December 1949] with Mazique introduction (my copy); interview with Edward Mazique, 8 January 1973.

58. CHH, untitled tape recording [c. December 1949], CHH Fam.

59. Ibid.

60. Interview with Edward Mazique, 8 January 1973.

61. HWH, "An Appeal to Whom It May Concern," typewritten notes, 19 and 20 January 1967, CHH Fam.; interview with Benjamin Amos, 17 January 1973; interview with Gardner Bishop, 2 March 1972. See *McCready*, 195 Md. 131 (1950); see also interviews with CMH, 1972–73; interview with Edward Mazique, 8 January 1973; and conversations with CHH Jr., 1974–78.

62. Interview with Edward Mazique, 8 January 1973; WLH to Collector of Taxes, D.C., 13 March 1950; CHH to Carl Murphy, 8 March 1950; file 1196, CHH/H&G.

63. "The People's Champion to Valhalla," *Pittsburgh Courier*, clipping, 6 May 1950, CHH vertical file, MSRC; interview with Edward Mazique, 9 January 1973.

64. Interview with Gardner Bishop, 2 March 1972. According to Nabrit, Houston also asked him to take the case during the last days in the hospital. (*Star News*, 12 May 1974, p. 1.)

65. Interviews with CMH, 1972–73.

66. Interview with Edward Mazique, 8 January 1973; HWH to CHH, 16 April 1950, CHH Fam.; conversations with CHH Jr., 3 and 4 January 1973.

67. Certificate of death (of CHH), file 1189, CHH/H&G firm files.

68. Harry S. Truman to Mrs. Charles Houston, 25 April 1950, President's personal file, private papers, HST Papers; letters and telegrams of condolence to Mrs. C. H. Houston, file 1167, CHH/H&G firm files.

69. "Supreme Court Justices, Cabinet Heads, Join 'Little Man' in Tribute to Houston," *Afro-American* (Washington, D.C.), clipping, 29 April 1950, CHH vertical file, MSRC.

70. Ibid.

71. WH, "Charles Hamilton Houston, 1895–1950," *Negro History Bulletin* 13 (June 1950): 208.

72. CHH's inscription to son in Joshua Liebman, *Peace of Mind* (New York: Simon & Schuster, 1946), p. 48 of copy among possessions of Clotill M. Houston.

CONCLUSION

1. CHH to Stephen Early, 16 August 1933, CHH/H&G firm case files.

2. Ibid.

3. CHH, "An Approach to Better Race Relations" (Address before the YWCA Convention, New York City, 5 May 1934).

4. CHH, untitled tape recording [c. December 1949], CHH Fam.

5. "Negro and Poor Whites Should Unite—Houston," untitled newspaper clipping, n.d. [c. 29 June 1934]. See Mary F. Berry, *Black Resistance/White Law: A History of Constitutional Racism in America* (Englewood Cliffs, N.J.: Prentice-Hall, 1971).

6. CHH, "Justice for All," December 19, 1934, CHH folders, Sp. cor., Adm. files, C64, NAACP Papers.

7. CHH, "Proposed Legal Attacks on Educational Discrimination," 1 August 1935, CHH Folder, Speeches, Adm. files C429, NAACP Records.

8. Ibid.

9. *Afro-American* (Baltimore), February 1, 1947, p. 8.

10. *Afro-American* (national edition), June 12, 1948, p. 4. Compare Berry, *Black Resistance* pp. ix–x, chaps. 9–13. See Dorothy B. Gilliam, *Paul Robeson, All-American* (Washington, D.C.: New Republic Book Co., 1976).

11. CHH, "Personal Observations on the Summary of Studies in Legal Education," ms., 28 May 1929, CHH-Howard Univ., CHH/H&G firm files.

12. CHH to F. M. LeMay, 30 March 1935, Scottsboro Correspondence, CHH/H&G firm files. See interview with WHH, 19 September 1972. See also 338 U.S. 851.

13. CHH, untitled address, 2 July 1933, 1933 folder, Annual Conference Files, B10, NAACP Papers.

14. CHH, "Memorandum to Joint Committee American Fund . . . NAACP," 26 October 1934, AFPS, Adm. files, C199, NAACP Papers.

15. CHH, "A Challenge to Negro Youth," *Crisis* 45 (January 1938): 15.

16. CHH to Franklin D. Roosevelt, 18 January 1943, 4245g, official file, FDR Papers.

17. CHH, "Personal Observations," 28 May 1929.

18. See above, Chapters 6 and 7.

19. CHH, "Personal Observations," 28 May 1929.

20. Ibid.

21. Ibid.

22. Ibid.

23. CHH, "Law as a Career," July 1932, CHH-Howard University, CHH/H&G firm files.

24. Ibid.

25. Interviews with E. Lovett, 18 January 1973, and O. Hill, 8 December 1972; and [CHH] "Use of Law as an Instrument Available to a Minority Unable to Adopt Direct Action . . . ," typescript, 12 December 1946, CHH/H&G firm files.

26. NAACP, *Annual Report, 1934*, p. 22.

27. CHH, Memo to Joint Committee . . . , 26 October 1934.

28. See Roscoe Pound, *Introduction to the Philosophy of Law* (New Haven: Yale University Press, 1922), chap. 3.

29. CHH to Monroe Berger, 10 February 1948, CHH/H&G firm files.

30. Interview with Oliver Hill, 8 December 1972.

31. CHH, "The Need for Negro Lawyers," *Journal of Negro Education*, 4 (January 1935): 49.

32. 347 U.S. 483 and 347 U.S. 427 (1954).

33. 305 U.S. 337 (1938); 323 U.S. 192 and 323 U.S. 210 (1944).

34. See Paulo Freire, *Education for Critical Consciousness* (New York: Herder & Herder, 1980), and Paulo Freire, *Pedagogy of the Oppressed* (New York: Herder & Herder, 1970).

35. Freire, *Education*; Freire, *Pedagogy*.

36. CHH, "Proposed Legal Attacks on Educational Discrimination," 1 August 1935.

37. See Jesse Jai McNeil, Jr., "A Critical Analysis of Planning for Social Change" (Ed. D. diss., University of Massachusetts, 1975).

38. See above, Chapters 10–12 and Jesse Jai McNeil, Jr., and Genna Rae McNeil, "'Consciousness and Action': Historical Observations on NAACP Planning and Litigation for Social Change, 1909–1954," *Lectures: Black Scholars on Black Issues*, ed. Vivian V. Gordon (Washington, D.C.: University Press of America, 1979).

39. CHH, "An Approach to Better Race Relations," 5 May 1934.

40. CHH, untitled tape recording [c. December 1949], CHH Fam.

41. CHH, "Statement of Certain Legal Activities Carried on Behalf of the Association," 24 June 1935, CHH/H&G firm files.

42. CHH to Colgate Darden, 22 June 1942, "W," CHH/H&G firm files.

43. CHH to WW, 18 October 1933, George Crawford file, Legal Files, D52, Cases Supported, NAACP Records.

44. CHH, "Educational Inequalities Must Go!" *Crisis* 42 (October 1935): 316.

45. CHH, "Proposed Legal Attacks on Educational Discrimination" 1 August 1935.

46. Derrick A. Bell, *Race, Racism, and American Law* (Boston: Little, Brown & Co., 1973).

47. CHH, untitled tape recording [c. December 1949], CHH Fam.

48. Ibid.

49. CHH inscription to son in Joshua Liebman, *Peace of Mind* (New York: Simon & Schuster, 1946), p. 48 of copy among possessions of Clotill M. Houston.

50. CHH, untitled tape recording [c. December 1949], CHH Fam.

51. Traditional African-American spiritual, sung by slaves exhorting each other not to grow weary of performing good works and to persevere in their efforts to be free.

Index of Names, Places, and Subjects

Index of Principal Cases Cited